Studies in Deprivation and Disadvantage

Continuites of Deprivation?

Studies in Deprivation and Disadvantage

1 Cycles of Disadvantage: A Review of Research
   Michael Rutter and Nicola Madge

2 A Cycle of Deprivation? A Case Study of Four Families
   Frank Coffield, Philip Robinson and Jacquie Sarsby

4 Disadvantage and Education
   Jo Mortimore and Tessa Blackstone

5 Mothers and Daughters: A Three-Generational Study of Health Attitudes
   and Behaviour
   Mildred Blaxter and Elizabeth Paterson

6 Continuities in Childhood Disadvantage
   Juliet Essen and Peter Wedge

7 Housing Inequality and Deprivation
   Alan Murie

8 Families at Risk
   Edited by Nicola Madge

9 Policies, Programmes and Disadvantage: A Review of the Literature
   Roger Fuller and Olive Stevenson

10 Parents and Children: Incomes in Two Generations
   A.B. Atkinson, A.K. Maynard and C.G. Trinder

11 The Money Problems of the Poor: A Literature Review
   Pauline Ashley

12 The Structure of Disadvantage
   Edited by Muriel Brown

13 Hard to Place: The Outcome of Adoption and Residential Care
   John Triseliotis and James Russell

14 Parenting Breakdown: The Making and Breaking of Intergenerational Links
   David Quinton and Michael Rutter

Studies in Deprivation and Disadvantage 15

Continuities of Deprivation?
The Newcastle 1000 Family Study

Israel Kolvin, F. J. W. Miller, D. McI. Scott,
S. R. M. Gatzanis, M. Fleeting

Avebury

Aldershot · Brookfield USA · Hong Kong · Singapore · Sydney

Published by
Avebury
Gower Publishing Company Limited
Gower House
Croft Road
Aldershot
Hants GU11 3HR
England

Gower Publishing Company
Old Post Road
Brookfield
Vermont 05036
USA

British Library Cataloguing in Publication Data

Continuities of Deprivation? the Newcastle 1000 family
  study. - (Studies in deprivation and disadvantage; 15)
  1. (Metropolitan County) Tyne and Wear. Newcastle upon
Tyne. Socially disadvantaged families
  I. Kolvin, Israel II. Series
362.8'2'0942876

ISBN 0 566 05799 9

Printed and bound in Great Britain by
Billing and Sons Ltd, Worcester

Contents

List of Figures   vii
List of Tables   ix
Foreword   xv
Acknowledgements   xvi

Part 1   ORIGIN AND METHOD OF STUDY
1   The background   3
2   The present study: planning and method   14

Part II   FAMILY AND ENVIRONMENT
3   Families of origin: the Red Spot children
    1947–62   37
4   Families of formation   50
5   Deprivation, occupational class and mobility   64
6   Family income and male unemployment   72
7   Housing and neighbourhood   90

**Part III   PERSONAL DEVELOPMENT
             AND DEPRIVATION**
8   The Red Spots as children 1947–62   105
9   The Red Spots and their spouses in 1979–80   120
10 The children of the Red Spots 1979–80   129

Part IV   CHANGING FAMILIES
11 Change within generation 1952–62   145
12 Change across generations 1952–80   166

Part V   ROUTES TO AND FROM DEPRIVATION
13 Statistical indicators   211

Part VI   CONTACT WITH THE LAW

14 Deprivation and offending   269
15 Non-deprived but delinquent:
    deprived but resilient   281
16 Prediction of criminality   290

Part VII   REVIEW AND CONCLUSIONS

17 Perspectives, associations and
    statistics of deprivation   325
18 Summary findings based on comparison
    of groups   338
19 Understanding deprivation   355
20 Final conclusions of the Newcastle study   370

Appendices   376
References   379
Index   395

List of figures

2.1   Flowchart of 1,000 family cohort: 1947–81   15

3.1   Profile of deprivation (criteria)   39

4.1   Profile of criteria of deprivation in the study
        groups in 1947 and 1979–80 at the 5th year
        (Generation I) and 33rd year (Generation II)   59

8.1   Generation II (children): height by age and
        weight by age curves   106

11.1   Profile of criteria of deprivation in the three
        selected groups at the 5th and 10th years
        (Generation I)   146

13.1   Prediction of performance (Generation I to II
        in the school years)   223

13.2   Prediction of performance – some dependent
        variables: Generations I to II   224

13.3   Prediction of performance (multiple
        regression analyses by stepwise procedures):
        Generations II to III   227

13.4   Prediction of performance – results of
        multiple regression analyses by stepwise
        procedures: Generations II to III   228

13.5   Path analysis: proposed model: child behaviour   242

13.6   Path analysis: revised model: path diagram
        with coefficients: antisocial behaviour   245

13.7   Path analysis: revised model: non-verbal
        reasoning ability   246

13.8   Path analysis: revised model: vocabulary
        ability   246

13.9   Path analysis: revised model: antisocial
        behaviour (Rutter)   247

13.10   Path analysis: revised model: reading ability   247

13.11   Path analysis: psychosocial model A:
        reading attainment   250

13.12   Vocabulary ability   251

13.13   Non-verbal reasoning ability   251
13.14   Antisocial behaviour at school   251
13.15   Neurotic behaviour at home   251
13.16   Path analysis: psychosocial model B:
        reading attainment   253
13.17   Vocabulary ability   254
13.18   Antisocial behaviour at school   254
13.19   Antisocial behaviour at home   254

14.1   Mean numbers of offences committed by
        males at each age to 33 years   276

15.1   Division of cohort into sub-groups   282

List of tables

2.1	The frequency of criteria of deprivation in 847 families in 1952	19
2.2	Distribution of criteria in 847 families in 1952	19
2.3	Percentage overlap in pairs of criteria 847 families in 1947	20
2.4	The criteria of deprivation in 1979–80: Red Spots (Generation II) as adults	23
2.5	Criteria of deprivation 1979–80	29
2.6	Distribution of families by number of criteria 1979–80	30
2.7	Post-school vocational attainments: families of formation (tertiary occupational training)	33
2.8	Distribution of educational insufficiency and educational attainment	33
3.1	Social, family and health data in 1947 at birth of 'Red Spot' child in 264 families visited in 1979–80	37
3.2	Social data of families of origin, 1947–52	38
3.3	Social data: families in 1962 categorized according to deprivation in 1952	40
3.4	The three groups of Red Spots classified according to deprivation in the family of origin in 1952 (i.e. the 5th year)	43
3.5	Correlation of criteria of deprivation gathered prospectively and retrospectively	44
3.6	Spouses' retrospective accounts of childhood experiences	44
3.7	Spouse early life experiences classified according to deprivation in families of Red Spots	47
4.1	Family of formation – 1979–80: recollections from Red Spots regarding parents	52
4.2	Families of formation 1979–80: women – current social and family data	52

4.3   Families of formation: physical and
      psychological health of women   54
4.4   Family of formation: social and family
      factors 1979–80   56
4.5   Families of formation: some items of
      deprivation 1980   57
4.6   Recent life events in family of formation   62

5.1   Social class distribution of study groups
      according to social class in 1952   66
5.2   Comparison of occupational class of 847
      families across generations based on estimates
      using 264 families in the first generation   69

6.1   Relationship of deprivation in first-generation
      families to categories of gross annual income
      of the second-generation families in 1980   73
6.2   Family income and deprivation 1979–80   73
6.3   Families and subsistence levels 1979–80   73
6.4   Unemployment in 847 families   77
6.5   Incidence of unemployment 1979–80   78
6.6   Social perceptions of men in families of
      formation   79
6.7   Housing and unemployment: families of
      formation   80
6.8   School experience, career training, verbal IQ
      and unemployment: families of formation   80
6.9   Psychological and physical illness and
      unemployment: families of formation
      1979–80   81
6.10 Family relationships in 1979–80: family
      of formation   82
6.11 Families of formation and unemployment:
      behaviour and cognition of first-born children   83
6.12 Precursors of unemployment   84

7.1   Families of origin 1952: electoral wards
      and deprivation   91
7.2   Overcrowding defined according to 'personal
      unit' according to severity of deprivation   93
7.3   Housing and deprivation 1952–79   94
7.4   House ownership, household factors
      and deprivation   96
7.5   Families, neighbourhood and ward rankings   98

8.1   Physical factors and deprivation in 1952:
      Red Spots aged 3 to 5 years   105
8.2   11-plus examination scores:
      1958 boys and girls   108
8.3   Type of secondary school attended   109
8.4   Siblings attending selective schools   110
8.5   Attendance during the last three terms at
      school (percentage of possible attendance)   111
8.6   Attitude to leaving school at 15 years   112
8.7   External examinations at 15–16 years   113
8.8   Red Spots' expressed preference for
      employment at 15 years   114
8.9   Behaviour at school as rated by teachers:
      Red Spots at 10 years of age   115
8.10 Red Spots: intentions, interests and
      attitudes in their last two years at
      primary school   117
8.11 Red Spots' behaviour at secondary school   118

9.1   Red Spot school examination successes
      (self-report)   121
9.2   Red Spots and spouses: self-report on
      qualifications   122
9.3   Parent testing: Mill Hill vocabulary IQ
      equivalent scores classified according to
      deprivation in family of origin   124
9.4   Behaviour and illness in women in families
      of formation: Red Spots and spouses
      combined   126

10.1 First-born schoolchildren, families of
      formation: Raven's Coloured/Standard
      Progressive Matrices   131
10.2 Raven's Coloured/Standard Progressive
      Matrices   131
10.3 Reading performance for Generation III
      first-born children: Holborn Reading Scale   133
10.4 Generation III schoolchildren: percentage
      of good, average and poor readers   133
10.5 Children of Red Spots: behaviour and
      temperament grouped according to
      deprivation in the family of formation   136

11.1	Deprivation in 810 families in 1952 and 1957	147
11.2	Prevalence of criteria	148
11.3	Improvement from 1952 to 1957	149
11.4	Social data in 1957	151
11.5	Year fifteen: social and family data	151
11.6	Last year in primary school 1958	153
11.7	Outcome: secondary school/early employment behavioural and cognitive data	153
11.8	Occupational class and movement into deprivation by 1957	154
11.9	Mental ability scores (mean quotients)	156
11.10	Red Spots aged 15 years: behaviour and attitude to school	157
11.11	The offence rates of men whose families moved in or out of deprivation	158
12.1	Change in deprivation: 1952–1979/80 in 264 families	168
12.2	Estimated changes in deprivation status in the families of 847 Red Spots from family of origin (1952) to family of formation (1980)	169
12.3	Families in 1952 and estimate of number of criteria in 1980	171
12.4	Occupational class (Registrar General)	177
12.5	Paternal provision, participation in the home and interest in the Red Spot child 5–15 years	179
12.6	Physical growth at age 5	180
12.7	Distribution of scores at 11-plus examination	181
12.8	Education of parents in families of formation 1980	181
12.9	Mill Hill vocabulary quotients in O–O and M–M groups	185
12.10	Schooling and vocational training: family of formation	186
12.11	Mean quotients of first-born schoolchildren	190
12.12	Mean Mill Hill quotients at 33 years: 10 Red Spots and 7 spouses	200
13.1	IQ of Red Spots at 11-plus examination	213

13.2   School attendance of the Red Spot
        children: last year at school   215
13.3   Classroom temperament and behaviour and
        growth during secondary school years:
        analysis of variance   215
13.4   Summary of effects of deprivation at five
        and ten years on later mental abilities and
        behaviour: analysis of variance   216
13.5   Influence of deprivation and other factors
        on children of family of formation: analysis
        of variance   219
13.6   Reading ability of children: family of
        formation   219
13.7   Mean 'antisocial' scores and degree of
        deprivation   220
13.8   Outcome variables in families of the Red
        Spots as adults significantly predicted by
        prior childhood factors: percentage of
        variance   235
13.9   Prediction of deprivation in the family
        of formation from deprivation in the
        family of origin and IQ at the 11-plus
        examination   237
13.10   Two-factor prediction of deprivation in
        family of formation   239
13.11   Path analysis: proportion of explained
        variance   263
14.1   Deprivation in Red Spot families when the
        children were five and ten years of age   270
14.2   Newcastle upon Tyne 1947–65 delinquency:
        children appearing in court by 18.5 years of
        age from 760 boys and girls   270
14.3   Offence rates in base cohort of 847
        families corrected for losses   273
14.4   Percentage of male offenders and non-
        offenders who experienced deprivation in
        early childhood   274
14.5   Convictions (CRO) in relation to
        deprivation (1952)   278
14.6   Predominant character traits of parents in
        relation to male Red Spots aged 15 years   279

15.1 Males: fifth-year and earlier — stress factors
      in the non-deprived; protective factors in
      the deprived   283
15.2 Females: fifth-year protective factors in
      the deprived   284
15.3 Stress and protective factors in boys
      10 and 11 years   286
15.4 Females: tenth-year protective factors
      in the deprived   286
15.5 Males: fifteenth-year: stress and protective
      factors   288
15.6 Females: fifteenth-year: protective factors
      (deprived group only)   288
16.1 Validity of predictors of delinquency   294
16.2 Data from '1,000 Family Study'   295
16.3 Correlation of neighbourhood factors
      and offending   296
16.4 Single-factor prediction: percentage correct
      in relation to different sub-populations   297
16.5 Two-factor prediction of male offending
      in Generation II   300
16.6 Discriminant function analysis   302

Foreword

In 1701 Richard Gough, then a 66 year-old widower, began his history of the Parish of Myddle in Shropshire. He continued until 1706, and his book offers case histories suggesting that the social and behavioural misdemeanours of one generation have their origins in the social and family pathology of its predecessor. One memorable vignette merits quotation:

> William [Bickley] was a faire dealeing person, and well to passe, butt hee was unfortunate in his marriage with Elizabeth, daughter of William Tyler, of Balderton. Shee was more commendable for her beauty than her chastity and was the ruin of the family . . . William Bickley has two sons — Thomas and William, and three daughers — Mary, Elizabeth and Susan. Thomas, practised his father's virtues, William imitated his Grandfather's villanyes, and the three daughters followed the mother's vices.

Man's destiny lies half within himself and half without
Philip Wylie: *Generation of Vipers*, 1942

To our wives: RK and SM

Acknowledgements

This study would not have been possible without the cooperation of families from the '1,000 Family' study of the years 1947–62. Our first thanks must be to them. The work has been carried out within the Human Development Unit of the Nuffield Psychology and Psychiatry Department, University of Newcastle upon Tyne, and, throughout the years it has taken to complete, all the authors have also been engaged on other tasks.

Early in the study the death of our experienced statistician and friend, Dr Roger Garside, deprived us of a senior member of the original team, but later we had great help from Mrs Hazel Fells, Mrs Mary Fleeting and Professor Robin Plackett. Mr Fred Wolstenholme, while a member of the unit, made a major contribution to the initial planning and preparation of the social interview proformas. Mrs Marjorie Blackburn, the Administrative Secretary to the Nuffield Unit, has throughout the whole period undertaken wide ranges of work beyond her ordinary commitment and the authors are deeply indebted to her. Mr Philip Alan Kolvin contributed to the chapter on contact with the law.

The onerous work of visiting the families locally was undertaken by Mrs Doris Fadden, Mrs Olwyn Pollinger and Mrs Nanette Nelson, who also visited those who lived outside Newcastle upon Tyne. We were able to arrange, through present and former members of the Nuffield Unit, for some families to be visited in Australia, Canada and South Africa.

Every facet of the study was essential and all were interdependent. Computer analysis was undertaken by Mrs Elaine Kennedy, Mrs Hazel Fells and Mrs Mary Fleeting.

The initial clerical work and contacts with the families were made by Mrs Lorna Wake and Mrs Dorothy Fisher. Several drafts of the book have been patiently typed by Miss Helen Davies and Mrs Kathleen McAneney. Mrs Nicola Sanderson and Mrs Anne Alexander prepared the final manuscript.

A record of all those who have worked in the study is listed in the nominal role given below.

Professor I. Kolvin
Dr F.J.W. Miller
Mr D. McI. Scott
Dr R.F. Garside (deceased)
Dr S.R.M. Gatzanis
Professor R. Plackett — statistical advice
Mr F. Wolstenholme
Mr P.A. Kolvin

Mrs D. Fadden
Mrs N. Nelson   } Family Interviews
Mrs O. Pollinger

Mrs N. Nelson   Criminality Codings

Dr S.R.M. Gatzanis
Mrs N. Nelson   } School Interviews
Mrs I. Smith

Mrs E. Kennedy
Mrs H. Fells   } Computer Analysis
Mrs M. Fleeting

Mrs M. Blackburn   Administration

Mrs A. Alexander
Miss H. Davies
Mrs D. Fisher   } Clerical/Secretarial
Mrs K. McAneney
Mrs N. Sanderson
Mrs L. Wake

The main financial support for the initial planning, printing, visiting and the computerization of the data was given by the DHSS/SSRC to whom an initial report was made in 1982. We have also had generous supplementary grants from the Joseph Rowntree Trust; the W.T. Grant Foundation, New York; the Newcastle Inner Cities Fund; and the Joel Joffe Trust, and for the study of delinquency and criminality from the Home Office. We are grateful for all this help and hope that we have justified it.

Certain aspects of the material have been presented in several previous communications (Kolvin *et al.*, 1983a;

Kolvin *et al.*, 1983b; Miller *et al.*, 1985; Kolvin *et al.*, 1988a; Kolvin *et al.*, 1988b; Kolvin *et al.*, 1988c).

Planning committee
We are indebted to our local planning committee which met on a regular basis. In addition to the four authors, it comprised the following membership: Psychology — Dr R.F. Garside; Newcastle Local Education Authority — Mr J.T. McLoughlin; Social Work — Mr F. Wolstenholme; Computing — Mrs E. Kennedy, Mrs H. Fells; Research Associate — Dr S.R.M. Gatzanis; and Mrs M. Blackburn — Administrative Secretary.

Steering committee
The Social Science Research Council Planning Committee made an invaluable contribution. We list here those who made regular contributions:

Representing the SSRC:	Professor P. Collison (Chairman)
	Mr M. Duggett (Secretary to Joint Working Party)
	Professor M. Rutter
	Professor H. Goldstein
Representing the University of Newcastle upon Tyne:	Professor D. Eccleston
	Professor I. Kolvin
Representing Research Team:	Dr R.F. Garside
	Dr F.J.W. Miller
	Mr F. Wolstenholme

General acknowledgements
A project of this magnitude needs the collaboration and co-operation of many individuals and agencies and we wish to thank the many Directors of Education and Heads of staff of the schools in Newcastle and elsewhere, who have been most helpful. We are also grateful to Mr Roycroft, the Director of Social Services, Newcastle upon Tyne, and his research department.

We are indebted to Professor M. Rutter for constructive criticisms of our method and our concept of resilience. We would also like to thank Professor A. Clarke and Professor P. Collison for helpful comments on earlier drafts. We are also grateful to Dr D. Farrington for his help with the analysis and interpretation of our criminality data. We are also indebted to Professor Donald Court for his interest, support and encouragement. Finally we would like to thank Jackie McDermott for the compilation of the index.

Fleming Nuffield Unit
University of Newcastle upon Tyne
NE2 3AE

PART I
ORIGIN AND METHOD
OF STUDY

1 The background

On Thursday 29 June 1972 Sir Keith Joseph, then Secretary of State for Social Services, made a speech at a conference for local authorities organized by the Pre-school Playgroups Association. That speech led to more than a decade of studies, of which this book is one. His actual words need to be remembered:

'The Paradox': Why is it that in spite of long periods of full employment and relative prosperity, and the improvement in community services since the Second World War, deprivation and problems of adjustment so conspicuously persist? . . . Deprivation is, I know, an imprecise term. What I am talking about are those circumstances which prevent people developing nearer their potential — physically, emotionally and intellectually, than many do now.

The Cycle of Deprivation: Perhaps there is at work here a process, apparent in many situations but imperfectly understood, by which problems reproduce themselves from generation to generation. But I am not suggesting that there is some single process by which social problems reproduce themselves — it is far more complex than that. I am saying that, in a proportion of cases occurring at all levels of society, the problems of one generation appear to reproduce themselves in the next . . . . In my view we need to study the phenomena of transmitted deprivation, what I have called the 'Cycle of Deprivation'.

I am hopeful that it will be possible to mount studies that will give us a better understanding of the nature of the 'Cycle of Deprivation'.

As a matter of experience social workers and medical practitioners familiar with history making are well aware that social attitudes and ways of life tend to recur in some families from one generation to the next. But what is even more surprising, this does not always happen, and whether there is a continuity or discontinuity between generations, the mechanism or mechanisms and the pathways of change or otherwise also require exploration and, if possible, explanation. The difficulty comes, however, in setting up a model for study, a model which makes it possible to explore many factors across one or more generations, and to assess the significance of physical, psychological, intellectual or social factors. This model must possess valid information on each generation involved and also be able to take into account alterations in social attitudes, economic change and indeed the expectancy which have occurred during the time under review.

As it happened, information of this type was available in Newcastle. A project, designed to collect the facts of health and illness in children during the first year of life had enrolled, as a study group, all children born to families in Newcastle upon Tyne during the months of May and June 1947. Although designed originally only for one year, the cooperation between the families and the workers was so good that it continued until the fifteenth year when the children either left school or continued with their education (Spence *et al.*, 1954; Miller *et al.*, 1960; Miller *et al.*, 1974).

The data of that survey had been carefully preserved and that relating to the cohort still living in the city in 1952 has been used as the basis of the present study. In 1979–80 some 300 members of the cohort were traced and interviewed. They were then 32 years of age and most were parents. The study was, and remains, local in emphasis and must be seen within the context of the City of Newcastle and its immediate neighbourhood of Tyneside and the North-East, although the 20 per cent of families who had moved from Newcastle after 1952 were visited wherever they lived.

The present study: the cycle of deprivation

Following the Minister's speech and the establishment of the joint working party of the SSRC and the DHSS, several studies of 'deprivation' were initiated and many publications followed. The literature on the subject to 1981 was summarized in *Despite the Welfare State* (Brown and Madge, 1982) and accounts of some of the projects specifically funded by the SSRC were brought together in *Families at Risk* (Madge, 1983a). From these publications it is evident that the concept of deprivation means different things to different people. It is thus necessary to state our own position as clearly and precisely as possible.

This study had its origin in a suggestion that the families who in 1952 had shown characteristics described as 'deficiencies in family wellbeing' (Miller *et al.*, 1960: 34–56) should be traced to discover whether the deficiencies continued into later childhood and adult life. Certainly, if the families could be traced and revisited, we could claim to satisfy the Minister's requirements. Our one shortcoming was that we lacked prospective data regarding the childhood of one spouse in each of the families of formation. But, accepting that difficulty, we thought that we should be able to describe how far children from severely deprived families in the first generation continued to show evidence of deprivation in later childhood, and whether their families did so in 1980.

In 1952 the families were assessed with regard to their potential to provide a happy and stable home for both parents and children. This was in the belief that such homes give children the best chances of developing their potential, first as children and then as adults. Thus, theoretically, if the families in the 1952 survey could be traced and if they could be interviewed in 1980, it should be possible, having adjusted the criteria used in 1952 to the standards of 1980, to describe the change or continuity in family conditions (within limits of our parameters) between the two dates and two generations.

It will be apparent that this study stands or falls by decisions made regarding the data relating to 1952 and by the basic acceptability and soundness of our concepts of deprivation. It was therefore comforting to find that Madge (1983a) in her introduction to *Families at Risk* approached the subject from the same direction as ourselves.

The concept of continuity and our hypotheses

Our study is based upon a belief that the total conditions under which a child lives influence his or her development and functioning in physical, social, emotional and intellectual terms. If this is correct, then family environments lacking the necessary requirements are likely to lead to less than optimal development unless the deficit is recognized and can be remedied at an appropriate time. If not, sub-optimal functioning may then continue into adult life, bringing the possibility that the next generation of children will, in their turn, also receive inadequate care.

In a more strict sense, 'continuity' can be defined as the repetition of the same criteria of deprivation in the next generation at an equivalent point in time in the life cycle. This concept can be used to study family circumstances both within generations and across generations. In this study the generations are as follows:

Generation I   The parents of the index children (Red Spot families) (see page 17).

Generation II   The 'Index' children (Red Spots) during their early and school years and their characteristics as adults.

Generation III   The children born to the Red Spots at the time of the interview of this study.

Hypotheses

In formulating hypotheses concerning the cycle of deprivation we needed to identify the frequency of criteria of deprivation, their effects, their continuity or discontinuity from one generation to the next and the mechanism of their transmission. We therefore formed the following hypotheses:

1   Children from families affected by deprivation (in the terms of our definitions) will show an association with poorer social, behavioural and educational functioning during their school years than the children of families not so affected.

2   Children from families affected by deprivation will show an association with poorer economic, social and emotional functioning when adult. This poorer functioning will reduce ability to care adequately for their own children.

3   Thus, from 1 and 2 above there will be a transmission of poorer social, emotional, behavioural and educational functioning from the first to the second and third generations.

4   Within one generation, specific criteria of deprivation will continue to be evident at different points in the life cycle.

5   Specific criteria of deprivation will repeat themselves in the next generation.

6   Multiple criteria of deprivation will have a stronger association than single specific criteria with all types of subsequent poorer functioning.

7   Certain forms of social and family deprivation will have specific and more harmful influences than others.

8   Certain social, family and personal factors will exert protective influences against the effects of deprivation.

The city of Newcastle upon Tyne

This study must be seen against the background of the historical development of the city, its neighbourhood, and the people who have lived, and who now live, therein.

Although the river Tyne was first bridged by the Romans the building of New-Castle, from which the town derives its name, began in 1080 during the consolidation of the North following the Norman victory at Hastings. The medieval town grew slowly but had strong walls and was always important both as a trading centre and as a base for military operations against the North or Scotland. From the thirteenth to the early nineteenth century, the city had a monopoly of coal export to London, yet until the second half of the eighteenth century remained for the most part within its ancient walls. Then, with the impetus of the Industrial Revolution, growth was rapid and continuous and Newcastle became the centre of a highly industrialized community dependent upon coal, chemicals, glass, shipbuilding and armaments. Industry brought great increases in population, met by immigration from neighbouring country districts and other parts of the United Kingdom and Ireland. A population of 28,000 in 1801 became 215,000 in 1901 and 286,000 in 1931.

In common with similar areas of rapid growth in that period, mortality rates were high at all ages, particularly in infancy and early childhood. From the 1870s the birth rate fell steadily, except for short periods in the early 1920s and late 1940s, so that the proportion of children in the population declined, while lengthening life expectancy increased the number and proportion of the elderly. By the 1970s the population structure of the city had dramatically changed from that of the 1930s, with great improvements in general health but with a smaller proportion of children and a larger one of elderly people.

In this century Tyneside has been unfortunate in depending too much on war. The First World War and its aftermath was followed by fifteen years of depression in heavy industry, high unemployment and economic hardship.

From 1936 more work became available and unemployment almost disappeared during the Second World War. At the same time nutrition was improved by the adequate rationing system, and mortality rates, sensitive to better nutrition and care, were lower in 1945 than ever before.

The '1,000 Family Study'

The '1,000 Family Study' can be traced to the early 1930s. In 1931, Dr A.J. Smith, the Medical Officer of Newcastle Dispensary, referred in his annual report to the great increase in poverty, sickness and malnutrition amongst the poorest classes in the city. Reported in both local and national press, this caused concern, and Dr J.A. Charles, the Medical Officer of Health (later Chief Medical Officer, Ministry of Health), asked Dr J.C. Spence (later Nuffield Professor of Child Health), then a physician on the staff of the Royal Victoria Infirmary, Newcastle, to investigate the situation. Spence did this by comparing the medical histories and the physical states of two groups of children under five; one group came from professional families and the other from children attending a Salvation Army Sunday School, a Child Welfare (Health) Centre, or accompanying their mothers, who were seeking advice on their own behalf at the Newcastle Dispensary.

Spence's (1932) conclusions were dramatic and can be summarized. They were that at least 56 per cent of the children from the poorer districts of the city were unhealthy or physically unfit, and appeared malnourished due to infective illnesses under conditions which prevented satisfactory recovery.

In the winter of 1938 Dr Spence's study was repeated with substantially the same results (Brewis, Davison and Miller, 1940). Employment amongst fathers had improved, but two of every three families interviewed spent less on food than the cost of a basic diet. In 1939 a study of infant mortality revealed the local importance of low birthweight and infection as causes of death and also how little was known about them (Spence and Miller, 1941).

In 1946 it was again possible to take up the study of child health. This was based in the new University Department but worked throughout the city with the active cooperation of the Newcastle Health Authority. The question we sought to answer was: 'What is the incidence and what types of acute infective illness occur in the first year of life in Newcastle upon Tyne?'

The resulting survey was designed to last one year and to record the period from birth to the first birthday of a sufficiently large and representative group of Newcastle infants. In the event, at the end of the first year it continued for a second, then until the children were fifteen, and finally for some purposes until they were eighteen and a half years old. The results were published in three volumes between 1954 and 1974 and provided a bridge between textbooks of paediatrics and manuals of social medicine. The authors hoped that 'this account of our experience over these years will help readers to understand the interdependence of physical growth, personal development, family function and social environment in determining the character of health and disease in childhood' (Miller *et al.*, 1974).

Organization

The study throughout was a joint undertaking of the University Department of Child Health at the Royal Victoria Infirmary, Newcastle upon Tyne, and of the Public Health Department of the Newcastle Corporation. It was only possible because a tradition of cooperation between the Medical College and the City Health Committee already existed and a research team could be formed from the existing staffs of the University Department of Child Health and the Maternal and Child Welfare section of the City Health Department. The medical staff undertook the work as part of their general commitment as departmental members, or after 1948 as Consultant Paediatricians. The health visitors were all volunteer members of the Health Department staff seconded for the purpose.

Three basic problems of organization were involved:

1 the enrolment at birth of a group of infants representing the infant population of the city, which was large enough to establish the incidence of the common acute infections;
2 the selection and training of a team of observers;
3 the development of a technique of family visiting, observation and record-keeping.

The study group was to involve one in six of the births in Newcastle during 1947. Since it was impracticable to isolate every sixth birth, all births taking place during two particular months were taken. May and June were chosen so that travelling and visiting could be done in favourable weather during a time when each health visitor would be required to meet more than 200 new families. This method had some epidemiological disadvantages, but it was necessary to accept what was practical and possible.

Preparation of the community

The outlines of the survey were agreed by July 1946; detailed planning began in the autumn and continued through the winter into 1947. The team met regularly, and records were designed and tested. Since the record was to begin at birth, the help of the city midwives was required for infants born at home, and that of matrons of the private nursing homes, and obstetric and paediatric staffs of the two large maternity hospitals for those born in hospital.

During the autumn of 1946 meetings were held with the domiciliary midwives. The nursing homes and maternity hospitals were visited and the object and design was explained to everyone concerned.

The team met all the health visitors working in the city and the medical staffs of the children's hospitals. Arrangements were made for the study to be notified of hospital admissions and to obtain copies of the notes and the growth charts of the infants who attended the child welfare centres. We knew we were very dependent on the support of the family doctors, and they were approached both through the British Medical Association and also individually.

Enrolment therefore began on 1 May, and by 30 June 1,142 infants from 1,132 families formed the study group. During the first year only four families 'contracted out', but 45 children died, and after removals from the city, 967 families were left. At the end of the fifth year the number was 847, and at the end of the fifteenth year there were continuous records for 750 families.

Records

Following the original plan, the records had been designed only for one year. As each notification of birth was received a register was compiled, the child was given a number and his or her dossier initiated. All relevant information went into that dossier, the records progressively expanded and ultimately came to contain the accumulated data of 15 years. During the school years several special studies and sub-surveys added to the available information and the end result was a bulky dossier for each child and his or her family. After the publication of the third report in 1974 these records were carefully stored and were available as the starting-point of the present study.

To identify correspondence and notes a small red 'legal' seal was placed on each document. This distinctive mark rapidly became widely known so that soon the children themselves were known as 'Red Spot' babies, a name which has persisted and 40 years later is still warmly remembered almost as a mark of club membership.

As the work proceeded the team became increasingly aware of complexities and uncertainties of family life, and how slowly understanding of families is attained. Patience was as important as observation. In the first five years, although many of the families were badly housed, in other respects they enjoyed material standards better than those of 20 years earlier. There was considerable regard for the health and welfare of children but only too often the families lacked one or more of the essentials required to establish a stable and happy home. To the team, these essentials seemed to be: a sound dwelling of sufficient size; parents who enjoyed a satisfying relationship with each other and were sensitive to the emotional and intellectual needs of their children; and a reasonable family income wisely used.

Family shortcomings
It was necessary to find criteria which would indicate families in which children would be 'at risk'. The data were reviewed and three major groups or categories of deprivation could be recognized, each group containing a number of related factors. These were as follows:

1 *Deprivation* (of parental care), which included a range of situations in which a child was bereft of parental care. This could be temporary or partial, or permanent by separation or death, and could affect one or both parents.

It included disruption of the family by death, desertion
or divorce, by illness or parental work.

2 *Deficiency*, which involved the more material aspects of
child care and failure to provide adequate food, clothing
or suitable sleeping arrangements, or a low standard of
personal or domestic cleanliness.

3 *Dependence on society*, which contained families whose
degree of breakdown was so extensive that they were a
burden to their neighbours and made demands on the
social services and financial resources of the community.

These were the families who later formed the major part of
the deprived groups of the present study.

The school years
The five years 1947–52 were a time of great social change as
the country recovered from war, and important legislation —
particularly the 1944 Education Act and the 1946 National
Health Service Act — became operative. New houses were
built, wages increased, and general living standards improved.
Significant advances, particularly in the treatment of
bacterial infections, reduced both morbidity and mortality.

In 1952 the children began school and we were still in
close touch with 847 families. Routine and emergency
visiting continued until the children were seven years of age.
However, by the end of the sixth year a change was noticeable: routine visiting was becoming more difficult as more
mothers were in paid employment, and it was evident that
the incidence of infective illnesses was declining and its
nature changing.

From the beginning of the school years the City Education
Committee and teachers who had 'Red Spot' children in their
classes agreed to notify the survey team whenever a child
was absent for more than two days. This notification brought
a special visit to the home by the health visitor or a medical
member of the team and was of very great assistance over the
next 10 years.

After seven years, therefore, the method of data collection
changed. Each family had only one routine annual visit, but
visits following a request from either family doctor or health
visitor continued, as did those when children were notified
absent from school. Throughout this time, hospital notes and

school health records were collected. The routine annual visit, made by arrangement with the family, was also made an occasion to seek answers to particular questions on, for example, stuttering, enuresis and age of menarche.

Throughout the school years attention was progressively directed towards the concept of 'performance' which formed the central theme of the third volume and involved several special enquiries and studies, each with an identity of its own yet within the overall project. Thus, studies were mounted in respect of respiratory disease, disturbed behaviour, attitudes to school, scholastic attainments, weekend activities in work and leisure, and secondary education and hopes and ambitions for the future.

Physical growth in height and weight was checked and recorded. A particular privilege was to be able to study the 'contact' of children with the law and to record juvenile court appearances.

Finally in 1966, four years after the collection of other systematic data had ceased, data was obtained on the entry of boys to employment or the results of continued education in those who had stayed at school. All these studies provided facets of 'performance' and were described in *The School Years in Newcastle upon Tyne* (Miller *et al.*, 1974).

2 The present study: planning and method

Exploiting longitudinal data
The flowchart (Figure 2.1) provides a chronology of the themes discussed in this book.

The base population
The 847 families remaining in the study in 1952 formed the base population for the present study. The recorded social and family information was then reconstituted to develop six criteria of deprivation (see Chapter 6) and the degree of deprivation was calculated for each family as follows:

1 *Non-deprived*: 482 (59 per cent) families had no adverse criteria.
2 *Deprived*: 246 (29 per cent) families had one or two criteria.
3 *Multiply deprived*: 118 (14 per cent) families had three or more criteria.
4 For certain analyses categories (2) and (3) have been combined to enable a study of all 364 (43 per cent) deprived; and for others the deprived families have been separated into those with one and those with two criteria.

The above categorization enabled us to use all the data to study the association of deprivation in the first generation with social functioning, with the cognitive and behavioural effects on Red Spot children and on their adult lives at the age of 32 years.

The tenth-year population
By 1957 the number of families had fallen to 812, almost all the loss being attributable to movement out of the city. Further psychosocial data were then collected allowing the families to be re-rated on five of the six criteria studied at

YEAR	COHORT	THEMES
1947	1142 children	Original sample
	1132 families	All births in Newcastle upon Tyne, May and June 1947
1952	847 families	Baseline cohort of 1978–1980 Study, Six criteria of deprivation, Severity of deprivation
1957	812 families	Five criteria of deprivation Severity of deprivation Becoming deprived Moving out of deprivation
1979–1981	266 families interviewed	A. Family of origin: stratified samples based on 1952 criteria
	264 families analysed	i Non-deprived (14% sub-sample)
		ii Deprived (50% sub-sample)
		iii Multiple deprivation (68% sub-sample)
		B. Family of formation: reorganized according to criteria of deprivation (types and severity) in the current families (families of formation)
		C. Retrospective data from spouses.
1981	812 (notional)	Contact with the law
		i Deprivation and offending
		ii Privileged but delinquent: deprived but resilient
		iii Prediction of delinquency
1979–1981	352 total children in 1979–80 179 first children	Third generation school-age children.

Figure 2.1   Flowchart of 1,000 family cohort: 1947–81

the fifth year. This made possible a comparison of families who had moved out of deprivation since 1952 with those who were not deprived in 1952 or 1957. The children were compared in relation to educational and behavioural progress, personality, temperament and attitudes until they left school.

As families left the city the numbers fell slowly during the school years. For instance in 1952, 483 families did not show any criteria of deprivation, and of these 477 remained in

1957 and 423 in 1962. No data relating to school were available for the children of families who left Newcastle but some were later visited in 1979 or 1980.

The 32–33 year families: the transmission of deprivation

Definition and selection of study groups
The 1979–80 follow-up was undertaken to study the extent and the effects of deprivation and the transmission from one generation to the next. Limitations of time and resources required the family visits to be confined to defined sub-samples of the base population, and four groups were isolated by random sampling:

1   *Non-deprived*: a sample 62 (13 per cent) of the 483 families without deprivation in 1952 (families of origin).
2   *Deprived*: 185 families, a one-in-two random sample of the base population with one or more criteria of deprivation in 1952. This would allow study of the progress of the children from these families, the effects of deprivation, cross-generational changes and also supply information about the importance of both type and degree of deprivation.
3   *Multiply deprived*: 78 families, a random two-in-three sample of the 118 families with three or more criteria of disadvantage in 1952. This sample overlapped with the *deprived* group. It allowed the same studies as for the deprived group.
4   *Random controls*: a random sample of 67 (8 per cent) of the base population of 847 families to allow inferences about the base population. Since this was a random sample there was some overlap with families in other groups. Subsequently we decided this complicated rather than clarified the picture and for most purposes it was abandoned.

There were 294 families in these three samples and eventually 264 were interviewed. For certain themes only the first three of the above four groups are described and the numbers fall to 220. However, one theme concerning the change in deprivational status from family of origin to family of formation uses all the 264 families. By 1979–80 there were 352 children of which 179 were first-born and of school age in the families of formation.

Method 1952: the definition of deprivation
We were faced with problems of definition, organization and procedure. These comprised:

1 The definition of criteria of deprivation and description of essential requirements for family life, reasonable for 1952 and 1980.
2 The design of questionnaires for family interviews. Only one home visit would be possible in most cases, and in all long-distance cases. Data were required concerning both parents (one in each family was not known to the original study) and for each child. Documentation of the school visits was also necessary. The result was a series of proformas which could also be used as transcription sheets for data storage.
3 From the 847 families in the study in 1952 it was necessary to identify those showing the criteria of deprivation and to obtain a comparable sample of families without criteria.
4 The families thus selected had to be traced and interviewed. About half had been seen in 1969 during a study of growth in adolescence (Miller *et al.*, 1971). Some had left the city between 1952–62, whilst others were still living in Newcastle.
5 After collection the data had to be stored and analysed.

The first step was to reassess the criteria used in the ascertainment of deprivation in 1952. These assessments were made in relationship to the standards of the time and the information available in the records of the 1,000 Family Study and to theoretical views about their relevance. That data yielded 14 items or circumstances which could be used and these were gathered into five groups:

1 family and marital disruption which included loss of father (almost half died), loss of mother (most died), marital instability, either parent incapacitated by illness;
2 poor care of child and home which included poor cleanliness of child, domestic cleanliness and clothing;

3   social dependence which included serious debt, un-
    employment, reliance on National Assistance;
4   inadequate housing as represented by overcrowding
    (Miller *et al.*, 1960: 269) and lack of amenities;
5   maternal failure to cope with management of children.

The frequency of each was calculated for the 847 families;
this ranged widely from 1 to 48 per cent. To reduce the
number of items, we calculated the percentage overlap
between pairs of items and the intercorrelation between
items. The family items were not well correlated with each
other (r=0.15). Furthermore, loss of father or mother included loss from death as well as from divorce, desertion or
separation, and death differs from other forms of loss. We
decided therefore to omit loss by death and to allow marital
disruption and parental illness to stand on their own as
separate criteria of deprivation (see Table 2.1).

On the other hand, the items grouped under poor physical
and domestic care correlated highly with each other (r=0.61),
and were therefore combined as a single criterion of overall
care. This group showed a moderate correlation with poor
mothering, but the latter was retained as a separate criterion
(see Table 2.1).

The three items of social dependency showed only
moderate intercorrelations (r=0.27), and also correlated
poorly with items in other groups. Nevertheless, we decided
they should form a single criterion (see Table 2.1).

The last group representing inadequate housing also intercorrelated only moderately (r=0.34) and there were no
important correlations between these items and those from
the other groups. Since lack of a fixed bath and a shared
lavatory affected as many as 48 per cent of families they
were omitted (see Table 2.1).

Thus, our final decision was to group the items that reflected similar concepts of deprivation; this gave rise to six
clusters and their frequency analysis is also presented in
Table 2.1. This decision was supported by intercorrelations
within clusters. All six criteria were identifiable when the
Red Spot children were five years of age in 1952, and the
first five were again identifiable in 1957 when the children
reached their tenth birthday. Assuming that each criterion
had the same 'value' as an indicator of family deprivation,

Table 2.1   *The frequency of criteria of deprivation*
             in 847 families in 1952

A.	Family/marital disruption i. Divorce/separation ii. Marital instability	14.5%
B.	Parental illness Parent incapacitated by illness	12.2%
C.	Poor physical and domestic care i. Personal cleanliness ii. Domestic cleanliness iii. Poor clothing	12.6%
D.	Social dependence i. Debt ii. Unemployment iii. National Assistance	17.5%
E.	Housing (overcrowding)	18.7%
F.	Poor mothering qualities (non-coping)	15.2%

Table 2.2   *Distribution of criteria in 847 families in 1952*

No. of Criteria	No. of Families		Percentage of Total		Combined Percentages
0	482	482	57.0	=	57% Non deprived
1 2	165 } 84 }	249	19.5 9.9	=	29% Deprived
3 4 5 6	61 30 17 8	116	7.2 3.5 2.0 0.9	=	14% Multiple deprivation

each family was given a score of '1' for each criterion exhibited. Families without any criterion scored zero. The definition score for any family then could range from 0 to 6. We confirmed that it was reasonable to sum the scores of deprivation by subjecting the data to factor analysis.

Table 2.2 shows that 482 (57 per cent) of the 847 families had no adverse criteria. One-fifth of families had one criterion and the number of families affected fell rapidly as the number of criteria increased until only 1 per cent were affected by all six criteria. In all, one family in seven (14 per cent) had three or more criteria and were in 'multiple deprivation'.

Agreement between pairs of criteria (Table 2.3)
This can be represented in terms of percentage overlap between pairs of criteria, by summing the cases with either of two criteria and calculating what percentage of the total have both. The highest overlap (50 per cent) occurred with poor care and poor mothering (Table 2.3). Further, each of the criteria correlate at least moderately highly with the summed score with correlations ranging from 0.52 to 0.70.

Table 2.3   Percentage overlap in pairs of criteria
            847 families in 1947

		A	B	C	D	E	F
Family/marital disruption	A	—					
Parental illness	B	16.5	—				
Poor care	C	17.4	18.6	—			
Social dependence	D	22.6	37.9	25.6	—		
Housing — overcrowding	E	14.7	15.0	27.4	25.4	—	
Poor maternal mothering (non-coping)	F	22.4	18.4	50.3	25.3	26.4	
Summed score and its correlation with each of the criteria		(0.52)	(0.57)	(0.70)	(0.70)	(0.59)	(0.70)

Previous assessment of deprivation

Wedge and Prosser (1973) using National Child Development Study data reported 6.2 per cent of families affected by low income, poor housing and adverse family situation. Stevenson and Graham (1983) reported that 6.6 per cent of their families showed three or more of their eight indices of family disadvantage. Both of these rates are lower than the 14 per cent we report for multiple deprivation. Berthoud (1980) used data collected during the 1975 General Household Survey to identify six adverse criteria: educational disadvantage (43 per cent); family (lone parent or divorced/separated, or four or more children) (19 per cent); poor housing (19 per cent); low income (24 per cent) sickness and work handicap (that is, unemployed, or in semi-skilled or unskilled work) (41 per cent). The educational and work criteria were rather broad and were unlikely to represent a severe deprivation and this affected a large percentage of families; accordingly 8.8 per cent of families had four or more criteria, which is higher than the 6.4 per cent in our study. The differences may be determined by definition and method. None of these workers included assessments of mothering skills and these may be fundamental to the problem. The method of aggregating the criteria may be crucial — for instance Stevenson and Graham (1983) define deprivation as the worst 10 per cent on each of the eight measures. Finally, no evidence is provided of the extent of overlaps between criteria and, until this information is available, it is difficult to compare deprivation across samples.

There are difficulties, and they have been well described by Brown and Madge (1982): 'Multiple deprivation comes in many shapes and forms, and is due to a variety of causes . . . in general deprivation of one kind attracts deprivation of another'. Irrespective of the method, it is evident that single deprivations are more widespread in the community than is often appreciated — 76 per cent in the Berthoud study, just over 50 per cent in the Stevenson and Graham research and just under 50 per cent in the Newcastle study.

Tracing and follow-up: isolating groups for study

Four groups of families to be interviewed were extracted by random sampling (see Chapter 5). In this procedure the following principles were considered. First, the random control group would provide a yardstick for comparison with other studies. Second, an important comparison was to be between the non-deprived group and the deprived groups. However, because a high percentage of the families had at least one criterion of deprivation, we might have concentrated on mild rather than severe deprivation. The use of a multiply deprived group would constitute an insurance against that possibility. Nevertheless, it was essential that our research strategy should allow a comparison between the non-deprived and the total group of deprived families.

There was also overlap between the two deprived groups, and they are not directly comparable. This created problems when mutually exclusive groups were needed for certain statistical analyses. To facilitate direct comparisons between different degrees of deprivation, the families were also regrouped into three categories of non-deprived (zero criteria), moderate deprivation (one or two criteria) and multiple deprivation (three or more criteria). Similar regrouping was undertaken in the families of the 266 'Red Spots' as adults and their spouses or partners.

Types of deprivation

It is also necessary to consider the effects of the different types of deprivation and whether there is constancy or change in types of deprivation across the generations. Six groups of families each representing a different type of deprivation were therefore isolated (see Table 2.1, p. 19). The numbers were as follows:

Marital Disruption	Parental Illness	Poor Care	Social Dependency	Over Crowding	Poor Mothering
70	63	66	89	92	81

Tracing and cooperation of the families

Our project depended upon an ability to trace and obtain the cooperation of the 300 families in the samples we had isolated (see Table 2.4). We first made an appeal over the local radio and in the local newspapers asking the parents of 'Red Spots' or the children themselves (then 33 years of age) to get in touch with us. The results were encouraging for we located 90 (31 per cent) of those we wished to visit. Only five responses came by letter, the rest by telephone from the

Table 2.4   *The criteria of deprivation in 1979–80:*
Red Spots (Generation II) as adults

Features considered additional to the six criteria used in 1952

Group 1   Psychological Disturbance of Parents
         1. Disturbance of mother
         2. Disturbance of father
         3. Alcoholism (excluded)

Group 2   Socio-economic Stress
         4. Unemployment
         5. Job mobility
         6. Poor maternal resources (excluded)
         7. Poor socio-economic status
         8. Poor domestic facilities (excluded)
         9. Large family size

Group 3   Education and Further Training
       10. Education – mother
       11. Education – father
       12. Further vocational training

Group 4   Parental Stress
       13. Marital stress
       14. Parental psychological stress
       15. Maternal over-concern about family
       16. Family mobility
       17. Problems of care and fostering (excluded)

'Red Spots', their spouses, their parents or other close relations. This was the easiest part of the search.

Next we located families through statutory agencies. We negotiated an arrangement with the Office of Population Census and Statistics who provided the details of Family Practitioner Committees with which the individuals were registered as patients. We then wrote to the Secretary of each of these Committees explaining our purpose and asked if we could be permitted to have the name of the family practitioner. We then got in touch with the family doctor, explained our purpose and asked his permission to approach or to send a letter to the family. Again, the cooperation was remarkable, and in this way we made contact with another 109 (37 per cent) of the families. We also pursued local searches. The housing list proved particularly useful and neighbours were helpful. This gave another 25 (8 per cent) families. We then extended the direct search by visiting relatives, friends and other 'Red Spot' families — particularly through local child health centres.

Searches of telephone directories and electoral registers were laborious rather than rewarding, but we did get six names in this way and these, with the 34 from the 'local gossip', gave 40 (13 per cent) including some valuable addresses for families who had gone abroad. Later we made contact with four more families in the armed forces.

In all we traced and obtained agreement to visit 268 families. This left 27 families who fell into two residual groups. First, there were some 15 families or individuals who were traced but could not be interviewed — of these five had died, six refused or did not reply to our letters, and four appeared to lead lives of irregular movement throughout the locality. That left 11 of whom we had no knowledge at that time. We learned later that two of these had died. Ultimately, therefore, we were able to trace and interview 266 Red Spots (264 families since two had married other Red Spots) all but five within the United Kingdom. Those abroad were interviewed in South Africa, Australia, the USA and Canada.

Comment

We were encouraged that we had been able to trace 96 per cent of those in the sample groups. In the end we interviewed 92 per cent of those still living. The success of our search, more than 15 years after the end of the original study, was due chiefly to two factors. First, the relative stability of the population and, second, the firm lasting relationship established in the first study between the families and the observers had brought its own reward. In 1979 only about 20 per cent of the second-generation 'Red Spot' families lived beyond Tyneside and the adjacent areas of Northumberland and Durham which might be fairly described as the North-East. Less than 3 per cent were known to have migrated beyond the United Kingdom.

In the United Kingdom there is one other study which has attempted to trace families studied over roughly the same period as the '1,000 Families'. Atkinson *et al.* (1980) set out to trace, as adults, the children of the 1,363 'Rowntree' parents who were studied in 1950. They concentrated on families headed by a man in full-time work, and using Kelly

Street Directories, voting lists and personal letters, they received a positive response from 567 families.

In the USA Robins (1966), studying deviant children, located 90 per cent of subjects, interviewed 82 per cent, and obtained adult agency records for 98 per cent. More recently, in Wisconsin, Clarridge *et al.* (1978) traced 92.5 per cent of high school graduates 17 years after they had left school by contacting parents and using telephone and taxation record searches, but they only obtained telephone interviews with 88 per cent.

The family interviews and school visits

The meetings with the families took place from 1979 to 1981 and altogether 264 were visited. In some families two or more visits were needed to complete the interview. The school visit was complementary to the home interview for all families with children at school.

The family interviews

The home visits were conducted by three trained interviewers each taking an agreed area of the city and its immediate neighbourhood. All long-distance visits — that is, journeys requiring an overnight stop — were undertaken by the same interviewer.

As addresses became known, the interviewer got in touch with each family either by letter or by a personal visit to arrange a satisfactory time for the interview. For each family the best time varied with the family composition and occupation of the adults. Where both parents or partners were employed, an evening visit was the only time convenient, and this also applied when the father was the Red Spot. If neither parent was working, visits could be arranged during the day. Occasionally a special visit was needed to interview the father. But, in practically every case, a mutually satisfactory arrangement was found. Long-distance visits were necessarily arranged by correspondence or by telephone, and many took place during the weekend, yet there was not a single instance in which the arrangements for a long distance visit failed, even though it was always necessary to complete the interview in one session.

Separate interviewing of each partner was not always possible. The interviewers estimated that, where only two adults were to be seen, the visit took about three hours. Each child added another hour, so that families with more than two children required a second or, exceptionally, a third visit. In a few cases, interviews were carried out in two different houses.

We knew we were asking much of the families both in time and in the content of the interviews, and we approached our task with care. This was well worthwhile, for with only one or two exceptions the interviewers were well received and the families were actively cooperative, perhaps particularly so when the mother had been the 'Red Spot' child. Occasionally the father's attitude was that of amused tolerance and, once, it was suggested the team should organize a Red Spot reunion with plenty of Newcastle Brown — a potent local brew — which would have been wonderful but was unfortunately beyond our resources.

At the completion of the interview the Mill Hill vocabulary test was taken by both husband and wife, occasionally provoking friendly rivalry. Dictionaries, sometimes hopefully regarded, were prohibited. Only one man declined the test cheerfully saying he was not a reader and had truanted from school most of the time.

Only in two families was the interview not completed and in each case special circumstances understandably gave rise to apprehension, despite good relationships with the interviewers. One of the Red Spots was severely mentally handicapped and only the parents were interviewed.

Despite the length and complexity of the subject matter, the interviews were successfully achieved in all but four instances.

Long distance children   These children were tested, weighed and measured in their own homes by the family interviewer who had travelled from Newcastle. At the same time permission to contact the school was obtained from the parents and, after approaching the headmaster, behavioural questionnaires were sent to the teacher; all were completed and returned.

Overseas families   Five families were visited outside the United Kingdom. The same procedure was followed, but the interviewers were contemporary or former members of the Newcastle University Department of Child Psychiatry.

The interview technique   The interviewers, all of whom had previous experience of systematic interviewing for research purposes, had received further instruction in the technique of the semi-structured, focused interview. Regular quality checks were undertaken to ensure the consistency of scoring of the information given, and problems were discussed. A satisfactory level of reliability was achieved. The interviewers had no previous access to information about the family backgrounds.

The school visits

At each family interview, the presence of schoolchildren was noted and details of name, sex and age recorded. Each family was then asked to agree that we should visit the school the children attended. This was given in every case and permission was usually obtained in writing.

The next step was to approach the Director of Education in each of the relevant areas. We sent details of the purpose and method of the study and asked for permission to get in touch with the head teachers in each school. It is pleasant to record that we had generous help from both local and distant areas and Directors of Education notified the heads of the schools concerned. We then sent details of the study to each teacher and arranged to visit the school. The visits to local and nearby schools were made by one of three qualified teachers who were also trained as interviewers.

Each interviewer had scales which were of the same type, were synchronized and had been purchased at the same time. The testing material comprised Holborn Reading Scale (Watts, 1948), Crichton and Mill Hill Vocabulary and Raven Progressive Matrices (junior and senior) (Raven, Court and Raven, 1976). At school, the interviewer met the head or class teacher, for the study had caused considerable interest, particularly in those who remembered the original 'Red Spot' study. Many asked if they could be told of the ultimate findings. Several times the interviewers accepted invitations to join in assembly, listen to concerts or see exhibitions of works.

Most of the children, aged from 6 to 17 years, were interested for they knew about the study in which their parents had taken part.

Each child was seen alone and the tests were given after a little general conversation. After the test, each child was measured for height and weight and given a card, similar to that used in 1962, recording the results. Each assessment took some 40–60 minutes. Finally, on taking leave of the teacher, a Rutter B behaviour scale was left with an addressed and stamped envelope — all were completed and returned. If a child was absent, a further appointment was arranged, and eventually all were assessed.

The help we had received was always acknowledged, all the data collected were scored, double-checked and transferred to a specially designed proforma and transcription sheet.

The method 1979–80: defining deprivation in 1979–80

Study of the Red Spots as adults and parents posed a new situation. Each family now contained a spouse or partner about whom we did not have any previous information. We faced also the problem of defining a series of criteria of deprivation which would be applicable to the standards of reasonable family life in 1979–81 and representative of current views of deprivation.

The selection of items

We began with a group of six criteria resembling those identified in 1952 — namely, marital instability, parental illness, poor personal care of the child and home, social dependence, overcrowding and poor mothering ability. We then identified 17 further features which we thought might be more appropriate for use in 1980 and these were divided into four groups as set out in Table 2.4 (p. 23).

First we looked at the frequency of each item and excluded four which did not occur often enough to merit further consideration. We then studied the average correlations of items within each group. The education items in group 3 showed an average correlation of 0.33 but those for socioeconomic stress in group 2 and parental stress in group 4 were lower at 0.21 and 0.15 respectively. The intercorrelations of items relating to psychological disturbance of parents in group 1 was low; but as they gave a correlation of 0.30 with the parental illness criterion, their effects were considered to be represented therein. Similarly the items in group 4, parental stress, seemed to be represented in the marital disruption criterion (average correlation 0.27).

From principal component and other analyses, seven major criteria of deprivation could be identified in 1980. Six of these coincided with those described in 1952. The frequencies with which the seven occurred in 266 families in 1979–81, are given in Table 2.5. Only one of the 1952 criteria, overcrowding, was of reduced importance (although defined differently), and a new criterion of 'educational deprivation' (that is, the absence of educational qualifications, no school examinations or vocational training after leaving school) had assumed major significance.

In the family of origin, we had been subject to constraints in choosing and defining criteria of deprivation. However, there were no such constraints in relation to the family of formation as we were free to elicit information we considered appropriate to the present times. Nevertheless, we concluded that the data in 1952 and 1980 yielded very similar profiles of deprivation at each period.

Following a major change in housing circumstances in Newcastle after 1952, overcrowding had been displaced as a useful criterion. Nevertheless a housing measure was available which represented a lesser degree of overcrowding and which could be used instead of 'educational insufficiency' in order to achieve a crude comparison between the 1952 and

Table 2.5   Criteria of deprivation 1979–80

Frequency of each criterion of deprivation in 264 family units

1.	Marital instability	71 (27%)	(NA = 18)
2.	Parental illness	58 (22%)	(NA = 12)
3.	Poor care of child and home	41 (16%)	
4.	Social dependence	63 (24%)	
5.	Educational insufficiency	119 (45%)	
6.	Housing (overcrowding)	28 (11%)	
7.	Poor mothering ability	48 (18%)	(NA = 20)

Many families had more than one criterion.

NA = This item not applicable to the stated number of cases on the grounds of their being single or childless.

1980 criteria. This is not comparable with 1952 'overcrowding' because different definitions were used and in 1980 only 28 families (11 per cent) were rated as overcrowded. Yet in nearly half the families the parents had left school without any qualifications and had not afterwards had any vocational training, so that the effect of substituting one for the other was marked.

We had hoped to consider deprivation using criteria which were broadly comparable in both generations, but this proved not to be a credible exercise. Table 2.6 shows the distribution of the summed deprivation scores.

*Table 2.6   Distribution of families by
             number of criteria 1979–80*

Number of criteria	n = 264
0	75 (28%)
1	82 (31%)
2	47 (18%)
3	30 (11%)
4	19 (7%)
5 or 6	11 (4%)
	1980 assessment of deprivation

The criteria of deprivation in the family of formation
We have already discussed the importance of devising contemporary concepts of deprivation. An account is now given of the criteria that were eventually chosen.

1   Marital instability
This was defined as the presence of divorce or separation or marital instability as reflected by serious conflict, fights and physical aggression. The percentage given in Table 2.5 (p. 29) constitutes a slight underestimate as it does not allow for 18 Red Spots who were not married or cohabiting.

2 Parental illness

On this occasion we decided to confine parental illness to illness in the mother, mainly because a number of mothers were not living with their spouses yet carried responsibility for care of their children. Furthermore, illness in these mothers was more likely to give rise to stress and distress in their children (the third generation). Support for this decision was available from the statistical analysis (principal component analysis) which highlighted a cluster of physical and psychological disorders particularly in mothers. The two defining illness features were serious physical illness in the previous five years, and a chronic or recurrent illness lasting at least a year and substantially affecting her capacity to work or ability to cope with housework.

3 Poor care and domestic cleanliness

This was characterized by a low standard of care of household or children. It correlated highly with family size.

4 Social dependence

This was characterized by debt, unemployment (two or more years), and voluntary or mandatory contact with Social Services concerning any children before their fifth birthday.

5 Poor mothering ability

This consisted of judgements by the social interviewers, on the basis of the family interview, of mothers' ability to cope with tasks of mothering.

We appreciated that the judgements about mothering ability in the first-generation families were likely to have had sounder foundations as they were based on long knowledge of the family by health visitors and paediatricians. This item correlated significantly with a variety of features reflecting psychiatric disturbance of mother, marital stress, and low socioeconomic status. Despite a link with social dependency in the factor analysis, it was decided that this criterion required consideration on its own merit.

6 Housing: overcrowding — the family of formation

In 1952 overcrowding was defined according to the 1936 Housing Act and affected 18.7 per cent of the 847 families. But by 1980, due to the greatly improved housing circumstances in the city and a major rehousing programme, the less rigorous criterion of 1.5 or more persons per room identified only a small proportion of our sample of 264 families. For the purpose of comparison, an operational decision was made to take a subsample that approximated to the lowest 10 per cent on the overcrowding index, and this amounted to 28 families. It is noted that only 11 of these overlapped with overcrowded families in the previous generation.

We have already established that 'overcrowding' is of reduced importance as a criterion of deprivation in the 1980s. We could not propose any other housing standard which could be viewed as a meaningful criterion of deprivation in the 1980s. Non-ownership of one's home was a possibility but there were many circumstances, such as being accommodated in satisfactory council housing, where this could not in itself be considered as a deprivation.

7   *Educational insufficiency*

Society is continuously changing and therefore what is not perceived as deprivation in one decade may be so perceived two or three decades later. Other workers have suggested lack of basic educational achievements and occupational skills constitute deprivation in the 1970s and 1980s. We therefore examined the situation in our families, defining educational insufficiency as absence of any examination success at school-leaving and absence of occupational training after school.

In our families between one-third and two-thirds of second-generation males and females (both Red Spots and their spouses) were without educational achievements and 20 per cent had training aspirations but no success (Table 2.7). These rates proved too high for use as meaningful criteria.

Only a minority of the girls had vocational training and, when present, this was traditional in character; few had degrees or their equivalents. On the other hand, two-thirds of the men did have vocational training, many with degrees or equivalents. For these reasons we decided to aggregate this information and define a criterion of educational insufficiency which encompassed both parents.

Table 2.8 shows the distribution of this information. We

Table 2.7 *Post-school vocational attainments: families of formation (tertiary occupational training)*

	Second Generation Males	Second Generation Females
No further training	76	160
Further training but no vocational qualification	43	26
Degree or equivalent (e.g. City & Guilds, Technical Diplomas, etc.)	54	3
Professional training (nurse/teacher, etc.)	5	10
General vocational qualifications (secretary, trade apprenticeship, etc.)	48	50
Other combinations	10	3
Total	236	252

Table 2.8 *Distribution of educational insufficiency and educational attainment*

a. educational insufficiency

		'n'
1. Two-Person Family Unit		
(i) Neither parent has school-leaving qualifications or vocational educational achievements		44
(ii) Neither has school-leaving qualifications One has vocational achievement		58
2. Single-person Unit		
Has neither school-leaving qualifications nor vocational achievement		17
Total		119

b. educational attainment

		'n'
1. Two-Person Family Unit		
(i) One has school-leaving qualifications Neither has vocational achievement		10
(ii) One has educational qualifications One has vocational achievements		29
(iii) Neither has school-leaving qualifications Both have vocational achievements		19
(iv) One has school-leaving qualifications Both have vocational achievements		23
(v) Both have school-leaving qualifications Only one has vocational achievements		15
(vi) Both have school-leaving qualifications and vocational achievements		25
2. Single-Person Unit		
(i) Has both school-leaving qualifications and vocational achievements		11
(ii) Has school-leaving qualifications only		11
(iii) Has vocational achievements only		2
Total		145

considered that the foundations of educational sufficiency should be school-leaving qualifications in one or both of the adult partners (or in a single person). This simple decision needed modification to allow for some of the complex contingencies revealed in the table where both adults in a two-person family unit had obtained vocational qualifications despite the absence of school-leaving qualifications. These were solved by adding the rider that a unit should be categorized as showing educational insufficiency when both the adults in the family unit lacked school-leaving qualifications and when, in addition, one of the adults lacked any tertiary occupational achievement (and the equivalent for the single-person unit).

These were rigorous criteria and 119 (45 per cent) of 264 family units were rated as deprived. But as this was the sum of stratified samples, each sub-population needed to be considered separately. When this was done, the incidence rose sharply from the non-deprived families (21 per cent) through the random control (38 per cent) and deprived groups (49 per cent) to 65 per cent of the multiply deprived. Thus, even in non-deprived families, one in five of the adults were without educational success or vocational training, and this was the situation in one in three of all the 847 families.

PART II
FAMILY AND
ENVIRONMENT

3 Families of origin: the Red Spot children 1947–62

Social data in 1947

When the extent and distribution of family deprivation in 1952 had been defined, we looked at the family data at the time of the child's birth. The social data of the families in 1947 is shown in Table 3.1 and reveals that the families in the three categories of deprivation in 1952 were likely to have been already deprived in 1947 when the Red Spot child was born.

Table 3.1   Social, family and health data in 1947 at
birth of Red Spot child in 264 families
visited in 1979–80

Situation in 1947	Degree of Deprivation in 1952					
	Non-Deprived		Deprived		Multiply Deprived	
	0 criteria		1 or more criteria		3 or more criteria	
	n	%	n	%	n	%
Illegitimate/uncertain	0	0	19	10**	13	17**
Marital instability	1	2	50	27**	36	46**
Overcrowding: (statutory)	1	2	42	23*	30	38**
Age at marriage: under 20	10	16	65	38**	37	51**
Persons in household (mean)	4.7		5.1*		5.6**	
Occupational class						
I + II	14%		2%		1%	
III	65%		47%		28%	
IV + V plus	21%		51%		71%	
Sleeps in parents' bed	0	0	50	27**	33	46**
Poor mothering	0	0	64	35	57	73
Total 'n'	62		170–185		72–78	

*   = p < .05
** = p < .01

Note: Tests of significance are one-tailed and refer to the non-deprived group.

Social data in 1952

Some of these data simply reflect the criteria of deprivation by which the families were selected, but others provide a more detailed picture of differences between the groups in terms of family, social and health factors. Table 3.2 shows how deprived families differ from non-deprived in terms of parental employment, family size and parental loss or ill-health. In every assessment the position of the multiply deprived was worse than that of the deprived.

Table 3.2   Social data of families of origin, 1947–52

	Non-Deprived		Any Deprivation		Multiply Deprived	
Total 'n'	63		185		78	
	n	%	n	%	n	%
Work						
i. Father unemployed	0	0	67	36**	48	62**
ii. Mother works full or part-time	16	25	60	32	31	40**
iii. Family on National Assistance	0	0	31	17*	27	35**
iv. Occupational class IV + V	13	21	93	50	50	64
Unclassified (unemployed etc.)	0	0	18	10	9	12
Ordinal Position and Family Size						
i. Third or subsequent child	9	14	72	39	45	58
ii. Number of children ($\bar{x}$)	2.2 (SD 1.1)		3.4 (SD 2.0)		4.3 (SD 2.2)**	
Illness and Parental Loss (excluding death)						
i. Parent illness	0	0	56	30**	41	53**
ii. Loss of father	3	5	45	24**	25	32**
iii. Loss of mother	0	0	10	5**	5	6**

*   = p < .05
** = p < .01

Notes: 1. The main criteria are presented in Figure 3.1.
2. The above items contributing to composites.
3. Tests of significance are one-tailed and refer to the non-deprived group.

Parental loss and illness in 1952

Just over one in four of the deprived Red Spots were born

into a household without a father or one from which he disappeared in the first five years; by definition, absence of the father, except by death, constituted one criterion of deprivation. Disappearance of father was common in the marital disruption group, but uncommon in the overcrowding group, while loss of mother, although it showed a similar pattern of associations, was much less frequent.

Significant parental illness, defined as sufficient to impair either parent's contribution to normal family life, whether for physical or psychological reasons, shows a similar steep gradient running at about one-third of the deprived and half of the multiply deprived groups.

The criteria of deprivation

The overall picture is best revealed in Figure 3.1 which shows the intermediate position of the curve of the deprived group in relation to all six criteria — running from 30 to 40 per cent — and the extreme position of the curve of the multiply deprived group where the percentages of families

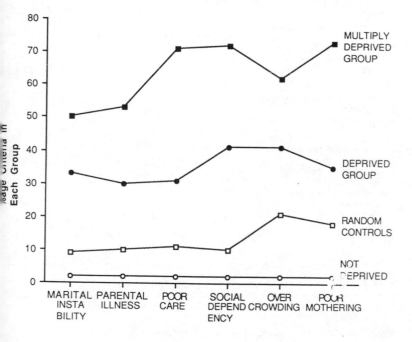

Figure 3.1 Profile of deprivation (criteria)

with a particular criterion run between 50 and 70 per cent. By definition, all points on the curve of the non-deprived group are zero.

Social and family factors in 1962
By 1962 about 15 per cent of the families had been lost by removal from the city. Nevertheless, the remaining 760 families provided a broad picture of the social and family circumstances of the different groups (see Table 3.3)

Table 3.3   Social data, families in 1962 categorized according to deprivation in 1952

	Non-Deprived		Deprived		Multiply Deprived	
	n	%	n	%	n	%
Child Loss within the Family						
i. Miscarriages	1	2	37	23**	18	26*
ii. Death of a sibling before 1962	0	0	14	9*	1ͅ	20**
Father's Presence						
Father present throughout 15 years	44	83	105	65**	37	53**
Father never present, divorced, permanently separated or died	4	8	29	18	19	27
Unemployment						
Father 1947–62 unemployed > 1 year	2	4	45	28**	31	44**
Parents and Home						
Poor participation by father in domestic tasks (where father present)	1	2	53	39**	35	66**
Poor parental interest in Red Spot	0	0	29	18**	27	39**
Father perceived as poor organizer	3	6	50	31**	35	50**
Child care: poor/incompetent	3	6	33	20*	30	43**
Personality — Effective, Kind and Considerate						
i. Father	28	53	30	19**	5	7**
ii. Mother	24	45	26	16**	2	3**
Total 'n'	50–53		159–161		70	

*   = p < .05
** = p < .01

Notes: 1. The main criteria are presented in Figure 3.1.
2. The above items contributing to composites.
3. Tests of significance are one-tailed and refer to the non-deprived group.

Miscarriages or deaths within the family indirectly reflected the social circumstances of the 1940s, as higher rates of loss were experienced by the less skilled occupational groups (Miller *et al.*, 1974). This is also reflected in relation to deprivation — for instance, 10 times as many of the mothers in the deprived groups had had a miscarriage as compared to the non-deprived. In addition, a sibling had died in one in five of the multiply deprived families but not in any of the non-deprived families. The 1940s were unusual times for child health and it is unlikely that such associations would still hold in the 1970s and 1980s.

One important family theme is the presence of a father throughout childhood. Parental roles within a family are important, the father giving both material and emotional support, and serving as a model for direction, guidance and identification. His mere presence does not ensure the existence of such qualities. In non-deprived families, 83 per cent of fathers were present throughout the whole of the 15 years 1947–62 but this held for only 53 per cent in the multiply deprived families. The use of the more stringent criterion of complete absence of the father during those first 15 years is seen to affect the multiply deprived group three times more frequently than the non-deprived. In deprived families the cumulative rate of fathers' absence at some time over the 15 years is considerable. A similar pattern occurs with unemployment where only 4 per cent of fathers in non-deprived families were unemployed for more than one year in the first 15 years. However, even when present, the fathers in the multiply deprived group participated poorly in domestic tasks whereas most of the non-deprived fathers were rated as participating well. Half the multiply deprived fathers were considered to be poor organizers and only a small minority were thought to be effective, kind and considerate, based on the judgement of the research team who had known these families for the entire period (Miller *et al.*, 1974).

In brief, the deprived groups were characterized by frequent absence of fathers and, even when present, these tended to be inadequate providers who made little contribution to domestic activities and were seldom thought to be competent or caring. Similar differences were apparent in respect of mothers. In the non-deprived group few rated as poor or incompetent housekeepers or as showing poor care of children, whereas almost half of those in the multiply deprived group were so considered and only an occasional mother in the multiply deprived group was described as having an effective, kind and considerate personality.

Finally, we looked at the data in relation to the six different types of deprivation and could find no distinctive patterns. There was a tendency for more adverse ratings on the variables listed in Table 3.3 in the case of the poor physical and domestic care group, and the least adverse ratings occurred in the parental illness group.

While none of the parents of the non-deprived was said to show poor interest in their children, about 40 per cent of the multiply deprived reportedly did so. The overall picture was that, in the multiply deprived group, the children were exposed to poor parenting either by omission or commission, and lack of parental interest in the children's development and progress were chiefly evident. It would not be unreasonable to suggest that these multiple factors must be acting directly or combining to produce a social and family environment which is inimical for child development.

The spouses

Spouses' retrospective accounts of their family experiences
It was necessary, despite the limitations of retrospective data, to consider whether the information obtainable from the Red Spot spouses in 1979–80 could be used to develop a comparable index of deprivation which would reflect the circumstances of their childhood homes and compare with recollections of the 'Red Spot' children themselves at a comparable age.

To check the validity of data collected in this way we had asked the Red Spots to try to recall their family circumstances during their school years. The material obtained tended to refer to the years in junior school and corresponded closely to our recorded data relating to 1957. That comparison was based on five criteria, omitting that relating to social dependency, since the Red Spots could not be expected to have knowledge of family reliance on state subsistence during their early childhood.

Table 3.4 provides a picture of the three criterion groups

Table 3.4   The three groups of Red Spots classified
according to deprivation in the family of
origin in 1952 (i.e. the 5th year)

Accounts from the parents of Red Spots in 1957	Non-Deprived Group (1952) %	Deprived Group (1952) %	Multiply Deprived Group (1952) %
Score 0	85	50	21
1 + 2	15	41	53
3 +	0	9	25
Accounts from memories in 1980 (retrospective)			
Score 0	62	37	24
1 + 2	33	49	54
3 +	5	14	22

Note: Comparisons of the percentage of families scoring zero, one or two, and three or more deprivation criteria in 1957 (i.e. 10th year) and also on retrospective enquiry in 1980 concerning deprivation in the families of origin.

classified according to the degree of deprivation in the family of origin in 1952. To obtain this we used data collected prospectively at year ten from the parents of the Red Spots and retrospectively from the Red Spots themselves recalling family life during their junior school years.

It is surprising how well the percentage distribution of these prospective and retrospective accounts coincided for the three criterion groups and this was particularly true of the multiply deprived. This level of agreement suggested that there was acceptable general validity. Furthermore, correlating the deprivation index scores based on retrospective and prospective enquiry in relation to Red Spot families gave rise to an overall coefficient 0.30. When the data were correlated in relation to specific criteria, the only satisfactory correlation was on marital disruption (0.52); poor mothering correlated only moderately (0.24), and the rest showed little in the way of specific agreement. It seemed therefore that retrospective memories (with the exception of marital disruption) were usually concerned with general aspects of deprivation rather than the specific types of deprivation we have defined (see Table 3.5).

*Table 3.5   Correlation of criteria of deprivation
gathered prospectively and retrospectively*

Data Gathered Retrospectively	Data Gathered Prospectively						
	A	B	C	D	E	F	G
A. Marital Disruption	0.52**					NA	0.34**
B. Parental Illness		0.00				NA	0.00
C. Personal Care			0.24***			NA	0.24***
D. Social Dependence	NA	NA	NA	NA	NA	NA	NA
E. Overcrowding					0.00	NA	0.14*
F. Maternal Care						NA	0.23***
G. Total of Five Criteria	0.25***	0.12*	0.27**	0.21***	0.00	NA	0.30***

*p < .05
**p < 0.1
***p < .001
NA = No data available.

We concluded that it was reasonable to use the retrospective data to reflect the early life of the Red Spot spouses in
the form of a global or total index of deprivation, and the
results are set out in Table 3.6. These agreed closely,
particularly in the deprived group with the recall data from
the Red Spots themselves. This suggests that many of the
Red Spots have married partners whose families had a similar
background to their own.

*Table 3.6   Spouses' retrospective accounts of
childhood experiences*

Retrospective Accounts from the Red Spot Spouses (families of formation)	Non-Deprived Group (1952) %	Deprived Group (1952) %	Multiply Deprived Group (1952) %
Non-deprived	58	36	32
Deprived	40	51	46
Multiple deprivation	2	13	22

Note: The three criterion groups classified according to deprivation in family
of origin in 1952.

The absolute numbers and percentages of our three groups defined according to deprivation in the family of origin of the Red Spots in 1952 are as follows:

1   Some 85 per cent of the non-deprived were married or cohabiting (n = 52).
2   Some 82 per cent of the deprived were married or cohabiting (n = 135).
3   Some 84 per cent of the multiply deprived were married or cohabiting (n = 58).

We earlier gave details about the families of origin of the Red Spots. We now provide some details concerning the families of origin of the spouses. An examination of family circumstances in the early life of the Red Spot spouses can provide answers to some important questions, such as whether groups of persons from deprived backgrounds reproduce similar circumstances in their own families. One way of answering this question is by ascertaining whether there is a link between adverse childhood experiences of the spouse and current family circumstances. We may hypothesize that, when couples set up house together, they would establish a new set of family conditions. However, if the presence of current depriving circumstances is predicted by previous experiences, then we have powerful evidence of the continuity of deprivation.

A relatively simple method was used to examine the above idea. First, the Red Spots were located in the appropriate category of deprivation according to the criteria of deprivation in their family of origin in 1952. Their spouses' early life experiences were then studied in relation to this classification. If specific early life experiences of the spouses proved to be related to the presence of deprivation in the family of origin of their Red Spot partners then we would have clues about the basis of the assortive mating. Second, each of the Red Spots and their spouses were located in categories according to the type and degree of deprivation in their current family circumstances (family of formation). If the spouses' early life experience proved to be linked significantly to the current circumstances of their families as adults, then it would mean that early life experiences of a spouse predict the type and degree of deprivation in his or her family in the next generation.

*Data concerning the spouses' early life experiences
in relation to category of deprivation in family of
origin of the Red Spots (Tables 3.6 and 3.7)*

When the Red Spot came from a non-deprived home, the
spouse usually reported few negative early life experiences.
Most of the families were Social Class II or III. Family size
was smaller than that of the deprived, and few reported loss
of a parent by separation or death. In 1957 one in four
families owned their own house and there was little overcrowding. Domestic and sanitary arrangements were generally
reasonable. Although one-third reported significant illness in
parents, the incidence of maternal nervous problems seemed
low, as did those relating to alcohol. About one in five
remembered parents receiving National Assistance. Less than
one in 20 reported any difficulties at school.

In contrast, the spouses in families with multiple
deprivation in 1979–80 remembered many negative early
life experiences. One in three had been separated from both
parents and one in six had experienced the loss of a parent
before they were 15 years old. In 10 per cent of families
parents had separated. Families were larger than those of the
non-deprived, there was little home ownership and domestic
facilities were often inadequate. Half remembered parents
with illnesses which affected their care of the family. Nearly
one in three remembered drink problems in parents. About
half remembered their families being on National Assistance.
Finally, one in five reported difficulties at school. Thus, the
spouses' early family circumstances related to the broad
deprivation status of their Red Spot partner.

A study of the spouses' life experiences in relation to the
different types of deprivation during the childhood of
the Red Spots revealed a similar pattern to that described in
the case of the deprived group. However, none of the six
different types of deprivation gave rise to a distinctive
pattern — that is, the patterns of adverse experiences did not
vary much one from the other. Such findings constitute an
argument against the notion of specificity of effects of
deprivation.

This proved true for evidence of separation, maternal
nervousness, family drink problems, rates of owner-
occupation, poor domestic facilities, and so on. Furthermore,
without producing data in table form, the spouses' early

Table 3.7 Spouse early life experiences classified
according to deprivation in families of Red Spots

		Red Spot Non-Deprived	Red Spot Deprived	Red Spot Multiply Deprived
		%	%	%
i	Lived with natural parents to age 15	92	78**	70**
ii	Death of either parent before 15	2	10**	16*
iii	Separation from mother after age of 5	6	18	25
iv	Separation from father after age of 5	11	29	37
v	Mean no. children in family when spouse 5 years	2.7	3.3	3.8
vi	Occupational class of father Year 5 classification			
	I and II	10	4	2
	III	61	49	47
	IV, V and Unemployed	29	47	51
vii	Significant illness in parents of Red Spot spouse	31	40	52*
viii	On National Assistance (social welfare)	20	34	46*
ix	Drink problems in parents	15	21	29*
x	Owner–occupier of home	27	10	2
	Council-rented	33	49	49*
xi	Overcrowding	17	42	50**
xii	Bathroom: sole use	69	61	48**

*p < .05
**p < 0.1
***p < .001

family circumstances also appear to predict their own deprivation status in the family of formation. It needs to be emphasized that these findings refer to deprivation as broadly perceived rather than as correlations of specific deprivations. For instance, the correlation between the composite indices of deprivation in the families of the Red Spots and those of their spouses while highly significant is low (r = 0.19; p < 0.01). The only criterion with a specific significant correlation is overcrowding in the family backgrounds of the Red Spots and their respective spouses but this is again low (r = 0.19; p < 0.05). Marital disruption in the Red Spot families correlated significantly with the *composite index of deprivation* in the Red Spot spouse family (r = 0.19; p < 0.01); as did overcrowding (r = 0.23; p < 0.01) and poor mothering (r = 0.19; p < 0.01). This supports the view that there is no specific assortive mating, but rather that individuals from poor or generally deprived homes are likely to consort with one another.

Discussion

The question arises as to whether spouses of Red Spots came from families with similar backgrounds to the Red Spots themselves. We are aware that spouses' recollections may have been affected by both distortions and defects in memory, but prospective and retrospective data from the Red Spot families indicate that memories seem to have surprising 'group validity'. It was noted that the majority of spouses of non-deprived Red Spots reported a background comparable to their partners/husbands and wives. Almost 60 per cent of the Red Spots who were not deprived in 1979–80 had partners who came from similar social and family backgrounds and only 2 per cent had a partner who came from a heavily deprived background. On the other hand, one-third of the spouses of Red Spots with multiple deprivation at the age of five claimed to have come from families which were reportedly free from deprivation.

From the data presented we concluded that it was reasonable to use the retrospective data from the spouses as reflecting their earlier life experiences. However, we did note that in the retrospective accounts, the Red Spots in the non-deprived group appear to over-report hardship, whereas those in the multiply deprived group give reports which more closely coincide with their actual earlier life experiences.

We have demonstrated a link between the early adverse experiences of Red Spot spouses and those of their Red Spot partners. All the above suggests that the Red Spots — men and women suffering different degrees of deprivation — tended to choose partners from a similar background of deprivation. However, there was little specificity about that choice.

Again, without going into details, there were also

indications that the couples who made up the families of formation tended to introduce into their own houses the same patterns of deprivation they had experienced in childhood — an important but not surprising tendency.

4   Families of formation

Social and family data 1980

Method
In this section we present our data on the second generation
as adults. We decided that a household unit would mean any
second-generation adult in any of the following circumstances, but only families in categories (a) and (c) could be
used when considering the children of the third generation:

(a)   a married or cohabiting couple with children
(b)   a couple without children
(c)   a single parent
(d)   a single person.

We also decided that, except for certain key variables, in
the new families men and women would be looked at collectively as Red Spots or spouses.
In addition, we had to decide whether to classify the
families according to archival evidence of deprivation in
the family of origin or current evidence of deprivation in the
family of formation. There were good reasons for doing
both. The former tells us about the social and family circumstances in 1980 of groups of Red Spots according to whether
they were categorized as deprived or not deprived in 1952.
The latter tells us about the social family circumstances of
groups of families who were categorized in 1980 as deprived
or not deprived.
Our tables provide distributions of social and family
factors reported in 1980 in the various groups defined
according to 1952. It will be evident that there is a degree
of repetition inherent in this exercise — but it is analogous to
the classification of disorders in psychiatry whereby cardinal
criteria are used to define a disorder and co-morbidity is
thereafter established by empirical research. In addition, a
distribution of such factors is provided in groups defined

according to the severity of deprivation in their families of formation.

In the second generation there are inevitably shifts both in and out of deprivation (see Part IV). If deprivation in the family of formation were unrelated to that in the family of origin, then the social and family data in the second generation as adults would be randomly distributed when the households are defined according to the degree of deprivation in the family of origin. If there are relatively close links in deprivation between the two generations, then the distributions of social and family data in the family of formation should reflect the original grouping. In fact, we found considerable excesses according to the original grouping.

Tables 4.1 and 4.2 record the recollections of the men and women in families of formation (1979–80) regarding their own parents and homes. The differences between the memories of families in the different categories of deprivation in 1979–80 can be seen.

Only half of those women who were multiply deprived as children had both parents still alive in 1980 as against two-thirds of those who were not deprived (Table 4.1). In the case of men, these differences are not so substantial. However, the surviving parents of the multiply deprived tended to live nearer their families than did those of the non-deprived, and contact was more regular. This is likely to reflect the reduced mobility of multiply deprived families.

The women in the multiply deprived group (both Red Spots and spouses) reported an excess of parents too busy or too ill to care for them during childhood and, when they did, the care given tended to be poor. They also reported more arguments between their parents than did those from other groups. A similar picture was obtained from the men, and the data have not been presented. Of considerable importance is the evidence of lower occupational status of the respondents' fathers in the multiply deprived group, as compared to the non-deprived, coded according to the Registrar General's classificatory system.

Table 4.2 gives current data. A higher proportion of the adults living in deprivation as compared to those living in multiply deprived circumstances claimed good relationships with their siblings. However, while the differences between

*Table 4.1   Family of formation — 1979–80
            Recollections from Red Spots regarding parents*

	Non-Deprived Group 1952		Deprived Group 1952		Multiply Deprived Group 1952	
	n	%	n	%	n	%
A. Women's Report						
1. Both parents alive 1979–80	37	66	96	61	30	47
2. Parents together	33	59	71	49	23	40
3. Parents live locally	24	43	98	67	46	79
4. Mother too busy or ill to care for daughter during childhood	14	25	54	35	29	46
5. Poor care by mother	4	7	11	7	12	19
6. Poor care by father	5	9	18	13	11	20
7. Parental arguments	11	20	40	28	24	39
B. Men's Report						
1. Both parents alive 1979–80	31	55	74	52	28	46
2. Parents together	25	47	58	42	23	40
C. Men and Women: Memory of Fathers' Occupational Class During 1958–62						
I + II		16		3		1
III		58		50		43
IV + V		25		43		49
Unclassified		1		3		7
Total 'n'	53–56		132–157		50–62	

*Table 4.2   Families of formation 1979–80
            Women — current social and family data*

Present Circumstances	Non-Deprived Group (1952)		Deprived Group (1952)		Multiply Deprived Group (1952)	
	n	%	n	%	n	%
1. Frequent contact with siblings (at least fortnightly)	19/51	37	82/141	58**	33/60	55**
2. Good relations with siblings	46/51	90	117/141	83	44/60	73*
3. Less than 3 years full-time employment since leaving school (cumulative)	2/57	4	27/157	17	18/64	28*
4. Supplementary benefit	4/57	7	25/157	16*	21/64	33**
5. Without training and unwilling to undertake training	18/33	55	82/122	67	41/65	63*
6. Society unfair to you	5/57	9	32/157	20*	17/64	27*
7. Authorities do enough for the poor	30/70	43	61/157	39	16/64	25

*p < .05
**p < .01

the groups are significant, only a minority of all families reported poor relationships between siblings.

Second-generation women without vocational training were asked whether they intended to undertake any training in the future; a greater proportion of those from a deprived childhood background were not willing to undertake further training (Table 4.2).

We also asked who had been employed full-time for a cumulative total of less than three years since leaving school and found that only 4 per cent of those from non-deprived background had been so employed against 28 per cent of the multiply deprived — also more of the latter had been in part-time employment. Further, more families from multiply deprived backgrounds were on supplementary benefit and more of the women from multiply deprived families thought that society was unfair and did not do enough for the poor. When the families are reorganized according to current deprivation, the distribution showing receipt of supplementary benefit broadly resembles that already listed in relation to early life deprivation. This was a common finding.

Information about health and other worries
and concerns of second-generation women
Table 4.3 records some of the physical and psychological health problems of the second-generation females as adults. Little differences were apparent when the families were classified according to early life family deprivation, but some substantial differences emerged when the families were classified according to family deprivation in 1980. In 1980, in terms of chronic physical problems, the difference between non-deprived and multiply deprived was 52 per cent.

However, these wide differences were true only in relation to illness that mothers reported about themselves rather than illnesses they reported in their spouses. One exception concerned alcohol problems that women reported in their male spouses where the rate is zero in the non-deprived group as compared to one in five in the multiply deprived group. We suspect that this underestimates the real situation as there was a general reluctance to talk about drink during the interviews.

Again, as occurred in the Red Spots as children, the

children from multiply deprived families of formation were twice as prone to accidents requiring treatment than the children of the non-deprived. Such an excess of accidents probably reflects more dangerous environmental circumstances as well as poorer care. It is interesting to note that, when the families are reorganized according to deprivation in 1952 in the family of origin, the pattern of percentages of accidents in the third-generation under fives is similar — that is, 26, 35 and 58 per cent respectively.

Table 4.3   Families of formation: physical and psychological health of women

	Non-Deprived Group (1979–80)		Deprived Group (1979–80)		Multiply Deprived Group (1979–80)	
	n	%	n	%	n	%
A. Chronic or Recurring Health Problems in Last 5 Years						
1. Amount	0/70	0	58/182	32	29/60	48
2. Type of problems						
Physical	0/70	0	45/182	25	31/60	52
Psychiatric	0/70	0	10/182	5	20/60	33
B. No Hospital Treatment in Previous Year	52/70	74	117/182	64	35/60	58
C. Reported Illness: Male Spouse						
1. Male partners drink problems	0/43	0	9/82	11	6/27	22
2. Nature of illness						
Physical	6/67	9	28/160	18	12/50	24
Psychiatric	1/67	1	4/160	3	1/50	2
Both	0/67	0	3/160	2	2/50	4
D. Third-Generation Children Treated for Accidents in First Five Years	7/28	25	25/67	37	12/23	52

Social and family factors in 1979–80

In 1980 the wife or cohabitee (girlfriend) in multiply deprived families was about two years younger than in the non-deprived. The men were about five years older than their partners but less than two years older in the non-deprived group.

In more than half of the families the partners had known each other for more than two years before marriage but the proportion was higher in the non-deprived than in the deprived group; more spouses in the multiply deprived group were living apart than in the non-deprived. There was a similar gradient in the rate with which couples became irritable with each other, reflecting the higher rates of marital disharmony in the multiply deprived group.

These gradients of percentages or rates of characteristics in families in 1980 are again remarkably similar when the families are reorganized according to deprivation in the family of origin in 1952, but the discrepancy between the non-deprived, deprived and multiply deprived groups is not so steep. For instance, the percentages of partners who knew each other for more than two years are 81, 59 and 58 per cent respectively, and irritability of couples with each other are 17, 25 and 37 per cent respectively.

In 1980 the home situation in any family appeared to be partly a reflection of conditions in the family of origin and partly due to the personal characteristics of the couple and their circumstances.

Table 4.4 shows that male unemployment was greater in the previous five years in the multiply deprived families than in the non-deprived, the difference between groups being far greater in relation to groupings of families based on deprivation in 1980 than in 1952. Second, there was a difference in the number of jobs an individual had held since leaving school — using the 1952 groupings, 16 per cent of the non-deprived had had nine or more posts since leaving school as compared to 29 per cent of the deprived and 36 per cent of the multiply deprived; but using the 1980 groupings the rates were 12, 31 and 51 per cent respectively.

It was clear that, just as with women, the parents of the multiply deprived men were more likely to live locally than those of the non-deprived. Contact with siblings appeared to be more frequent in the case of the multiply deprived than the non-deprived, probably because of their proximity. Just as with women, more of the men from families with multiple deprivation thought that society did not do enough for the poor and was unfair to them but the differences are significant only when the data is distributed according to definitions of family deprivation based on 1980 rather than

1952 criteria. Even so, the rate in the multiply deprived was a mere 27 per cent, suggesting either a relatively poor appreciation of social and economic differences or a remarkable generosity of attitude in the face of wide inequalities in society.

Table 4.4   Family of formation 1979–80
          Social and family factors

	Non-Deprived Group (1979–80)		Deprived Group (1979–80)		Multiply Deprived Group (1979–80)	
	n	%	n	%	n	%
A. Females						
Age of female partner when first married or cohabited	21.4 yrs		20.2 yrs		19.5 yrs	
Age of male partner when first married or cohabited	22.8 yrs		23.9 yrs		24.5 yrs	
Partners knew each other more than 2 years prior to current marriage/co-habitation	48/67	72	104/168	62*	31/53	58*
Either partner married before	0/74	0	52/180	29	24/59	41**
Couple get irritable with each other once a week or more	5/67	7	47/157	30	25/50	50
B. Males	Non-Deprived		Deprived		Multiply Deprived	
Employment in previous 5 years						
Mean length of time unemployed	0.9 months		9.1 months		14.6 months	
Family						
Contact with siblings at least fortnightly	24/63	38	83/149	56	28/48	58
Society						
Society unfair to you	4/72	6	27/163	17	14/51	27
C. Unemployment in 1980 According to 1952 Criteria	Non-Deprived Group (1952)		Deprived Group (1952)		Multiply Deprived Group (1952)	
Male unemployment previous 5 years: mean length of time unemployed	3.6 months		6.2 months		11.7 months	

*p < .05
**p < .01

Table 4.5 shows other individual items or features which reflect deprivation in 1980. They demonstrate expected patterns — for instance, marital quarrels were more common in the multiply deprived than the non-deprived. We see similar differences in respect of family size and family mobility. On the item 'no educational achievements of men and women' the rates were high in all groups but particularly so in the multiply deprived.

Table 4.5   *Families of formation: some items of deprivation 1980*

	Non-Deprived Group 1980		Deprived Group 1980		Multiply Deprived Group 1980	
	n	%	n	%	n	%
A. Items of Deprivation						
Marital rows	0	00	27	17	18	36
Family mobility	19	21	47	25	17	28
Three or more children	9	13	56	32	33	56
Family size: current family	1.9		2.3		2.7	
No educational achievement of women	24	34	142	78	55	92
No educational achievement of men	33	46	126	77	47	92
B. Criteria of Deprivation						
Marital disruption	0	0	71	40	36	62
Parent illness (mother)	0	0	58	32	29	48
Poor care and cleanliness	0	0	41	22	29	48
Social dependence	0	0	63	33	44	73
Poor mothering	0	0	48	27	35	58
Educational handicap	0	0	119	63	51	85
Total 'n'	67–75		164–189		50–60	

Percentages only	Non-Deprived Group 1952	Deprived Group 1952	Multiply Deprived Group 1952
Marital disruption	21	31	44

Data are also given relating to the frequency of the criteria of deprivation in 1980 and reveal a similar frequency distribution to other variables. When the families were classified according to earlier deprivation in the family of origin, marital disruption rates ran between 21 per cent in the non-deprived and 44 per cent in the multiply deprived; when defining family deprivation using the 1980 criteria, they run from nil to over 60 per cent. Similar patterns occurred in the other five criteria. Thus the differences are always greater between non-deprived and multiply deprived families when the defining criteria relate to the family of formation rather than the family of origin.

Figure 4.1 gives the prevalence of the indices of deprivation in the families in 1952 and 1980. The percentages of each of the criteria were estimated in 1980 in relation to the self-same groups. It must be emphasized that the 1952 data were based on the total population; the 1980 curves are that self-same population and are based on estimates for that population. We have tried to ensure that the defined deprivations were broadly comparable, although in some (such as illness) this was less so than in others. It will be noted that, while there is a marked convergence of the curves, the convergence is not even.

Nevertheless, these constitute important life cycle changes. Some might consider them merely a manifestation of a regression to the mean, but this is too simple an explanation. We see considerable divergence of the curves in relation to marital disruption, dependence on social welfare and poor mothering. The most dramatic changes occur in our two extreme groups: the group which is defined as non-deprived in the first generation shows evidence of some disadvantage in the second generation, notably in the areas of marital disruption and parental illness; the multiply deprived group, by contrast, shows considerable reduction in the areas of overcrowding and poor care. However, in marital disruption, poor mothering and social dependence, the multiply deprived still show considerable differences from the non-deprived group. Finally, the high rates of educational insufficiency must have a basis in factors associated with deprivation in family of origin.

The interpretation of these findings is essentially dependent on the methodology of the longitudinal design. Over the last three decades there have been both changes in living conditions and changes in standards. The life cycle changes described above, represented by a reduction in the incidence of all types of disadvantage, probably reflect a real change in social circumstances. This was the time of the economic expansion from 1950–65 (when the Prime Minister of the day, Harold Macmillan, was reminding the British electorate that

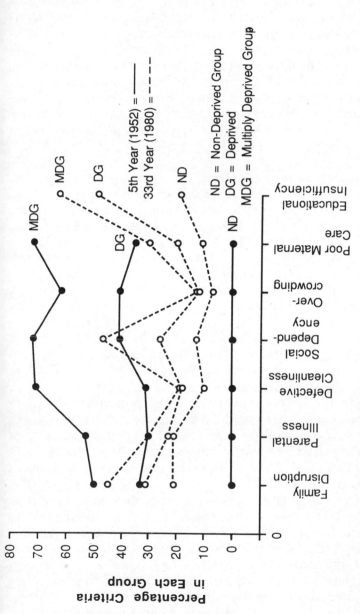

Figure 4.1   Profile of criteria of deprivation in the study groups in 1947 and 1979–80 at the 5th year (Generation I) and 33rd year (Generation II)

they had 'never had it so good'). The assessment of disadvantage in the second generation was undertaken during a harsh economic era of financial inflation and recession, and we think that the rate of social dependency reflects the social circumstances of the time. In times of economic recession families who were previously the most disadvantaged will prove to be the most vulnerable. Lower rates of overcrowding reflect not only differences of definition but real and considerable improvement in housing circumstances in post-war Newcastle to 1980. Finally, the high rates of marital disruption are likely to represent a real phenomenon of modern times.

Recent life events

While there have been extensive studies of the impact of recent life events on adult disorders (Holmes and Rahe, 1967) particularly in relation to depression (Brown and Harris, 1978; Paykel, 1974), research into the impact on child development and child disorder is less well advanced. The adult research, together with the early methodological papers of Coddington (1972) and Gersten *et al.* (1974), provided a groundwork for applications to children by Monaghan *et al.* (1979) and Goodyer *et al.* (1985).

A variety of conditions have now been studied: asthma (Zlatich *et al.*, 1982); adolescent pregnancies (Coddington *et al.*, 1979); behaviour problems in pre-school children (Earls, 1980). Correlations have been reported between negative life events and adolescent pregnancies, and also between marital stress and behaviour problems in pre-school children. Some workers have looked specifically at children attending child psychiatric clinics and have found clear-cut causal relationships with adolescent psychiatric disorder as compared to controls (Vincent and Rosenstock, 1979); others report variable associations (Goodyer *et al.*, 1985) or merely limited associations (Steinhausen and Radtke, 1986) or none at all (Steinhausen, 1983). Steinhausen and his colleagues explored the value of differentially weighting the life events rather than merely giving equal weight to each event, but concluded this was not a fruitful exercise. They did, however, demonstrate that distant, rather than recent, undesirable life events seemed to be more predictive of psychiatric disorder, and in this respect pointed to the effect of lack of family warmth, inconsistency of control and lack of stimulation.

In contrast, research in Newcastle has demonstrated that recent stressful life events occurring over a twelve-month period increased the relative risk of psychiatric disorder by between three to six times (Goodyer *et al.*, 1985, 1986).

Any work in this area needs to consider the impact of desirable and undesirable events, entrance and exit events and those with variable degrees of threat. In a small number of vulnerable individuals, even pleasant events may constitute stresses but, on balance, recent research has led to the conclusion that the association with psychiatric disorder is mostly confined to unpleasant events (Rutter, 1981a; Paykel, 1974; Tennant and Andrews, 1978). Exit events (such as a child marrying) were more strongly associated with psychiatric disorder than entrance events (such as birth of a child); similarly with events beyond the control of an individual (such as serious family illness) as compared with events within his control (such as an engagement) (Paykel, 1974). Brown and Harris (1978) also report that it is only events with a long-term threat which appear to predispose to psychiatric disorder.

Our object was to investigate the hypothesis that recent adverse life events are more common in deprived families (Coffield *et al.*, 1981). More specifically, we expected that deprived families, because of their greater social and psychological vulnerability, would be prone to an accumulation of undesirable experiences throughout their lifetimes. We wished to explore this vulnerability both in the family of origin and in relation to current deprivation in the family of formation. For these purposes we adapted Coddington's Recent Life Event Schedule (1972) which had been developed specifically for use in relation to families with children and focuses on any undesirable events occurring within those families. We then examined these events from the point of view of the eldest child. Since we were concerned to study the impact of adverse life experiences in groups rather than the relationship between specific events and specific disorders, we did not grade the severity of their presumed impact on individuals or families.

The Recent Life Events Schedule was a semi-structured standard questionnaire submitted by the social interviewer during the home interview. The interviewers concerned themselves only with those life events occurring in the twelve months prior to the interview. Before commencing the questions they gave the family a standard explanatory introduction. For this purpose, the term 'family' included all forms of household unit listed on p. 50. For the questions relating to children, the eldest child in each family was treated as the index person and all the other children in the family were viewed as siblings. Thirteen categories of events were considered to cover the major life events likely to occur within a family in the span of a year, some of which are listed in Table 4.6.

Table 4.6   Recent life events in family of formation

A. Groups Defined According to Deprivation in Family of Origin						
	Non-Deprived Group		Deprived Group		Multiply Deprived Group	
	n	%	n	%	n	%
Family illness	12	19.7	48	29.6	25	36.8*
Mean total score	2.31		2.67**		3.09***	
Standard deviation	2.01		2.01		2.50	
Total 'n'	61		162		68	

B. Groups Defined According to Deprivation in Family of Formation						
Distribution of some events	Non-Deprived Group		Deprived Group		Multiply Deprived Group	
	n	%	n	%	n	%
Family illness (includes children)	13	17.3	66	34.9**	28	46.7**
Family accidents	14	18.7	42	22.2	20	33.3*
Increase in family arguments/tension	18	24.0	59	31.2	23	38.3*
Problems of progress at school	3	4.0	22	11.6*	11	18.3**
Adult difficulties with the law	3	4.0	10	5.3	8	13.3*
Financial deterioration	3	4.0	20	10.6	9	15.0*
Total score (2 +)	44	58.7	139	73.5*	49	81.7**
Mean total score	2.13		2.83***		3.73***	
Standard deviation	1.72		2.12		2.72	
Total 'n'	75		189		60	

Note: Significant difference from the NDG: all one-tailed test.
  All one-tailed: *p < .05
                **p < .01
               ***p < .01 (test)

Relationship of deprivation in the family of origin
and recent life events in family of formation

Table 4.6 shows that the only significant difference between the three criterion groups was in family illness, and that occurred only in the multiply deprived. However, on average, the multiply deprived had more children than the deprived, and therefore more opportunities for family illness. Comparing the summed scores of undesirable recent life events for each of the three groups shows that significant differences exist between the non-deprived and the deprived and also the multiply deprived groups. Thus it would appear that on average, both deprived groups experienced significantly more adverse life events than the non-deprived.

The families were then reclassified according to deprivation in the family of formation, and significantly more from both deprived groups experienced a wide range of undesirable recent life events − more family illness and more children showing problems in progress at school. In addition, the multiply deprived families experienced significantly more family accidents, arguments or tensions, adult difficulties with the law and deterioration in finances than did the non-deprived families. Because significance levels were based on a one-tailed test, the magnitude of significant differences was not necessarily great. No differences occurred on entrance and exit events, family and school mobility, and employment events. When the undesirable recent life events are summed there are very significant differences between non-deprived and both of the deprived groups. This overall pattern is similar to the picture with the previous classification, except that the differences between the criterion groups are greater when the groups are defined according to their current deprivation circumstances.

Inevitably some of the items which constitute undesirable recent life events may also be indirectly represented in the criteria used to define deprivation in the family of formation, and questions therefore arise regarding the extent of circularity of this data. But, even so, there remained an excess of undesirable experiences during the previous year in families who are currently categorized as deprived.

5 Deprivation, occupational class and mobility

Method
The short occupational classification of the Registrar General (1951) which employs five basic categories was used at both five years and 33 years. This classification has limitations as it depends upon the employment of the father or male wage-earner, and does not therefore provide for the classification of unmarried women or the unemployed.

Many research workers who have used the classification have divided Class III into manual and non-manual, but our samples were too small to use this device. We assigned men who had worked within the last year to the category appropriate to their last occupation.

Our families
In 1952, the mean age of mothers was 33.5 years and therefore almost the same as the female Red Spots in 1980. It was therefore considered reasonable to use a similar index to compare occupations at an equivalent point in the life cycle across the two generations. In 1952 there was little unemployment of skilled or able bodied men who wanted to work, and the Registrar General's classification was a broad indicator of status and of relative family incomes and ways of life. The unemployed were not included. The second classification was in 1980 when the Red Spots were in their thirty-third year, and all but 19 of the 264 had married and most were bringing up their own children. A few marriages had already failed and the partners had gone their own ways, either alone or with a new partner. The deaths of two husbands and one wife had broken three families. Three unmarried mothers were living alone with their children. In all, 14 Red Spots had divorced. The children of one family had been taken into care after their parents' divorce and remained there despite the fact that one parent remarried. In all, by

33 years of age, 244 of the 264 Red Spots had married, but some 10 per cent of these first marriages had already failed.

Findings

The distribution of occupational class at ages 15 and 33
The classification of social class (see Table 5.2) was not identical at five and 33 years. At five years, unemployment and absence of fathers were recorded as 'not classifiable', whereas at 33 years the unemployed were classified as category VI, and others, with absent fathers or without information, were grouped as not classifiable.

The figures for 1952 represent the occupations of the fathers in the original families, whereas those for 1980 represent the male Red Spots and partners of the female Red Spots. Noticeably more families (55 as against 19) were unemployed or not classifiable in 1980 compared with 1952. Nevertheless it is evident that there had been an upward movement into categories II, and III (occupations which demand skills) and a striking reduction in the numbers occupied in semi- and unskilled work.

Occupational class and deprivation
Table 5.1 shows the social class distribution of the study groups according to social class in 1952. While there are the expected significant differences between the groups, it is evident that deprived families were found in every occupational class but the greater the degree of deprivation, the greater the percentage of families in the lower occupational strata.

Since it is determined only by the one indicator, the Registrar General's classification hardly seems suitable to meet the social complexities which arise in families and which determine the environment into which children are born and spend their formative years. An alternative way of describing children living in the most seriously disadvantaged situations was devised by Wedge and Prosser (1973) in their book, *Born to Fail*. Their index comprised four factors: more than four children in the family; single-parent family; low income; and poor housing. They studied the 6 per cent of 11 year-old children in their sample who fulfilled all these conditions and thus they compared the

Table 5.1   Social class distribution of study groups according to social class in 1952

A. Occupational Classes of Men: England and Wales (1951 and 1971) (Ex Townsend 1979) '1000' Family Data (1952 and 1979-80)

Occupational Class	National Sample 1951	Newcastle Total Group 1952	Newcastle Non-Deprived Group 1952	Newcastle Deprived Group 1952	Newcastle Multiply Deprived Group 1952
	%	%	%	%	%
I + II	17.5	10.3	16.2	2.5	0.9
III	53.4	53.0	61.8	41.4	26.7
IV + V	29.1	32.3	21.8	46.3	59.5
Unclassified	?	4.4	0.2	9.9	12.9
Total	14064	847	482	365	116

B. Second Generation as Adults (1979-80) Classified According to Deprivation in Family of Origin

Occupational Class in 1952	National Sample ex 'Child Health and Education' 1977	Not Deprived Group 1952	Deprived Group 1952	Multiply Deprived Group 1952
	%	%	%	%
I + II	29.5	30.4	17.5	13.1
III	51.8	51.8	50.3	44.3
IV + V	18.7	16.1	20.3	14.8
Unclassified		1.8	11.9	27.9
Total	1917	56	143	61

C. Second Generation as Adults in 1980 Classified According to Deprivation in Family of Formation

Occupational Class in 1980	Not Deprived Group 1979-80	Deprived Group 1979-80	Multiply Deprived Group 1979-80
	%	%	%
I + II	31.9	16.4	10.0
III	56.9	51.4	34.0
IV + V	9.7	30.7	24.0
Unclassified	1.4	1.4	32.0
Total	72	140	50

Note: Section A relates to 847 families; B and C to subsamples.

most disadvantaged of the population with the 'normal' 94 per cent. With our index we were able to compare the multiply deprived (14 per cent) and the deprived (43 per cent) with both a random sample and the 57 per cent of families who did not present any of the indices of deprivation.

Our criteria provided measures when social class is not easily rated, covered situations of deprivation not necessarily tied to social class, and directly tapped adverse life experiences relevant to the development of children. Using them, we have shown that, in 1952, although multiple deprivation occurred mainly in families where the father was in semi-skilled or unskilled employment or was unemployed, a sizeable minority did come from artisan or other skilled occupational groups. In the non-deprived families, the gradient was the reverse of this. Thus, deprivation, according to our criteria, is related to, but not necessarily synonymous with, social class as defined by the Registrar General. This is simply demonstrated in Table 5.1, which shows that, when the Registrar General's social class alone is used, the number of deprived families in social classes IV and V may be underestimated because some are unclassifiable. Our method avoids this potential difficulty but depends upon the possession of information available only by special enquiry.

*Occupational mobility and deprivation
over generations*
Table 5.1 illustrates how Newcastle had lower percentages of families in the upper social strata when compared with the national distribution. This was partly because one of the suburbs was, until 1974, outside the municipal boundary.

The next question was the relationship between occupational class and severity of deprivation. In Generation I, occupational class was strongly related to deprivation, and this is well illustrated in relation to the national distribution (see Table 5.1). In the families of origin, it was only the non-deprived group which approximated to the national distribution of occupational class. This confirms the economic and occupational deprivation of Newcastle in the immediate post-war period, as compared to national 'norms'. Further, it highlights the social and economic disadvantages experienced by the multiply deprived families over 70 per cent of whom fall into the social classes of IV, V and unclassified.

The upward social mobility of our non-deprived group proved dramatic, with the percentage of families in occupational classes I and II almost doubling over the two decades. The distribution of this group is now almost identical to that of Osborn *et al.* (1984) in their National Study of Child Health and Education. However, the upward mobility of the deprived and multiply deprived was even more dramatic, the former increasing from under 3 per cent to over 17 per cent, and the latter from 1 per cent to 13 per cent. Nevertheless, deprivation in the previous generation still strongly influenced the occupational class of the next, and rather more than 40 per cent of the second-generation adults who came from multiply deprived families of origin were still in occupational class IV or V or were unclassified in 1980.

There was also a close relationship between the severity of deprivation in Generation I and occupational class for that generation. Almost three-quarters of the multiply deprived in Generation I fell into classes IV and V, but only one-quarter of the non-deprived did so. This indirectly supports Townsend's contention that, although occupational class is strongly correlated with poverty, the two are certainly not synonymous. When the 1980 families are classified according to deprivation in their families of origin and contemporary occupational class, they show a discrepancy which is even more marked; for instance, two-thirds of the deprived group do not then fall into social classes IV or V or unclassified, nor do over half of the multiply deprived. Further, twice the number of multiply deprived now fall into the unclassified category, a high proportion of these probably being unemployed. Thus, deprivation in one generation is an important indicator of the occupational class distribution in the next.

The next question is the relationship of deprivation defined according to contemporary family circumstances and contemporary occupational class. Almost all the non-deprived group and about two-thirds of the deprived group are contained within occupational classes I, II and III while 56 per cent of the multiply deprived are in classes IV and V.

Occupational mobility over generations
To this point, occupational mobility in families has been

considered by looking at the frequency distribution of the various populations. We also looked at occupational mobility both within and across generations. Mobility from 1947–54 had previously been described in *Growing Up in Newcastle upon Tyne* (Miller *et al.*, 1960).

To study intergeneration change we calculated whether the sons and sons-in-law of our population differed for each of the groups and we found few differences between the percentage distributions of occupational class of fathers in Generation I in 1952 and of their sons or their sons-in-law in Generation II. A minor trend was for sons-in-law in the non-deprived group to fall into higher occupational strata than sons. We therefore decided to combine the data for sons and sons-in-law and estimated the occupational class distribution within the original cohort (Table 5.2). When we look at occupational classes I and II in the families of origin we see, in the next generation, that two-thirds of these remain in the same categories; from occupational class III, just less than a half remain the same while about a quarter move up into classes I and II. From occupational classes IV

Table 5.2   *Comparison of occupational class of 847 families across generations based on estimates using 264 families in first generation*

Occupational Class of Family of Origin	Occupational Class of Families in 1980 Family of Formation					
	Class I + II	Class III	Class IV + V	Unclassified	Father Absent	Distribution at 5 Years Total
Class I + II	52(66)	11(14)	8(10)	0(0)	8(10)	79 9%
III	114(26)	204(46)	54(12)	20(4)	53(12)	445 52%
IV + V	17(6)	150(52)	80(27)	24(8)	20(7)	291 34%
Unclassified	6(18)	17(52)	2(6)	2(6)	6(18)	33 4%
Total Distribution at 33 Years	189(22)	382(45)	144(17)	46(5)	87(10)	848

Note: The figures in brackets are percentages of subtotals and may be summed horizontally.

and V, almost 60 per cent move up to classes III or I and II (although only a small percentage rose into the latter). When we look at the unclassified group we see, in the next generation, that almost a fifth fall into classes I and II and half fall into class III. One explanation is that the original unclassified category contained a proportion of students.

The numbers in the margins of the table confirm the fact of upward mobility. The estimated numbers in occupational classes I and II in 1952 were 79 (9 per cent) and in 1980 189 (22 per cent); and in III in 1952 they were 445 (52 per cent) and in 1980 382 (45 per cent). However, in 1952, the unclassified represented only 4 per cent of the sample but rose steeply to 15 per cent in 1980.

Occupational class and deprivation

Although we have examined the relationship between the degree of deprivation and occupational class in 1952 and 1980, we have not presented data in tabular form; this is, however, available on request to the authors. In the non-deprived group in occupational classes I and II in 1952, 25 per cent moved down; of those in class III, 31 per cent moved up and 14 per cent down; of those in classes IV and V, 71 per cent moved up. The numbers of the deprived group from occupational classes I and II are too small for analysis; of the families from occupational class III, 24 per cent moved up and 25 per cent moved down; and of those in IV and V, 60 per cent moved up. Finally, in the case of the multiply deprived, almost 50 per cent of those coming from occupational classes IV and V moved up. Overall, 77 per cent of the non-deprived families in 1952 and 76 per cent in 1980 were in occupational classes I, II or III while the same classes contained 41 per cent and 59 per cent of the deprived group respectively. This constituted considerable upward mobility. In the multiply deprived group it was 24 per cent and 45 per cent respectively. This suggests that a larger proportion of people moved upwards in the groups which were initially deprived. However, the most dramatic change was the numbers who fell into the unclassified categories in 1980, which range from 10 per cent of the non-deprived to 37 per cent of the multiply deprived.

We compared the occupational class distribution of our families with the national norms and saw again the social and economic disadvantages experienced by Newcastle in the 1950s. Social mobility was estimated for the total original population of 847 and this provided evidence of upward occupational mobility across generations even with respect to the deprived and multiply deprived. Such analysis also reveals how deprivation in the families of origin in 1952 was significantly related to contemporary occupational status in 1980. Occupational class in 1980 was found to be significantly related to contemporary deprivation.

Finally, we turned to mobility across the generations in relation to the degree of deprivation. It was found that a larger percentage of deprived families were upwardly mobile compared with the non-deprived. On the other hand, there was a substantial increase in downward mobility with an increase in severity of deprivation. We conclude that 'averages' masked major movements in both directions.

6 Family income and male unemployment

Introduction

When studying low income, a principal issue is the definition of poverty. Should the criterion be the lowest 10 per cent of income levels irrespective of material and marital circumstances and the number of children in the family? Or should there be a series of defined levels which specify a minimum subsistence for a particular family unit? We have used the latter concept of 'persons and families whose incomes fall below certain levels' (Brown and Madge, 1982). This raised two issues: first, to what extent was deprivation in 1980 associated with poverty as then defined? Second, did deprivation in the family of origin predict poverty in the family of formation?

Method

At first, each adult interviewed was shown a card with 13 bands of gross family income and asked to indicate which most closely reflected the family's gross weekly income. This was not successful. Some people considered the bands too narrow and were unwilling to select too precise an account of income. The bands were thereupon reduced to seven (Table 6.1).

Findings

The income of second generation families in 1980 according to deprivation in their family of origin in 1952

Table 6.1 shows that the main differences are at the extremes. For instance, when summing categories A and B, C, D and E, F and G, Red Spots reared in non-deprived families had 36 per cent in the top band, 51 per cent in the middle and 8 per cent in the lowest. In contrast, the reverse occurred in those reared in multiply deprived families with percentages of

Table 6.1 **Relationship of deprivation in first-generation families to categories of gross annual income of the second-generation families in 1980**

| | Deprivation in Family of Origin | | | | | |
| | Non-Deprived Group 1952 | | Deprived Group 1952 | | Multiply Deprived Group 1952 | |
Income Bands 1979–80	n	%	n	%	n	%
A £2,340 or less	0	0	8	5.0	9	13.0
B £2,341–£3,379	5	8.2	25	15.5	15	21.7
C £3,380–£4,371	10	16.4	25	15.5	13	18.8
D £4,372–£5,719	9	14.8	37	23.0	8	11.6
E £5,720–£7,279	12	19.7	26	16.1	11	15.9
F £7,280–£8,319	8	13.1	13	8.1	4	5.8
G £8,320 or more	14	23.0	22	13.7	7	10.1
Not classified	3	4.9	5	3.1	2	2.9
Total	61		161		69	

Table 6.2 **Family income and deprivation 1979–80**

| | Non-Deprived Group 1979–80 | | Deprived Group 1979–80 | | Multiply Deprived Group 1979–80 | |
Income Bands 1979–80	n	%	n	%	n	%
A/B up to £3,379	0	0	49	25.9	27	45.0
C/D/E £3,380–£7,279	48	64.0	93	49.2	24	40.0
F/G over £7,280	25	33.3	41	21.7	8	13.4
Not classified	2	2.7	6	3.2	1	1.7
Total	75		189		60	

Table 6.3 **Families and subsistence levels 1979–80**

| | Non-Deprived Group 1979–80 | | Mildly Deprived Group 1979–80 | | Multiply Deprived Group 1979–80 | |
| Minimal Subsistence Levels | | | Score 1 or 2 | | Score 3 or more | |
	Below	Above	Below	Above	Below	Above
Single Adult						
No children	0	7	0	9	0	2
One/two children	0	0	1	4	0	1
Three children	0	0	0	0	3	2
Couple						
No children	0	11	0	9	1	2
One/two children	0	46	10	68	7	14
Three children	0	9	5	18	14	13
Total	0	73	16	108	25	34
Percentage	0	100	13	87	42	58

16.5, 46 and 35 respectively. The Red Spots coming from deprived families proved intermediate. Thus, four times more of the multiply deprived, as compared to non-deprived, fall into the lowest income band and less than half in the highest band. This emphasizes that to come from a family without deprivation carries the likelihood of having a higher rather than a lower total family income in adulthood.

Current deprivation and current income, taking
into consideration theoretical poverty levels
For this analysis we were assisted by Mr Graham Charles (a clinical and social science research colleague at the Fleming Nuffield Unit), who calculated poverty lines based on supplementary benefit levels for the period November 1979 to November 1980. He also produced tables derived from the formula proposed by Abel-Smith and Townsend (1965): the amount of supplementary benefit multiplied by 140 per cent plus average housing allowance. These were calculated both for single householders according to the number of children and repeated for couples and their children.

Table 6.2 shows family income in relation to deprivation in 1979–80. There were clear-cut associations at the extremes: 20 per cent of non-deprived families had incomes in the bottom three bands (all in the highest of these) but 55 per cent were in the top three bands. Of the multiply deprived, almost 60 per cent were in the bottom three bands but there were 25 per cent with 'higher' incomes. We then applied the defined poverty levels to the stated incomes and found that, in families of formation about which we had data, 8 per cent (5/61) of those who were non-deprived in 1980, 8 per cent (13/161) of those who were deprived and 33 per cent (23/69) of those who were multiply deprived in 1980 were living below the 'poverty line'. By recreating the original population it was possible to estimate that in 1980 about 12 per cent of the Red Spots were living at or below the poverty level of which about half were from families who had been multiply deprived in 1952.

Income in relation to nature and size of the family:
family of formation
Table 6.2 does however obscure the extent to which single-parent or large families were living on minimal subsistence

levels. These levels have been defined, and the numbers of families living below subsistence level are shown in Table 6.3. All the non-deprived were above that level, even those with two or three children. We estimate that, of the original 847 families, the non-deprived in the family of formation consisted of about 300 family units with more than 500 children and all of these units had incomes above 'poverty' levels.

Some 20 per cent of deprived and multiply deprived families were at or below subsistence levels and most of these were multiply deprived, particularly if the family was large. Indeed, more than 50 per cent of the 27 families who were multiply deprived and who had three children were at or below subsistence level.

We estimate that, in 1980, the deprived group (with one or two criteria) contained over 400 families with more than 900 children and about 100 of these children were living at the margin of, or in, poverty. Of the 100 multiply deprived families with about 300 children, about one-third were living at the margins of, or in, poverty. It will be remembered that half of the 14 per cent of the multiply deprived Red Spots were themselves multiply deprived as adults and therefore must have contributed their full share of families with incomes below the subsistence level.

To summarize, our data relate to an income at or below 140 per cent of the supplementary benefit level. This is not an official poverty level but is a widely accepted definition. Those with incomes below the 100 per cent level are regarded as being in poverty whereas those between 100 and 140 per cent are on the margins of poverty. Using these definitions, the Family Expenditure Survey (DOE, 1978) showed that 5 per cent of all families were eligible for, but did not receive, supplementary benefit; 10 per cent received benefit; another 8 per cent were within 20 per cent of this standard. This suggests that approximately 15 per cent of families were in poverty and, overall, that nearly 25 per cent were in or near the range of poverty levels. From our Newcastle figures about 12 per cent of the second generation, as adults, were living in 1979–80 at or on the margins of poverty.

Male unemployment

Employment and unemployment

We had data relating to the employment of the parents of the Red Spot children when they were five years of age and had noted how the situation changed from 1952 to 1962 as two-thirds more mothers worked at some time outside the home. During the same period 82 (9 per cent) fathers were unemployed for between one and two years and 38 (5 per cent) for more than five years (Miller *et al.*, 1974).

Using data collected in 1979–80 on the employment experience of the Red Spots or male spouses for the previous five years, we then examined unemployment from 1975–80. We did this by a study of 80 families where there was male unemployment, of which 35 had experienced short-term and 45 long-term unemployment. We used 72 non-deprived families as a control group.

Changing patterns of unemployment 1952–82

In 1981, Moss estimated that, nationally, over 16 per cent of children had unemployed fathers. We could not provide a precisely comparable estimate for the Newcastle cohort but data were available both for sporadic, short-term unemployment — defined as three or more months in the preceding five years — and for long-term unemployment — defined as cumulative unemployment of one or more years in the preceding five years. Table 6.4 gives the unemployment figures for the fathers of the Red Spots in 1952, 1957 and 1962 and the estimated rates for the Red Spots as adults. In 1952 the rate for short-term unemployment was 15 per cent and by 1957 it had dropped to below 11 per cent. However, in the next generation in 1980 it had risen to over 27 per cent. This criterion is not a rigorous one, being merely three months' unemployment in the previous five years — the same criterion as was used in 1952.

When we look at long-term unemployment we see that the rate in 1980 was 50 per cent higher than in 1962. This finding has to be interpreted in relation to national and local economic circumstances. The 1950s and 1960s were times of economic expansion and it is not surprising that the short-term rate had dropped. The figure for the second generation as adults represents the harsher economic era of world economic recession and inflation and is more than twice the rate for 1957.

Table 6.4 Unemployment in 847 families

	Generation	Year	Rate
A. Short-term or Sporadic (At least 3 months in previous five years)			
Fathers of Red Spots	I	1952	14.9%
Fathers of Red Spots	II	1957	10.7%
Men 1979–80	II	1979–80	27.3% (estimate)
B. Long-term (Cumulative: one or more years in previous five years)			
Fathers of Red Spots	I	1962	14.2%
Men 1979–80	II	1979–80	21.5% (estimate)

Duration and history of unemployment (Table 6.4)

In the long-term group the mean duration of unemployment was two and a half years. Only two men had held their current post for more than three years, half had lost two or more jobs, and one-third had had as many as seven changes since leaving school. In contrast, few of the controls had lost two or more jobs or had had seven or more changes since leaving school, and more than two-thirds had held their current post for more than three years.

Unemployment in 1952 and 1980

We can compare previous unemployment in the three groups of second-generation families. Of the 80 unemployed in the study group, 35 per cent came from families where the father had been unemployed, compared to only 12 per cent of the controls. Current short-term unemployment (29 per cent) was associated with twice the rate, and long-term unemployment (40 per cent) with three times the rates in the controls (Table 6.5).

Table 6.5   Incidence of unemployment 1979–80

	Non-Deprived Controls	Unemployment Short-term	Long-term
	n = 72	n = 35	n = 45
Two or more jobs lost/redundant	11%	29%	53%
Seven or more job changes since leaving school	17%	48%	33%
Holding current post for more than three years	68%	32%	4%
Mean months unemployed in previous five years	0.9	5.4	29.5

Relationship of long-term unemployment to types of deprivation

In 1952 parental illness (51 per cent) and overcrowding (41 per cent) were both frequently associated with long-term unemployment, whereas in 1980 the former was rare (16 per cent) and overcrowding, as defined in the Housing Act 1936 had virtually disappeared. In 1980 by far the strongest association was with educational insufficiency (68 per cent) associations with the remaining criteria all being weaker (16–33 per cent).

Recollections of parental care by Generation II

In 1980 the wives of 45 per cent of the long-term and 26 per cent of the short-term unemployed had recollections of 'poor' childhood care, compared with 17 per cent of the women in the control families, suggesting a link between poor care in one generation and unemployment in the next. The mechanism by which this occurs is not clear.

These findings demonstrate the difficulties of disentangling the effects of unemployment and other social and family deprivations. They also demonstrate the importance of distinguishing between short and chronic unemployment.

Social perceptions (Generation II) (Table 6.6)

Surprisingly, three-quarters of the men in the long-term unemployed group considered that society had been fair to them, and only one-quarter unfair. Again a surprisingly high percentage also thought that people in poor circumstances had a fair chance of improving themselves — a magnanimous perception of the fairness of contemporary society. However, twice as many long-term unemployed (62 per cent) compared to the controls (32 per cent) considered that those in authority did insufficient for the poor.

*Table 6.6   Social perceptions of men
in families of formation*

	Controls	Short-term Unemployment	Longer Unemployment
	n=72	n=35	n=45
	%	%	%
a. Is society fair to you?			
Very fair	39	17	0
Fair	54	74	71
Unfair	5	9	24
Not sure	1	0	4
b. Chance of improvement of people in poor circumstances:			
Yes	76	63	58
Almost none	21	34	42
Don't know	3	3	—
c. Chance of improvement for their children:			
Yes	72	57	62
Almost none	25	43	36
Don't know	3	—	2
d. The amount those in authority do for the poor:			
Too much	10	11	7
About right	29	34	22
Too little	32	43	62
Other	29	12	9

The home and housing circumstances of the currently unemployed (1980)

Table 6.7 shows that the unemployed were at a disadvantage in all the aspects examined. Few were living in owner-occupied homes, compared with most of the controls. They were less satisfied with their current accommodation and living circumstances and there were great differences in the adequacy of furnishing and tidiness of the homes.

Table 6.7   Housing and unemployment:
families of formation

	Controls n=75 %	Short-term Unemployment n=35 %	Longer Unemployment n=45 %
Owner-occupied (i.e. mortgaged etc.)	72	34	7
Total persons in household (mean)	3.5	3.7	4.3
Satisfaction (expressed) in housing	91	77	64
Furniture Good quality	65	36	9
Untidy home	0	20	29

School and career: Generation II (Table 6.8)
The strong association between previous educational insufficiency and unemployment has already been mentioned. While school achievements or work training qualifications provide opportunities for upward occupational mobility, lack

Table 6.8   School experience, career training, verbal IQ
and unemployment: families of formation

School	Controls n-72	Short-term Unemployment n=35	Long-term Unemployment n=45
Attended grammar school or equivalent	31%	9%	7%
Left school at earliest age: males	62%	86%	96%
Took exams at school	56%	26%	18%
Further career training	82%	63%	53%
Mean Vocabulary Quotient (at age 33)	102	97	96

of these increase the likelihood of unemployment. The unemployed had a poorer experience of school, had taken fewer exams, had been less successful at public examinations and had had less career training than the controls. This suggests that inadequate scholastic and career training experience increased the risk of subsequent unemployment. A rider to this hypothesis is that lower intellectual ability increases the risk of unemployment, but a vocabulary test provided no evidence in support of this hypothesis as the mean vocabulary quotients were rather similar.

Psychological and physical malaise:
adults Generation II (Table 6.9)
Unemployment was associated with a significant excess of psychological disturbance and feelings of depression especially in the long-term unemployed group, but we had no way of ascertaining whether this was caused by unemployment or other associated social and family deprivations. It

Table 6.9 Psychological and physical illness and unemployment: families of formation 1979-80

	Controls n=72 %	Short-term Unemployment n=35 %	Long-term Unemployment n=45 %
Phobic/anxiety attacks:			
males	3	9	0
females	9	24	17
Lack energy:			
males	11	23	27
females	16	29	37
Sleep disturbance:			
males	9	14	27
females	13	12	32
Depression:			
males	3	9	31
females	10	21	34
Emotional disturbance:			
males	5	18	29
females	7	38	32
Physical:			
Recent physical illness	17	31	40

may well be that long-term unemployment interacts with deprivation to give rise to high rates of depression, and it was notable that 10 per cent of these men and women had had serious thoughts of suicide, whereas this was a non-existent occurrence in other groups. Short-term unemployment appeared to be associated with phobias and anxieties in women. Although recent illness in the family was two and a half times as frequent in the long-term unemployed and almost twice as great in the short-term unemployed as in the controls we could not tell how much was caused by, or resulted from, unemployment.

Family relationships (Table 6.10)

A number of interesting patterns emerged. First, unemployment was associated with a high rate of irritability and open rows between the spouses in both unemployed groups, these being four times more frequent than in the controls.

Despite unemployment, over half of the husbands went out to clubs or other regular social activities and there was little difference in this respect between the unemployed and the controls. Wives in all groups went on social outings less often than their husbands, and the wives in families suffering long-term unemployment appeared to spend much less in social clubs. It appears that, in such families, more money for social activities outside the home was available for husband than wife.

*Table 6.10   Family relationships in 1979–80:
family of formation*

	Controls n=72 %	Short-term Unemployment n=35 %	Longer-term Unemployment n=45 %
Spouse irritability: Once weekly	7	33	30
Spouse rows: Monthly	8	21	26
Wife attends club etc.	49	38	27
Husband attends club etc.	67	66	54

The first-born children of the unemployed
(Generation III) (Table 6.11)

We thought that the children of unemployed parents might be adversely affected in respect of behaviour, social relationships and scholastic activities. Antisocial behaviour was the only trait in which this seemed apparent and we recorded, from the unemployed parents, rates of 32 per cent and 40 per cent of antisocial behaviour in children in comparison with 13 per cent in the controls. Support to this was given by information from the school (Rutter B Scale) where there were significant differences of antisocial, but not of neurotic, behaviour. This was particularly so in the children of the short-term unemployment group (24 per cent), suggesting that recent unemployment was a particular hazard for them.

Lower levels of intelligence scores and achievement were related to parental unemployment but it is difficult to know how much was due to genetic factors. Differences in vocabulary quotient proved twice as great in the grandchildren (Generation III) as in the parents themselves (Generation II), and these findings suggest that environmental factors are crucial in influencing and exaggerating differences.

Table 6.11 *Families of formation and unemployment:*
behaviour and cognition of first-born children

	Control n=46	Short-term Unemployment n=22	Longer-term Unemployment n=37
Behaviour			
Parental interview: Antisocial behaviour	13%	32%	40%

Teacher Scale (Rutter B):
  Antisocial score
  (Newcastle version
  cut off 4)
	2%	24%	11%

Cognition			
Vocabulary quotient (mean)	113	101	96
Reading quotient (mean)	109	98	92

Precursors of unemployment in 1979–80
Substantial data concerning precursors of unemployment are available from the authors. These, together with data already reported, provide a profile of the statistically significant antecedents of current unemployment. They are listed in Table 6.12 according to whether they were identified in the preceding generation or the current generation.

Table 6.12   Precursors of unemployment

Adverse Factors in Family of Origin	Adverse Factors in Family of Formation
A. Mothers (of Red Spots) 1. Poor mothering 2. Poor care of the child and the home B. Fathers (of Red Spots) 1. Lower occupational status 2. Lesser participation in domestic tasks 3. Frequent job dismissal C. Both Parents Poor Providers 1. Parents show poor interest in child during school years 2. Marital breakdown 3. Dependence on social welfare 4. Poor housing circumstances	A. Teenage children 1. Poor interest in family activities 2. Eager to leave school 3. Disturbed behaviour (antisocial) 4. Poorer measured IQ 5. Poorer scholastic attainment 6. Not selected for grammar school B. Adults 1. Educational disadvantage

Unemployment: discussion
Rising levels of unemployment affected both the young and the middle-aged. Much of the modern work on unemployment concerns the young unemployed — those recent school-leavers who fail to attract employment. That particular sub-group should be distinguished from older persons who have both shorter and longer periods out of work.

Duration of unemployment
It would be natural to expect that prolonged unemployment would be associated with diminished psychological well-being and reduced self-esteem (Warr *et al.*, 1982) but cross-section research on men has not always supported this hypothesis. Goodchilds and Smith (1963) studying a cohort

in their mid-twenties found a lack of correlation between duration of unemployment (up to five months) and self-confidence scores, and Little (1976), studying older unemployed professional people, found no correlation between attitudes and duration of unemployment. Yet Hepworth (1980) found that longer-term unemployment in men with a median age of 34.5 years had a low, but significant, correlation (0.22) with minor psychiatric morbidity.

School-leavers are different, never having been in work. If they fail to get work, they may be expected to become increasingly demoralized. Contrary to expectation, recent cross-section research has failed to demonstrate a correlation between longer unemployment in the young and lowered psychological well-being. Surprisingly, some unemployed young women, perhaps because of a stronger personal involvement in family matters, actually exhibit a greater sense of well-being (Warr *et al.*, 1982).

The effects of unemployment: minor psychiatric morbidity

When unemployment has been studied without regard to the effects of its duration, adverse consequences have undoubtedly been demonstrated. For instance, Banks and Jackson (1982), studying poorly qualified school-leavers in Leeds, found evidence of a close association between unemployment and elevated General Health Questionnaire scores used as a measure of minor psychiatric morbidity. They also showed a significant decrease in scores in those who left school and found work, suggesting that work had a protective effect (Brown and Harris, 1978).

Risk of unemployment

A number of factors may accentuate or moderate the risk of unemployment. These include poorer qualifications, a family history of unemployment, low work motivation, membership of an ethnic minority and feminality (Allen and Smith, 1975).

Our study provided useful information about a number of factors which appeared to be predictors of unemployment in 1979–80. Chiefly implicated was a deprived childhood in association with a poor quality of personal care, social dependence and parental unemployment. But we identified associations, not causal mechanisms. In order to bridge the gap, we needed to postulate the basis of such associations in psychosocial terms. Our data suggest that one important family process may be a combination of poor care and under-stimulation, causing poor motivation and lack of interest in success and achievement. This in turn is translated into poor interest in scholastic and vocational activities and forms the basis of educational disadvantage in the post-school years. This set of processes may be heightened in individuals who experience parental unemployment during childhood.

When attempting to identify explanatory factors and the effects of unemployment it is important to specify the nature of that unemployment. For instance, the effects of short-term unemployment may be different from those of long-term; unemployment due to illness may be different from that due to redundancy; and older persons long unemployed will differ from school-leavers never employed (Warr *et al.*, 1982). Furthermore, as our data show, there may be variations over time: there was a much closer relationship of illness to unemployment in the 1950s than in the 1980s.

Short-term versus chronic unemployment

In 1980 our group of wage-earners with only short-term unemployment stood in contrast to those with a longer period of cumulative unemployment who experienced a variety of social and family deprivations. However, our data did not support the notion that this long-term unemployment was entirely due to contemporary economic factors. Indeed, unemployment in 1979–80 correlated with many factors in the preceding generation, particularly with regard to long-term unemployment. Other significant factors include childhood exposure to poor parenting, low parental regard for children, marital breakdown, low occupational status and poor work record of father, and overcrowding. On average, these children had poor scholastic achievements and were eager to leave school at the earliest opportunity. After school they were less likely to have had vocational training.

Another question is the extent to which recent unemployment was directly related to redundancies. Our research suggests that, while the relationship may be simple in some circumstances, it may be more complex in the case of chronic unemployment where longstanding social and family disadvantages may have intensified the effects of, or even interacted with, recent unemployment.

The impact of unemployment on the first child in the family varied according to its duration. For instance, although antisocial behaviour was apparently the child's only behavioural manifestation of long-term unemployment, school reports indicated a higher rate of such disturbance in the children whose parents had short-term, rather than long-term, unemployment. Perhaps recent short-term unemployment constitutes a greater stress because the family has not had time to adapt.

Long-term unemployment of the breadwinner was associated with poorer performance of the child in cognitive and educational tests. Thus the antecedents of unemployment proved to be social, familial, educational and intellectual, were particularly associated with longer-term unemployment, and both determine the risk of becoming unemployed and contribute to its effects. Nevertheless, it is difficult to tease out specific adverse effects of unemployment from the range of associated socio-cultural and educational factors. We must emphasize therefore that any conclusions drawn from the current analysis must remain at the level of hypotheses.

Social circumstances of unemployment, 1950–80
Unemployment in the 1950s seems to have been associated with greater economic and material hardship for children in terms of poorer care and housing conditions than in the 1980s. This was to be expected, as standards of living are now much higher (Madge, 1983b). Nevertheless, the unemployed tend to come from the lower income groups (Sinfield, 1981), and unemployment frequently affects both partners in a marriage simultaneously (Moylan and Davis, 1980).

Family relationships
Our work supports the notion that unemployment places additional strain on family relationships, but we have been unable to allow for other social and family disadvantages which may precede or accompany unemployment. We did

not set out to study unemployment specifically and therefore did not look at the associated changes in status and family relationships which suggest that fathers who become unemployed lose their sense of self-esteem and their authority in the family (Elder, 1974). On the other hand, it should not be assumed that unemployment always has adverse family effects, for it is known that strengthening or 'steeling' effects may occur, whereby certain families draw closer together following adverse experiences.

Impact on parents
Our data suggest that the long-term unemployed in particular often show characteristics reflecting depression, which accords with the literature (Jahoda, 1979; Fagin, 1981). Wives particularly may show an excess of phobic–anxiety states following their husbands' short-term unemployment, and depression following their long-term unemployment. We see that 10 per cent of both husbands and wives had serious thoughts of suicide during long unemployment, and the important conclusion is that the families of the unemployed have a higher risk of psychological ill-health, which endorses the findings of Banks and Jackson (1982) and Hepworth (1980). There is also evidence that return to work is associated with reduction in minor psychiatric morbidity, which suggests that work has a positive and protective influence.

Children of the unemployed
We did not find any excess of neurotic symptoms in the children of families where there was unemployment. This experience is contrary to the findings of Brennan and Stoten (1976) and Fagin (1981).

Scholastic progress and cognitive functioning
Essen and Wedge in 1982 demonstrated a relationship between income levels and scholastic progress, and Brown and Madge (1982) suggested, therefore, that children of the unemployed are likely to do less well at school than their contemporaries since their families are usually relatively poor even when in work. The National Survey of Health and Development also described a cognitive relationship with unemployment, with lower mean test scores for non-verbal and

verbal IQ at 11 years and mathematics and reading test scores at 15 years (Douglas, 1964; Douglas *et al.*, 1968). Our work showed the same trend, but poor progress could not be linked directly to unemployment in the presence of coexisting criteria of deprivation or possible genetic factors. One may speculate that the poor in one generation are those who are less intelligent and therefore less likely to maintain their way in work in the next generation. However, while it is not easy to exclude a significant genetic component, our data show that the discrepancy on mean verbal quotients between the unemployed fathers and controls is almost half that of the children and their controls, which suggests an important environmental influence. These findings emphasize the importance of a longitudinal design when attempting to explain poor scholastic progress and cognitive functioning.

7 Housing and neighbourhood

Introduction

In this chapter we present the changes in housing circumstances in Newcastle upon Tyne as they affected our Red Spot families over the 30-year study period. We first describe the housing conditions in 1952 when the Red Spot children were five years of age, then the changes they had experienced by 15 years, and finally the situation in their early thirties as the Newcastle housing authority advanced its housing development programme. We shall look at a variety of aspects of housing over that period: the decline of overcrowding, the change in the housing stock available, the increase in home ownership, and improvements in household amenities and neighbourhood standards. Finally, we shall review the attitudes expressed by families in 1979–80 towards their housing circumstances.

In the twentieth century the northern sector of Newcastle became a relatively prosperous and well-housed area, whereas the riverside districts, sharing as they did the housing of the mid- and late nineteenth-century expansion, contained, by the 1930s the oldest and poorest properties.

Until 1974 Newcastle was divided into 20 electoral wards. We grouped these into three broad categories (Table 7.1), among which there was appreciable variation. Those to the west of the city centre had a disadvantaged subcultural quality; those to the east also had poor-quality housing but displayed a less unsatisfactory community ethos. The northern wards had higher housing standards but did not share the homogeneous quality of living.

Despite the variation in environmental quality among the wards, and in the housing stock within them, Table 7.1 shows that in 1952 the families rated as non-deprived were evenly distributed throughout the three groups of wards. In comparison with the non-deprived, both deprived groups showed a statistically significant population distribution between the

Table 7.1 Families of origin 1952: electoral wards and deprivation

	Non-Deprived		Deprived		Multiply Deprived	
Electoral Wards (Newcastle) 1952)						
Families of origin	(n=63)		(n=165)		(n=78)	
North District	21	33%	28	15%	10	13%
East District	21	33%	71	38%	21	27%
West District	21	33%	66	46%	47	60%
Neighbourhood (Newcastle and other) 1980						
Families categorized according to criteria of deprivation in 1952	(n=59)		(n=157)		(n=67)	
Poor-quality urban neighbourhood	1	2%	20	13%	6	9%
Average-quality urban neighbourhood	29	49%	104	66%	44	66%
High-quality urban neighbourhood	23	39%	26	17%	13	19%
Rural neighbourhood	6	10%	7	4%	4	6%
Families categorized according to criteria of deprivation in 1979–80	(n=73)		(n=184)		(n=58)	
Poor-quality urban neighbourhood	2	3%	23	12%	10	17%
Average-quality urban neighbourhood	41	56%	119	65%	43	74%
High-quality urban neighbourhood	29	40%	27	15%	1	2%
Rural neighbourhood	1	1%	15	8%	4	7%

Note: Table based on data available.

ward districts. Only 13 per cent of the multiply deprived lived within the desirable north district whereas 60 per cent were in the disadvantaged west district. By 1962 council rehousing development, chiefly in the north-west side of the city, had allowed many families in all three groups to move into the northern district. Yet 40 per cent of the multiply deprived groups still lived in the most disadvantaged wards as compared to 27 per cent and 23 per cent respectively of the deprived and non-deprived.

After the Local Government Act of 1974 it became impossible to pursue district comparisons on the same basis as before and we classified the now enlarged city area on the basis of housing density and standard of upkeep.

When we looked at our Red Spots as adults, classified into the three groups according to deprivation in their families of origin, we saw that, as a result of the post-war rehousing programme, the greatest proportions of all three groups were housed in neighbourhoods of average quality while only a minority of the non-deprived lived in a poor-quality neighbourhood. These findings do not provide evidence of familial intergeneration continuity of residence within an unsatisfactory neighbourhood. Although immediately after the war most of the parents of our study children were living in an unfavourable district, by 1979–80 most of their offspring lived in acceptable neighbourhood settings.

When we looked at families of formation grouped according to current data and criteria of deprivation we found a similar pattern, with 17 per cent of multiply deprived and only 3 per cent of non-deprived living in a poor-quality neighbourhood. Furthermore, only 2 per cent of the multiply deprived group, compared with 40 per cent of the non-deprived families, lived in a high-quality neighbourhood.

Housing type and quality

Overcrowding

Overcrowding is usually defined in terms of the ratio of household residents to the number of rooms in a property. A working definition adopted in the original 1947 study proved suitable for our purposes including, as it did, all persons within the household and all rooms within the property. This unofficial standard was termed the 'personal unit'; it included young children and infants on an equal basis with adults, and did not exclude kitchens, if large enough, or other small rooms able to accommodate one or more persons.

Overcrowding in 1952 was a basic criterion of deprivation in the study. Table 7.2 shows that no families had more than two persons per room in 1979–80 according to the 'personal unit' standard. By definition, no cases of overcrowding occurred in the non-deprived group. This was the basic level against which we made all subsequent comparisons.

In 1952 overcrowding, defined on the 'personal unit' criterion, was the most common of all criteria, affecting 18.7 per cent of the families. Table 7.2 shows that, in 1952, as many as six out of ten families in the multiply deprived

Table 7.2   Overcrowding defined according to 'personal unit' according to severity of deprivation

Families of Origin	Non-Deprived Group (1952)		Deprived Group (1952)		Multiply Deprived Group (1952)	
More than 2 persons per room (1952)	0 (n=63)	—	76 (n=185)	41%**	48 (n=78)	62%**
More than 2 persons per room (1962)	2 (n=53)	4%	32 (n=158)	22%**	17 (n=78)	25%**
More than 1 person per room (1980)	4	7%	17	10%	9	13%
More than 1.5 persons per room (1980)	0	—	1	1%	1	1%
More than 2 persons per room (1980)	0 (n=61)	—	0 (n=162)	—	0 (n=68)	—

Families of Formation	Non-Deprived Group (1980)		Deprived Group (1980)		Multiply Deprived Group (1980)	
More than 1 person per room (1980)	4	5%	24	13%	13	22%
More than 1.5 persons per room (1980)	0	—	1	1%	1	2%
More than 2 persons per room (1980)	0 (n=75)	—	0 (n=189)	—	0 (n=60)	—

** p < .01

group and four out of ten families in the deprived group were significantly overcrowded. By 1962, however, when the study children were 15 years of age, the picture had changed appreciably. The families in the worst housing had received priority allocation of new accommodation with the result that the deprived and multiply deprived groups were both experiencing 20–25 per cent overcrowding.

By 1980 conditions had again changed, and families of formation were living in their own homes, in conditions very different from those of their childhood. Overcrowding, with more than two persons per room, had totally disappeared and the criterion of 1.5 or more persons per room identified only 1 per cent of families with multiple deprivation. If the criterion was merely more than one person per room, we recorded some overcrowding in all groups with more in the deprived, but there were no statistical differences. We have to conclude that overcrowding *per se* as a social problem or potential health hazard has ceased to be a critical issue for the great majority of the population of Newcastle. This has been brought about by the trend towards smaller families, the local authority's large-scale rehousing programme and the growth of house ownership.

Type of housing

Post-war Newcastle contained a great deal of nineteenth-century housing. The chief example of this was the type of 'two up–two down' dwellings which were found everywhere on Tyneside. The oldest of these had a single shared entrance from the street approached through a dark unventilated passageway. Alternatively, downstairs flats had front entrances opening directly on to the street with a third street door leading to the dwellings above. Later dwellings all had

Table 7.3   Housing and deprivation 1952–79

		Non-Deprived Group (1952)		Deprived Group (1952)		Multiply Deprived Group (1952)	
Family of Origin							
1952	Adequate (Private & Council Detached, Semi, Terrace, Bungalow)	26 n=63)	41%	40** n=184	22%	16** n=77	21%
1962	Adequate	36 n=52)	69%	90 n=184	57%	40 n=77	58%
1979–80	Adequate	60 n=61	98%	162 n=162	100%	67 n=68	99%
		Non-Deprived Group (1979–80)		Deprived Group (1979–80)		Multiply Deprived Group (1979–80)	
1979–80	Adequate	75 n=75	100%	187 n=189	99%	59 n=60	98%

** = p < .01

separate street entrances. While originally sound in structure, the majority of these properties had suffered dilapidation over the years. Almost without exception, they were un-hygienic and were viewed as undesirable. We categorized these properties under the heading of poor housing together with the few other types of accommodation generally re-garded as unsatisfactory for family living — for example, sublet rooms in larger properties or post-war 'prefabs'. All other types, detached or semi-detached, bungalows or terraces, whether private or council-owned, were considered to be 'adequate housing'.

Table 7.3 shows that, in 1952, at least half the non-deprived families and more than three-quarters of the deprived group lived in properties viewed as substandard. But the next decade saw a great expansion of housing provision, reflected by the reduction in the proportion of families living in poor housing in 1962, which became less than 2 per cent by 1979–80. Thus we could not use the quality of housing provision as a measure of deprivation in Newcastle in 1979–80.

House ownership

Table 7.4 shows the distribution and increase of home ownership from 1952–80 and the decrease of private renting over those 27 years; council renting decreased in the non-deprived and increased in the deprived groups. These figures were recorded before the legislation which enabled estab-lished council tenants to purchase their own property and, since then, the move to private ownership will probably have continued.

Household amenities

At the end of the war, only a minority of the population lived in an average family semi-detached property. In 1952 many houses had inadequate plumbing and lacked indoor sanitation. Only half the non-deprived families had their own fixed bath and one-fifth did not have an indoor lavatory. The multiply deprived fared much worse, only a quarter having a fixed bath and a half their own lavatory. By 1962 all but an occasional family possessed both amenities.

To this point we have described household amenities which were recorded systematically from 1947. During the

Table 7.4   House ownership, household factors and deprivation

		Non-Deprived Group (1952)	Deprived Group (1952)	Multiply Deprived Group (1952)
Families of Origin		(n=58)	(n=185)	(n=78)
1952	Owned – Personal	12.1%	4.9%	1.3%
	Rented – Private	67.2%	68.1%	73.1%
	Rented – Council	20.7%	27.0%	25.6%
		(n=52)	(n=157)	(n=68)
1962	Owned – Personal	25.0%	6.4%	–
	Rented – Private	32.7%	24.2%	20.6%
	Rented – Council	42.3%	69.4%	79.4%
1979–80	Owned – Personal	68.3%	43.8%	28.8%
	Rented – Private	10.0%	6.3%	7.6%
	Rented – Council	21.7%	50.0%	63.6%
		Group (1979–80)	Group (1979–80)	Group (1979–80)
Families of Formation		(n=74)	(n=186)	(n=59)
1979–80	Owned – Personal	73.0%	38.2%	11.9%
	Rented – Private	9.5%	7.0%	3.4%
	Rented – Council	17.6%	54.8%	84.7%
Tidy home		93.3%	78.2%	52.5%
Satisfactory furniture/equipment		93.3%	81.9%	52.5%
Dissatisfaction with neighbourhood		9.3%	18.5%	30.0%

interviews in 1979–80, we gathered other information about current household amenities and expectations and sought to discover if home and neighbourhood were seen as satisfactory. At the same time we made our own assessment of the domestic equipment and state of tidiness of the home (Table 7.4). At this time only one in six of the non-deprived expressed dissatisfaction with their house or neighbourhood and usually their homes were tidy and had satisfactory amenities. In contrast, when classified according to the 1980 criteria of deprivation, the multiply deprived group were rated as being at a significant disadvantage, often with untidy, poorly equipped homes. They also voiced appreciably more criticism of their home conditions and the quality of life in their neighbourhood, despite the fact that, as a group, they were accommodated in housing of adequate quality.

Housing and deprivation

Type of deprivation and housing

The quality of housing was then compared in relation to each of the six criteria of deprivation in 1979–80. There was little difference one from the other except that those families deprived by parental illness appeared to be in better housing than any of the other five, with 50 per cent living in detached or semi-detached accommodation and 45 per cent in owner-occupied accommodation.

Neighbourhood factors and deprivation

The demographic, housing and economic characteristics of each of the wards of the city in 1973 and 1983 in relation to Census data of 1971 and 1981 respectively had been published by the Social Services Department of the Newcastle Corporation. This enabled us to prepare a rank order for each characteristic in each ward. For car ownership it was found that, on both occasions, all nine of the top third rankings coincided, but only seven out of nine of the bottom third. For unemployment the score was six out of eight and seven out of nine respectively. We concluded that there was sufficient stability from 1971–81 to presume the rankings would have been broadly the same from 1963–73.

On that basis we allocated each family to the top, middle or bottom third of the distribution for a variety of social and economic circumstances and grouped them according to their deprivation category in 1952. For 1962 we could allocate only 772 of the 847 families to a specific ward. Of that number 439 were non-deprived and 333 were deprived including 109 who were multiply deprived.

Table 7.5 gives the percentages of selected neighbourhood circumstances for these 772 families and shows that a significant proportion of our deprived families lived in neighbourhoods or wards which fell into the bottom third of the ranks on the following features:

1   less affluence, represented by a low percentage of households with their own cars;

2   high rates of male unemployment;
3   excess of children given free school meals;
4   financial difficulties as reflected by cut-off gas and electricity supplies (and by rent arrears, not listed);
5   more adult crime (and drunkenness, not listed);
6   higher incidence of concern to the local authority (and children in care, not listed).

In all these characteristics from one and a half to almost twice as many families from the multiply deprived group fell into the bottom third of the rankings compared with the non-deprived, and the deprived were usually intermediate. However, the differences in the case of the top third of the rankings were even more dramatic, with the percentages running from twice as high to about seven times as high when the non-deprived group is compared to the multiply deprived group.

Table 7.5   Families, neighbourhood and ward rankings

Ward Rankings and Neighbourhood Factors	Non-Deprived	All Deprived	Multiply Deprived
Size of sample	439	333	109
Neighbourhood affluence			
Top third	25.1%	17.1%***	11.9%***
Bottom third	33.9%	52.0%	59.6%
Adult males unemployed			
Top third	26.4%	11.1%***	3.7%***
Bottom third	45.3%	64.3%	61.7%
Free school meals			
Top third	21.9%	12.0%***	2.8%***
Bottom third	46.7%	65.8%	83.5%
Indicators of family financial difficulties — electricity and gas cut off			
Top third	24.1%	14.4%	10.1%
Bottom third	33.7%	51.7%	59.6%
Adult crime			
Top third	14.6%	9.6%***	2.8%***
Bottom third	44.9%	61.9%	75.2%
Families of concern to LA			
Top third	34.2%	20.4%***	11.0%***
Bottom third	33.7%	45.9%	45.9%

***Significant difference from 'non-deprived' at p < .001 (one-tailed).

These findings demonstrate that families categorized as deprived in 1952 were likely to have lived in neighbourhoods with the highest incidence of poor social circumstances and to be exposed to a variety of adverse neighbourhood influences.

Discussion

Review of literature
Townsend (1979) identified three principal measures of poor housing circumstances: inadequate structure, poor amenities and inadequate space in relation to the number of users. The Morris (Parker) Committee (1961) established a standard definition of overcrowding of 1.5 persons per room. The General Household Survey (OPCS, 1973) stated that, in 1961, 2.1 per cent of households in England and Wales and 3.8 per cent in Great Britain were overcrowded by that standard but that, by 1966, the proportions had fallen to 1.2 per cent and 2.1 per cent respectively. However, Townsend claimed that the true prevalence was underestimated by the use of outdated absolute standards. He held that:

1 politicians did not appreciate that the 'twilight' houses of one era become in time unfit for habitation;
2 standards change as society becomes more affluent;
3 disproportionate attention is given to the physical appearance of housing;
4 the term 'slum' is variously applied to houses unfit for human habitation or beyond repair at a reasonable cost.

Townsend developed his own 'housing facilities index' and, on this basis, identified 21 per cent of households as deficient in one or more respects and 22 per cent with structural defects. Many would be uneasy about such high rates since these are likely to include a high proportion of substantial housing with some minor defect.

The findings in our families
In the immediate post-war era the majority of houses were substandard by modern standards, and approximately 80 per cent of the multiply deprived lived in this type of house.

Home ownership was the exception in all groups but particularly in the multiply deprived. Council housing was developing, but most housing was rented from private landlords. This was still a time when basic household amenities and facilities were not widely available, the general level of housing was low and there were vast inequalities.

We have described the three broad geographical areas in Newcastle — north, east and west — with the north area, which could be described as inner city, having the least poor housing, the east having more and the west having most of it. One in three of the non-deprived group and three in five of the multiply deprived were living in the west area.

Since by 1962, three-quarters of all the families were free from overcrowding and the majority were in adequate circumstances, we therefore also looked at home ownership as a possible alternative criterion of housing deficiency. Here, there were great inequalities with none of the multiply deprived living in their own houses and 80 per cent of them in council-owned property. There had been a major movement in housing in the case of the non-deprived, 25 per cent of which owned their houses by this time. Overall, the major difference between 1952 and 1962 was that less than one-third of all groups lived in privately rented accommodation — a 50 per cent decrease over the 10 years. However, despite the increase in council housing, the growth of private ownership for the non-deprived seems to have given rise to a different type of inequality. Similarly, an analysis of the available facilities and amenities indicate how much had changed between 1952 and 1962.

The City Profiles

From the Newcastle *City Profiles* we know that, in 1971, 32 per cent of households were living in owner-occupied premises and, in 1981, 39 per cent. These rates were lower than those reported in our study groups even when we estimate rates for our whole population. However, the figures are not comparable as, by 1980, a substantial proportion of our families had moved outside the city boundaries. Similarly, our estimated rates for council-rented houses were below those for the *City Profiles*. The census data did reveal a significant fall in overcrowding within the city which the *City Profiles* attributed to smaller families and improved housing, since the frequency of families with more than 1.5 persons per room dropped from 2.2 in 1971 to 0.7 per cent in 1981. This supports our claim that 'overcrowding' is no longer a useful indicator of housing inequality.

While the grosser deficiencies of household circumstances have clearly been reduced, the question arises whether, when using relative criteria, there would still be inequalities. The answer must be that the inequalities remain but are of a different type. While we agree with Townsend that it is important to modify one's standards according to the times, it cannot be denied that there have been great changes for the better in Newcastle and, in particular, for those who had lived in the poorest housing circumstances.

We studied household facilities of the families of formation classified according to deprivation in the families of origin and identified discrepancies between groups which indicated continuities across generations. A significantly higher percentage of the previously multiply deprived had no access to a garden or yard; the quality of care and the decor and furnishings of the homes were substantially poorer in those from deprived circumstances in early life and particularly in those from multiple deprivation. We were interested to note some of the attitudes of the families living in these circumstances. Despite all the evidence of inequality listed above, a small proportion of those from multiply deprived backgrounds were apparently satisfied with their housing and the area in which they lived.

In summary, the grim and unhealthy housing and living circumstances of those families who were deprived or multiply deprived improved over the period 1952–62, but there still remained considerable inequalities between the non-deprived and the multiply deprived in terms of type of accommodation, type of district in which the families lived and frequency of home ownership.

We also had an objective standard in the Acorn Classification (see again Table 7.1, p. 91) which allowed us to compare the housing situations of our three groups with a national standard and to examine the 1980 housing circumstances of families who had experienced deprivation in 1952. The families who remained in Newcastle were more likely to live in council housing and less likely to live in higher-status housing compared with the national norm.

However, the picture was not all bleak, with 44 per cent of Red Spots who were not deprived in 1952 located in higher-status housing in 1980; the comparable percentages for the deprived and multiply deprived were 26 per cent and 17 per cent respectively.

PART III
PERSONAL
DEVELOPMENT AND
DEPRIVATION

8 The Red Spots as children 1947–62

In the '1,000 Family Study' the weight of the children was recorded at birth and there was no significant difference in mean birthweight among children experiencing deficiency of care (Miller *et al.*, 1960). Subsequent analysis in relation to deprivation has shown a similar finding.

The measurements of height and weight taken in 1950 and at five other ages to 15 years were re-analysed in 1980 to compare the growth of children in the non-deprived and the multiply deprived groups. Significant differences were found at every age with regard to height and at all but one age with regard to weight (Figure 8.1). We concluded that the relationship between deprivation and reduced height and weight is due to impaired post-natal growth.

The accident rate in the multiply deprived children was one and a half to three times as great as in the non-deprived. A similar picture emerged concerning burns, scalds and defects of speech at five years (Table 8.1).

Table 8.1   Physical factors and deprivation: Red Spots aged 3 to 5 years

	Non-Deprived		Deprived		Multiply Deprived	
	n	%	n	%	n	%
Third Year (1950)						
One or more accidents	8	(13)	51	(28)*	27	(35)**
Fifth Year (1952)						
Speech defect	11	(18)	55	(30)	29	(37)*
One or more accidents	28	(45)	103	(56)*	51	(65)**
Burns and scalds	4	(6)	28	(15)*	18	(23)**
Hospital inpatient admissions	7	(11)	50	(28)**	21	(27)**

*Different from non-deprived (p < .05)
**(p < .01) (one-tailed)

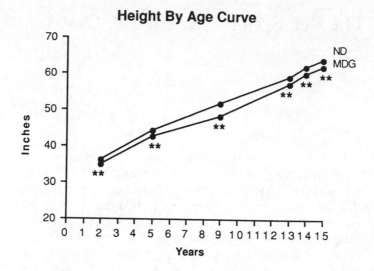

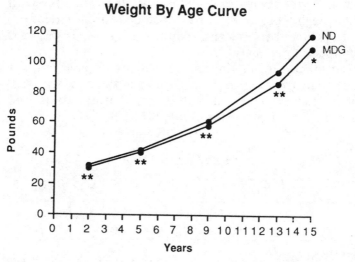

*Significant difference from non-deprived group at p < .05 (one-tailed tests)
**Significant difference from non-deprived group at p < .01 (one-tailed tests)

ND = non-deprived group
MDG = multiply deprived group

*Figure 8.1   Generation II (children):
height by age and weight by age curves*

**The Red Spots at school 1952–62: intelligence
and attainments in relation to deprivation**

We were fortunate in having results of ability testing concerning the Red Spots obtained during their school years, to which was added information of their performance when adult and, in turn, of their own children at school.

This information was gathered at various times:

(a) 1958: in the last year at junior school at the time of the statutory 11-plus examination, which determined the type of secondary education judged most suitable for the child (Generation II);

(b) 1959–62: in senior school where a variety of assessments were undertaken (Generation II);

(c) 1979–80: when adult, at this point both the Red Spots and their partners were tested (Generation II as adults);

(d) 1979–80: when the children of the Red Spots were assessed (Generation III).

In 1958 in Newcastle, as in the majority of local education authorities, the 11-plus examination consisted of written papers involving tests of intelligence, English and arithmetic. The examination results were made available to the 1,000 Family Survey by the Newcastle Local Education Authority (Table 8.2). Striking and highly significant differences were seen between the non-deprived and deprived groups, with the multiply deprived group clearly at a disadvantage in all three areas. The non-deprived children returned average scores, the deprived low average, while the multiply deprived functioned at a still lower level. There was no significant difference in intelligence between girls and boys.

Differences in intellectual and scholastic performance are likely to reflect differences in social background and quality of schooling. We therefore identified the extent to which the children might have attended private schools, but the numbers were so small that they could not have influenced the picture.

At the time of sitting the examination 22 per cent of the deprived group and 30 per cent of the multiply deprived group attended denominational maintained schools, compared with only 9 per cent of the non-deprived.

Table 8.2   11-plus examination scores:
1958 boys and girls

Families	Intelligence		Arithmetic		English		
	Mean	SD	Mean	SD	Mean	SD	No.
Non-deprived	104.3	13.3	108.4	14.0	105.9	14.0	52
Deprived	93.9**	13.3	97.1**	12.7	94.7**	14.4	158
Multiply deprived	86.7**	9.2	90.8**	10.7	87.5**	11.9	68

**Significant difference from the NDG at p < .01 (one-tailed test)

School selection following the 11-plus examination
In the years before national comprehensive school provision the decision by the educational authority to offer or withhold a grammar school place was viewed by many parents and children as crucial for the child's future. Within the country as a whole about one-quarter of the children could be expected to be allocated to a selective school, but the proportion varied somewhat in the individual local education authorities (Douglas *et al.*, 1968).

In Newcastle in 1958 17.6 per cent of the Red Spot children were placed in state selective secondary schooling — slightly more boys than girls (Miller *et al.*, 1974). For the majority of parents a selective school was regarded as the most successful and desirable outcome to their children's primary schooling. A further 1.5 per cent of boys and 1.3 per cent of girls were successful in competition for a direct grant place in independent schools. Both grammar and direct grant schools offered a range of academic subjects and specialization together with relatively smaller classes than were available to children in other forms of schooling. Until the raising of the school-leaving age to sixteen years in 1972, almost all children in secondary modern school left school after their fifteenth birthday.

An alternative to the secondary modern school, largely for pupils who had not succeeded in obtaining a selective placement, was offered by the commercial secondary school, which was generally a privately run school for children seeking grounding in commercial and clerical subjects as a preparation for employment in forms of skilled non-manual work.

Table 8.3 shows the great differences which existed between the non-deprived and the deprived categories in respect of their allotted schools.

Table 8.3 *Type of secondary school attended*

	Non-Deprived		Deprived**		Multiply Deprived**	
Grammar, direct grant, technical, commercial	16	29.1%	18	11.1%	3	4.3%
Secondary modern	35	63.6%	140	86.4%	65	92.9%
Private	4	7.3%	1	0.6%	0	0.0%
ESN Res. special	—	—	3	1.9%	2	2.9%
Total	55		162		70	

**p < .01 (one tailed test)

Generation II: intellectual assessment in
first year of secondary school
The children made the transition to secondary schooling when the national debate regarding the inequalities of separate provision was at its height (Table 8.3). Comprehensive school provision was not introduced in Newcastle until the 1960s, but the fairness and appropriateness of allocation was already a lively talking-point in most schools and homes. It has long been known that practice in group intelligence testing could generally raise IQ scores by some five points, and the degree to which this was practised varied. In the Easter term of 1959 when the children had begun their secondary education they were again tested using Raven's Progressive Matrices and the Mill Hill Vocabulary Tests (Miller *et al.*, 1974). The former was considered one of the more culture-free tests available and relatively free from the effects of prior practice. The Mill Hill Test, by comparison, being essentially a vocabulary test, was more susceptible to the effects of educational and cultural exposure. The results,

however, showed the same pattern of differences as existed with the 11-plus test.

Intellectual reassessment at 15 years
The same tests were repeated in the fifteenth year as most children approached the end of statutory education. The results, with one notable exception, were similar to those obtained in the earlier years. The exception was the Matrices score for the deprived group which, although still coming midway between the non-deprived and multiply deprived groups, did not depart significantly from the score obtained by the non-deprived group. Again, there was no significant difference between boys and girls.

Generation II: type of school attended by brothers and sisters of 'Red Spot' children
School placements also seemed to reflect family attitudes towards the value of schooling. We did not have information about the secondary schooling of the parents of the 'Red Spot' children, but fortunately we did have information gathered in 1962 of the type of school attended by their siblings (Table 8.4). The data of that table seemed to indicate that a selective school placement for an older child increased the chances for a younger.

Table 8.4   Siblings attending selective schools

	Non-Deprived (n=41)		Deprived (n=128)		Multiply Deprived (n=62)	
Yes	21	51.2%	22	17.2%	4	6.5%

Generation II: school attendance
School attendance rates show a decline as children progress through their teenage years, and absenteeism reaches a peak in the final year of statutory schooling. Our data (Table 8.5) revealed significant differences. Average attendance in the non-deprived group was as high as 93 per cent and as low as

80 per cent in the multiply deprived group. When this was examined in relation to the six criteria of deprivation, similar significant differences were found. It might have been expected that illness in parents would produce higher school absenteeism rates if children were kept from school to help with domestic tasks. However, the reverse was true, and parental illness showed the weakest associations with absenteeism, while poor care and poor mothering showed the strongest.

Table 8.5 Attendance during the last three terms at school (percentage of possible attendance)

	Non-Deprived	Deprived	Multiply Deprived
Pupil numbers	43	141	59
Mean per cent	93.4	85.6	80.5
SD	7.9	12.1	15.2
Less than 90 per cent attendance	21%	53%	71%

Generation II: school-leaving attitudes

In the last year of statutory schooling the children had been asked about their attitudes towards school-leaving or readiness to continue with education (Table 8.6). At that time a noticeably higher proportion of non-deprived children said they were willing to continue school after their fifteenth birthday, while half the multiply deprived were anxious to leave. We were particularly interested to discover the path taken by those children described as 'neutral' in their attitude to school-leaving, since presumably they might have remained at school and progressed into further education had they been encouraged to do so. We therefore combined the categories 'neutral' and 'willing to continue' in order to determine the pool of potential candidates for further secondary education. Since we had available the number of children who in fact continued their secondary education, we were in a position to estimate the difference in proportion between pupils potentially available for further schooling and those who actually stayed on. Nineteen per cent of the non-deprived who had expressed themselves as willing or available for further schooling failed to continue but 29 per cent in the deprived group and 37 per cent in the multiply deprived group left school.

Table 8.6   Attitude to leaving school at 15 years

	Non-Deprived Group (n=44)		Deprived Group* (n=140)		Multiply Deprived Group** (n=59)	
Eager to leave	10	22.7%	58	41.4%	30	50.8%
Neutral	16	36.4%	50	35.7%	23	39.0%
Willing to continue	18	40.9%	32	22.9%	6	10.2%

*Difference from NDG at p < .05
**p < .01 (one-tailed)

Generation II: external examinations attempted at 15–16 years

Children attending secondary modern schools, if considered capable of taking a formal school-leaving examination, would normally have been entered for the Northern Counties examination before reaching school-leaving age at 15 plus. This examination was for a certificate of general educational proficiency. Children taking GCE 'O' level examinations would normally attend selective schools and would sit the examination in their sixteenth year. Table 8.7 shows the proportions of children entered for external examinations.

Most children in both deprived groups were not entered for any examination; indeed only 57 per cent of the non-deprived children were entered. Some 22 per cent of the non-deprived group, largely in secondary modern schools, entered the Northern Counties examination and 35 per cent, largely at selective schools, attempted GCE 'O' levels. These rates were significantly higher than in the deprived groups. The success rate was considerably greater for the non-deprived (39 per cent) than for the deprived (16 per cent), while only 5 per cent (n=3) of the multiply deprived group passed.

Table 8.7   External examinations at 15–16 years

	Non-Deprived Group (n=51)		Deprived Group** (n=154)		Multiply Deprived Group** (n=66)	
None attempted	22	43.1%	121	78.6%	62	93.9%
Northern Counties	11	21.6%	15	9.7%	2	3.0%
GCE 'O' level	18	35.3%	18	11.7%	2	3.0%

**Significant differences from the NDG at $p < .01$ (one-tailed)

Preference for employment
During the final year of schooling children were interviewed by staff from the Youth Employment Service and were offered advice about work and training prospects in relation to their own expressed preferences. Table 8.8 gives information about preferences for occupations and skills grouped under three headings descriptive of the type and length of training required. The category 'most trained' includes all forms of trade apprenticeships and all professional training including nursing and training within the armed forces; the category 'more trained' comprises the training necessary for clerical, secretarial and machine-operative work; the category 'least trained' includes the least skilled types of work required in shopkeeping and distributive trades, in unskilled factory work and in general labouring.

Children in each group gave a marked similarity of preference for the most skilled categories of employment, an aspiration unlikely to be fulfilled for many. But half the children in the multiply deprived group expressed interest in occupations requiring the least training. The pattern of recommendation by careers officers per skill category correspond fairly broadly to the preference expressed by the children in the multiply deprived families, and the careers officers appear to have appreciated the potential of many of

Table 8.8   *Red Spots' expressed preference for*
employment at 15 years

	Non-Deprived Group (n=35)		Deprived Group (n=126)		Multiply Deprived Group (n=51)	
Most trained	16	45.7%	62	49.2%	21	41.2%
More trained	12	34.3%	21	16.7%	4	7.8%
Least trained	7	20.0%	43	34.1%	26	51.0%

the multiply deprived even though it may not have been realized.

There was, however, a tendency for all groups of children to aspire to training demanding higher levels of skill than the career officers recommended. We cannot know whether they were unrealistic or whether the Careers Advisory Service was cautious and guided the children into jobs they could obviously cope with. We know that some children expressed their preferences before, and some after, their interviews with the careers training officers, and this might have influenced their choice.

School attended after 15 years of age
Apart from two girls, friends from deprived families, the children in selective schooling remained for at least one more year to sit school-leaving examinations. On the other hand, almost all children attending secondary modern schools left to enter the labour market and full-time employment. Only a few continued some education and training through day and evening class work at Colleges of Further Education; 88.2 per cent of the multiply deprived and even 42 per cent of the non-deprived had ceased all education or training.

The Red Spots at school 1952–62: behaviour
When the children were 10 years old teachers were asked to rate them on a five-point scale on the assumption that the abilities and personal qualities rated were normally distributed. A wide range of items was rated but subsequently reduced to three-point scales covering the top band of 30 per

cent, the middle 40 per cent and the bottom 30 per cent, corresponding to good, average and poor categories of functioning (Table 8.9). The overall pattern of differences seen between deprived and non-deprived groups proved basically the same item for item, with a steady increase of poorer function or problematic behaviour as the degree of deprivation increased.

Table 8.9 *Behaviour at school as rated by teachers:*
Red Spots at 10 years of age

	Non-Deprived %	Deprived %	Multiply Deprived %
Craft Ability			
1	41	13	2
3	9	27	39
Handwriting			
1	34	18	11
3	18	32	46
Reading			
1	44	22	11
3	18	32	48
Response in class			
1	33	17	13
3	29	31	39
Classroom reliability			
1	60	54	29
3	2	15	31
Classroom initiative			
1	20	13	10
3	42	51	60
Classroom concentration			
1	20	16	5
3	31	35	55
Classroom persistence			
1	22	12	3
3	27	38	61
Sociability			
1	40	30	24
3	9	10	13
Maximum 'n'	45	144	62

Note: Each attribute is graded into   1 = top 30% (good)
                                         3 = bottom 30% (poor)

The patterns and significant differences were similar but the percentages varied with the theme. For craft ability, 41 per cent of the non-deprived were in the top band but only 2 per cent of multiply deprived; only 9 per cent of the non-deprived 'functioned poorly' compared with 39 per cent of the multiply deprived. Reading skills showed distributions similar to craft ability, and the same broad patterns held for personal characteristics such as response in class, classroom reliability, initiative, concentration and persistence.

We also reorganized the data by looking at the bottom band of the five-point scales for a combination of three items: concentration, classroom persistence and reading. Averages of the percentages showed that the non-deprived gave zero, the deprived 4 per cent and the multiply deprived 7 per cent. This shows that this particular trio of characteristics was rare except in the multiply deprived group, and even there it is uncommon.

Two explanations seem possible. First, the poorer intellectual level of the multiply deprived group might alone account for their weaker scholastic performance and poorer response to classroom discipline. Second is the possibility that inadequate concentration and attention may result in poor scholastic performance. In the 1970s the concept of impaired attention had become central in descriptions of hyperactivity and subsequently disorders of attention had become the cardinal condition to which hyperactivity was the qualifier (Shaffer, 1985).

Data concerning the intentions, interests and attitudes of the 'Red Spot' children in their last two years at primary school are given in Table 8.10. Even at this early stage a large percentage of children, and even half the non-deprived, had already decided to leave school as early as possible. A detailed account of the wishes of the children according to the type of school attended is given in *The School Years* (Miller *et al.*, 1974: ch. 21).

Information was also available about membership of clubs or participation in spare-time activities at the age of twelve. More than double the non-deprived than the multiply deprived belonged to a school music group and more of the non-deprived played a musical instrument. In the 1950s cinema-going was a particularly common activity for the multiply deprived (1 in 2) and much less so for the non-deprived who

*Table 8.10   Red Spots: intentions, interests, attitudes
in their last two years at primary school*

	Non-Deprived		Deprived		Multiply Deprived	
	n	%	n	%	n	%
Intended leaving school at 15 years	25	(49)	94	(66)*	35	(67)*
Membership of school musical group	11	(21)	17	(12)	4	(8)*
Did not play musical instrument	21	(42)	83	(59)	31	(60)*
Frequently visited cinema	12	(23)	66	(46)	26	(50)*
Enjoyed listening to the radio	17	(35)	32	(24)	7	(15)*
Enjoyed reading comics	28	(54)	95	(69)*	36	(71)*

*Significant difference from non-deprived (p < .05) (one-tailed)

listened more to the radio. With their poorer reading skills it is not surprising that some 7 out of 10 of the multiply deprived read comics as against only 5 out of 10 of the non-deprived.

The data were also examined in relation to the six criteria of deprivation. The children in families with parental illness again presented the same broad pattern as the control group. In contrast, those from families characterized by poor maternal care and cleanliness wished to leave school as early as possible and had the worst rates for all the six items examined.

Behaviour at 10–15 years

When the children were 12 years old their teachers were asked to rate them on the possibility that they would become delinquent, emotionally disturbed or both (Table 8.11). The prediction of 15 per cent for non-deprived and nearly 40 per cent for multiply deprived children constituted a clear association between degree of deprivation and the prediction of delinquency or behaviour disturbance. By 15 years, police probation records showed the rate of delinquency was four times as great in the multiply deprived as in the non-deprived group.

Table 8.11 Red Spots' behaviour at secondary school

	Non-Deprived		Deprived		Multiply Deprived	
	n	%	n	%	n	%
Year 12 Prediction of delinquency/ maladjustment	8	(15)	46	(26)	27	(39)**
Year 15 Police/probation record at 15	3/53	(6)	21/153	(13)	19/67	(28)**
Families with record of delinquent sibling by age of 15	1/61	(2)	16/172	(9)	15/73	(21)**
Interest in games at 15th year	23/51	(45)	50/153	(33)	14/67	(21)*
Activities outside home in the local community	10/52	(19)	13/151	(9)*	3/67	(4)*
Interest in family activities	38/53	(72)	46/152	(30)**	10/67	(15)**
Interest in studying	27/53	(51)	30/153	(20)**	3/67	(4)**

Note: Differences from non-deprived group
  * = p < .05
  ** = p < .01
  (one-tailed tests)

Both school absenteeism and eagerness to leave were highly correlated with family deprivation, and school absenteeism was three times as great in the multiply deprived.

Table 8.11 also provides information about the children's interests. More of the non-deprived declared their interest in study, games, activities in the local community, and were more likely to be involved in family activities.

Personal attributes: the last year at school,
performance and behaviour
School information, relating to 1962, was available on 80 per cent of the original 847 Red Spots. Absence of information did not necessarily mean that the family had moved from Newcastle; the child may simply have been absent from school on a particular day. Here we limit ourselves to the data from those Red Spots who were followed up in 1980.

According to the teachers' ratings, the non-deprived children consistently performed better in school, and their percentage within the top reading band is double that of the multiply deprived whose percentage in the bottom band of reading is three times that of the non-deprived. This picture recurred even more markedly in relation to mathematics and manual dexterity where none of the non-deprived fell into the bottom band, but almost 40 per cent of the multiply deprived did so.

In respect of athletic ability the picture was not so extreme because, although the distribution of the multiply deprived was about the same as in manual dexterity, on this occasion about a fifth of the non-deprived fell into the bottom band.

In other personal attributes, such as initiative, concentration, persistence and good attitude to schoolwork, the non-deprived children also received significantly more favourable ratings than the multiply deprived.

9   The Red Spots and their spouses in 1979–80

The 'catch-up' longitudinal phase: self-report data
The data so far presented came from the original Red Spot study. This section covers the educational and occupational data of the Red Spots as reported by themselves in 1979–80. By 33 years of age, 92 per cent had married and we also obtained data from their spouses, male and female.

Self-report on examination successes at school
Table 9.1 shows that both the male and female multiply deprived Red Spot children had significantly lower success rates in school-leaving examinations than the non-deprived. A far higher proportion of deprived and twice as many multiply deprived boys and girls were not even entered. Red Spot boys and girls in non-deprived families had a much higher success rate at both 'O' and 'A' levels than the multiply deprived.

Female spouses' results followed the pattern in the female Red Spots (see Appendix Table 10). In contrast, the results for the male spouses do not show the difference in the deprived group, and this was the first indication that the spouses of women in the deprived groups show differences from their Red Spot equivalents. The nature and extent of these differences became more apparent later.

Training after school
The Red Spots and their spouses told us about all the occupational training they had undertaken after leaving school. We have not grouped the data according to a professional level but have simply divided respondents into those who did not attempt training or failed and those who completed training and obtained a job qualification.

A first glance at Table 9.2 suggests that deprived females undertook significantly less training than the non-deprived,

Table 9.1 Red Spot school examination successes (self-report)

| | Males | | | | | | Females | | | | | |
| | Non-Deprived (n=31) | | Deprived** (n=80) | | Multiply Deprived** (n=32) | | Non-Deprived (n=30) | | Deprived** (n=83) | | Multiply Deprived** (n=36) | |
	n	%	n	%	n	%	n	%	n	%	n	%
No exams	10	32	54	67	27	84	12	40	63	76	30	83
Sat exams but failed	2	6	3	4	–	–	1	3	–	–	–	–
CSE/Northern Counties	6	19	10	12	3	9	8	27	10	12	4	11
School Certificate												
'O' level	6	19	11	14	1	3	5	17	5	6	1	2
'A' level	7	23	2	2	1	3	4	13	5	6	1	2

**Significant differences from the non-deprived group at p < .01 (one-tailed)

Table 9.2 Red Spots and spouses: self-report on qualifications

A. Red Spot adults

| | Males | | | | | | Females | | | | | |
| | Non-Deprived | | Deprived | | Multiply Deprived | | Non-Deprived | | Deprived* | | Multiply Deprived** | |
	n	%	n	%	n	%	n	%	n	%	n	%
Qualifications – No	11	36	42	52	17	53	17	57	64	77	33	92
Qualifications – Yes	20	64	38	47	15	47	13	43	19	23	3	8

B. Spouses

| | Males | | | | | | Females | | | | | |
| | Non-Deprived | | Deprived | | Multiply Deprived | | Non-Deprived | | Deprived* | | Multiply Deprived** | |
	n	%	n	%	n	%	n	%	n	%	n	%
Qualifications – No	10	40	29	47	14	48	16	59	57	78	24	86
Qualifications – Yes	15	60	32	52	15	52	11	41	16	22	4	14

*Significant difference from the non-deprived group at $p < .05$ (one-tailed)

**$p < .01$

whereas such differences do not readily appear in males. Yet almost half the deprived male Red Spots obtained some job qualification despite their low school examination success, while less than a quarter of deprived females did so.

We also recorded a lack of correspondence between self-reported occupational history of male and female spouses. The wives of deprived males clearly lacked adequate job training experience, whereas the husbands of deprived females did not.

Parents in families of formation: ability testing

The Red Spots were well aware that many aspects of their physical development and scholastic progress had been documented during their school years and neither they nor their spouses appeared to resent being asked to undergo further tests when they were interviewed in their homes. Years earlier, aged 12 and 14 years, they had completed the Mill Hill Vocabulary Scale and the same test was used again because it was both comparable and convenient.

In most homes both man and wife were tested during the same visit. The usual standardized procedures were observed and neither partner had knowledge of the other's responses. Only the synonym selection part of the test was required and was completed by both participants simultaneously whilst under scrutiny. All the Red Spot adults, male and female, had entered their thirty-third year. As expected, the female spouses of the Red Spots were, on average, slightly younger (30 years 1 month) and the male spouses slightly older (34 years 8 months). The scores are given in Table 9.3 and show significant differences in the Mill Hill vocabulary quotients between the non-deprived and the two deprived groups of Red Spot men. For Red Spot women the same pattern is seen between the non-deprived and multiply deprived groups but the differences in the deprived group fails to reach statistical significance. The scores of the male spouses in all three groups lie close to the mean of 100, whereas for the spouse females, like the Red Spot females, there is a highly significant difference between the non-deprived and the multiply deprived but not the deprived group.

A surprising result from Table 9.3 was the superiority of male over female scores for every grouping both for Red Spots and spouses. This is contrary to expectation for two

Table 9.3   *Parent testing: Mill Hill vocabulary IQ*
equivalent scores classified according to
deprivation in family of origin

		Males			Females		
		Mean	SD	n	Mean	SD	n
Red Spots	NDG	103.3	12.7	29	98.4	8.4	31
	DG**	97.3	9.1	79	95.0	10.8	78
	MDG**	92.9	7.9	32	90.6**	7.0	34
Spouses	NDG	100.8	9.5	25	97.6	8.5	25
	DG	99.6	10.9	56	94.2	9.1	74
	MDG	99.4	11.6	26	90.7**	7.8	29

**Significant differences from the NDG at $p < .01$ (one-tailed)

NDG = Non Deprived Group ; DG = Deprived Group; MDG = Multiply Deprived Group

reasons: first, on purely verbal measures females tend to show superiority over males; and second, when the children were tested at 11 years there were no differences between the sexes.

The picture becomes much more complicated when we divide the total group according to the degree of deprivation and whether Red Spot or spouse. Then, although non-deprived Red Spot males scored significantly higher on vocabulary quotient than the non-deprived females ($p < .05$), that did not hold for the Red Spot deprived groups. Further, the scores for the spouse groups show significant differences in favour of the males, in both non-deprived and deprived groups ($p < .01$). When we turn to consider females (Red Spots and spouses) for the three categories, we note that there are no differences between the three groups of Red Spots and the spouse groups. But that was not true for male equivalents, as the spouses of multiply deprived females are distinctly superior to multiply deprived Red Spot males.

Behaviour and health: the Red Spots as adults

Findings: Generation II as adults
Significant illnesses were studied for women and men separately. The definition of a chronic or recurrent illness

was one of at least a year's duration which substantially impaired working capacity either in a job or at home. Table 9.4 shows that women whose family of origin was deprived had only a slight excess of physical illness, but there were significant differences in those currently living in deprived circumstances.

As might have been expected, women who were reared in deprived and multiply deprived families in 1952 had more worries over a range of matters including their own children's health, money, housing, husband's employment and their own ability to cope. However, the rate of worries proved even greater in those women who, in 1980, were living in deprived circumstances. The percentage difference between the non-deprived and the multiply deprived when comparing findings between those reared and those currently living in deprived circumstances doubled for some of the items such as money, housing and ability to cope.

The recorded psychiatric symptoms, as represented by current emotional disturbance, disclosed a similar pattern when the data were classified according to early or current deprivation. Important features in this respect were those which might reflect depression, such as dysphoric mood, lack of energy and suicidal thoughts. The pattern with psychiatric treatment was similar with rates of 5 per cent for the non-deprived and 16 per cent for those reared in deprivation and 1 per cent and 24 per cent respectively in relation to current deprivation. In the family of formation substantial illness was one of the identifying criteria of deprivation and thus more symptoms could be expected in the deprived than in the non-deprived.

Data relating to men show lower rates overall and smaller differences between non-deprived men and those reared in deprivation than in women, and the nature of the problems were not always the same. First, problems with alcohol, uncommon in women, were significant in men. Second, the men seemed to worry about their spouse's or partner's health to a much greater extent than the women. This probably reflected the excess of ill-health in the women themselves. The pattern of cigarette smoking, however, was the same in men and women. Broadly similar patterns of worry concerning their children's health, finance, housing and coping ability were seen in men and women. However,

Table 9.4   Behaviour and illness in women in families of formation: Red Spots and spouses combined

	Family of origin			Family of formation		
	Non-Deprived %	Deprived %	Multiply Deprived %	Non-Deprived %	Deprived %	Multiply Deprived %
A. Significant Illness:						
Physical	18	17	22	0	25**	33**
Psychiatric	4	5	6	0	6*	12*
Both physical and psychiatric	0	1	2	0	2	3
Total illness (%)	22	23	30	0	33**	48**
B. Worried About:						
Children's health	31	50*	55*	23	53**	74**
Finances	18	23	33*	32	51**	73**
Housing	9	19	22*	3	26*	43**
Husband's work	6	15	32**	6	18**	33**
Ability to cope	18	17	30	3	23**	38**
Mean number of worries:						
Worries in last year	3.4	4.7*	5.5*	2.4	5.3**	7.3**
Worries interfering with sleep, work and leisure	32	45	44	29	46*	62**
C. Psychiatric Symptoms:						
Lack of energy (moderate/marked)	26	31	42	16	37**	52**
Dysphoric mood (moderate/marked)	21	28	41*	10	33**	52**
Suicidal thoughts	9	18	22*	3	18**	33**
'End of tether'	26	35	41*	20	39**	48**
Non situational 'panics'	12	20	31*	4	24**	38**
On tranquillizers	9	13	17	3	16**	30**
Psychiatric treatment	5	11	16	1	12**	24**
Current emotional disturbance (marked)	9	17	27	3	22**	24**
Phobias	1.4	1.6	2.1	0.8	1.9	2.7
D. Smoking:	44	52	64	26	60	72
E. Marital Friction: Two Parent Families Only						
Irritability at least once a week	17	25	37*	8	30*	50*
Sum score of marital problems (i.e. 5+)	9	16	24*	2	19**	36**

Note: Difference from non-deprived group: * = p < .05, ** = p < .01 (one-tailed)

there were some differences: for instance, men reared in deprivation showed a high rate of worry about jobs irrespective of degree of deprivation. It would seem that the non-deprived women expressed less concern about their husband's employment than did the men themselves. Psychiatric and emotional symptoms were less frequent in men than in women; there was less of a gradient in men from non-deprived to deprived than in women.

The results for men currently living in deprivation show many differences: drink problems show a clear pattern, being absent among those not currently deprived; rates of smoking in the deprived were double those of the non-deprived and admitted worries increased with the degree of deprivation. Thus, worry interfering with sleep, work and leisure rose from 12 per cent in the non-deprived to 37 per cent in the multiply deprived and worry about jobs from 28 to 49 per cent. On most items the rates of worries were twice to three times as high among multiply deprived than among non-deprived men. Even so, on most items the rates were far lower than in women.

When the data on marital friction were classified according to deprivation in the family of origin, the rates were twice as high in the multiply deprived compared to the non-deprived. One way of obtaining an overall picture was to look at the sum score of marital problems in families where there was quarrelling, marital separation or physical conflict between partners. These events were on 4-point scales and, when summed, the maximum score was 12. Table 9.4 gives percentages of women where the summed scores of marital problems were five or more. The picture changes according to the classification used. In families currently living in deprivation, weekly irritability between partners occurred in about one in ten of the non-deprived, but in as much as one in two of multiply deprived families. When marital problems were totalled and a cut-off taken of five or more, only 2 per cent of non-deprived families were identified against 36 per cent of the multiply deprived.

Sex differences in behaviour
We selected a few major behavioural variables in an attempt to investigate sex differences. Because of the low incidence

of these features in the non-deprived we confined ourselves to the multiply deprived.

The multiply deprived Red Spot adults had twice the rate of health problems (34 per cent) as compared to their spouses (16 per cent), but there were no male/female differences. The overall rate of drink problems was three times as high in males (18 per cent) than females (5 per cent). The rates of adults taking tranquillizers were twice as high in the Red Spots (18 per cent) as in their spouses (7 per cent) and the rate among females was more than twice that of their spouses. Dysphoric mood, a symptom likely to reflect depression, was particularly high in females (41 per cent as against 16 per cent in males) and suicidal thinking, while not high, was more frequent in women (21 per cent) than men (8 per cent). Again, multiply deprived Red Spot adults had twice the rate of suicidal thinking (21 per cent) as their spouses (9 per cent); this was more frequent in women than men.

Physical growth
The heights of the Red Spots and their partners were recorded in 1979–80 when aged between 32 and 34 years and the picture remained the same as in childhood. For example, the mean heights of the deprived group were significantly less than the non-deprived.

10   The children of the Red Spots 1979–80

Children of the Red Spots at school: cognitive development of the first-born

At the time of the 1979–80 interview, the Red Spot (Generation II) families included 473 children, 252 (53.3 per cent) of which were boys and 221 (46.7 per cent) girls. Although data were gathered on all children, detailed information about level of general ability and school progress could only be obtained on children over five years of age. Of the 352 at school, 179 (51 per cent) were first-born, and we used their data to avoid statistical difficulties of differences due to birth order (Altus, 1966).

Pre-school stimulatory experience

One index of parental readiness to provide an early educational experience for their children is the use made of attendance at pre-school playgroups; three-quarters of those from the non-deprived and half of the deprived had attended playgroups, the difference being significant. This suggests that significantly more non-deprived children began formal infant schooling with an appreciable advantage.

Schooling

The mean age of the first-born of the non-deprived was 105.7 months (n=45), of the deprived 133.1 months (n=129), and of the multiply deprived 140.7 months (n=47). The non-deprived group were significantly younger than the deprived and, at the time of our interview, only 18 per cent of the non-deprived had entered secondary school in contrast to 34 per cent of the deprived and 37 per cent of the multiply deprived groups. This reflects the earlier marriages of the deprived groups.

We were thus faced with an appreciable age spread among

the children whereas, in the previous generation, the Red
Spots had been comparable in terms of educational
experience.

Neither in 1962 nor 1980 did any of the children of non-
deprived families attend special schools, whereas in each
period a few from deprived families did so.

Parent–school contacts
We attempted to measure parents' interest in school by
enquiring whether they had consulted the child's teacher
during the year preceding the home visit and learned that
87 per cent of non-deprived, 75 per cent of deprived and 68
per cent of multiply deprived parents had done so.

Testing
The tests used were:

1   Raven's Progressive Matrices (Raven, Court and Raven,
    1976)
    (a)   Coloured Progressive Matrices for children under
          11 years
    (b)   Standard Progressive Matrices for children 11 years
          and older
2   Vocabulary (Definition Form) Scale (Raven, Court and
    Raven, 1976)
    (a)   Crichton Vocabulary Scale for children under 11
          years
    (b)   Mill Hill Vocabulary Scale — Junior 1 form for
          children of 11 years and over
3   The Holborn Reading Scale (Word-Recognition) (Watts,
    1948) for all children.

Test results: first-born children

Raven's Coloured/Standard Progressive Matrices   Table 10.1
shows scores expressed as quotients for all the groups of boys
and girls according to deprivation in the families of origin.
The mean score for the children in non-deprived families
(IQ=109) was not significantly different from that of their
parents at the same age (IQ=106), but was significantly
greater than the mean for children in both deprived groups.
Greater differences between non-deprived and deprived are

Table 10.1   First-born schoolchildren — families of
formation: Raven's Coloured/Standard
Progressive Matrices (classified according
to 1952 criteria of deprivation)

	Boys and Girls			Boys			Girls		
	$\bar{x}$	SD	n	$\bar{x}$	SD	n	$\bar{x}$	SD	n
Non-Deprived	109.5	13.0	40	109.7	12.6	19	109.2	13.6	21
Deprived	103.1**	14.9	106	104.6	15.8	58	101.3*	13.6	48
Multiply Deprived	101.9**	14.8	48	101.4*	14.7	26	102.6	15.2	22

*Difference from non-deprived group at p < .05
**p < .01 (one-tailed)

Table 10.2   Raven's Coloured/Standard Progressive
Matrices (classified according to 1980
criteria of deprivation)

	Boys and Girls			Boys			Girls		
	$\bar{x}$	SD	n	$\bar{x}$	SD	n	$\bar{x}$	SD	n
Non-Deprived	112.2	13.3	45	113.9	13.5	26	109.8	13.0	19
Deprived	102.1**	13.9	129	101.8*	13.9	64	102.5	13.9	65
Multiply Deprived	98.8**	14.7	47	97.7	13.3	23	99.9	16.2	24

*Difference from non-deprived group at p < .05
**p < .01 (one-tailed)

shown if the grouping of deprivation in 1980 is used (see
Table 10.2). This suggests, as might have been expected, that
contemporary deprivation has a greater effect on children
than that which affected their parents.

Five of the six groups defined by deprivation in the family
of origin yielded significantly lower mean scores than the
non-deprived group. The exception was parental illness which
was merely two points below the non-deprived suggesting
that parental illness is different in nature and effect from the
other criteria. The other five factors all appear to be in-
criminated in giving rise to lower non-verbal cognitive
performance across the generations, but the mechanism is

not clear. Further, poor care and poor mothering, with means of 99 and 101 respectively, were particularly low in the deprived group.

Crichton/Mill Hill Vocabulary Scales   When the children were grouped according to deprivation in the families of origin non-deprived boys showed an 8-point vocabulary difference over multiply deprived (p < .05), and the non-deprived girls a 12-point difference both over the deprived and multiply deprived (p < .01).

When classified according to contemporary deprivation non-deprived boys scored 17 points higher than multiply deprived and 14 higher than the deprived; non-deprived girls scored 20 and 19 points higher than the deprived groups respectively. No significant sex difference was seen in vocabulary scores.

The Holborn Reading Scale   All the children attempted the Holborn Reading Scale — a test of reading sentences aloud. The scale assigns a reading age ranging from 5 years 9 months at the simplest level to 13 years 9 months at the most difficult. For the purpose of converting scores into reading quotients, any child unable to make sense of the first sentence on the scale was arbitrarily assigned a reading age level of 5 years 6 months; and children older than 13 years 9 months were assumed to have a chronological age at the test ceiling age. Table 10.3 gives average reading quotients for first-born boys and girls separately and shows consistently better performance of non-deprived over deprived children for classification, both according to family of origin and family of formation, again with greater differences in the latter case. Throughout the groups girls scored higher than boys.

Table 10.4 confirms that appreciably more good readers were found within the non-deprived groups, and this difference was especially noticeable for the very good readers (reading quotient 130+), few of whom were from the multiply deprived group. The reverse gradient held good for those children rated very poor readers (quotient 69 or less), all of whom were deprived or multiply deprived.

Table 10.3 Reading performance for Generation III first-born children: Holborn Reading Scale

	Boys			Girls		
	Non-Deprived	Deprived	Multiply Deprived	Non-Deprived	Deprived	Multiply Deprived
Fifth Year Classification: Mean Reading Quotient	98.9 (n=19)	94.9 (n=58)	90.7 (n=26)	109.8 (n=21)	99.0** (n=48)	96.4** (n=22)
Thirty-third Year Classification: Mean Reading Quotient	106.2 (n=26)	91.5** (n=64)	90.8** (n=23)	112.9 (n=19)	97.2** (n=65)	95.5** (n=24)

**Difference from non-deprived group at $p < .01$ (one-tailed)

Table 10.4 Generation III schoolchildren: percentage of good, average and poor readers (thirty-third year classification)

		Boys			Girls		
Reading Quotient		Non-Deprived (n=26) %	Deprived (n=64) %	Multiply Deprived (n=23) %	Non-Deprived (n=19) %	Deprived (n=65) %	Multiply Deprived (n=24) %
115 and above	GOOD	23	–	–	42	17	21
85–114	AVERAGE	77	64	65	58	63	54
84 and less	POOR	–	36	35	–	20	25

Physical growth

In the follow-up study, the heights and weights of children over five years of age up to 17 were recorded at the time of the interview but, with the wide age range, these children could not be treated as a homogeneous cohort. When the schoolchildren were divided into age groups and the growth of non-deprived compared with the multiply deprived, the number of children in each cell was small. The schoolchildren also came from families of different sizes and were of different birth order. These factors made comparisons difficult and we therefore simply plotted whether or not weights and heights of first-born children were above or below the 50th percentile for height and weight (using Tanner percentile charts). When that was done, and the non-deprived and multiply deprived compared, significantly more of the non-deprived were above that percentile for height (63 per cent as to 38 per cent) but not for weight (58 per cent as to 50 per cent).

Behaviour: Generation III

Behaviour in the first-born children of Generation III was studied using the Rutter Teacher and Parent Questionnaires covering behaviour and temperament.

Method

The Rutter Teacher Scale (B2) (Rutter, 1967)   This is completed by teachers regarding children's behaviour in school. It yields a total score plus neurotic and antisocial subscores. Rutter (1967) and Rutter, Tizard and Whitemore (1970) found that a cut-off of nine or more on the total score had discriminative value. In the Isle of Wight study it selected 10 per cent of boys and 4 per cent of girls. Test–retest reliability for total scores over a three-month interval was 0.89; and inter-rater reliability 0.72 (Rutter, 1976). With regard to validity, it was reported that total scores on a sample of normal nine to 13 year-old children were significantly lower than those on a group of children attending a psychiatric clinic.

Child behaviour and temperament, based on parental reports
Behaviour   An inventory, administered as a semi-structured,

open-ended interview with mothers, was used to quantify behaviour (Kolvin *et al.*, 1975). It consists of 29 questions with appropriate probes which relate to the three or four scales originally developed: neurotic behaviour (Scale A); antisocial behaviour (Scale B); and psychosomatic behaviour (Scale C). The interrelated reliability of the original scales was all above 0.9.

Temperament   An inventory, also administered as a semi-structured, open-ended interview with mothers, was used to measure temperament (Garside *et al.*, 1975). This was also slightly modified for the current study. There were 29 questions with appropriate probes which relate to four dimensions: withdrawal, activity, mood and irregularity. (Inter-rater reliabilities of these dimensions were all above 0.9.)

Findings

When we examined the data according to whether a parent had been reared in deprivation in the family of origin there were few significant differences except in relation to anti-social behaviour but, when analysed according to current family deprivation, a number were apparent (see Table 10.5). The rates of antisocial behaviour, based on information from teachers, were almost three times as great in the multiply deprived as in the non-deprived, but there was virtually no difference for neurotic behaviour. We also had measures of behaviour based on information provided by the parents and here the multiply deprived showed an excess of disturbance on the total score. Again, there was no difference in relation to neurotic behaviour, while higher rates of antisocial behaviour and psychosomatic symptoms were recorded.

The multiply deprived group showed higher rates of activity and moodiness than the non-deprived but there was no difference on the other temperamental dimensions. The Teacher Scale showed more than twice as many multiply deprived boys than girls had high antisocial scores, but there were no sex differences on the ratings of behaviour and temperament gathered from mothers.

Table 10.5   Children of Red Spots: behaviour and temperament grouped according to deprivation in the family of formation

	Non-Deprived		Deprived		Multiply Deprived	
	n	%	n	%	n	%
School Behaviour (Rutter Scale):						
i. Antisocial score of 3+ (Newcastle Variation)	4/46	(8.7)	23/129	(17.8)	12/47	(25.5
ii. Neurotic score 4+	8/46	(17.4)	20/129	(15.5)	10/47	(21.3
iii. Total score of 9+	6/46	(13.0)	20/129	(15.5)	9/47	(19.1
Home Behaviour:						
i. Antisocial score of 16+	6/46	(13.0)	24/131	(18.3)	15/48	(31.2
ii. Somatic score (20+)	10/46	(21.7)	35/131	(26.7)	20/48	(41.7
iii. Motor score (3+)	1/46	(2.2)	14/131	(10.7)	7/48	(14.6
iv. Total score (48+)	3/46	(6.5)	20/131	(15.3)	11/48	(22.9
Temperament:						
Activity (13+)	9/46	(19.6)	35/131	(26.7)	16/48	(33.3
Mood (12+)	3/46	(6.5)	16/131	(12.2)	8/48	(16.7

*Significance of difference (one-tailed) p < .05

Childhood accidents:
the children of the Red Spots

We have already described an early excess of childhood accidents in the Red Spots who came from multiply deprived families. A similar excess occurred in the children of the Red Spots who had been exposed to multiple deprivation. In families with children under the age of five who had had accidents which merited medical attention, the rates were 26 per cent, 35 per cent and 58 per cent respectively for the non-deprived, deprived and multiply deprived.

Summary and comment on findings presented in Chapters 8, 9 and 10

In the preceding chapters, development has been addressed from a chronological perspective. Here we draw together and comment on similar areas of performance throughout the period 1947–80.

Cognitive and scholastic performance

When a selective examination system was operative, more than one in three of the Red Spots from non-deprived families entered grammar or private schools after the 11-plus examination. This was true for only one in eight of the deprived and one in 25 of the multiply deprived. Striking differences in measured intelligence were also found at 11-plus examinations between the non-deprived and deprived groups, with the multiply deprived at an even greater disadvantage. However, by fifteen years, the gap on the Progressive Matrices score between the deprived and non-deprived had much reduced and the difference was no longer significant. The reasons for this are speculative but call to mind explanations in terms of the capacity of moderately disadvantaged children given the passage of time to show an improvement in those general abilities not greatly influenced by cultural factors. Other possibilities are that the effects of early life deprivation may 'wash out' by 15 years or that there are compensatory effects of more positive later environmental influences.

At the age of 10 and 11 there was a wide pattern of poorer performance, classroom behaviour and attitudes of the deprived as viewed by the teachers. These data raise a number of unanswered questions. For instance, does performance reflect the life experiences or the innate ability of the multiply deprived? Why had more of the multiply deprived failed to catch up in basic attainments, skills and attitudes after some five years at secondary school? How much did these ratings reflect predetermined expectation by teachers? Why did we see the same pattern of inferior performance in physical and athletic pursuits? It is well known that intelligence and physique are positively correlated. Is this the basis of the poorer athletic ability of the multiply deprived or is it because they lack the opportunity?

Our data did not reveal patterns distinctive for the different types of deprivation, but children coming from families of origin where there was poor care and cleanliness tended to perform and behave more poorly in adolescence.

At school-leaving age a higher proportion of the non-deprived continued school, although roughly the same proportion of children in all three groups (between 36 per cent and 39 per cent) had been neutral over remaining at school.

While still at school, 20 per cent of the non-deprived, as against 51 per cent of the multiply deprived, expressed an option for unskilled work. However, nearly half of the multiply deprived were hoping for more than unskilled employment. While this may have been unrealistic, it does suggest that educational authorities should seek alternative ways of stimulating children from deprived home backgrounds towards realizing their ambitions.

We found that a relatively high success rate at 'O' and 'A' level examinations was obtained by non-deprived Red Spots in comparison with the multiply deprived. This was also true for post-school training. When the Red Spots were adult, we saw that deprived males married women with a comparable or greater lack of examination success and job training whereas some deprived women married men who were relatively successful in their school examinations and occupational training.

There were other sex differences. Red Spot females from the multiply deprived group, while not differing significantly from their Red Spot male counterparts in verbal ability, showed a decided tendency to associate themselves with males who proved to be significantly superior to their Red Spot male counterparts. The same trend was apparent for the deprived Red Spot females, but not at a statistically significant level. We were naturally interested to know whether a similar trend held true for the deprived males. However, inspection of the data revealed that multiply deprived Red Spot men associated with spouses not significantly different from the female Red Spot counterparts. In other words, there was evidence of assortive mating on the measure of verbal ability in the case of multiply deprived males and a general trend in this direction for the deprived males. This did not occur in the multiply deprived Red Spot females who tended to marry men brighter than their deprived male Red Spot counterparts.

In the third-generation children there was a surprisingly similar gradient for verbal and reading quotients in the groups according to degree of deprivation. In general, the impact of deprivation on Generation III children was stronger when we studied influences from the current family

(Generation II) rather than from the previous generation (Generation I).

Behavioural performance

For the Red Spots in the pre-school period, a broad pattern emerged of a steady increase of poorer function or problematic behaviour as the degree of deprivation increased. In the primary school, at the age of 10, multiply deprived children were rated by their teachers as doing worse than non-deprived. Nevertheless, on every item studied, a sizeable proportion of the multiply deprived were rated as showing average functioning; for 'response in class' over 60 per cent, for classroom concentration and classroom persistence 40 per cent, and for sociability almost 90 per cent. Thus, towards the end of their primary school careers, many of the children from multiply deprived homes were showing adequate standards of performance and classroom behaviour. However, we need to ask how far ratings of a child's personal qualities were influenced by perceptions of that child's scholastic abilities and vice versa; that this might have happened is supported by the similarity in the patterns of scholastic ability and behavioural functioning.

While in the 1950s the concept of an attention deficit disorder had not yet been developed, our fifteenth-year data provided evidence of some of the features which nowadays are held to be characteristic of attention-deficit disorder: poor concentration, poor persistence and initiative in the classroom and learning problems. These features were present only in a small proportion of the deprived groups — particularly in the multiply deprived. These findings are consistent with those of Bosco and Robins (1980) suggesting an incidence of hyperactivity in about 1 per cent of schoolchildren under 11 years of age. They lead to the suggestion that some attention-deficit disorders may have origins in deprivation and are supported by the work of Tizard and his colleagues on the psychological problems of children reared in institutions (Tizard and Rees, 1974; Tizard and Hodges, 1978).

The Red Spots' interests provided a picture of 10 and 11 year-olds in the late 1950s. It suggested that children coming from non-deprived families would tend to have more stimulation and enjoy listening to the radio. The most deprived children wished to leave school early and would not seek their enjoyment through membership of a school musical group or by playing a musical instrument, or even listening to the radio. However, they went more frequently to the cinema and read more comics.

In senior school, the same broad pattern was identified in relation to indicators of delinquency or behaviour disturbance; in their fifteenth year, eagerness to leave school and poor school attendance markedly increased, especially in the multiply deprived. However, this was the school-leaving year when absenteeism traditionally tends to be higher.

All data were examined to ascertain if there were differences of disturbed behaviour between boys and girls, but these were significant only in the antisocial behaviour of boys.

Health
When we considered the Red Spots as adults and their spouses in terms of health, the individual symptoms tell us about the response of females to adverse life experiences: for instance, about one-sixth of the non-deprived, but one-half of the deprived, complained of lack of energy over the previous year, and the same picture was found in the case of a sadness of mood sufficient to interfere with work or housework. Few of the non-deprived group had contemplated suicide, whereas one in every three of the multiply deprived said they had. They also showed higher rates of non-situational panics, specific fears and other psychological problems. All these findings indicate that women living in deprived circumstances are at considerable risk of psychological morbidity and particularly of depression. This risk is increased if the deprivation is current rather than in their childhood. In the former, few non-deprived but almost one-third of the multiply deprived had been on tranquillizers for more than a year. Another factor which reflects both the burden of deprivation and life stresses is smoking. In families of formation only a quarter of non-deprived women smoked, whereas three-quarters of the multiply deprived did so. Deprived males did not seem to manifest the same affective-depressive pattern of disturbance but were at greater risk from problems of alcoholism and the development of antisocial behaviour.

Previous workers have reported high rates of psychiatric disorder in problem families (Tonge *et al.*, 1975). Our findings show that women appear to carry most of the burden of family deprivation. The presence of psychiatric problems in 40 per cent of women in the multiply deprived group must make even more difficult their attempts to cope with the everyday activities of their families and care of their children. Our data lead us to suggest that the children in families in which there is a combination of multiple deprivation and parental psychiatric disturbance are at greater risk than those children whose parents have psychiatric problems alone. We do not find it surprising that other authors consider that children of depressed mothers are more at risk from accidents (Brown and Harris, 1978), and we would speculate that such mothers are not only depressed but likely to have been beset by other social difficulties. In a similar way, we can begin to understand the links between family deprivation, maternal psychological problems and antisocial behaviour in childhood.

We saw that from multiply deprived families have come two subsequent generations manifesting a significant degree of antisocial behaviour. This form of transmission is not replicated in the case of other types of disturbed behaviour, such as neurotic and psychosomatic conditions. However, in Generation III there was an excess of psychosomatic symptoms in the multiply deprived. Finally, deprivation in the family of formation was associated with temperamental abnormalities in children consisting of high levels of high activity and moodiness. These latter qualities are likely to be related to antisocial behaviour.

Physical growth and development

It is well known that the mean height and weight of children as they enter school and thereafter during their school years has increased steadily during the present century. On the other hand, many studies, including the '1,000 Families' have shown that the downward gradient through occupational groups I–V (Registrar General's classification) has persisted. These studies have been documented by Blaxter (1981). We too provide evidence of a significant failure of growth in height and weight in the multiply deprived group of Red Spots at the age of three years, with relative growth failure continuing for all ages up to 15 years. Since there did not appear to be any significant difference in the mean birth-weight of children in that group, we considered that the poorer physical growth was related to post-natal factors, and that such differences between children of deprived and multiply deprived families should be regarded as environmentally, rather than as genetically, determined. It is therefore theoretically avoidable.

PART IV
CHANGING FAMILIES

11   Change within generation 1952–62

This chapter describes change in individual families within one generation. First, the families who became deprived while their children attended primary school are compared with families who remained non-deprived and then with the same families who remained deprived. Second, families who were deprived in 1952 but moved out of deprivation are compared with those who remained deprived.

Changes in deprivation

Prevalence and change

Data were recorded concerning deprivation in the family of origin in 1952 when the children were aged five and in 1957 when they were 10. These data allowed a study of changes between 1952 and 1957 — a period when deprivation was substantially reduced. The families with most deprivation showed the greatest reduction while a few others moved into deprivation (see Figure 11.1). By 1957 the differences between the deprived and non-deprived groups were reduced, much of the reduction being due to improvements in housing and less overcrowding, reflecting the Newcastle City Post-War Rehousing Programme — but there was some reduction in every criterion.

With the small movement into deprivation from the non-deprived group, it was important to know whether there was likely to have been an overall reduction of criteria of deprivation in our families in Newcastle. That this was so is shown in Table 11.1.

We also compared the sums of the same five criteria at the fifth and tenth years and we found that:

(a)   of families scoring zero at year 5, 10 per cent scored more at year 10;

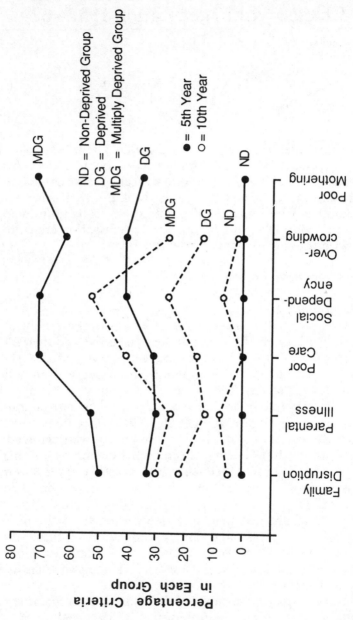

Figure 11.1 Profile of criteria of deprivation in the three selected groups at the 5th and 10th years (Generation I)

Table 11.1   Deprivation in 810 families in 1952 and 1957

		\multicolumn{7}{c}{Number of Criteria in 1952}	
		0	1	2	3	4	5	10th year	
Number	0	444	112	33	6	3	0	598	0
of	1	38	44	28	15	6	1	132	1
criteria	2	11	10	11	12	4	1	49	2
in	3	0	0	7	3	2	3	15	3
1957	4	0	1	2	2	3	1	9	4
	5	0	0	1	3	2	1	7	5
	5th Year	493	167	82	41	20	7	810	

Note: Based on five criteria in 1952 and 1957

(b) of those scoring one at year 5, 67 per cent scored zero and 7 per cent scored more at year 10;

(c) of those scoring two at year 5, 74 per cent scored zero and 12 per cent scored more at year 10;

(d) of those scoring three or more at year 5, 80 per cent scored less and 12 per cent scored more at year 10;

(e) of those scoring four at year 5, 75 per cent scored less and 10 per cent scored more at year 10;

(f) of those scoring five at year 5, 86 per cent scored less at year 10.

We also wished to know whether deprivation continued in the same families. We studied this by correlating our criteria at the fifth and tenth years and found that, while all correlations were positive and significant, only those of marital/family disruption and poor care were moderate ($r = 0.57$ and 0.58 respectively), while parental illness proved low ($r = 0.17$). The other criteria were intermediate (social dependence $r = 0.46$; and overcrowding $r = 0.32$). This implied that marital/family disruption and poor care of children were comparatively stable phenomena. We also correlated the sum of the scores on five criteria of deprivation in 1952 (total score) with each of the criteria at both 1952 and 1957 and, similarly, the total score of deprivation at 1957. All the correlations proved substantial at the fifth year but were considerably lower at year 10. Only those in relation to poor care and social dependency were moderately high ($r = 0.50$ and 0.47 respectively), suggesting that the stability of total deprivation was particularly dependent on these criteria. Total deprivation, too, proved a fairly stable phenomenon (r = 0.61) and further analysis suggested this was particularly owing to its association with poor care and social dependence.

Changes in the individual criteria

The prevalence of the various criteria of deprivation at the fifth and tenth years are shown in Table 11.2. Those at the tenth year include families which remained deprived and those which moved into deprivation. Nevertheless, it was evident that in the five years there had been an overall reduction in deprivation; this was most marked in respect of overcrowding and was least for marital disruption and social dependency.

Table 11.2   Prevalence of criteria

| | Percentage of Families Showing Each of Five Criteria | | | | |
	Marital Disruption	Parental Illness	Poor Care	Social Dependency	Overcrowding
5th Year (n=847)	14.5	12.2	12.6	17.5	18.7
10th Year (n=812)	10.7	6.2	6.7	12.7	6.6

Improvement in individual families

However, such evidence of crude reduction of deprivation tells us little about the percentage of families who were 'deprived' initially but were free from deprivation at the tenth year. We defined improvement as follows:

- Deprived group: a deprivation score reduced to zero.
- Multiply deprived group: the deprivation score reduced to zero or one.
- Each of the single groups: the score reduced from one to zero.

To do this, we used the 812 families still in touch with the research team when the 'Red Spots' were 10 years old. Table 11.3 shows that about half of both the deprived and multiply deprived groups had improved by the tenth year, with parental illness and overcrowding groups showing considerable improvement, and marital disruption less improvement.

Table 11.3   Improvement from 1952 to 1957

		Families		Criteria			
		Deprived	Multiply Deprived	Marital In- stability	Parent Illness	Poor Care	Social Depen- dency	Over- crowding
Total	n =	331	103	112	88	98	130	147
Improved	n =	167	51	51	72	53	68	113
% Improvement		50.5	49.5	45.5	81.8	54.1	52.3	76.9
				Poor mothering was not recorded at the 10th year				

Note: Based on a population of 812

This categorization allowed us to look at 47 non-deprived families (10 per cent) who, for the first time, had moved into deprivation between 1952 and 1957. Using the above defini- tions and the total original sample, we had sufficient cases to study short-term changes of deprivation status of families and to ask whether such changes had implications for the later functioning of the children in these families.

Becoming deprived 1952–57

Aims and hypotheses

Little has been written about families who move into depri- vation. We had two hypotheses in relation to downward mobility:

1   That the main factors which precede movement into deprivation would be change in social and family circum- stances, and that these could be defined.

2   That deterioration in family status would be associated
with   poorer   behavioural,   cognitive   and   educational
functioning of children in the families concerned.

The group studied were families which were not deprived
in 1952, but were so by 1957 — about 10 per cent of all non-
deprived in 1952. We do not comment on variations in
sample size from analysis to analysis unless the differences
are greater than 5 per cent.

This is an attempt to highlight factors which were predictive of movement into deprivation between 1952 and 1957.
A few hints were available from the large pool of data
gathered during the first year of their children's lives but
none proved substantial. The clues obtained related only to
social influences such as poor occupational status which
affected 23 per cent of families who were not deprived at
any time and 36 per cent of those who had moved into
deprivation; larger family size with household averages of
4.5 and 5.1 persons respectively; and families not living in
owner–occupier situations. By the time the children were
five years old, a greater number of risk factors were identifiable. Again, they were usually social in nature or reflected
poor social circumstances, such as a large family, poor home
circumstances (inadequate sleeping arrangements) and not
owning one's home. Also, there was an excess of respiratory
infections and poor speech development when compared to
the families who would remain non-deprived (Miller *et al.*,
1985).

Defining differences between the groups
Comparison of the groups at the tenth year revealed three
main differences (Table 11.4). First, despite general improvement in social and economic circumstances, some families
remained static or deteriorated in these respects. Second,
the father became unemployed or left the family. Third,
housing and material circumstances deteriorated.

Later progress of the 47 families
Table 11.5 shows the social and family data for the 47
families in 1962. The picture had now become much clearer
in that the central importance of the father was emphasized.
In many of the families he was of low status or had

Table 11.4 Social data in 1957

	A Families not deprived in 1952 or 1957		B Families moving into deprivation 1952–1957		C Families deprived in 1952	
	Total n	% of n	n	%	n	%
i. Loss of father	430	2	47	17**	335	18
ii. Unemployment	430	0	47	45**	335	20
iii. Defective sleeping arrangements	430	< 1	43	8**	335	14
iv. Housing: owner– occupier	472	29	43	5**	308	6
v. Persons in household (mean)		4.4		5.2**		5.6

Notes: 1. Items ii, iv and v showed similar differences at year 15 (1962).
2. One-tailed tests of significance to A versus B; **p < .01.

Table 11.5 Year fifteen: social and family data

	A Not deprived 1952–1957		B Moved into deprivation 1952–57		C Families deprived in 1952	
	n	%	n	%	n	%
Father:						
Permanently present	377	88	44	66**	314	65
Substitute father in family	377	5	44	23**	313	15
Personality good	336	79	31	61**	255	45
Aspirant job status (success & promotion)	373	39	37	22**	279	14
Inadequate provider	372	8	38	34**	279	40
Poorly participates in domestic tasks	358	7	33	21**	262	38
Poor organizer	350	9	34	29**	281	37
Mother:						
Poor standard of house- keeping	357	2	44	16**	306	27
Poor child care	376	3	43	14**	306	25
Good premarital employ- ment history	270	30	44	7**	309	5
Psychiatric illness	377	11	44	23**	304	19
Family:						
Activities which include child	374	70	42	45**	303	31
Maximum size sample	377		44		314	

Notes: One-tailed test of significance: A versus B, **p < .01
'n' refers to the sample upon which the percentage is derived: for
example, 81 out of 270 mothers = 30%

disappeared and sometimes had been replaced. When he was present, unemployment was a frequent problem, and in one-third of families he did not make adequate provision, was a poor organizer and was recorded as having a difficult or complex personality. In reality, the loss or absence of the father is not only a key factor in its own right but complicates many of the other analyses that relate to the father figure. For instance, no information about his personality was available in 30 per cent of the families which became deprived and in 10 per cent of families without deprivation. Absence of the father also meant that both the number of persons in the family and the rate of overcrowding were underrepresented. A similar set of factors related to the mother — particularly poor housekeeping, poor child and family care, and a higher rate of psychiatric illness. The third series of factors related to housing; the families who became deprived were both larger than the non-deprived and lived in houses with a low rateable value (Table 11.4).

Intellectual, educational and behavioural data

School reports on behaviour and test scores are given in Tables 11.6 and 11.7. Although, as a group, the children of families who moved into deprivation always did worse than the non-deprived, formal tests seldom gave rise to significant differences.

Differences reported by teachers were mainly concerned with poor reading performance. Children in families entering deprivation read fewer library books, were thought to have poorer concentration, to be less persistent in the classroom, and were generally considered less reliable pupils.

Table 11.7 gives more information derived from school. Children from families entering deprivation were absent from school more often, and their teachers thought they were more eager to leave and also more likely to become maladjusted than their peers from non-deprived families. Further, three times as many children from non-deprived families hoped for skilled employment. Formal ability tests showed poorer vocabulary and performance scores. There were no significant differences between boys and girls.

*Table 11.6   Last year in primary school 1958
(approx. 11 years of age)*

	Intellectual, Educational and Behavioural					
	A Not Deprived 1952 or 1957		B Moved into Deprivation 1952–57		C Families Deprived in 1952	
Test Scores:						
Mean IQ (11+ exam)	104.4		103.3		92.9	
English	105.8		103.7		94.0	
Maximum 'n'	367		45		305	
Achievements:						
Reading poor	314	16%	42	33%	285	31%
Does not read library books	347	57%	45	73%	274	55%
Classroom Behaviour:						
Good reliability	316	72%	42	45%*	286	51%
Poor concentration	316	20%	42	40%	286	37%
Poor persistence	316	21%	42	38%	285	47%
Maximum 'n'	316		47			

Note: One-tailed test of significance: A versus B, *p < .05

*Table 11.7   Outcome: secondary school/early employment
Behavioural and cognitive data*

	A Not Deprived 1952–57		B Moved into Deprivation 1952–57		C Families Deprived in 1952	
	Base 'n'	%	Base 'n'	%	Base 'n'	%
Behaviour:						
Less than 90% school attendance during last year	301	22	38	42	375	53
Children considered at age 12 likely to become delinquent (by teacher)	374	13	43	26	320	37
Eager to leave school	304	24	38	42	272	42
Aspiring to skilled employment of those who left school at 15	374	42	42	12	311	25
Test Scores:						
Mill Hill Vocabulary Test (mean)	257	42.8	38	39.8*	223	36.0
Progressive Matrices (mean)	257	46.2	38	43.2*	223	41.2

*p < .05

Relationship between occupational class
and movement into deprivation

Data relevant to social class are shown in Table 11.8 which
shows that, if one's family comes from a lower occupational
class and moves into deprivation, then the effects appear to
be considerable. This is reflected in classroom behaviour and
achievements, intellectual ability, examination successes and
teachers' judgements about the probability of delinquency
when the children are 12 years old. This is particularly so in
performance ability as shown by Raven's Matrices and very
much less evident in vocabulary ability. The data also suggest
that it is not simply a matter of occupational class, based on
the nature of father's employment, but rather those
additional factors inimical to family well-being that correlate
with the social grouping which are most crucial. This is
exemplified by the presence of a series of adverse paternal
characteristics which loomed large in the lower social group
which then moved into deprivation.

Table 11.8   Occupational class and movement
into deprivation by 1957

Groups	Remained Not Deprived		Moved into Deprivation	
	Social Class of Family of Origin		Social Class of Family of Origin	
	1–3	4–5	1–3	4–5
Father:				
Generation I				
Good personality	82%	69%	80%	20%
Good provider	87%	57%	64%	20%
Poorly participates in domestic tasks	4%	16%	11%	39%
Child:				
Aged 15: Generation II				
Classroom behaviour:				
Poor concentration in class	19%	25%	35%	53%
Poor persistence in class	20%	27%	31%	53%
Poor reading	13%	23%	23%	53%
Teacher Prediction (1959)				
Delinquency and maladjustment	11%	20%	15%	44%
Public Examination Successes, Age 15–16	49%	24%	45%	0%
Test of Ability				
Ravens Matrices (mean)	46.3	45.6	45.7	38.9
Mill Hill Vocabulary (mean)	43.7	39.6	40.5	38.7

**Comparison of families deprived in 1952 with
those who moved into deprivation between 1952-57**
We did not undertake statistical comparison between these
groups of families but compared selected data.

The deprived group in 1952 had larger households than
those who moved into deprivation (Table 11.4) and had
poorer sleeping arrangements. Children in both groups had
similar levels of respiratory infections; on the other hand
children of families who moved into deprivation had higher
rates of poor speech than children whose families were
originally deprived (Miller *et al.*, 1985). We concluded that
the circumstances of families who moved into deprivation
soon approximated to those who had started as deprived, but
their social circumstances were never as dysfunctional, apart
from unemployment. (When the Red Spots were 10, we saw
no differences in rates of loss of father or house ownership –
Table 11.4.)

Data on the Red Spots at 15 years old showed a few
interesting differences (Table 11.5). Fathers in the families
who started as deprived tended to be less adequate providers;
a high proportion participated poorly in domestic tasks and
were poor organizers. Fewer were 'good' personalities. A
similar picture was found with the mothers far more of
whom showed poor housekeeping standards and poor care
of children.

There were some clear-cut differences in mental performance and behaviour. Red Spots deprived in 1952 had
lower intelligence and poorer educational achievements than
those who moved into deprivation (Table 11.6). Differences
in classroom behaviour proved marginal although 50 per cent
more children in the always deprived group were predicted as
likely to become delinquent or maladjusted. We concluded
that the children of families who had moved into deprivation
usually performed less well on measures of intelligence,
attainment and behaviour than those who had never been
deprived, but better than those whose families were rated
as deprived in their fifth year of life.

Moving out of deprivation

Aim
We wanted to know whether children from families whose

deprivation improved showed better progress than those whose family situation did not improve. About half the deprived and multiply deprived groups improved between the fifth and tenth year (Table 11.2, p. 148). We have allocated data according to improved and static sub-groups.

Findings: physical development

In absolute terms, children from deprived families in 1952 whose deprivation subsequently improved were significantly heavier and taller at 10 and 15 years than children from deprived families who did not improve. At the ninth year their weight difference was 2.5 lb, and by the fifteenth year almost 8 lb. At ten years their height difference was 0.8 inches, and at fifteen years 1.1 inches. There were no differences in children from multiply deprived families which improved, compared with those in families who remained deprived (Kolvin *et al.*, 1983b).

Intellectual development

Table 11.9 shows that children from deprived and multiply deprived families in which there was a lessening of deprivation during the junior school years performed better on intellectual tests at the tenth year than children in families who remained unchanged. Many of the differences were significant and the absolute differences were always greater in the deprived than in the multiply deprived families. By 15 years, the differences in the multiply deprived group were no longer significant.

Table 11.9   Mental ability scores (mean quotients)

Children	Deprived Families			Multiply Deprived Families		
	Improved	Static	Sig.	Improved	Static	Sig.
Aged 11 Years:						
IQ	95.2	90.6	< .01	89.2	84.8	< .05
Ravens Matrices	37.0	31.1	< .01	31.1	27.2	< .05
Mill Hill Vocabulary	31.7	27.7	< .01	27.1	24.0	< .05
Aged 15 Years:						
Ravens Matrices	43.2	38.8	< .01	39.5	36.9	NS
Mill Hill Vocabulary	37.9	33.7	< .01	33.6	32.4	NS

General behaviour and attitude to school (Table 11.10)
We did not have comparable behavioural data at both the
tenth and fifteenth years, and data were not available for all
children at age 15. However, there were no differences at the
tenth year. At the fifteenth year more children from the
static deprived (but not the static multiply deprived) families
showed poorer concentration in class, were viewed by the
teacher as likely to become maladjusted, and showed poorer
interest in family activities. In addition, more were eager to
leave school. A significant number of the group whose deprivation had improved continued at school after 15 years
whilst most of the multiply deprived left.

*Table 11.10   Red Spots aged 15 years: behaviour
and attitude to school*

Children	Deprived Families			Multiply Deprived Families		
	Improved %	Static %	Sig.	Improved %	Static %	Sig.
Eager to leave school	35.9	47.7	< .05	35.7	59.1	< .01
Continued school after 15 years school attendance	30.0	17.3	< .01	14.0	4.2	NS
Interest in family activities	56.5	39.9	< .01	48.0	20.0	< .01
Police probation record	9.0	17.9	< .05	10.0	37.7	< .01
Sibling delinquency (15 year data)	5.0	21.5	< .01	15.0	35.0	< .05
Teacher prediction: likely to become maladjusted	27.0	44.7	< .01	34.0	60.0	< .01
Good concentration in class	54.5	25.2	< .01	31.8	27.2	NS

Note: Tests of significance are one-tailed

School attendance (Table 11.10)
Children from either deprived or multiply deprived families
who improved had significantly better records of attendance
at school than children from static families. The highest rates
of attendance occurred in the children from deprived families

who improved and the lowest rates in multiply deprived families who remained static.

Police record (Table 11.11)
Fewer children from families who improved had a police record. Improvement was associated with a substantially lower risk of court appearance in both deprived and multiply deprived families. This was true both for the Red Spots and their siblings.

Table 11.11   The offence rates of men whose families moved in or out of deprivation

	Family Never Deprived	Family Moving Into Deprivation 1952–57	Family Moving Out of Deprivation 1952–57	Family Always Deprived
'n'	207	19	92	84
% offending	16	26	32	54

Not corrected for attrition

Continuities and discontinuities of risk factors and criminality
The question arises whether an increase in family deprivation over time (that is, from 1952 to 1957) increases the risk of offending as defined in Chapter 14 or, conversely, whether a reduction of family deprivation acts as a protective factor in relation to offending. To examine this question, the families were divided into those who were never deprived, those who moved into deprivation over that period, those who moved out of deprivation, and those who were deprived in both 1952 and 1957. The data in Table 11.11 suggest that, if the family moved into deprivation, there was a 50 per cent increase in the rate of offending. If the family moved out of deprivation, there was a 40 per cent decrease in the rate of offending.

Change in deprivation status in one generation — implications for housing circumstances in the next
We used the Acorn system to examine the housing circumstances in 1980 of families who changed their deprivation

status over the period 1952–57. For 1980 we had access to 761 addresses. As the findings are complex we focus on local authority housing data alone. More of the Red Spots whose families were downwardly mobile between 1952 and 1957, when compared to the non-deprived who did not change their status, lived in urban local authority housing. Thus, downward mobility in one generation appeared to have a small effect on the housing circumstances of the next generation. Most of the deprived Red Spot families who were upwardly mobile in 1957 were living in urban local authority housing in 1980.

Another way of looking at second-generation housing in 1980 is in relation to those families which were overcrowded in 1952. Of those 131 families, three-quarters were no longer rated so in 1957. Although numbers are small, we see that 71 per cent of the Red Spots whose homes were overcrowded at both times were living in council houses in 1980 in contrast to 41 per cent of those whose homes were over-crowded only in 1952. Only 28 per cent of Red Spots coming from families who were not overcrowded in 1952 were living in council housing.

Certain social factors, which did not appear sufficient in themselves to represent deprivation at an earlier period in time, appeared to make families more vulnerable to sub-sequent environmental stress when they occurred together. Examination of the 1957 data indicates that the key factors were unemployment, absence or loss of father and large families associated with overcrowding.

Subsequent circumstances

Five years after moving into deprivation (1962), the picture had become clearer. There was a series of unusual or adverse circumstances relating to fathers and also deterioration of care given by mothers. The differences, while significant, were not substantial, but they provided indications of associated mechanisms.

As to children, there were few differences in intellectual abilities between those coming from non-deprived families and those who moved into deprivation. Some of the important indicators of poor functioning derive from the school where there were significant judgements about delinquency, eagerness to leave school and poor aspirations of children from families who moved into disadvantage. There were also some signs of poorer achievements in reading, concentration and persistence. This implies that good early foundations are important and that subsequent breakdown of caring circumstances are not so damaging to psychological development.

Thus we identified effects which were behavioural and scholastic in nature, although we have not identified any substantial intellectual effects. It is not clear why there should be this distinction or why disadvantage in the primary school years had so little impact when it has marked impact in the pre-school years. We can only speculate about possible reasons. For instance, the foundation for intellectual development may have already been laid down in the pre-school years and become sufficiently robust to resist later adverse influences. Alternatively, the effects of deprivation on intelligence may be transient at this stage. There may also be some substantial self-correcting mechanisms operative at this time (Hinde, 1982). Another possible hypothesis is that there are age-dependent sensitivities to life stresses (Rutter, 1981a), so that intelligence is more sensitive in the pre-school years and scholastic achievements and behaviour is more sensitive during the school years. The first of these alternatives seems to fit the facts best.

We have not yet answered the question whether the second-generation children who showed immediate reactions to psychosocial stresses continued to show these effects into adulthood. Nor have we been able, so far, to study chain effects, such as early psychosocial stress giving rise to lack of educational qualifications and in turn to employment difficulties.

There is an extensive literature on deprivation and its consequences, but relatively little about families who are suddenly plunged into deprivation as occurred during the Great Depression. The classic American research on families who lived through the Depression was that of Elder (1974); Elder and Rockwell (1978); Elder (1979). He studied families with younger and older children and examined mechanisms by which the effects were mediated. His work encapsulated the best of the sociological approach, taking hard data and adding to it information about stability and change in families in relation to socioeconomic changes in the community in order to understand the relationship between these changes over time. The above work has been well reviewed by Bronfenbrenner (1979).

Elder studied two cohorts of families exposed to the Depression, the first born in 1922 at Oakland and thus exposed to this economic disaster in later childhood. The second set were born in 1928–1929 into the more affluent community of Berkeley and thus spent their earliest years during the depths of the Depression.

In the Oakland study (Elder, 1974), two family groups were examined — those with and those without exposure to the full impact of the Depression. In the latter there was an emergent dominance of mothers often accompanied by lowered status of fathers. Elder interpreted this as perceived role failure in the father and consequent shift of economic responsibility to the mother. In addition to showing preference for mothers, the children also showed strong identification with the peer group, manifested in a desire to have many friends rather than a few. In the deprived homes there was role differentiation in that girls specialized in domestic roles and boys in economic roles, seeking work outside the home. Both boys and girls developed an earlier sense of independence. Nevertheless, there were some paradoxical findings in that sons whose families were hardest hit appeared to profit from the experience by showing vocational motivation and maturation ahead of the non-deprived youths. In contrast, those whose families escaped the Depression proved less successful in adulthood educationally and vocationally. Elder concluded that childhood which shelters the young from hardship may not facilitate adaptive capacity in subsequent life crises. Nevertheless, boys coped better if they were supported by their fathers, which suggests a beneficial effect of social cohesion (Brown and Madge, 1982).

The Oakland study is not strictly comparable with ours. A greater similarity exists with the Berkeley cohort in which Elder and Rockwell (1978) hypothesized that adverse and enduring outcomes would be seen more in those who experienced the Depression when more dependent developmentally. Yet, they found that sons of both middle and working-class families who entered first school while their families were suffering from the Depression did not show any disadvantage in psychological stability, social relationship or school achievement. Subsequently in adolescence, however, the sons of middle and working-class families who had suffered the full force of the Depression had poorer academic aspirations, achieved lower rankings on high school performance, showed a lack of self-esteem and a tendency to withdraw from adversity, and were also less likely to complete college. They naturally tended to enter work earlier than those who had not suffered the Depression, and they spent much of their working life in manual jobs and unstable work patterns. They showed an excess of health problems, chronic fatigue and problem drinking, and these trends were surprisingly most common among those who had achieved scholastic success. It is notable that these effects emerged only in their adolescent years during World War II, a period of rising prosperity. Elder and Rockwell did not see these as 'sleeper' effects but rather as maladaptive responses in youngsters previously cushioned from environmental pressures when confronted with demanding situations in adolescence that call for adaptive responses. However, despite these adolescent problems, many of the previously deprived youngsters achieved occupational success and no longer had a sense of inadequacy but showed greater inner strength and effectiveness. It has been suggested that such positive changes may have been prompted by adult independence, work or marriage.

We may conclude that family deprivation produced greater disadvantage for the work and health of the Berkeley than the Oakland cohort, this being evidence in lowered aspirations and self-esteem in early adolescence and failure to make full use of opportunities at high school. Elder (1979) also reported that Berkeley girls from deprived families paradoxically fared well and proved more self-assertive than girls from non-deprived families, emerging as competent and resourceful adolescents (Bronfenbrenner, 1979). Elder surmised that even when parental relationship remained harmonious, boys under hardship lost their affection and identification with fathers, while girls developed a stronger tie with mothers.

Our Newcastle research concerns families which moved into deprivation against a general trend of economic advance, although we did not have comparable data into adulthood, only until school leaving age and early employment. Some of our findings concerning the early secondary school period described in this report are in accord with the Berkeley findings for boys. However, the picture for Berkeley girls is rather different from ours. Thus there are diverse effects of adverse life experiences, and in the case of boys the question arises whether these are persistent or transient effects. Of those Berkeley boys who attended university, the formerly deprived were more likely than the non-deprived to produce substantial achievements despite previously appearing in adolescence as unambitious, passive and indecisive. The higher achievers from deprived backgrounds moved increasingly to confidence and health. So for certain of the deprived children, deprivation proved to be a strengthening and steeling experience. It would, therefore, be unwise to predict a negative, developmental pathway for all the children of the Newcastle families who moved into deprivation and appeared to show effects in adolescence. Some may have unexpected successes in later life (see Part IV).

An additional finding in our research was the demonstration that if a family starts as non-deprived then moves into deprivation, and if the breadwinner comes from a lower occupational status, the effects appear to be considerable.

Next we compared those families who started deprived with those who moved into deprivation. We anticipated that the families who were deprived would subsequently show higher rates of social and family dysfunction than those who had recently moved into deprivation and this proved to be so. However, the differences were not substantial; the most evident being larger family size. By the time the children were 10 years old, unemployment was the most likely reason for families moving into deprivation. We examined a number of other family factors and found that the fathers concerned tended to have less adequate personalities, and were poorer providers or participators in family life but, again, the differences were not substantial. Similarly, mothers in the families which started in deprivation showed poorer standards of housekeeping and child care.

It is also important to note that there were different effects on intelligence and behaviour. Those who were deprived in their pre-school years ended up with lower mean mental ability scores than those who moved into deprivation. This suggests that being protected from deprivation for the first five years of a child's life has important protective effects as far as intellect is concerned. However, there do not appear to be similar protective effects in relation to behaviour as the rates of difficult behaviour usually proved to be similar in the offspring of Red Spot families moving into deprivation to those who started in deprivation. The exception was for delinquency, where the rates proved higher in those Red Spot children who had always been deprived.

We also examined the implications of life cycle changes in one generation for the next and found that life cycle changes of deprivation status in the direction of improvement in one generation were associated with evidence of improved functioning of physical development, intelligence and behaviour in the next generation, provided that the deprivation was not severe. Where deprivation was severe, reduction in family deprivation was associated with better intellectual functioning in the next generation, when the children were 10 years of age, but this had disappeared by the time they were 15. While improvement in family circumstances did not seem to affect physical development, there were some effects on behaviour and attitude to school.

It is important to try to understand the mechanisms that determine these differences. One approach is to attribute the differences between the groups of children to the changes in family circumstances over their second five years of life. This would give rise to the suggestion that the adverse effects of milder deprivation can be appreciably mitigated by later reduction in deprivation.

Another possibility is that the differences between the groups of children are mostly determined by the intelligence of the parents which in turn determines both the reduction in family deprivation and their children's performance. For instance, the lessening of deprivation may in part reflect the greater social competence of intellectually more able parents, which then re-emerges as identifiable differences between the groups of children in the next generation. This theory would carry with it the implication that, where deprivation is not severe, the range of intellectual abilities is wide, allowing differences between the group of children to emerge. However, where deprivation is severe, not only is the range of intellectual abilities narrow, but the mean level is low, and these factors hamper the appearance of differences.

We also studied the implications of change in deprivation status in one generation for housing circumstances in the next, and found that a substantial proportion of children from deprived families who were upwardly mobile were likely, as adults, to live in council accommodation. This was also the case for those from overcrowded families. Further, the data suggest that the offspring of families in satisfactory housing circumstances in one generation are likely to find their way into satisfactory housing in the next.

12 Change across generations 1952–80

Change and the measurement of change in a particular population is of the main purpose of this study. Do families in severe deprivation remain so from generation to generation? If not, what proportion escape and what are the characteristics of those who do? The same questions can be asked about families who are not deprived; do they remain so and, if not, what proportion moves into deprivation in its various degrees and why does this happen?

Our six criteria of deprivation have been described in Chapter 2, but here it must be noted that, while they can each be quantified, they are different in nature and not of equal 'value'. These differences have been described (Chapters 2 and 13) and must be taken into account when the reasons for movement into or out of deprivation or change in degree or type of deprivation are considered. To record quantitative changes in the various groups of non-deprived, deprived and multiply deprived is not, in itself, sufficient. We need to know the movement of each of the Red Spot children in their family of origin through their childhood and then to their thirty-third year (1979–80) when all but a small group who had never married were living in a family of formation. If the position of each individual with regard to deprivation can be determined in 1952 and in 1980 then his or her movement can be described both in terms of degree of change according to the number of criteria, and also in relation to the kind of criteria. This, in turn, allows a study of the specific continuity and discontinuity of criteria from one generation to the next as the index cases passed through childhood into adult life.

Resumé of method
There were 847 families in 1952, and the group of 264 families interviewed in 1979–80 was composed of stratified

samples from those 847 families. For the purposes of this exercise we have analysed data on all the 264 families: 62 without deprivation; 124 with mild deprivation (one or two criteria); and 78 with multiple deprivation (three or more criteria) at five years of age. Only the movement of the 264 Red Spots can be detailed but, as the proportion of each of the samples is representative of the total group from which it was selected, the degree of movement in relation to the 847 can be estimated.

The final stage in the analysis of movement is, therefore, to trace the change of each of the 264 families containing a Red Spot boy or girl through that child's life until the assessment can be made of his or her condition or family in 1980. This analysis of movement is in two parts: first, according to degrees of deprivation in 1952 and 1980; second, in terms of the criteria demonstrated by each individual's family. In reviewing changes in criteria between 1952 and 1980 it must be remembered that, although the criteria shown in 1980 will have been influenced by the characteristics of the Red Spot spouse, he or she was likely to have come from a broadly similar family of origin (see Chapter 4).

Measurement of change between 1952–80
The data of Table 12.1 are derived from a comparison of the situation in the families of the Red Spot children in 1952 with that in their families as adults and parents in 1979–80. The 264 families are all those persons interviewed and contain some 20 persons who had never married, were one-parent families or were living alone after separating from their spouse. In the sense in which we are using it 'family' does not necessarily require the presence of children or of both spouses or partners.

Change is the dominant feature. Thus, of the sample of 62 children whose families did not show any deprivation in 1952, only 43.5 per cent of their families of formation remained non-deprived in 1980; 29 per cent had acquired one criterion (D1); 22.6 per cent two criteria (D2) and 4.8 per cent were in multiple deprivation (D3). The same degree of movement was apparent in multiply deprived families, for only 43.6 per cent remained in the same group in 1980 — remarkably, the same proportion as of the non-deprived; 12.8 per cent had moved free from all deprivation; 16.7 per

*Table 12.1   Change in deprivation: 1952–1979/80
in 264 families*

Number of criteria		0	%	Distribution in 1952 D1	D2	%	M	%	Tota
Distribution 1979–80	0	27	(43.5)	24	14	(30.6)	10	(12.8)	7
	D1	18	(29.0)	28	15	(34.7)	21	(26.9)	8
	D2	14	(22.6)	17	3	(16.1)	13	(16.7)	4
	M	3	(4.8)	16	7	(18.5)	34	(43.6)	6
Total		62		85	39		78		26
					124				

Notes: All 16 categories in this table are mutually exclusive
D1 = Single criterion of deprivation
D2 = Two criteria
M = Three or more criteria

cent had improved into D2; and 27 per cent had improved
into D1. Movement from, or within, the D1 and D2 sample
was the characteristic most frequent of most families; in D1
only 33 per cent of families remained unchanged while 28
per cent moved out of all deprivation and 39 per cent moved
into deeper deprivation. Red Spots with two criteria at five
years (D2) seemed very prone to change, for at age 33 only
8 per cent remained in that category whilst 18 per cent had
entered multiple deprivation and 29 had improved, 36 per
cent moving to the non-deprived and the other 38 per cent to
D1.

Since the groups of non-deprived, deprived and multiply
deprived were stratified samples of these categories from our
population of 847, the changes occurring in the entire population of 847 families could be estimated. This was done by
multiplying the data in each cell by the proportion of the
sample to the whole of the group in 1952 (Table 12.2). The
number of families without deprivation had decreased from
483 (57 per cent) to 301 (35.5 per cent); those with one or
two criteria had increased from 246 (29 per cent) to 426
(50.3 per cent). Thus, from 1952–80, there was a decrease in
the number of families without any criteria, an increase in
those with one or two adverse criteria, but virtually no
change in the number of families in multiple deprivation.

Table 12.2   *Estimated changes in deprivation status in
the families of 847 Red Spots from family
of origin (1952) to family of formation
(1980): calculated from Table 12.1*

| | Families of Origin | | | Totals |
	(0)	(D1 + D2)	(D3 or more)	Families of Formation 1980
Sample size	62	124	78	264
Factor	7.8	1.98	1.51	
0	211	75	15	301
D1	140	85	32	257
D2	109	40	20	169
M	23	46	51	120
at 5 years	483	246	118	847

The position, however, looks different when we consider
the movement of individual families from one category to
another (Table 12.2). Only 211 (43.7 per cent) of the
original 483 families without deprivation in 1952 remained
so at 33 years; and 125 (50.8 per cent) of the 246 deprived
families (D1 and D2) and 51 (43.2 per cent) of the 118
families in multiple deprivation did likewise. In all, therefore,
45.7 per cent (387 of the 847) would have remained in the
same category in the two periods and 54.3 per cent changed,
with 37.5 per cent (318) moving into greater deprivation
(nearly half with only one criterion) and 16.8 per cent (142)
moving from, or reducing, their degree of deprivation.

Thus, in summary, whilst proportions changed relatively
little, rather more than half of all families would have
changed category between 1952 and 1980.

Analysis of groups and change 1952–80
Having looked at the change in degree of deprivation in terms
of numbers of criteria it is necessary to consider the individual families represented in Table 12.1 and ascertain
which criteria occurred in each group in 1952 and 1980,
and the degree of continuity or otherwise from one
generation to the next. Thus, for example, the 27 families
who remained without deprivation in both 1952 and 1980,
and the 34 families who were in multiple deprivation at both

periods both constitute 43.5 per cent of the samples of 62 and 78 families who were studied. These groups can therefore represent the features of these two extreme classes of family.

Families from the two degrees of deprivation who moved either out of or into deprivation can also be examined and a search made for differences between the groups of families; similarly, the few families originally not deprived who moved into multiple deprivation can be examined beside those who moved from multiple deprivation to no deprivation.

But the first stage was the examination of the criteria present in 1952 and 1979–80 in each of the 16 groups which make up Table 12.1 and which are represented in the grid in Table 12.2. From that examination it was possible to examine the continuity, or otherwise, of the same criteria from 1952 to 1979–80.

The numerical values in terms of 'Red Spot' families (264) have been given in Table 12.1. Using those figures, it was possible to estimate the addition or removal of each criterion experienced by the 'Red Spot' girl or boy as children in their family of origin and 33 years later in their family of formation. Since the groups of 0, D1 and D2 and M families were samples of the total number of the families in those categories in the 1952 study population of 847 families, this allowed comparison of families within, but not across, the 1952 categories. Thus one can attempt two operations: first, to examine the appearance and disappearance of criteria in a reconstituted population; and, second, to describe the characteristics of families in each cell in an attempt to compare the characteristics of families who changed, or did not change, their positions.

Criteria and change in criteria 1952–80 in 847 families

Here, by reference to Table 12.2, we demonstrate the number of criteria experienced, the change in criteria between 1952–80, and the degree of continuity of each criterion.

Families without deprivation in 1952 (Table 12.3)

1 . Group 0–0: In 1980, 27 (45 per cent) of the 62 families

in the sample remained without any deprivation – an estimated 211 of the original 847 families.

2   Group 0–D1: Eighteen (29 per cent) of the 62 families in 1952 had one criterion of deprivation in 1980, the numbers being estimated as 140 (79 boys and 61 girls). By definition there was no continuity of criteria from 1952 to 1980. Three-quarters of the criteria in 1980 comprised marital disharmony, parental illness and educational insufficiency.

3   Group 0–D2: Fourteen (23 per cent) of the 62 had acquired two criteria by 1980. This was estimated as 109 Red Spots (23 boys and 86 girls). In this group the most prominent criteria in 1980 are social dependence, educational deficit and parental illness.

4   Group 0–M: Only three (5 per cent) of the children from the 62 families without deprivation in 1952 had fallen into multiple deprivation by 33 years. This is too small a number to make a reasonable estimate and detailed case histories are given on p. 190.

All in all, Table 12.3 suggests that movement into deprivation from non-deprivation from 1952–80 was chiefly due to educational insufficiency, marital disruption and parental illness.

Table 12.3   Families in 1952 and estimated number of criteria in 1980

Estimated Criteria in 1980	Non-Deprived 1952	One or Two Criteria 1952	Three or More Criteria 1952	Estimated Specific Continuity 1952–80
Marital disruption	93	62	42	36.0%
Parental illness	93	52	30	21.9%
Poor care	47	38	24	21.9%
Social dependency	62	40	53	31.1%
Educational in-sufficiency	101	110	77	–
Poor mothering	47	40	33	26.2%
Total criteria	443	342	259	
Sample size in 1952	483	249	116	
Mean per family in 1980	0.92	1.37	2.23	

Families with one criterion in 1952 (Table 12.3)

1   Group D1–0: Twenty-four (21 per cent) of the 85 families with one criterion at five years were free from deprivation in 1980 — an estimated 48 of 847. In half of these the only adverse criterion in 1952 was that they were in overcrowded houses.

2   Group D1–D1: Twenty-eight (83 per cent) Red Spots were in the 85 families which showed one criterion, but not necessarily the same one in 1952 and 1980 (estimated 56). Again as with Group D1–0 the largest group in 1952 was 'overcrowding'. Only in four families were there any continuity of criteria from one generation to the next — two in marital disharmony and one each in parental illness and social dependency. In 1980, the most frequent criteria were educational insufficiency and marital disharmony.

3   Group D1–D2: This group of 17 (20 per cent) of 85 families — all male, except one girl who remained un-married — increased from one to two criteria between 1952 to 1979–80 (estimated 34). In 1952 most of the criteria were equally divided between overcrowding and marital disruption. At 33 years the most common criterion was educational insufficiency. There was con-tinuity of specific criteria only in three cases of marital disharmony and two of parental illness.

4   Group D1–M: Sixteen (19 per cent) of 85 families with only one criterion at five years had by 1980 become deeply involved in deprivation with at least three criteria (estimated at 32 individuals — 16 boys and 16 girls). Looking at this group, the marked increase of poor mothering, poor care and social dependence is very apparent, and all showed educational insufficiency. This is the picture of increasing social failure but little evidence of specific continuity of criteria.

Table 12.3 indicates that deprivation in 1980 in families who started with one criterion in 1952 was determined by educational insufficiency followed by marital disruption and parental illness. This is similar to the pattern of the families who started without deprivation.

Families with two criteria in 1952 (Table 12.3)

1   Group D2–0: Fourteen (36 per cent) of the 39 families
    with two criteria in 1952 had no deprivation in 1979–
    80 (estimated at 28 Red Spots — 16 boys and 12 girls).
    Two boys remained unmarried. In 1952 social depen-
    dency was the most common criterion, and poor care and
    poor mothering were the least common. The pattern of
    poor care and poor mothering proved very similar to
    Group D1–0. Thus, recovery from D1 or D2 to 0 at 33
    seems associated with low scores in family caring items
    but substantial scores in combined marital disharmony
    and parental illness which did not appear in the next
    generation.
2   Group D2–D1: This comprised 15 of 39 families (20 male
    and 10 female Red Spots). At age five, this group
    showed a high level of poor mothering but by 1980 all
    mothering failure, social dependency and poor care had
    disappeared and the remaining criteria were almost
    equally represented by marital disruption, parental illness
    and educational insufficiency. There was continuity of
    specific criteria in three cases of marital disruption and
    two of parental illness.
3   Group D2–D2: This group, which is too small to be used
    in an estimate, comprised only three Red Spots — two
    married each other and the third remained single.
4   Group D2–M: Only seven of the 39 families (14 Red
    Spots), increased their deprivation score from two to at
    least three criteria at 33 years. At 33 years, of the 26
    criteria they displayed half were associated with social
    dependency and educational insufficiency. Specific con-
    tinuity was also apparent particularly in social depen-
    dency, with three families and poor mothering with two.

Table 12.3 indicates that the increased deprivation in
families in 1980 was largely due to educational insufficiency,
and that social dependency, parental illness and marital disruption all make contributions.

Families with multiple deprivation in 1952 (Table 12.3)

1   Group M–0: Ten of 78 (13 per cent) multiply deprived

families (estimated at 15 families) lost all criteria and joined the non-deprived at 33 years. The distribution of the criteria within those families in 1952 was fairly equal. A more detailed account of these families is given in the description of movement to extremes.

2   Group M–D1: Twenty-one (27 per cent) of 78 families, multiply deprived at age five, had improved at 33 years (estimated at 32). In 1952 the criteria were fairly evenly distributed within the families. At 33 years half the families were handicapped by educational insufficiency, and each of the other criteria were sparsely represented. There was specific continuity of marital disruption in three families.

3   Group M–D2: Thirteen (17 per cent) families, multiply deprived at age five, were somewhat improved at 33 years (estimated at 20). By then, educational insufficiency was a criterion in three-quarters of the families and poor care was uncommon; indeed the latter had decreased. There was no specific continuity.

4   Group M–M: Thirty-four (44 per cent) of 78 Red Spots (an estimated 51 of the 847) were born into families with multiple deprivation at age five and remained in that category in their families of formation at 33 years. At five years, the variation was not great and poor care, social dependency and poor mothering were the most common criteria. At 33 years, while social dependency had increased, the other two criteria had been substantially reduced. Marital disharmony was present in half these families at age five and slightly more than that at 33 years, while parental illness was recorded in rather more than half at both assessments. Finally, in 1980 no less than 30 (about 90 per cent) of the families lacked any educational success or vocational training. Not surprisingly, this group showed the greatest continuity of specific criteria, particularly in social dependency in 21 families, poor mothering in 11, marital disruption in 10, poor care in 9 and parental illness in 5.

Table 12.3 has indicated that deprivation in 1980 in families who started with multiple criteria in 1952 was again primarily determined by educational insufficiency (30), social dependency (29) and marital disruption (20). The other three criteria made smaller contributions.

Overall, in 1980, deprivation in families who started without, or with only a low level of, deprivation in 1952 appeared to be determined by educational insufficiency followed by marital disruption and parental illness. As the levels of deprivation in 1952 increased, social dependency emerged as important and eventually was second only to educational insufficiency.

Continuity from one generation to the next
Finally, from the estimated distribution in the 847 families in 1952 and 1980 it is possible to give a total for each of the six criteria and to indicate the degree of continuity from one generation to the next (Table 12.3). The strongest evidence of continuity from 1952 to 1980 occurred with marital disruption (36 per cent) followed by social dependency (31 per cent). The remaining criteria all had rather over 20 per cent continuity.

These 1980 rates have to be compared with the group that was not deprived in 1952. In this latter group in 1980 marital disruption, parental illness and educational insufficiency occurred in about one in five, in one in ten of the poor care and poor mothering groups, and finally, in one in eight of the social dependency group.

Characteristics of families with different entries into or out of deprivation from 1952–80
The previous sections have demonstrated the way in which the 'Red Spot' child, in his or her development from childhood at five years of age to adult life at 33 years, fared both in degree of deprivation and in the various criteria which, we believe, are indications of family well-being or otherwise.

Comparisons of extremes:
never deprived–always deprived
To be without deprivation at both five and 33 years was the prerogative of 27 Red Spots and their families, while 34 experienced multiple deprivation at both these times. These groups were, by chance, both 43.5 per cent of the samples of which they were a part and are estimated to represent 211 and 51 respectively of the groups of 483 and 118

non-deprived and multiply deprived families in 1952. That being so, it was likely that these two groups, although they were not large, did represent the conditions which accompanied stability of either 'good' or 'poor' quality of personal and family life. In this section we offer an analysis and comparison of the two groups: 0–0, the non-deprived; and M–M, the multiply deprived.

Composition of Groups 0–0 and M–M

The group in 0–0 consisted of 16 men and 11 women Red Spots. In 1980 all but two, who remained single, were living with their spouses. One female Red Spot from a family without deprivation married another Red Spot from a family who showed two criteria (parental illness and social dependency), but in 1980 at the time of the interview the new family did not manifest any criteria and also remained in 0–0, the husband having improved from D2. Two others, one man and one woman, had not married but had made successful careers for themselves, and certainly neither had any evidence of material deprivation. Interestingly, the man had not been successful or happy at school and not until he was engaged in an occupation which aroused his interest did he take advantage of opportunities to acquire technical training; but the will was certainly evident. The woman was described as a lively and sociable person who, after appropriate training, was also successful in her career.

In the M–M group there were 19 men and 15 women. Two of the latter had never married; in each there were two individuals who had remarried after divorce, and several were cohabiting, having been separated or divorced from previous partners.

The occupational class distribution was assessed at both five and 33 years, and Table 12.4 indicates that, at both times, at least four-fifths of Group 0–0 families were in social groups I–III; in 1980 there was even a higher proportion. Group M–M was very different. At five years two-thirds were in social classes IV and V, and the other third in social class III. By 1980 the category of semi-skilled and unskilled workers had been greatly reduced and, while the category of the non-skilled workers had virtually disappeared, the unemployed and not classifiable had increased. (Unemployed

Table 12.4 *Occupational class (Registrar General)*

Group	Social Class	I + II	III	IV + V	Unemployed	NC	Total
0–0	1952	6	16	5	0	0	27
	1979–80	7	19	1	0	0	27
M–M	1952	0	10	22	0	2	34
	1979–80	2	8	5	14	5	34

in that context meant at least one year without work in the previous five.)

Other differences were apparent. In 1947 the average number of children in the never deprived families had been 1.6, and 3.35 in the always deprived. By 1952 the children in 0–0 families had experienced little loss of parental care, and all the mothers except one were described as coping with the family organization; two fathers had been temporarily absent from the family but there had not been any permanent loss. Only two mothers had worked outside the home. No serious psychological problems were noted in the parents. Nearly two-thirds of the group were first-born children and none were fifth or later-born.

The situation of the children in the other group was very different. Thirty per cent were sixth or later-born; only six (18 per cent) of the mothers were thought to be coping with the family while 17 (50 per cent) were unable to manage. One parent had died, five fathers had 'disappeared' and four had been temporarily absent, while four mothers were working full-time and five part-time. Seven parents seemed to have severe psychological problems associated with epilepsy (4) and behaviour difficulties (3).

In 1952 about a third of each group were living in local authority council housing and a further quarter of Group 0–0 were owner–occupiers, but that was rare in Group M–M.

Family and child care recorded in 1962 (15th year)
In making this comparison it must be remembered that, in 1980, the families in the groups were revisited whether or not they were still domiciled in Newcastle. This had not been possible in the original study and therefore, in a few families,

information regarding the school years was not available for the fifteenth-year analysis. This applied to four families in Group 0–0 but to only one family in Group M–M — so the general picture of the comparison was not distorted.

Families without deprivation (0–0)   Information on 23 families was available in 1962. These families were characterized by the continued presence of both parents and a normal pattern of child care. Twenty of the fathers and 21 of the mothers had always been present and had given good support to the family. During the 10 years (5–15) one divorce had taken place, one father had had a chronic illness, one had had psychological care, and one had been away from home by the nature of his work for a total of four of the 15 years. One mother had had a chronic illness, and one had died. Half of the mothers and fathers were rated as being effective and kind.

In 19 of the 23 families the pattern of child care could be described as normal for the modern nuclear family. Paternal provision for the home during these 15 years was described as constant and full in over two-thirds; and three-quarters helped with domestic tasks. Only six of these 23 mothers had worked full-time outside the home, one for less than one year, another for less than two years and the remaining four for more than five years. Paternal interest in the child or children was rated as good in 17 of the families, average in five, and one was not assessed.

Families with multiple deprivation (M–M)   Similar information was available in 1962 for most of the parents in the group of 34 families. Three fathers and four mothers died between 1947 and 1962; 28 (84 per cent) mothers but only 19 (57 per cent) fathers were continuously present; and four had been divorced or had deserted. Three had been intermittently present. In only 21 (63 per cent) families was the child care pattern assessed as normal — in four, the children lived in more than one family, one child was with grandparents, and some were in residential schools. Only three of the fathers were said to be constant and full providers (Table 12.5); during the 15 years, nine had been dismissed from, or demoted within, jobs and 11 had more than three changes of jobs without improvement in situation.

Table 12.5   Paternal provision, participation in the home
and interest in the Red Spot child 5–15 years

		0–0	M–M
Paternal Provision:	n =	26	34
Constant and full		17	3
Constant but inadequate		4	11
Domestic Participation:	n =	27	32
Good/Average		20	6
Interest in Child:	n =	26	32
Good/Average		23	13
Poor		—	14

Paternal interest in the children was described as poor in 14 cases (42 per cent). Only one father was described as effective, kind and considerate; four as ineffectual but well meaning; two as ineffectual and apathetic; and no less than 14 (of the 24 rated) as aggressive and inconsiderate. Only a minority seemed to help with domestic tasks. Three were known to be criminal and two alcoholic. Nine mothers had worked full-time, six of these for more than five years, nine mothers had had psychiatric disturbances or received psychiatric care, four complained of chronic fatigue and two suffered from depression. None of the mothers had been rated as effective and kind and 10 (40 per cent of the 26 rated) were considered ineffective.

These comparisons indicate that the quality of the home and family life was very different in the two groups throughout the early and school years of the Red Spot children.

There are few indications of the children's behaviour within their families, but 14 of the Red Spot children in Group 0–0 were recorded as helping in the house but none of those in Group M–M. In half of the 0–0 families where there were older children they had been to selective schools, whereas in only three of 27 deprived children had that occurred.

Comparisons of the children in the school years
Not all the children in each group were measured on each

occasion, but at five years Group M–M were on average 2.6 lb lighter and 1.3 inches shorter than those in Group 0–0; at nine, they were 5.5 lb lighter and 1.5 inches shorter. Thus, at both ages, there was a significant difference in physical growth between the groups (Table 12.6).

Table 12.6   Physical growth at age 5

Groups	n	Weight (lbs)	Height (ins)
M–0	10	42.0	42.9
0–0	24	43.3	43.1
M–M	29	40.7	41.8

Children's attitude to leaving school
An attempt was made to describe the attitude of the children of both groups to school, but the numbers were small, and for about one-third of Group M–M information had not been recorded. This in itself was perhaps significant. All that can be said is that, whereas most children in both groups thought they would like to leave school at 15 or 16 years, more were willing to stay on in Group 0–0 than in Group M–M, and in Group M–M there were many who wished to leave even before 14 years.

Results of the 11-plus examination
All the children, apart from two in Group 0–0 in private schools, took their 11-plus examination. The results showed wide and highly significant differences in measured intelligence and in arithmetic and English assessments. Indeed, it can be seen that the distribution of intelligence was so wide that the groups hardly overlapped (Table 12.7).

Parent's attitude to the 11-plus examination
In the last term at the junior school the parents of all the survey children were asked their preference with regard to the type of school they wished their child to attend (Miller

Table 12.7   Distribution of scores at 11-plus examination[1]

	-85	86-99	100-115	115+	mean	SD
Intelligence Quotient						
0-0	1	6	8	6	106.2	13.09
M-M	21	7	2	0	84.5	6.7
Arithmetic Quotient						
0-0	0	3	9	8	112.8	12.28
M-M	9	18	3	0	88.4	7.97
English Quotient						
0-0	0	7	7	7	109.2	12.89
M-M	19	9	2	0	84.4	9.69

[1]Numbers of children: Group 0-0 = 21; Group M-M = 30

Table 12.8   Education of parents in families of formation 1980

	Group 0-0			Group M-M		
	Wife	Husband	Total	Wife	Husband	Total
Grammar or Technical School	10	11	21	0	0	0
Comprehensive/ Secondary Modern	15	15	30	33	27	60
Approved/Maladjusted	0	0	0	0	1	1
Other	1	—	1	1	2	3
Total	26	26	52	34	30	64

et al., 1974). In Group 0–0 69 per cent chose grammar schools, 8 per cent chose technical or commercial, and 4 per cent chose secondary modern. In Group M–M the corresponding percentages were 44, 25 and 22 respectively. However, the schools the Red Spot children attended were very different from the parents' preferences: 35 per cent of Group 0–0 went to grammar or technical schools, 54 per cent to secondary modern and 8 per cent to private schools, but none of Group M–M went to a selective school and almost all went to comprehensive or secondary modern schools.

Thus in 1980 40 per cent of parents in the 0–0 families had been to grammar or technical schools and the mothers and fathers were almost equally represented (although not necessarily in the same families) while none of the parents of Group M–M had been to a selective school (Table 12.8).

Red Spot children in senior schools

In the senior schools, the teachers assessed the personal attributes of the children on five-point scales, and each child was given the Raven's Progressive Matrices and Mill Hill Vocabulary Test at both 12 and 14 years. The results of the Matrices and the Vocabulary Tests at both ages showed similar differences to those of the 11-plus examination in their previous schools.

Personal attributes

The scores for initiative, ability to mix, self-confidence, assertiveness, sensitivity and emotional stability did not reveal any significant difference between the groups, but those for concentration and persistence did, with the children in Group 0–0 showing greater ability to concentrate and more persistence in the classroom than those in Group M–M. The children in Group M–M also showed a more hostile attitude towards school which fitted with their declared wish to leave school earlier than Group 0–0.

School attendance in the last year

The record of school attendance showed that two-thirds of the M–M children during the final year at school attended less than 85 per cent of possible days and only 12.5 per cent attended more than 95 per cent. This was compatible with other measurements of attitudes to school and of the valuation of education displayed by both children and parents. Group 0–0, on the other hand, showed much better attendance.

Appearance in juvenile courts

Before 1963 only two boys of the 0–0 children had been charged with an offence; one had a conditional discharge and the other was fined. However, no less than eight of the 19 boys in Group M–M had appeared at the juvenile court: five were on probation, one was in an approved school, one had been fined, and one had been given a conditional discharge; one girl was in care of the social services.

Families of formation in 1980: Red Spots as adults

Only two of the 27 0–0 Red Spots had not married; all the others were living with their spouses and families. Only three couples did not have any children, four had one child, 15 had two and three had three children, making 43 in all. Of the 34 Red Spots in Group M–M, two women had never married, one still lived with her mother and the other, deserted by her partner, was also alone except for her infant with Down's Syndrome; one woman was widowed but had been separated from her husband before he was killed; three men were divorced and cohabiting, while four other men and two women were cohabiting with a partner. The marital situation was therefore very different in the groups. There were 88 children in 31 families or partnerships in Group M–M in contrast to 43 in 25 families in Group 0–0. The mean numbers of children in the families were 2.84 and 1.72 respectively.

In Group M–M, when families had split up the children usually stayed with the mother; seven women had children from previous marriages and three did not appear to have any from the current marriage or partnership; it seemed that only 56 of the 88 children in the families at the time of the interview were living with both natural parents. No child had died in Group 0–0 and one had died in Group M–M.

The men and women in Group M–M had left their childhood homes earlier than those in Group 0–0, but in both groups girls left earlier than boys. Thus in Group 0–0, only two of 24 men and seven of 26 women had left by their 20th birthdays, whilst in Group M–M the figures were 17 of

30 men and 22 of 33 women. Most of the remainder in both groups left between 20 and 25 years. It is known that the age of partners at marriage is a strong predictor of later family well-being. In Group 0–0 the wife's age at first marriage was 22.2 years on average and the husband's 23.3 years, whereas those in the M–M families were 18.1 and 20.1 years respectively. Certainly this difference was reflected in the stability of the marriages.

Differences in the types of houses occupied were not so illuminating as differences in the ownership of the dwellings occupied in 1980, with 20 of the 0–0 families owning their own homes as compared to merely three of the M–M group.

Lifestyles

Since education and training for adult life significantly affect future lifestyle and attitudes, we should examine the lifestyles of parents in the families of formation.

An individual's consumption of tobacco or alcohol is important in two respects; first in its implications for health and second in its cost, so an attempt was made to quantify the use of tobacco and to ascertain if any of the parents were conscious that they might have an alcohol problem. In Group 0–0 nearly half the men and three-quarters of the women did not smoke, but in four families the consumption of cigarettes may have been as many as 40 per day while 11 men and five women smoked more than ten per day. No man admitted any awareness of a problem with alcohol, but one wife was dubious about herself. The situation seemed very different in the M–M families where only four of 29 men and nine of 34 women claimed to be non-smokers. Twenty men and women said they smoked more than 10 cigarettes a day; another 25 (13 men and 12 women) more than 20 each day, and 14 claimed more than 40 cigarettes per day. We had no means of checking that claim but, if true, it represented an expenditure of more than £2 per day in each of those families — a substantial proportion of their budget. Four of the men and one woman also had definite drink problems. While none of the 0–0 families was on supplementary benefit, 21 in the M–M families were receiving that aid, including six of the families where tobacco consumption was heaviest.

Employment
Of the 26 women in Group 0–0, 12 had not worked outside the home during the previous six months, while 10 had worked part-time and four full-time. In Group M–M 18 had not worked while 12 had part-time and four full-time employment. The work records of the women were therefore very similar. In most cases no special arrangements had been made for the care of children but in two 0–0 families and five M–M families relatives were helping. However, when we looked at the employment of the men, the positions of the two groups were very different. In 1980 26 of the men in Group 0–0 were known to be in employment, 22 had held their current job for more than five years and only one had been without work for as long as three months in the previous five years. Of the 30 in Group M–M only 13 were in employment, eight of whom had held the same job for more than five years. Furthermore, only seven of 30 had not been out of work in that time and, of the other 23, six had been unemployed for periods up to two years and eight for varying periods up to five years.

Thus the groups exhibited very different patterns as well as types of employment. From unemployment in Group M–M came differences in dependence on social services.

Vocabulary quotients
The Mill Hill Vocabulary Test scores, expressed as quotients, are given in Table 12.9. The difference between the total groups was not as great as when the Red Spots were children, but, if only the Red Spots are included, the difference increased to approach that found in the 11-plus scores and became statistically significant.

Table 12.9   Mill Hill Vocabulary quotients in 0–0 and M–M groups

| | Group 0–0 | | Group M–M | |
	Women	Men	Women	Men
'n'	26	25	32	28
Mean	98.65	103.9	89.33	92.7

Previous schooling and vocational training (Table 12.10)
Notable points about the educational comparisons were the
large number of men and women in Group M–M who recalled
an active dislike of school (39 per cent), who left at the first
opportunity without attempting any examinations (97 per
cent against 28 per cent), and who did not thereafter gain
any qualifications by further vocational training (85 per
cent against 37 per cent).

Table 12.10   Schooling and vocational training:
family of formation

	Group 0–0 Men and Women	Group M–M Men and Women
Age at leaving:		
15	26 (50%)	58 (91%)
16	15	6
17 or later	11	0
Examinations:		
None	13 (28%)	62 (97%)
CSE	14	2
O/A Level	20	0
Qualifications:		
Yes	33 (63%)	10 (15%)
Disliked School?		
Yes	9 (17%)	25 (39%)

Family income
To this point there has been no consideration of family income, although it was noted that the gross declared income
of more than half (56 per cent) the M–M families was below
that of the lowest group of 0–0 families.

Health of parents
Enquiries were made regarding the health and emotional state
of each parent.
  The M–M parents appeared to have a much higher
incidence of both physical (11 of 29 men and 15 of 33
women) and emotional problems (11 of 29 men and 20 of
33 women) than those in Group 0–0 (physical: two of 26

men and none of 25 women; emotional: one of 25 men and four of 26 women). The complex relationship between physical and emotional illness and deprivation requires further study.

Health and development of children

Mother's attitude to pregnancy and 'completed families'   In the 25 0–0 families only one mother appeared to have had any reservations about either her first or second pregnancy, whereas in M–M families no less than 11 of 26 women were reported to have had reservations about their first pregnancy, and this sentiment was found also in those who had second, third or fourth pregnancies. This suggests unplanned rather than planned pregnancies.

We have already noted that, whereas all the 43 children in Group 0–0 were living with both their natural parents, 36 per cent (32 of 88) of Group M–M were not doing so, largely because their original family had split up by separation or divorce. Some of these were with their natural mothers alone (7) but in four families a stepfather or cohabitor was present. One mother had died and the children lived with her relatives.

The children at birth and the time of walking   The data available concerned only children of school age — some 29 in the 25 0–0 families and 78 in 28 M–M families. In Group 0–0 one child's birthweight fell below 5lb 8oz, but only by three ounces and without ill-effects; none had required oxygen at birth, but in six some incident was recorded in the perinatal period; only one child was as late as 16–18 months in walking and none had had trouble with eyes or ears.

Altogether five of the 78 M–M children had low birth-weights. One, whose weight was 4lb 9oz, did not walk until two years of age and, at the time of the interview in 1980, was manifesting both educational and behavioural difficulties. Another had required oxygen at birth and special care in the perinatal period. In 13 (16.7 per cent) some untoward incident had been noted in the perinatal period. In marked contrast to the non-deprived families, 10 children were 'late' in walking (after 16 months); 12 had received attention for eyes and seven for ears; again the same families, although not necessarily the same children, had been involved in difficulties at birth.

Hospital attendances or admissions   The use of hospital in-patient facilities was also unequal. About half the children in each group had attended hospital as outpatients, but only 3 of Group 0–0 had been admitted for operation and none had been in hospital for more than seven days. In contrast, 34 (43.6 per cent) of Group M–M had been inpatients and 24 had had operations. None of the 0–0 children, but three of the M–M children, had attended psychiatric clinics.

The Rutter Behaviour Scale had been completed by teachers at school and the usual cut-off point (score 9) used to indicate those children likely to be disturbed. The percentages were broadly similar in both the 0–0 and M–M groups.

Separation from parents in first five years   For Group 0–0 no separation from mother for more than a month was recorded and only one separation of 3–6 months from a father. In Group M–M four separations from mothers were recorded for an equivalent period. Separations from fathers were much more frequent and affected 13 of the 78 children for more than three months. Thus there is no doubt that a substantial proportion of children in the families with continued deprivation had experienced family disruption before they were five years of age.

Home provision   The interview and the school visit also provided an opportunity to obtain information on certain aspects of home provision and home management. Thus, in a situation when overcrowding in houses to the extent seen in 1952 had vanished, enquiry was made into the sleeping accommodation provided for the school-age children. In Group 0–0 all but five of the 29 children had their own bedroom and all had their own bed. In Group M–M, of 78 children 21 had their own room, 40 shared a room but had their own bed, nine slept with a sibling and, in one family, two children shared a bed in the parents' room.

All children watch television as part of normal home life and all families in both groups seemed to have sets available, but the duration of viewing varied widely between families in the two groups, with Group M–M reported as spending more time watching. However, many in that group were older than those in the 0–0 families.

Child management   The response of parents concerning feelings of irritation and the use of physical 'punishment' are also signs which have bearing on the parents' own emotional control and their feeling towards their children. This was studied and mothers and fathers were asked about the frequency with which they showed irritation with the children and how often they had used physical punishment.

The questions related only to the previous six months and obviously begged the problem of the reasons for punishment — whether it was something which irritated the parents, whether it endangered the child, or whether it was behaviour affecting others of which the parent disapproved or regarded as 'wrong'. The answers therefore seem to throw more light on the parents' reaction to what was thought to be the child's inappropriate or annoying behaviour rather than to any attempt to train or educate the child. The data referred only to children of school age.

There were four questions. The first related to the use of physical blows such as 'slaps' or 'spanking' as practised during the previous six months. In both groups about one-third of children had been spanked, but frequent spankings — that is, more than once a month — were apparently more common in Group M–M, and two children, both aged six years, were said to be spanked several times weekly. The second question referred to the withdrawal of privileges which affected about the same number of children as 'smacking' and seemed to be largely used by the same families. The third method, that of sending the child out of the room, was used relatively more in the 0–0 families than in the M–M, but in both was said to be used more than either of the other two methods. Finally, talking to the child was claimed to be the most frequently used method and much more so in the M–M than in the 0–0 group and, in fact, most children in both groups were, or appeared to be, managed in that manner.

Education and 'social behaviour'   Pre-school playgroups and nursery schools are now accepted as the norm. Approximately three-quarters of Group 0–0 and one-half of the M–M children had attended before going to school at five years. All but two of the parents in Group 0–0 had been to school to see the teacher (90 per cent), but only in two cases had a special appointment been requested. Not surprisingly, fewer of the parents in Group M–M had seen the teacher, but 25 had done so once and 19 more than once.

The mean ability quotients of the 0–0 and M–M children, as measured by Raven's Matrices and Mill Hill Vocabulary Tests, are shown in Table 12.11. There were very significant differences between the mean scores both for first children and for all schoolchildren in the two groups of families, and the gap was rather wider for the vocabulary test than for the non-verbal ability test.

One in five of the children in Group M–M and one in 10 in Group 0–0 were said to be experiencing educational difficulties, behavioural difficulties or trouble with other children. None of the latter had been in contact with the social services nor with the police, whereas in Group M–M five families had had voluntary, and four families compulsory, contact with the social services.

Table 12.11   Mean quotients of first-born schoolchildren

	Group 0–0 (n=18)	Group M–M (n=26)
Raven's Matrices	115.5 (10.7) SD	96.8 (13.6) SD
Mill Hill Vocabulary Test	115.5 (14.1) SD	93.6 (13.2) SD

Movement to and from extremes 0–M and M–0

We next looked at those who, on the one hand, changed from no deprivation at age five to multiple deprivation at 33 years, and, on the other, those who escaped from multiple deprivation at five and by 33 years had established themselves as non-deprived.

Movement into multiple deprivation: Group 0–M

In the 264 families visited, only three Red Spots who spent their childhood in non-deprived families were, at 33 years, parents in families rated with three or more criteria of deprivation. These three families represented only 5 per cent of the sample of non-deprived families or an estimated 23 families from the 483 non-deprived families in 1952. They are too few to treat as a group and are best considered by their personal histories, detailed below.

The 'group' was one woman and two men, the former from an occupational class I home and the men from skilled and semi-skilled homes. The woman was from a stable family. Both her father and mother were good managers and were described as effective, kind and considerate parents. Her parents themselves did not quarrel and appeared to enjoy a good marriage. The woman's early childhood seemed un-eventful, and after scoring well in the 11-plus examination with an above-average IQ, she went to a commercial school which she accepted rather than positively liked. Her school-teachers thought her highly strung and lacking in self-confidence. She stayed at school to take the School Leaving Certificate, but left immediately afterwards at 16 years of age. Then, during the next year, despite her parents' objec-tions, she left home to move into lodgings. She did further training but did not get any formal qualifications. In adult life she remembered that, before leaving home, she had had frequent disagreements with her mother about friends, clothes and staying out at night. She was a single parent at 17 and soon married, but in a couple of years her marriage ended in divorce after two more children. By her early thirties she was living in council accommodation with her three children, working and receiving supplementary benefit. She appeared to have emotional problems and was a poor family manager. She remained in regular contact with her family and claimed a good relationship with them, but admitted that her life and her personal relationships had generally fallen short of her expectations. On the basis of her history she was rated on marital disharmony, ill-health, social dependency and poor mothering. We could speculate that this unhappy story appeared to originate in child–parent relationships in adolescence, but the precise cause is beyond the scope of this study.

The two men were very different from each other. One was born into a stable artisan family and had had an unevent-ful early childhood. At the 11-plus examination he scored well above average on IQ tests and went to grammar school which he enjoyed, staying to do 'O' and 'A' Levels and leaving at 18 years. He left home with his parents' agreement and, after vocational training, entered the employment which he still had in 1980. He married in his early twenties when his wife was in her late teens. She also had been to a selective school but disliked it and left at 16 after taking 'O' Levels. She did not have any further vocational training but obtained and held full-time employment for 10 years. The couple lived in a comfortable, but poorly kept, house and the wife was depressed and taking tranquillizers. Both had a drink most days but denied any alcohol problem. At the time of the interview the couple were having frequent major disagreements, although both denied these were severe. Husband and wife viewed their own parents' relationships very differently; the former thought his parents had been happy in their marriage and he got on well with them, whereas the wife remembered that her parents argued a great deal and that she did not get on with them, although she 'took to' her mother rather than her father. They also viewed their own lives differently, for the husband thought he had achieved more than he could have expected, while the wife thought she had not done as well as she hoped. This family, therefore, had adverse scores on marital disharmony, poor care of the home and maternal illness.

The third Red Spot's father was a semi-skilled worker. The mother also worked, but there were no family difficulties or major problems. Like the Red Spots in the other two families his childhood seemed uneventful and his physical growth was satisfactory. He claimed to have liked school but was said to lack self-confidence, show poor initiative and be hostile to schoolwork. His home conditions were good, his father was considered to be kind and effective but his mother, although her housekeeping was said to be good, was anxious and had received psychiatric care. In the 11-plus examination his test scores were average. He then went to a secondary modern school which he disliked, and left at 15 years without taking any examinations. He did not have further vocational training. At 19, with his parents' agreement, he left home in order to marry, but that marriage lasted only seven years and there were four children before divorce was initiated by his wife. By the age of 33 in 1980 he had remarried; his second wife also had one child whom she brought into this marriage. At the time of the interview, this marriage was of almost three years' standing and all four children of the first marriage had been taken into care. Their council house was well-equipped and tidy. Although the father had changed jobs seven times since leaving school, either because the job was lost or he was made redundant, he was satisfied with his current job. Yet he had many worries and complained of sleeplessness because of worry about his wife's health, about their marriage which was very troubled and beset with physical aggression, about his own ability to cope with life in general; he seemed indeed to be mildly depressed and to have definite emotional problems.

His wife had also gone to secondary modern school which she disliked and had left, aged 15, without having taken any examinations. Although without any further training, she did work full-time. At the time of the interview she regarded herself as chronically ill and had been in hospital. She was also worried about her child's health and was depressed and had bouts of weeping. She denied drinking but said that her husband did and that it was regarded as a problem affecting the marriage. Thus, this unhappy family was categorized on marital disharmony, parental ill-health and educational insufficiency, and finally there was evidence of poor mothercraft.

Movement into deprivation: Group 0–D2
This group consisted of 14 families, the Red Spot members of which found themselves two steps into deprivation in 1980 after spending their early years in families free from deprivation. The pattern of deprivation includes illness (six families), marital disharmony (four families), educational handicap (seven families), social dependency (five families) and poor care (four families).

Eleven of these 14 Red Spots were girls. Eleven families were artisan with fathers skilled workers, the others were professional (1) and semi-skilled (2). In 1952 only one family owned their own house and all the others rented from private landlords. In only one family was the father away temporarily; the parents' health was good and the children progressed well having the same order of growth in height and weight as the children in Group 0–D1 but not so good as those in Group 0–0. At the 11-plus examination the mean IQ of the Red Spots was 98.4. When personal attributes were assessed in the secondary school the main characteristic was that four of the nine assessed were extremely inattentive. Parental interest in their schoolchildren was rated as good in half and average in the rest, but parental provision to the home was described as inadequate in four families.

At the time of the interview in 1980 there were 13 families, including 29 children. Only one man had not married and was a 'drop-out' living in poor conditions. In four of the families one or both parents had had previous marriages. Eight families either owned, or were buying, their houses, five were in council-owned property, and one rented from a private landlord. All the couples claimed to have known each other for more than two years before the present marriage. Of the 11 women interviewed in 1980, only three had stayed at school until 16, two women had taken CSEs and two 'O' Levels; three of those had had further training. The men, nine of whom were Red Spot spouses and the other three single Red Spots, had fared rather better. Eight had gone to secondary modern schools, four to selective grammar schools or to private schools; only four seemed to have a liking for school and eight were either indifferent or hostile; six left at 15 without taking any examinations, two took CSE examinations but left as soon as possible. Eight then went on to occupational training but one of these, who had taken 'A' Levels and seemed to have the greatest potential, did only one year of his university course.

Two families admitted to rows at least once a month and one had considered separation; none admitted fighting. Altogether 16 of the 26 parents did not smoke. There were no problems over alcohol. Six women had worked in the previous six months, but only one full-time; however, as many as six claimed to have chronic or recurrent illnesses (five physical, one emotional) and two had been in hospital. Only one wife thought her husband, who had been in hospital, chronically ill, and this family was one of three on supplementary benefit.

Four women could remember times when their mothers were too ill or too upset to take care of them properly but only two thought their parents had looked after them less well than they should have done; four remembered parental arguments most of their childhood, although at five years of age no marital disharmony had been recorded.

Turning now to the men, all except three were Red Spot

spouses. One of the three Red Spots, of good education, had psychological difficulties and had 'dropped out'. Both the others were rated on illness and social criteria but neither had been out of work in the previous five years. Altogether, seven had experienced some period of unemployment in the last five years — four for over six months.

Seven of the men remembered arguments between their parents and nearly half were critical of care they received from their father or mother or both; only half thought their parents' marriage satisfactory to each parent.

From the adult vocabulary test, the mean quotient for the women was 94.3 and for the men was 99.9. The 10 families had 22 schoolchildren between them, and their results in the reading test gave a mean quotient of 98.0, and non-verbal and verbal ability quotients of 103.8 and 103.9 respectively.

Movement into deprivation 0–D1
Here we look at the 18 Red Spots whose families had no adverse scores in 1952 and yet had one criterion of deprivation at 33 years. The sexes were almost equally divided with 10 males and eight females. Three were single and one woman had been divorced. There were three chief causes of deprivation in 1980: marital disharmony (5), parental illness (4), and educational insufficiency (5). Thus the families in this group were more affected by illness, difficulty in marital relationships or with the all too frequent failure of education and occupational training, the criteria associated with social and family disintegration. At the 11-plus examination the mean IQ was 102.7. The personal attributes of 15 children as rated by teachers showed that only three children had good initiative and only three high persistence, while seven showed poor concentration. Only two children were rated as very interested in school. Most lacked self-confidence and assertiveness but none was emotionally unstable.

Seven of the 10 Red Spot men went to secondary modern schools and three attended grammar schools; only three of the eight women went to grammar or to private schools. While four of the women had liked their school, three did not and the other was indifferent. With that mixture of reactions it is not surprising that four of the women had not taken any examinations and had left at 15. Three of the eight women did occupational training. Of the 10 men, two of the three at selective schools took 'O' Levels and one at a secondary modern school also took 'O' Levels. Five had further occupational training. Of the seven male Red Spot spouses, three went to a selective grammar or technical school. Again antipathy to school was marked and only two had any examination success and only two had any occupational training. Four of the eight female Red Spot spouses went to grammar schools but only two took any school-leaving examinations; four went on to occupational training. In this group of Red Spots and their spouses, there was evidence of school underachievement, and only 14 from the 34 people had had any occupational training.

In 1980, at the time of the interview, only two of the Red Spots had not married, and four men and one woman had made previous marriages. Most families were buying their houses; three rented from the council and one from a private landlord, whilst two were living in tied property. Of 16 families where we had information, 10 adults did not smoke; one man had a definite alcohol problem; no men had been in hospital; no less than 11 of the 16 women had left home by 20 years of age.

In 1980 five of the women were working full-time and three part-time. All the men were in work, only one had been in his present occupation less than one year, and many had been in their present jobs for more than five years. However, in the previous five years four had been without work for a cumulative period of less than six months and three others for more than six months. Only one had been unemployed during the preceding twelve months. Half had had a maximum of three job changes since leaving school, but many had changed more than 10 times. Yet only four had lost a job or had been made redundant, so most of the changes must have been self-initiated.

The mean vocabulary quotients of men and women were 99, with little in the way of variation between sub-groups. There were 16 children of school age from 10 families, and the mean scores were: non-verbal ability 108.6; verbal ability 107.4 and reading quotient 102.1.

Movement from deprivation M–0

In contrast to the three Red Spots who moved into multiple deprivation, there were ten Red Spots (five men and five women) brought up in families with multiple deprivation at the age of five years, who at the age of 33 had no adverse score. This represented 13 per cent of the sample of 78 families from the 118 in multiple deprivation in 1952. In that year, seven of these families had three criteria, one had four and two had five; in five families, parental illness and social dependence were linked with either marital disharmony or poor mothering or with both.

Within this group, three sub-groups could be recognized:

1   Three families where the Red Spot in 1952 was deprived by marital disharmony and social dependence; two families also had parental illness and poor care and the other also had poor mothering.
2   Four families all without marital disharmony, but with parental illness and social dependence, also had poor care, poor mothering and overcrowding.
3   Three single persons. At five years all their families showed marital disharmony, two had parental illness, two social dependency and two poor mothering, and one each poor care and overcrowding.

Only in four of those 10 families was the father always present; in two others the parents had divorced, in one they were separated, in two the father was intermittently present, and in one he was always absent. In five families the father failed to provide for as long as a year, and in three the provision was constant but inadequate. Only one was described as giving full provision but even then it was irregular. Only one father in the seven whose personalities were assessed was thought to be kind and effective. Six mothers were always present, three others were present but chronically ill, and one died. Their personality assessments were very varied, only one being described as kind and effective, three kind but ineffective, two kind but aggressive and the other three were characterized by anxiety. Five mothers worked full-time for more than five years. It is not surprising therefore that the standard of child care was rated as good only in one family; four were considered average, two poor and two variable. A similar pattern occurred with housekeeping standards. Two fathers and one mother had received psychiatric care.

Throughout early childhood, however, the physical growth of these 10 children was better than that of Group M–M although not as good as the children in the non-deprived families (Table 12.6, p. 180). The children took part in the 11-plus examination and in the assessments conducted as part of the '1,000 Family Study'. The results of the former may be compared with those of Groups 0–0 and M–M in Table 12.7 (p. 181), and show that, although only one child went to a selective school, Group M–0 had a mean intelligence (94) and arithmetic quotient (100) some 10 points higher than those in Group M–M, but lower than Group 0–0 by the same margin.

Within this group of 10 children there were two sub groups – three children with IQ, English and arithmetic scores of less than 90, and the other six with considerably higher scores which were sufficient to raise the mean score for the whole group.

At age 12, only one pupil wished to leave school before 15 years and five wished to stay on until 16 or 17 years These are indications of greater interest and application at school than in Group M–M and were supported by the scores for personal attributes which approximated much more closely to the children of Group 0–0 than to Group M–M. Nevertheless, only two stayed at school after the age of 15 or achieved any examination success – the girl at the selective school who got more than six 'O' Levels but left at 16 years, and one other who took the Northern Counties examination.

In 1980 three of the 10 were still single, but four of the girls and three of the men had married. The mean age of the girls at marriage was 20 and of the men 23; in only one family were both partners under 20. There were 13 children in seven families and all the marriages seemed stable and secure; none admitted rows or disturbances. All the husbands and wives said that they had known their spouses for more than two years before marriage. One family lived in rented furnished accommodation, one in a house tied to occupation and the other eight were buying their own houses which were in good areas, well kept, with ample accommodation.

Of the women interviewed (three of whom were Red Spot spouses), four had liked school, two had been indifferent and two, including the only Red Spot girl to go to a selective school, claimed to have actively disliked school. Three had

taken CSE examinations, one 'O' Levels and one spouse 'A'
Levels, but all except the last two had left at 15 years. Only
four obtained vocational qualifications. Two had worked
full-time in the previous six months and both had held supervisory jobs. None had any chronic illnesses or emotional
disturbances. There did not appear to be any drinking
problems.

We had information on 10 men, five of whom were Red
Spots and the others spouses of the five Red Spot girls. Only
one spouse went to a selective school and he reached 'A'
Levels, while three others took CSE; two stayed at school
after fifteen years. All did vocational training and were in
employment at the time of interview, most having held their
jobs for more than five years. Only one had been unemployed for as long as six months in the previous five years.
Only one man appeared to have any emotional problems, and
all except two thought they came from happy homes where
their parents were happy and contented.

Life stories are always complex and difficult to describe
but the following short histories may help to indicate something of the difference between these families and those who
remained in double deprivation. The first was a male Red
Spot from an overcrowded home where there was poor care
and mothering. His father worked in a semi-skilled capacity,
but was described as a poor provider. His mother was rated as
aggressive. The Red Spot was of dull average intelligence and
had attended a secondary modern school which he had left
at the earliest opportunity, without having taken examinations. Nonetheless, he reported that he liked school and
indeed, he went on to obtain vocational training. When interviewed at 33 he had only been out of work for one month in
the last five years. His wife had attended a grammar school
and had taken public examinations. They had married in
their twenties, and neither was described as a drinker or a
smoker. They had two children, and lived in their own house
which was in a good neighbourhood.

The second was a female Red Spot also from an overcrowded council home, where there was chronic parental
illness and dependency on the social services. Her father was
unemployed in 1952 and later changed jobs many times. The
family remained united, however. The girl was of above-
average intelligence, attended a grammar school which she

disliked, but did take 'O' Level examinations. Her husband
had attended a secondary modern school, which he too disliked but he did have vocational training afterwards. He had
not been unemployed in the previous five years. They had
two children and owned their house. The striking thing about
these families was the steadiness and balance of their lives.

Table 12.12 gives the mean vocabulary quotient scores at
33 for all 10 of the Red Spots and the seven spouses of those
who were married; it suggests the mean was rather higher at
33 than when at school, but this was based on different tests.
The mean of the four male spouses was higher than that of
the Red Spots themselves, suggesting that four girls had
married men with higher abilities than their own.

Table 12.12   Mean Mill Hill quotients at 33 years:
10 Red Spots and 7 spouses

	Moving out of Deprivation: M–0		
Red Spots		Red Spot Spouses	
5 Men	97.8	4 Men	107.5
5 Women	96.6	3 Women	95.3

These 10 Red Spots had therefore succeeded in moving from
multiple deprivation in childhood to a family situation at the
age of 33 years which displayed no adverse criteria. We have
shown that, collectively, they had better school careers than
those who were brought up in deprivation and remained
there. Three — one woman and two men — remained un-
married at 33 years of age, but had their own careers, and
the others seem to have achieved both stable marriages and
settled employment.

We also looked at the 14 children of the seven marriages,
all living with their natural parents and 11 being of school
age. None of the children had been in hospital in the previous
year, and none had had any significant separation from their
parents. All the children slept in their own rooms. Eight had
attended playgroup or nursery school and all were then
attending local education authority schools. Only two

parents had not seen the teachers. School was well liked by all but one child, who seemed indifferent, and there were no educational or behavioural problems. The scores for the Raven's Matrices and Mill Hill Vocabulary Tests were high, the mean quotient for the Matrices being 111. Probably half of these 10 would have qualified for selective schools in the days of the 11-plus examination.

Movement out of deprivation: Group M–D1

This substantial group of 21 Red Spots were all members of families with at least three or more criteria of deprivation at five years of age (only one had as many as six criteria), yet they all 'lost' at least two criteria (eight losing three or more criteria) in their family of formation, so that at 33 years each had only one adverse criterion. In no less than 11 families that criterion was educational disadvantage; marital disharmony occurred in another four. By 1980, 76 criteria in those 21 families had reduced to 21 with a marked increase in family well-being and social occupational status. There was, in fact, little transmission of criteria from five to 33 years and, in three instances, marital discord was the only criterion to be present at both times.

In 1952 only two of the fathers were artisans, and none of the families owned their own homes, 18 were living in rented, privately owned dwellings and only three in council-owned property. More than half the marriages were undergoing stress. Only in eight of these families was the father always present throughout the first 15 years; five fathers had left permanently. The situation regarding mothers was quite different — all except one, who died, were present throughout the 15 years. In two families the mother's housekeeping was good and in 11, average.

The group's mean 11-plus scores (90), whilst higher than those of Group M–M (84), were substantially lower than Group 0–0 (106). Assessments of personal attributes at school showed that many of the children had low powers of concentration and initiative, poor persistence and a hostile attitude to school; only three seemed to show initiative, concentration, persistence at tasks and a good attitude to schoolwork.

In 1980 there were 21 female Red Spots or female spouses and all except one left school at 15 years of age. The exception had attended a selective school. Only seven liked school and six actively disliked it. Of the 19 male Red Spots or male spouses, five had been to selective or technical schools and had taken 'O' Levels, but only one stayed to take 'A' Levels. Only two of the 19 liked school whilst 12 were indifferent or showed positive dislike. Ten did not have any further training. Lack of training of both men and women was found in 11 families who in 1980 were categorized as having educational handicap as the sole criterion of disadvantage.

At the time of the interview in 1980 there were 17 couples with children: two families had three children and two one child, all the others having two. Eight couples were buying their own houses and 12 (including the single people) were living in council-owned property and had been settled there for more than two years. The marriages seemed stable; 11 couples had known each other for more than two years and only one admitted 'rows' about once a month, none admitted physical aggression and none had considered separation. Six couples said they got out together less than once a month and the same number that they managed once weekly.

Only three of the women had some significant emotional problems. Six men and six women claimed to smoke more than 20 cigarettes per day. One husband had a definite drink problem which affected his health and another had a problem sufficient to give rise to some social disruption. Only two men were unemployed at the time of the interview.

Only 10 of the men thought their mothers had looked after them very well during their childhood; seven thought the same of their fathers. All except five remembered frequent arguments between their parents, and only five thought both their parents were happy in their own marriages. Despite their poor origins, only three thought that their mothers had failed in their care.

In 1980 the women had a mean vocabulary quotient of 98.9 and the men 93.4. In the third generation, 26 children from 14 families had a mean reading quotient of 95.7; mean non-verbal IQ of 104.5; and vocabulary quotient of 99.5.

Movement out of deprivation: Group M–D2
These 13 Red Spots spent their early childhood in multiple deprivation and, at 33 in their new families of formation, had

moved out of that category, albeit retaining two criteria.

At five years the families of the Red Spots had 49 criteria, three of these were due to marital disharmony and five to parental illness, and 41 were grouped as poor care, social dependency, overcrowding and poor mothering — all criteria associated with family and social failure. At 33 none of these families were overcrowded, but then 10 families showed educational handicap, and 16 other criteria in 13 families. Only marital disharmony had shown any increase and there had been a significant reduction in poor care and mothering and social dependency, all being indications that the families of formation at 33 years had better social organization than those from which one of the parents had come. There was little continuity of specific criteria. In 1952 most of the fathers were in semi-skilled or unskilled work and there was no home ownership. One father had disappeared, one was temporarily absent, and one mother died before the child's fifth birthday.

Only two children wished to stay on at school after 15 years of age, and the secondary school assessment of personal attributes was revealing. No less than 10 of the children were hostile to school and the ratings on self-confidence, emotional stability and self-regard were lower than those in any other group, except Group M–M. The Red Spots all left school at 15, as did the majority of their spouses. However, three male Red Spot spouses went to selective schools and two took 'O' or 'A' Levels. All three spouses went on to further training, unlike all of the Red Spots.

In 1980, of the 13 families, two women and two men had had previous marriages and, in two of these, the present marriage showed signs of stress. Only three families had more than two children. The mean age of women at marriage had been 20.8 years and of men 24.3. Unlike most other groups who had less deprivation at 33 than at five, only one family was buying their home. Only six families denied having any rows, but none admitted physical fights. Three women claimed chronic physical illness, but only one had been in hospital; six women had severe emotional problems. Only six women and two men did not smoke and there was no family in which at least one partner did not smoke. There did not seem to be any serious alcohol-related health problems. Five wives reported that their husbands had recurring or chronic health problems, but none had been in hospital during the previous year.

Only five men were satisfied with their jobs, and most had changed jobs several times; half had experienced redundancy or had lost a job at least once. Nevertheless, all except two thought that society had been quite fair and that there were fewer poor people than ten years previously. Only three did not think they had a chance of improving their circumstances.

The mean vocabulary quotient of the adult males was 106 and of the females 95. The Red Spots scored higher than at the 11-plus examination. In 1980 there were 23 children of school age in 10 families: they showed a mean reading quotient of 91.4, almost the lowest of any group, a non-verbal quotient of 101.6 and a vocabulary quotient of 98.6.

Change across generations

This was an attempt to show the change or otherwise of the Red Spots as they established their own families. By so doing, the movement of families by degree of deprivation could be determined, and we compared two groups of families — one group never-deprived and the other always multiply deprived. During childhood, the first group showed superior intellectual and scholastic performance, whether in selective or non-selective schooling. Those who left school at the age of 15 were more likely to learn a skill which could command a stable occupation later. Their adult life was stable and, although not free from adverse chance events, they showed powers of adaptability and resilience in forming and rearing their own families. Their offspring, in turn, proved scholastically competent.

The families with multiple deprivation presented a very different picture of homes, which were often incomplete, or where parents might be absent. About half, when confronted with chronic social and family adversity, appeared bereft of problem-solving skills or retreated into a state of apathy and helplessness. Further, they were unable to produce the conditions in which children can develop to the best of their capacity. The reasons are undoubtedly complex and it may be asked how far can adults who have never themselves experienced a caring, organized and secure childhood and who may not possess sufficient intellectual capacity or motivation to change, be expected to regulate, organize and stimulate their children to acquire a scale of values different from their own? To what extent does a cycle of deprivation have foundations in constitutional factors, such as intelligence, and how much in learned values from one generation to the next? If it is the latter, then how is it to be changed — a change which requires emotional as well as intellectual strengths?

From information collected during the 15 years of the first study, together with that from the 1980 interview, it is possible to construct brief group profiles to show the factors involved in the maintenance or breaking of the cycle.

In comparing the two groups of families who continued over the generations either without deprivation or with multiple deprivation, we have seen the wide gap which exists between them on almost every indicator. In every respect, Group M–M were at a disadvantage both in their family of origin and in their family of formation: as children they did not experience a normal family life where parental care and support were manifest; in many, even physical needs were not met; and both home and neighbourhood effects mitigated against a desire to learn in the type of education provided. School was often abandoned as soon as possible, and too few had any incentives to learn skills or trades.

We have demonstrated continuity of multiple deprivation in 34 of the 78 families in the stratified sample which represents 45.5 per cent (an estimated 57 of the 118 families in the 1952 population of 847). At 33 years neither the men nor the women in 28 of the 34 families had achieved any educational success or training in occupational skills. This was linked with social dependency in no less than 26 families, reflecting the virtual disappearance of unskilled occupations for men, and it was not surprising to find this linked with marital disharmony in 12 families. Therefore, at 33 years, the most important associations were with social dependency, lack of mothercraft skills and with the intrafamilial disturbance caused by marital disharmony, or with combinations of these factors. These factors are operating in individuals whose family environment did not ensure them an adequate milieu in which to grow up and learn to cope with the world.

Short histories of the three Red Spots from non-deprived

backgrounds who fell into multiple deprivation in adulthood illustrate clearly the importance of personality in both sides of marriage and the formation of a stable relationship. The causes of deprivation in these families were not primarily financial or intellectual, but were bound up with the personal difficulties and relationships and possible inadequate career motivation and success and, in two of the three families, with larger than average family size.

Many of these themes recur when we examine the families who moved into less severe grades of deprivation. They reinforce the importance of factors of personal relationships, illness and lack of educational/vocational training after good family beginnings.

The characteristics of the group of 10 Red Spots who escaped from multiple deprivation were that they had longer courtships, made stable satisfactory marriages and that one or both members of the family of formation received adequate vocational training and thereafter steady employment. They had higher intelligence and more successful school careers, including scholastic achievements, than the always deprived. Three had remained single and they also had responsible employment. In women, we again noted the trend to marry upwards — that is, to spouses of higher intelligence. Numerically they represent one in eight of those who were living in multiple deprivation in 1952.

Life cycle changes in deprivation in the same generation

Study of change from 1952–57 illustrated the important fact that change, or its possibility, is always present in family life and is not only a generational phenomenon. Families deprived in 1952 moved out of deprivation, as we had defined it, by escape from overcrowding and ill-health, whereas marital unhappiness, poor care and social dependence remained more resistant to change. But change was not all improvement, for there were families who moved into deprivation during the same few years. Children remain vulnerable to adverse influences throughout childhood (Rutter, 1981a) and it is important to know if the effects of inimical influences are transient or more permanent (Kagan, 1980b). We found that moving into deprivation during the primary school years had effects in terms of intelligence and behaviour in the secondary school period, entry to employment and continued education. Elsewhere we described adverse experiences which created an impact in the pre-school years and showed that deprivation then had an enduring impact in the school years and in adult life (Kolvin *et al.*, 1983a, 1983b; Kolvin *et al.*, 1988a; Miller *et al.*, 1985). This is not to say that all children who experience these circumstances will have a poor outcome, but rather that the risks are substantially greater (Rutter, 1981).

Reduction of deprivation may also attenuate the effects on physical development, cognition and behaviour provided that previous adversities were mild (Chapter 11). If the adversities were severe, there was little improvement and even that may soon disappear. These effects are not merely a reflection of the persistence of environmental influences (Rutter, 1983). Our evidence also supports the view that the effects of adverse experiences in later childhood and adolescence are not as noxious or enduring as those of earlier childhood. Thus, early childhood experiences appear to be more critical than later ones, or putting it another way, children appear more resilient to life stresses and chronic adverse experiences from 5–10 years of age than before five.

PART V
ROUTES TO AND FROM DEPRIVATION

13 Statistical indicators

Introduction
The previous chapters describe the effects of family deprivation on the children. We wished also to study:

1 The effects of living conditions and occupational status upon the families and to do this we used analysis of variance which allowed us to compare differences within and between groups of families.
2 Whether there were patterns of prediction to the Red Spots themselves from their parents, and later patterns between the Red Spots and their own children. Allied to this was the question of the relative effects of the various explanatory variables used in different combinations. For this we used multiple regression analysis (MRA). We tried to use similar sets of explanatory variables and types and numbers of performance measures when studying prediction across the two generations but we could not obtain precise comparability.
3 The susceptibility of children falling into different categories to these influences — for instance, differences in susceptibility of boys and girls.
4 The effects of different factors on performance when the data were presented as proportions in various categories rather than exact measurements. To do this we used log linear analysis.
5 The patterns revealed by MRA, which were revealed using path analysis — an extension of regression techniques.

The effects of pairs of explanatory factors
using analysis of variance
We had no difficulty in determining significant differences in the functioning of children experiencing various degrees of deprivation in their families of origin — that is in showing the effects of a single explanatory variable. But we were often

confronted with the problem of determining whether, and to what extent, each of two explanatory variables had an independent effect. An example of this was our desire to understand how much the performance of the Red Spots was influenced by deprivation in early life and how much by occupational class of the family. For this we used two-factor analysis of variance which shows the significant separate effects of each of a pair of explanatory variables and whether there is interaction between them.

Analysis of variance is used to determine whether the average score of a particular measure of performance varies between different groups in a population to a greater extent than by chance. A population may be assessed in several different ways and this allows a determination of whether measures of performance are affected by different influences considered separately or in combination. If there is no interaction between the factors, the measured variance is the sum of the contributions from each factor together with those from other unidentified sources. However, if there is a significant interaction, the effect of each factor is dependent on the value of the other and is therefore not well defined, nor is it possible to simplify the structure of the data. Further, if the explanatory factors are correlated, it is more difficult to determine the effects of individual factors (Iverson and Norpoth, 1976). Ideally there should be equal frequencies of individuals in each of the groups, but in epidemiological research, in contrast to experimental studies, there is less control over numbers. Group frequencies were unequal in our study, thus complicating analyses.

Effects of family deprivation and other factors
Analyses were undertaken to determine the contribution of a range of explanatory factors studied in pairs. The measures of performance or outcome used were ability, achievements, school attendance, behaviour and growth.

Family of origin: deprivation and occupational status

Outcome: ability and achievements   We examined various ways of classifying these two explanatory variables, but the overall picture remained the same. We therefore divided the data to give substantial numbers in each category. The occupational status of the parents of the Red Spots was split into two categories by combining strata: higher status consisted of social classes I, II, and III, while IV and V plus were grouped as lower status. Deprivation in the family of origin was categorized as nil (zero); some (score 1); more severe (score of 2 or more). This division did not coincide with that used in the earlier simple analyses, but was necessary to ensure sufficient numbers in the categories. The data were analysed for boys and girls separately.

The first analysis was of intelligence at the 11-plus examination (Table 13.1). The mean scores of sub-groups varied from 87.8 to 105.3 for boys and 90.5 and 104.4 for girls. For boys there was an evident decrease in mean IQ from families of higher to lower occupational status but this was less clear in girls. However, the decrease in mean IQ across the categories of deprivation was equally steep for both girls and boys.

Table 13.1   IQ of Red Spots at 11-plus examination

| | Males | | | Females | | |
| | Family Occupational Status | | | Family Occupational Status | | |
	I, II, III Higher Status	IV, V Lower Status	Total	I, II, III Higher Status	IV, V Lower Status	Total
Deprivation in Family of Origin						
a. Non-deprived	105.3 (n=157)	100.1 (n=40)	104.3	104.4 (n=189)	103.5 (n=26)	104.3
b. One criterion	97.3 (n=38)	92.6 (n=36)	95.0	96.3 (n=47)	96.7 (n=24)	96.5
c. Two or more criteria	92.7 (n=35)	87.8 (n=50)	89.8	92.8 (n=24)	90.5 (n=51)	91.2
Total	102.1	93.1		101.9	95.3	
Analysis of Variance						
Main effects		$p < .001$			$p < .001$	
Effects of explanatory variables due to:						
deprivation		$p < .001$			$p < .001$	
occupational class		$p < .001$			$p < .05$	
interaction		NS			NS	
Residual mean square		158.28			156.22	

This analysis showed that measured intelligence was significantly related to both occupation and family deprivation. Further, the effects of deprivation in boys was similar to that in girls, but parental occupation had a lesser effect for girls. There was no interaction between occupational class and family deprivation, so that the pattern of association between intelligence and parental occupation was similar within all the levels of deprivation.

The second analysis concerned the measure of English ability. In males the findings were similar to those for intelligence, but in females the effects of the explanatory factors were not so clearly defined; the data suggest that there was a strong effect in the case of deprivation in the family, but the effects of parental occupation are complex.

Similar effects were found with arithmetic at the 11-plus, with reading and spelling as rated by the class teacher and with Raven's Matrices and the Mill Hill Vocabulary Test undertaken during the twelfth year. These last two tests, when repeated at 15 years, were significantly affected by deprivation but not by occupational class.

We concluded that deprivation in the pre-school years had a powerful and lasting effect on mental ability and scholastic achievement in both boys and girls. Occupational status of the breadwinner had an important effect on boys but less so on girls, and its effects mostly disappeared by mid-adolescence.

Outcome: school attendance in the last year at school (Table 13.2)   The mean attendance of both boys and girls fell as deprivation increased. Boys showed a smaller, but significant, decrease in attendance rate in relation to lower occupational status; however, in girls, this was not statistically significant. Thus deprivation in the pre-school period had a greater effect than occupational status on the school attendance of both boys and girls during their 15th year.

Outcome: teacher ratings of behaviour and temperament; and growth in the secondary school years (Table 13.3)   Temperament can be viewed as the manner in which a person behaves, as distinct from the behaviour itself. Deprivation proved to be strongly associated with temperamental qualities of concentration, persistence and initiative and of

Table 13.2　School attendance of the Red Spot
　　　　　　children: last year at school

| | | Males | | | Females | | |
| | | Family Occupational Status | | | Family Occupational Status | | |
		I, II, III Higher Status	IV, V Lower Status	Total	I, II, III Higher Status	IV, V Lower Status	Total
Deprivation in Family of Origin							
Non-Deprived	Mean %	94	93	94	92	89	91
	n	129	34	163	130	46	176
One criterion	Mean %	92	90	91	85	87	86
	n	32	31	63	37	27	64
Two or more criteria	Mean %	87	83	85	81	84	84
	n	31	42	73	21	54	75
Total	Mean %	93	88		90	86	
	n	192	107		188	127	
Analysis of Variance							
Main effect		$p < .01$			$p < .01$		
Effect of explanatory variables due to:							
deprivation		$p < .01$			$p < .01$		
occupational status		$< .05$			NS		
interaction		NS			NS		
Residual mean squares		54.84			85.18		

Table 13.3　Classroom temperament and behaviour
　　　　　　during secondary school years: analysis
　　　　　　of variance

		Main Effects	Deprivation in Pre-School Years	Occupational Status of Parents
Concentration at age of 15	Boys	$p < .01$	$p < .01$	NS
	Girls	$p < .01$	$p < .01$	NS
Persistence at age of 15	Boys	$p < .01$	$p < .01$	NS
	Girls	$p < .05$	$p < .05$	NS
Initiative at age of 15	Boys	$p < .01$	$p < .05$	NS
	Girls	$p < .01$	$p < .01$	NS
Criminality Index	Boys	$< .01$	$< .01$	NS
Height at age of 13	Boys	$< .01$	$< .01$	$< .01$
	Girls	$< .01$	NS	NS

Note:　Interaction was not significant in any of the analyses.

delinquent and criminal behaviour in males during both secondary school years and in early adulthood, whereas occupational status had no effect. Neither deprivation nor occupational status had an effect on emotional stability as rated when the boys were 12 years of age. While deprivation exerted a small, but significant, effect on height of boys at age 13, none was apparent in girls, and occupational status as we have grouped it had no effect.

Deprivation in family of origin at five and 10 years
of age in relation to performance in adolescence
An important question was whether family deprivation before five years of age exerted effects independent of deprivation continuing during the child's junior school years. However, we appreciated that, as these variables were correlated, the analysis could only provide clues about their relative importance. The effects are summarized in Table 13.4 where it appears that deprivation in the pre-school years was the more important factor overall for temperament,

Table 13.4   Summary of effects of deprivation at
five and ten years on later mental abilities
and behaviour: analysis of variance

		Main Effects	Effects Due to Deprivation at 5 Years	Effects Due to Deprivation at 10 Years
IQ at 11+ examination	Boys	p < .01	p < .01	NS
	Girls	< .01	< .01	NS
Reading at 11+	Boys	p < .01	< .01	NS
	Girls	< .01	< .05	NS
Concentration at 15	Boys	< .01	< .01	NS
	Girls	< .01	< .05	NS
Criminality	Boys	< .01	< .05	NS
Height at 13	Boys	< .01	< .05	NS
	Girls	< .05	NS	< .05
Mill Hill Vocabulary at 15 years	Boys	< .01	< .01	< .01
	Girls	< .01	< .01	NS
Prog. Matrices at 15 years	Boys	< .01	< .01	NS
	Girls	< .01	< .05	< .01
School attendance at at 15 years	Boys	< .01	< .01	< .01
	Girls	< .01	< .01	NS

Notes: 1. Interaction never significant.
2. Persistence and concentration gave patterns similar to concentration.

criminality and growth. However, later deprivation had important effects on intellectual ability measured in the fifteenth year, Mill Hill scores in boys and Raven's Matrices in girls, and also on school attendance of boys.

*Deprivation at five and 10 years in relation
to functioning in adult life*
The areas studied were:

1 social factors: unemployment (males only);
2 physical factors: growth (height only);
3 vocabulary ability at age 33;
4 behaviour: dysphoric mood, worries, fears.

There were few positive findings and they have not been tabulated. In men the only significant effect of pre-school deprivation was in relation to vocabulary ability (p < .05). In women there were two significant results: pre-school deprivation related to vocabulary quotient (p < .05) and to worry about many family problems in adult life (p < .05). When all the women (Red Spots and spouses) were studied, adult height was significantly and adversely affected by deprivation before five years of age.

*Family deprivation and occupational status (in 1952)
in relation to the functioning of children in adult life*
Again there were few positive findings. In male Red Spots, deprivation had only one significant effect, in relation to vocabulary scores. In women, deprivation in the pre-school years had significant effects on vocabulary scores, height, and an index of the worries of wives about family stress. Occupational status, as we have defined it, has no such effect.

*Deprivation in both family of origin and
formation and adult performance in the
family of formation*
This analysis was confined to the following four features of psychological functioning in adults:

1 an index of 'worry';
2 an index reflecting depressed mood in women;
3 an index of 'fear' in women (not tabulated);
4 vocabulary ability.

In women, deprivation in the family of origin always had a lesser effect than deprivation in the family of formation. While the effect of the former was significant only in relation to vocabulary ability ($p < .05$), the effect of the latter was highly significant in relation to worrying and depressed mood ($p < .01$) but less so in relation to vocabulary ability ($p < .05$). On measures of psychological functioning in men there was either a lack of significant effects or there was interaction so that the effects of the explanatory variables were not well defined. Yet, on the Mill Hill vocabulary measure, the effects of deprivation in both families of origin and formation were significant ($p < .01$).

Deprivation and other factors in relation to the third generation

The behaviour, growth and ability of the first-born children of school age in the families of formation were studied in relation to the following factors:

1   deprivation in the family of formation;
2   deprivation in the family of origin;
3   occupational status;
4   recent life events;
5   an index of parental vocabulary level (the average of the father's and mother's score for each child (see Tables 13.5 and 13.6).

The pictures for boys and girls were similar and have been combined.

Table 13.5 summarizes the effects on behaviour at home (parental report of antisocial behaviour) and at school (Rutter antisocial scale), reading ability and vocabulary and non-verbal quotients. None of the factors had a significant effect on growth and this has been omitted. Deprivation in the family of formation was the most important factor affecting reading, verbal and non-verbal intelligence and behaviour, at home but not at school; occupational status and parental vocabulary level had some effect, particularly in relation to the cognitive variables and parental occupational status in relation to antisocial behaviour at home for boys, but not for girls. Deprivation in the family of origin and recent life events had no effects.

*Table 13.5 Influence of deprivation and other factors
on children of family of formation (analysis
of variance)*

Explanatory Factors	Antisocial Behaviour Home	Antisocial Behaviour School	Reading	Non-Verbal Quotient	Vocabulary Quotient
1. Deprivation at 33	> .05	NS	< .01	< .01	< .01
Deprivation at 5	NS	NS	NS	NS	NS
2. Deprivation at 33	< .01	NS	< .01	< .01	< .01
Life Events at 33	NS	NS	NS	NS	NS
3. Deprivation at 33	< .05	NS	< .01	< .01	< .01
Occupational class 32	NS	< .05	< .01	NS	NS
4. Deprivation at 33	< .05	NS	< .01	< .01	< .01
Parents Vocabulary level at 33	NS	NS	< .05	< .01	NS
5. Deprivation at 33	NS	NS	< .01 [interaction]	< .05	< .01
Occupational class 32	NS	NS	< .01 [interaction]	NS	NS
Parents Vocabulary level at 33	NS	NS	< .05	< .01	NS

Note: None of the explanatory factors had a significant effect on growth.

*Table 13.6 Reading ability of children:
family of formation*

		Deprivation in Family of Origin			
	Non-Deprived	0	1	2 or more	Total
Deprivation	One criterion	112.8	109.8	101.9	109.1
in Family	Two or more criteria	96.3	103.6	94.8	97.0
of Formation	Much	99.3	92.0	91.7	92.9
	Total	104.5	100.1	94.2	

Not surprisingly, all the significant effects of deprivation in the children of the third generation were in relation to their own families' recent deprivation. Thus antisocial behaviour increased from no deprivation to multiple deprivation less in relation to the family of origin than to that of formation. More impressive was the drop in the mean reading quotient (Table 13.6) being 10.3 points in relation to deprivation in the family of origin but 16.2 in relation to the family of formation. While recent deprivation significantly explained antisocial behaviour within the home, educational achievements and vocabulary level, occupational class of parents explained antisocial behaviour and achievements. Finally, parental vocabulary level explained the children's educational achievements and the non-verbal intelligence but, surprisingly, not their vocabulary level.

So far, we have considered only the first-born children in the families of formation, and it is known that the eldest child may differ significantly from subsequent siblings. We therefore repeated the analyses using the average of the scores of all the school age children in each family as a single outcome variable. The most important effect of this change was in relation to antisocial behaviour of boys at school (Rutter scale). The average scores were higher than for the eldest boys (Table 13.7) and deprivation in both the families of origin and formation had significant effects ($p < .05$).

Table 13.7   Mean 'antisocial' scores and
degree of deprivation

	Eldest Boys	All Boys
No deprivation at 33	0.88	1.06
One criterion at 33	1.08	1.38
Two or more criteria at 33	1.85	2.19

Prediction by multivariate analyses

Some theoretical considerations

This section is concerned with the relationship between a

group of explanatory variables and a number of performance variables. The association of these variables can be studied by calculating correlation coefficients between each of the explanatory variables and each of the measures of performance. However, prediction of performance is better studied by multiple regression analysis.[1]

Multiple regression analyses were carried out using selected sets of explanatory variables to predict a range of measures of subsequent performance. Stepwise regression was used to identify the most important predictors within the set of explanatory variables in relation to each measure of performance and to compute the proportion of the total variance accounted for by each of these. These proportions were summed for each predictor across the complete set of performance measures to give an indication of the relative importance overall of the various predictors within the set. These totals are shown in graphical form in Figures 13.1 to 13.4. While such visual presentations of data have a degree of imprecision and roughness, they facilitate comparison without any grave distortions.

The interpretation of the results of multiple regression analysis is complex for several reasons. First, there is likely to be some variation in numbers of children studied — for example, some of the children may have been ill on the day of the 11-plus examination and must therefore be excluded from that analysis. While the quantity of missing data may be slight it may give rise to some distortion in the findings. Second, a high proportion of the total predictive power may be contained in a few of the variables employed, and so selection from all available predictive measures will be necessary. However, it is occasionally possible to combine groups of related variables so that a group may be represented by one overall score. Third, high correlation between the various explanatory variables, ('multi-collinearity'), may give rise to serious estimation problems (Iverson and Norpoth, 1976). There are two possible solutions i.e. either combining highly correlated predictive variables or discarding one or more of the variables. Interpretation is therefore not straightforward.[2]

*Findings: prediction of performance of
the Red Spots in childhood*

Analysis including all available families (the total group)   It
proved possible to use the maximal samples of 560 to 780
families and their children – the numbers being dependent
on the completeness of the data (Figures 13.1 and 13.2).
There were maximally 14 explanatory and 13 performance
variables as follows:

A. 14 Explanatory Variables: 'Red Spot' Families, 1952

- 7 indices of deprivation
- Age of mothers of Red Spots when married
- Birthweight
- Ordinal position in family
- Occupational class
- Home ownership
- Unemployment
- Sex of child

B. 13 Performance Variables During School Years

Mental ability and achievement	4
School attendance	1
Growth (height and weight)	2
Behaviour	3
Temperament	2
Attitude to school	1

The analyses show that the explanatory variable with the
greatest sum of the proportions of variance with regard to
the 13 performance variables was poor care of the child
followed by ordinal birth position. Others of importance are
occupational status, home ownership and poor mothering.
The proportion of the variance attributable to the set of
variables was up to 25 per cent in relation to the mental
ability variables, with smaller proportions in relation to
growth and least in relation to behaviour variables.
It was also helpful to study the pattern of importance of
the different explanatory variables in relation to the main
measures of performance during the school years. For

INDEPENDENT VARIABLES (family of origin) GI	N1 All Families 100/200/300	N2 All Families With Girls 100/200/300	N4 All Families With Boys 100/200/300	N5 All Deprived Families 100/200/300	N6 All Families Includes New Unemployment Index 100/200/300
1 Marital Disruption					
2 Parent Illness					
3 Poor care of Child & Home					
4 Overcrowding					
5 Poor Mothering					
6 Old Social Dependency Index					X
7 New Social Dependency Index	X	X	X	X	
8 Unemployment	X	X	X	X	
9 Mother's Age					X
10 Birth Weight					X
11 Occupational Class					
12 Home Ownership					
13 Ordinal Position					X
14 Sex of Child		X	X		
Note **X** = not included in the analysis					
'N' = Size of Population	568 to 780 A	279 to 336 B	277 to 395 C	250 to 330 D	592 to 691 E

Figure 13.1 Prediction of performance (Generation I to II in the school years)
Multiple regression analysis by stepwise procedure. Sum of coefficients of prediction of all significant independent variables (see text)

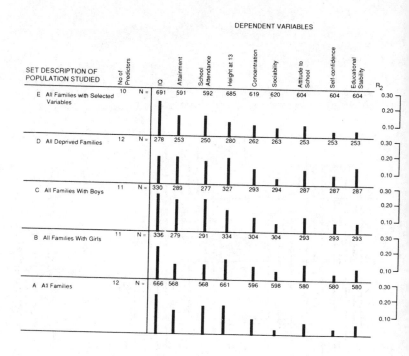

*Figure 13.2   Prediction of performance — some dependent
variables: Generations I–II*

instance, poor care of the child and ordinal position were
good predictors both of intellectual ability and child behaviour. Birthweight was a good predictor only of growth.
Prediction of behaviour also varied according to the sex of
the child, probably because deviant behaviour is more
common in boys.

*Analysis confined to boys during their school years (Figures
13.1C and 13.2C)*   In this analysis only eleven explanatory
variables were used. The most important explanatory variable
proved to be poor care of the child and home followed by
ordinal position. Other variables of some importance were

occupational class and home ownership and parental illness. This predictive set accounted for more than 25 per cent of the variance for intellectual ability and school attendance, but accounted for little of the variance of behaviour.

Analyses confined to girls during school years (Figures 13.1B and 13.2B) The pattern proved similar to that found for boys with impressive contributions of poor care and ordinal position, but the total effects of the explanatory variables were smaller than with boys. Furthermore, while social factors appeared to make a relatively smaller contribution to overall prediction, poor mothering assumed greater importance.

Analyses confined to deprived families (Figures 13.1D and 13.2D) The best overall predictor was poor care of the child; second was ordinal position; third was birthweight but only in relation to later height and weight. Occupational status did not emerge as important and we think that this was a result of its truncation in the sample which contained few families in the upper social strata. The proportion of variance accounted for by the explanatory variables was not great, being at best 20 per cent in the case of intellectual ability and height.

The contribution of unemployment (Figures 13.1E and 13.2E) In order to study the independent contribution of unemployment as an explanatory variable in the 1950s, the social dependence index was divided into residual social dependence and unemployment. However, these proved of little importance and the contribution of unemployment was probably submerged by its correlation with other associated adverse social influences.

Predicting the performance of the children of the Red Spots

For these purposes we used the 179 families with first-born children of school age and a similar set of variables to that used before:

1　the six criteria of deprivation;
2　occupational status;

3   home ownership;
4   family size;
5   age of mother at first marriage or cohabitation;
6   birthweight;
7   sex of child.

We would have preferred to use performance measures identical to those in the previous analyses but the best we could achieve was broad comparability: mental ability and achievement were represented by vocabulary, non-verbal reasoning and reading abilities; growth by height and weight (in standard form); school behaviour by neurotic and anti-social subscores (Rutter B2) and school attendance; behaviour at home by neurotic and antisocial behaviour scores (Kolvin *et al.*, 1975); and temperament by withdrawal and irregularity scores (Garside *et al.*, 1975).

The different types of performance variables relating to children were thus:

	Generation I to II	Generation II to III
Mental ability	4	3
School attendance	1	1
Growth	2	2
Behaviour	3	4
Temperament	2	3
Attitude to school	1	1
Total	13	14

Analysis including all available families (total group)
The most important predictor overall was occupational status (Figure 13.3), followed in turn by mother's age at first marriage, inadequate physical care of the child and home, birthweight and poor mothering. The remaining variables made little contribution to the overall pattern.

This predictive set accounted for a considerable proportion of the variance of vocabulary ability (36 per cent), non-verbal ability (20 per cent) and reading (25 per cent) (Figure 13.4). The proportion of variance accounted for in relation to behavioural and temperamental performance proved small. We noted which explanatory variables best predicted specific measures of performance: occupational class predicted intellectual functioning and antisocial behaviour; poor mothering

INDEPENDENT VARIABLES	N1 100/200/300	N2 100/200/300	N4 100/200/300	N5 100/200/300	N6 100/200/300
1 Marital Disruption	X	—	X	X	X
2 Parent Illness	X	—	X	X	X
3 Poor care of child & house	—	—	X	X	X
4 Overcrowding	X	—	X	X	X
5 Poor mothering	—	—	X	X	X
6 Educational Insufficiency	X	—	X	X	X
7 Old Social Dependency Index	—	X	X	X	X
8 New Social Dependency Index	X	—	X	X	X
9 Unemployment	X	—	X	X	X
10 Mother's Age at Marriage	—	—	—	—	—
11 Birth Weight	—	—	—	—	—
12 Occupational Class	—	—	—	X	X
13 Home Ownership	—	—	X	X	X
14 Family Size	-	-	X	X	X
15 Sex	-	-	-		—
16 Pregnancy Reaction	X	X			
17 Deprivation Summed Index	X	X			
18 Index of Management Techniques	X	X			
19 Recent Life Events	X	X			
20 Separation Index	X	X			
21 Marital Problems	X	X		X	X
22 Family Worries	X	X		X	X
23 Maternal Disturbance	X	X			
Note **X** = not included in the analysis	All Families	All Families	All Families	All Families	Deprived Families Only

Figure 13.3   *Prediction of performance (multiple regression analyses by stepwise procedures): Generations II to III*

predicted behavioural and temperamental factors: birth-weight predicted only growth.

Varying the predictors
First, we divided social dependency into unemployment and other indices of social dependence and also included educational disadvantage in the predictor set (see Figures 13.3N2 and 13.4N2). Neither unemployment nor the residual social dependency index appeared to have any influence.

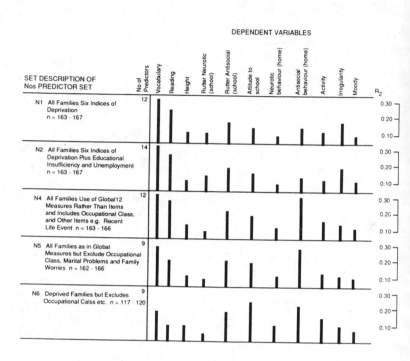

Figure 13.4   *Prediction of performance — results of multiple regression analyses by stepwise procedures: Generations II to III*

Educational disadvantage gave rise to the second greatest score when the proportions of variance in relation to the different measures of performance were summed, and it appeared to have an important influence on all the intellectual measures. Occupational status remained the most important explanatory variable overall.

All the indices of deprivation were next combined into a single score. Six different parental management techniques which, on theoretical grounds, were considered to be undesirable experiences for children were combined into a single score. These were smacking, under-use of rewards, exclusion from family setting, not reasoning with the child, and maternal irritability or loss of control. An index reflecting the sum of recent life events and the following individual variables were then added: mother's reaction to pregnancy; separations of child from parents; marital problems falling short of disruption; family worries and psychiatric disturbance. Some of these made so little contribution that we decided to reduce the predictive set to the following 12 main variables (Figures 13.3N4 and 13.4N4): deprivation, summed score; mother's age at first marriage; mother's reaction to pregnancy; birthweight; occupational class; child management techniques, summed score; recent life events; parent–child separations; marital problems; family worries; maternal psychiatric disturbance; sex of child.

Using this second variation of the predictive set, the strongest predictors proved to be occupational class and child management techniques followed in order by the summed deprivation index, mother's age at first marriage and recent life events. The only other predictors of any consequence were reaction to pregnancy and birthweight. This set of predictors accounted for 39 per cent of the variance of vocabulary ability, 36 per cent of home reports of antisocial behaviour and 23 per cent of school antisocial behaviour, but for only 15 per cent of activity level.

The best predictors of individual performance measures were: occupational status predictive of intellectual measures and school reports of antisocial behaviour; poor child management techniques predictive of antisocial behaviour at home and school; the deprivation index predictive of intellectual measures and antisocial behaviour reported by parents; mother's age at marriage predictive of vocabulary level and school attendance; recent life events predictive of school attendance and antisocial behaviour; and pregnancy reaction predictive of performance at school.

The third variation excluded three explanatory variables which correlated highly with deprivation — namely, marital problems, family worries and occupational status (Figures 13.3N5 and 13.4N5). The summed deprivation index was then the most important predictor, followed by child management techniques, mother's age at marriage and recent life events. Birthweight and pregnancy reaction also appeared influential but at a lower level. This set of predictors accounted for a moderate proportion of variance for vocabulary ability and antisocial behaviour in the home.

Analysis confined to the 'deprived' group (Figures 13.3N6 and 13.4N6)

In this instance the best predictor was child management techniques, followed by recent life events and mother's age at marriage. The deprivation index now had only marginal influence, probably because of the reduction of its variation within the deprived group. However, on this occasion the predictors used accounted for a more impressive proportion of the variance in behaviour than in intellectual performance.

The statistical data were too extensive for detailed reporting but general patterns were identified. The most important predictors of intellectual performance and attainments were the parental standard of education, family size and care of the child and home. The three main predictors of behaviour were care of the child and home, child-rearing techniques and recent life events. Occupational status and family size made some contribution. The only features which predicted temperament were poor mothering and poor child-rearing techniques. Thus it seemed that different predictors mostly predicted different elements of performance.

We judged it important to examine the relative significance of other potential predictors of performance. Unemployment as such did not emerge as a strong predictor; its impact was probably attenuated or submerged by other social and family factors. On the other hand, educational insufficiency of the parents proved a powerful predictor of children's performance. Two other important predictors were poor child management techniques and adverse recent life events, and it was surprising to discover that the mother's memory of distress in pregnancy adversely affected the child's later development while neither early separation nor maternal psychiatric disturbance appeared to contribute to later disturbance of the child. This was against expectations and we do not understand why; perhaps the influence of these variables was submerged in our analyses by more powerful predictors with which they were highly correlated.

From our findings seven key factors emerged and are listed

n historical sequence in relation to the way they might nfluence child development and behaviour.

Factors	Historical Sequence
1 Mother's age at first marriage or cohabitation	1 Prenatal and later
2 Pregnancy reaction	2 Prenatal
3 Deprivation experiences	3 Early formative years
4 Occupational status	4 Subsequent years and current
5 Educational insufficiency	5 Subsequent years and current
6 Child-rearing practices	6 Subsequent years and current
7 Recent life events	7 Recent times

Many mothers who marry early tend to find themselves in poor economic and social circumstances early in their marriage, yet the correlations with adverse factors identified are low. Our work highlighted the central role of inadequate care and poor mothering of children, and it is reasonable to suggest that poor mothering skills in the pre-school years subsequently result in inadequate child-rearing practices and thus continue to influence the child's behaviour over the middle years of childhood. Another set of important influences are recent life events which have been found to have powerful effects both in childhood and adulthood.

Also important is the impact of parental socioeconomic status at either end of the scale. Middle and higher occupational scores are likely to be associated with greater verbal and educational stimulation in childhood. We have already reported a significant association between occupational status and deprivation and suggest that, at the lower end of the occupational scale, the psychological mechanisms are similar to those operating in deprivation — that is, they may bring about their effects through poor child care and mothering. Educational disadvantage in parents is also likely to affect their children through poor stimulation over a wide range of functioning in play, in language and intellectual activities. This will be particularly true in the pre-school and early school years. Yet educational insufficiency is unlikely to act alone, but in combination with other adverse influences.

Prediction of behaviour from factors
intrinsic to the child

We have seen how little of the variance of behaviour was
accounted for when mainly background psychosocial and
family variables were used. It is likely that environmental
influences interact with factors intrinsic to the child which
themselves must receive consideration in the prediction
exercise. For this purpose we chose three factors — temperament, vocabulary and educational attainments — and, in so
doing, some performance variables in the previous subsection
were transferred to the status of explanatory variables.

Difficult–easy child index

Certain temperamental patterns in children may clash with
those of parents, particularly the mother, and result in disturbed behaviour (Thomas and Chess, 1980). To explore this
we decided to combine certain dimensions of temperament —
namely mood, overactivity, intensity and irregularity. This
constituted our measure of difficult–easy temperament, with
a high score reflecting difficulty.

Educational attainment

The literature suggests a relationship between sense of failure
at school and the later emergence of behavioural problems.

Language and verbal ability

Poor language development often precedes disturbed behaviour (Fundudis *et al.*, 1979; Richman *et al.*, 1982). Since
vocabulary level correlates well with verbal ability and even
with general intelligence, we were happy to rely on the Mill
Hill Vocabulary Test. For multiple regression analysis we
used the following 10 explanatory variables in the predictor
set:

1   summed deprivation index;
2   mother's age at first marriage;
3   summed child management index;
4   recent life events;
5   mother's reaction to pregnancy;
6   parent–child separation index;
7   an index of maternal psychiatric disorder;
8   summed child temperament index;

9   child's reading ability;
10   child's vocabulary ability.

We also employed three home-based and three school-based performance measures:

School-based	Home-based
Antisocial score (Rutter scale)	Antisocial score (reports by parents)
Neurotic score (Rutter scale)	Neurotic score (reports by parents)
School attendance problems	Psychosomatic score

Findings   The most important predictor proved to be the child's temperament. It predicted behaviour described by the parents as neurotic, antisocial, psychosomatic and school-avoiding. Since temperament was assessed at the same time as behaviour, prediction could well be spuriously inflated by a measure which indirectly reflects behaviour. So while it is likely that temperament is an important predictor of behaviour (Graham *et al.*, 1973), our data are not suitable to test this.

When temperament was excluded, the picture became clearer. The measure of the mother's child management techniques was a good predictor, particularly of antisocial behaviour as reported by mother and teacher. Recent life events was a good predictor of antisocial behaviour as reported by mother, and also of problems with school attendance. Mother's age when first married was the next best predictor, but chiefly for psychosomatic disturbance. A few other explanatory variables proved significant as predictors of antisocial behaviour; they include the summed deprivation index, low vocabulary level and poor reading ability.

The proportion of variance accounted for by the above set of predictors in 132 children was 32 per cent for parent reports of antisocial behaviour, 14 per cent for problems of school attendance and 11 per cent for psychosomatic problems. There were no substantial effects of maternal psychiatric disturbance or reaction to pregnancy and only limited effects of early life parent–child separation. It has to be assumed that any correlation of these latter explanatory variables with the outcome variables has been absorbed by other predictors.

We concluded that the most powerful influences were insensitive maternal management of children and recent undesirable life events.

Predicting adult family functioning from prior childhood factors

The next task was to examine the ability of factors operating during childhood to predict adult functioning. In this exercise some of the performance variables from earlier sections have been converted to the status of explanatory variables. We selected nine explanatory variables from the pre-school and school periods:

1   accidents before the fifth birthday;
2   classroom concentration/persistence;
3   sociability at school;
4   self-confidence;
5   attitude to schoolwork;
6   school attendance during the fifteenth year;
7   intelligence at age 11;
8   emotional stability;
9   juvenile delinquency.

Outcome variables, all relating to the same children as adults were:

1   the six criteria of deprivation in the family of formation;
2   occupational status in 1980;
3   unemployment;
4   home ownership;
5   wife's age at first marriage;
6   mother's reaction to her first pregnancy;
7   size of family in 1980;
8   mother's techniques of child management;
9   recent life events.

Analyses were undertaken separately for male and female Red Spots and significant predictions are shown in Table 13.8. Only two-thirds of the family 'performance' variables were significantly predicted by childhood 'explanatory'

Table 13.8   *Outcome variables in families of the Red Spots as adults significantly predicted by prior childhood factors: percentage of variance*

	Males %	Females %
Poor care and cleanliness of the child and home	21	—
Overcrowding	—	19
Educational insufficiency	26	40
Occupational class	31	—
Unemployment	23	—
House ownership	27	32
Wife's age at first marriage	23	—
Pregnancy reaction	34	—
Family size	29	—
Management techniques	25	30

Note: Recent life events, marital disruption, parental illness, poor mothering and social dependence were not significantly predicted.

variables. Significant prediction proved twice as common in males as in females. Only three factors were significantly predicted for both sexes: educational insufficiency, house ownership and the management of children. In males, occupational status, the wife's age at first marriage, wife's reaction to pregnancy, family size, unemployment and poor care of children were significantly predicted; and overcrowding in females. The only criteria of deprivation in Generation II which were predicted by childhood explanatory variables were poor care in men, overcrowding in women and educational insufficiency in both men and women. All the other significant predictions relate to social factors.

There were three important childhood predictors of adult outcome in men: IQ at the 11-plus examination, delinquent behaviour and poor school attendance. Explanatory variables reflecting personality and temperament were less important. In women, the most important predictors were IQ at the 11-plus examination and attitude to schoolwork, with school attendance emerging at a lower level; again, self-confidence and sociability made only a small contribution.

Finally we considered the role of the explanatory variables

in predicting individual measures of performance. The most important was IQ at the age of 11, being predictive of educational disadvantage, occupational status and home ownership in both men and women; in women it also predicted age at first marriage and in men family size. Attitude to schoolwork in girls was predictive of educational disadvantage, child management techniques, family size, overcrowding and age at first marriage. Male juvenile delinquency powerfully predicted the spouse's reaction to her pregnancy, poor school attendance, social dependency in women and unemployment in men. In girls, poor sociability in childhood predicted marital instability, and low self-confidence in adolescence predicted poor mothering abilities. There were two other suggestive predictions in males, first that poor concentration/persistence in adolescence predicted poor mothering of their children by their spouses and, second, that accidents in childhood predicted social dependency in adulthood.

The effects of two explanatory variables in predicting deprivation in the family of formation (Generation II)

We now turn to the use of two explanatory variables to predict the extent of deprivation in the family of formation.

Table 13.9A shows the joint effect of deprivation in the family of origin and the IQ of the Red Spot at the 11-plus examination upon the level of deprivation in the family of formation. The families of formation in our sample were divided into three groups according to the level of deprivation in their families of origin and then subdivided according to the IQ of the Red Spot (> 110, 91–110, < 91). Finally, each of the nine sub-groups was divided again according to the level of deprivation in Generation II.

Both childhood deprivation and IQ at age 11 had important effects on the level of adult deprivation. Taking the two extremes, only 13 per cent of those with good intelligence and no childhood deprivation became multiply deprived as adults; the corresponding figure for those of dull intelligence and multiple deprivation was 48 per cent. Further, few of those with good intelligence, despite some experience of deprivation in childhood, were multiply deprived in adult life, whereas a quarter of those with dull

Table 13.9 *Prediction of deprivation in the family of formation from deprivation in the family of origin and IQ at the 11-plus examination*

IQ at 11+	Deprivation in Generation II		Deprivation in Generation I					Total
			None		Some		Much	
			n	(%)	n	(%)	n	(%)	
A Actual Numbers								
> 111	None	0	8	(50)	9	(64)	1	(50)	18
	Some	1 + 2 crit.	6	(38	4	(29)	1	(50)	11
	Much	3 +	2	(13)	1	(7)	0	(0)	3
91–110	None	0	12	(41)	17	(32)	3	(20)	32
	Some	1 + 2 crit.	16	(55)	26	(49)	7	(47)	49
	Much	3 +	1	(3)	10	(19)	5	(33)	16
< 90	None	0	1	(14)	8	(20)	5	(10)	14
	Some	1 + 2 crit.	6	(86)	23	(58)	22	(42)	51
	Much	3 +	0	(0)	9	(22)	25	(48)	34
Total			52		107		69		228
B Predicted Numbers								
> 111	None	0	74		21		2		97
	Some	1 + 2 crit.	56		8		2		66
	Much	3 +	19		2		0		21
91–110	None	0	111		40		5		156
	Some	1 + 2 crit.	149		63		12		224
	Much	3 +	9		23		8		40
< 90	None	0	9		19		8		36
	Some	1 + 2 crit.	56		51		36		143
	Much	3 +	0		21		42		63
Total			483		248		115		846

Notes: 1.   Here the categories of deprivation are mutually exclusive.
2.   B reflects the reconstituted sample.

intelligence became so. Few without deprivation at five years of age, were in multiple deprivation in 1980, irrespective of their intelligence score at 11 years. Both good intelligence and absence of deprivation in childhood appeared to have good protective effects.

As explained in Chapter 2, the sample of families which we followed up in 1979–80 was biased towards deprivation and included only about one in eight of the original non-deprived families but one in two of the deprived and two in three of the multiply deprived. It was therefore of interest to reconstitute the original population of 847 families using the appropriate multiplier for each of the three subsamples, and these figures are presented in Table 13.9B. It must be emphasized that these are merely estimates based, in some cases, on very small samples and there may be some distortion.

The figures in Table 13.9 were analysed formally using log–linear analysis which is used when the data consist of proportions rather than measurements and which gives an estimate of the independent effects of each of the explanatory factors and of any interaction between them. The measure of these effects is the Likelihood Ratio Chi Square which is denoted by G2. In this analysis the actual, rather than the estimated, figures were used. The results (Table 13.10) show significant effects for both intelligence ($p < .01$) and deprivation in Generation I ($p < .05$) and no significant interaction. In the same way, we analysed the effects of deprivation in Generation I in combination with other childhood variables.

In all the analyses the effect of deprivation in Generation I was clear to see and statistically significant. In no case was there a significant interaction between the two explanatory variables. The other factors are discussed below.

Intelligence and arithmetic at the 11-plus examination
The picture for arithmetic was similar to that for intelligence and showed the same significant effects.

School-based personality and attitude factors
These factors comprised response in class, initiative, self-confidence and concentration/persistence based on teachers' ratings at the age of 10 years. Concentration/persistence was a composite score obtained by summing two variables. Inspection of the full data (not shown) suggested that these factors were of little importance in the non-deprived but may have had some effect in the case of the multiply deprived group. For instance, fewer of the multiply deprived whose teachers perceived them as good responders (as compared to those who were poor responders) ended up in multiple deprivation in adult life. This was also true of concentration/

Table 13.10   *Two factor prediction of deprivation in family of formation*

Analysis	n	Explanatory Variables	dF	G2	Significance
A	228	Deprivation in Generation I	4	11.10	p < .05
		IQ at 11-plus examination	4	11.77	p < .01
B	228	Deprivation in Generation I	4	11.68	p < .05
		Arithmetic at 11-plus examination	4	15.27	p < .01
C	207	Deprivation in Generation I	4	16.34	p > .01
		Attitude to school work	4	10.95	p > .05
D	200	Deprivation in Generation I	4	10.42	p < .05
		School attendance at 15	4	15.08	p < .01
E	207	Deprivation in Generation I	4	16.42	p < .01
		Response in class	4	4.85	NS
F	207	Deprivation in Generation I	4	12.58	< .05
		Initiative in class	4	3.85	NS
G	207	Deprivation in Generation I	4	11.58	< .05
		Concentration/persistence	4	8.92	NS
H	264	Deprivation in Generation I	4	37.92	< .01
		Occupational class	4	1.86	NS
I	256	Deprivation in Generation I	4	32.05	< .01
		Family size	4	NS	
J	264	Deprivation in Generation I	4	29.43	< .01
		Accidents to year 5	4	NS	
K	229	Deprivation in Generation I	4	22.42	< .01
		Height 1956	4	NS	
L	228	IQ at 11-plus examination	4	29.71	< .01
		Occupational class in 1952	4	NS	

Notes: Separate effects of two explanatory variables on deprivation in family of formation using log–linear analysis.
Interaction never significant.

persistence. Furthermore, when poor concentration/persistence in class and multiple deprivation at five years were combined they appeared to contribute to deprivation in the next generation. However, none of the effects was statistically significant.

Attitude to schoolwork was rated by teachers in the fifteenth year. The pattern was the same as in concentration/

persistence, but attitude to school also proved a significant predictor (p < .05) of the level of adult deprivation.

School attendance in the fifteenth year

Good attendance at school also seemed to enhance resilience in the face of severe early life deprivation. No one from a non-deprived home who was a good attender at school was subsequently multiply deprived in adulthood. Further, when poor school attendance was combined with multiple deprivation in the early years few escaped deprivation in the family of formation. When applying log–linear analysis, school attendance proved to be strongly predictive (p < .01) of the future level of deprivation.

Family factors

Those tested were family size at five years of age and the number of accidents in the first five years. Neither proved a significant predictor of adult deprivation, although inspection of the full data suggested some influence of larger family size among the multiply deprived. It is possible that their effect had been absorbed by family deprivation.

Growth

The child's weight at nine years showed no effect.

Path analysis

Introduction

Our next step was to use path analysis in an attempt to develop a model depicting the ways in which the biological, social and family background variables might influence child development and behaviour. The method consists in proposing a set of causal sequences in which explanatory variables are examined logically in sequence in relation to subsequent growth, intellectual functioning and behaviour. Such a path analysis cannot itself 'elucidate the direction of a causal sequence and therefore it has to be assumed a priori that the causal sequence proposed is correct' (Stevenson and Graham, 1983). Nevertheless it is possible on both theoretical and empirical grounds to propose a series of causal sequences which can be examined using path analysis. Regression and log–linear analyses are based on models describing how explanatory variables affect performance. Path analysis merely unravels the patterns depicted by these two methods over time.

Some theoretical considerations

Previous intergeneration research seeking evidence concerning relationships or causation has tended to rely on simple bivariate correlations or changes in proportions. Usually these studies have not investigated anything more detailed than the presence or absence of relationships in terms of simple associations between factors. Thus it seemed that a more detailed examination was required, first of the causal processes by which inter- and intra-generation influences operate and, second, of the way in which social, family and environmental factors causally influence a child's development and functioning. In a review, Rutter and Madge (1976, p. 311) pointed out that much of the literature on inter-generation continuities report only the proportion of disadvantaged adults who had disadvantaged parents or children. They consider that these data on their own mean very little and that simple estimates of the extent of inter-generational continuities provide no guide to social policy or political action. Furthermore, Kenny (1979) has demonstrated the pitfalls that can result when simple bivariate correlations alone are used to justify causal links.

This section concerns itself with causal processes which refer to an interconnecting network of causal influences rather than the identification of any supposed single basic cause.

Background to causal path analysis

In most cases, causation involves an interaction between several different types of influences. Thus the causal processes for a specific set of factors, both within and across generations, should be considered as a whole. There are two other considerations. First, the causes are likely to vary according to the type of functioning (such as performance) which is being studied; and second, the process of causation will usually involve a chain of circumstances no one of which can be identified reasonably as direct and basic.

Fuller accounts of the statistical theory of causal modelling or path analysis are available elsewhere (Asher, 1983;

Kenny, 1979; Macdonald, 1977). Path analysis is a technique which structures multiple regression analysis around considered theories. It investigates the causal links *a priori* between measured variables. These proposed, or hypothesized, networks of causal associations are generally referred to as path models. The choice of variables for any model is based both on theoretical knowledge of the area under study, and on substantive reasoning. In the context of this study, such a structure of causal links is termed a psychosocial model. Having generated a psychosocial model a path diagram can then be constructed as a pictorial representation of that model.

Figure 13.5 represents a proposed model and Figures 13.6–13.10 revised models. The unbroken arrowed lines represent causal links where the association between the two factors in question is significantly different from zero. The relevant coefficient is termed a path coefficient. The broken arrow lines represent proposed paths which have been omitted and which

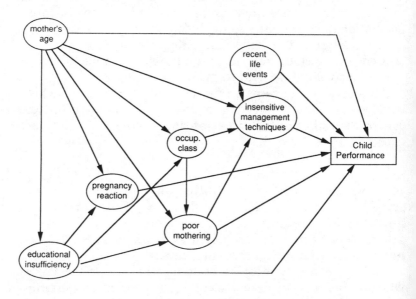

Figure 13.5   Path analysis: proposed model:
child performance

are, therefore, implicitly set equal to zero. Proposed linkages are omitted if no significant causal association for a proposed linkage emerged from the multiple regression analysis. When two or more predictors are highly correlated (multicollinearity), the result is a very imprecise estimate of the magnitude of their causal influences on performance, and can sometimes result in some of the predictors apparently having no significant causal influence, when in fact they do (Kenny, 1979). The choice of factors to include or to omit, should, as far as possible, be made on logical grounds. The curved double-headed arrow lines represent simple non-causal associations. Their relevant coefficients are termed correlation coefficients. The arrows marked with an E represent all those unspecified factors which may influence the performance variable in question, but which have not been identified or measured and included in the proposed psychosocial model. Their coefficients are termed residual coefficients which, when squared, give the proportion of variance of the performance variable which has not been explained by the proposed predictor or explanatory variables.

A path analysis covering two generations

The independent and dependent variables

This set of analyses concerns itself with studying the way social and family background variables influence child performance and behaviour. For these purposes, the eldest children of school age of the third generation were included in the analyses (Gatzanis, 1985). School age children were selected because two of the areas of child functioning being investigated were specifically concerned with educational attainment (reading) and psychological adjustment (neurotic and antisocial behaviour) as reported by the children's teachers in the school setting. Data were required for all the explanatory and dependent variables under consideration, so that only the 162 Generation II families with complete data could be included in the analysis.

A small number of social and family factors (explanatory variables) were selected on both theoretical grounds and the results of the previous analysis. They were:

1   mother's age at first marriage or cohabitation;

2   mother's reaction to her pregnancy;
3   the quality of mothering (for these purposes the two measures of poor care of the child and poor mothering were summed to give an index of quality of mothering);
4   mother's child management techniques;
5   an index of educational sufficiency of parents;
6   occupational status of the breadwinner;
7   recent life events index — the sum of the negative recent life events.

The third-generation children were assessed in four broad areas of performance:

(a)   reading competence;
(b)   vocabulary ability;
(c)   non-verbal reasoning ability;
(d)   psychological adjustment with regard to neurotic and antisocial behaviour in two settings (home and school).

The psychosocial model
A single psychosocial model was proposed and was investigated with respect to six third-generation factors. In the following section, path diagrams are presented only when there were significant causal links to the Generation III factors under study, since the emphasis of this sub-study is to investigate social, family and environmental influences on children's performance. In this model (Figure 13.5), the proposed set of explanatory variables was ordered in a chronological sequence which seemed sensible on theoretical grounds. First came mother's age when first married; next, educational insufficiency, as we have defined it, which may in part be contemporaneous but might also reflect an irresponsible attitude in youth or an unwillingness to seek vocational training; third came lack of occupational success and an adverse reaction to pregnancy; the latter is followed by poor mothering in the infant years and insensitive child management techniques; and, finally, there was the total of adverse recent life events.

It was necessary to establish whether any of the factors in this psychosocial model were so correlated with each other as to distort the patterns that emerge, but in fact the correlations proved only moderate — the highest being between educational insufficiency and occupational class (0.37).

This path model (Figures 13.6–13.10) suggested that factors associated with mother's age at first marriage had an influence on educational and vocational attainments and also on reactions to pregnancy but did not significantly influence the occupational status of the family or the quality of mothering. While educational insufficiency did not significantly influence the reaction to pregnancies, it did influence the quality of mothering and also the occupational status of the breadwinner. Although these patterns were according to expectation, there were some surprises. For instance, mother's age at marriage, occupational class, and poor mothering skills did not appear to be significant prior causal influences of insensitive child management techniques.

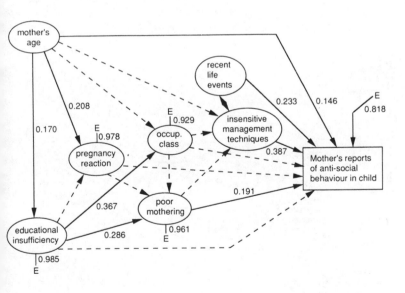

Figure 13.6   Path analysis: revised model: path diagram with coefficients: antisocial behaviour

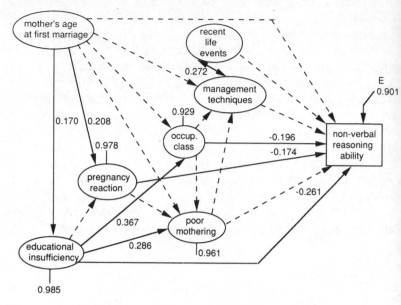

Figure 13.7   Path analysis: revised model:
non-verbal reasoning ability

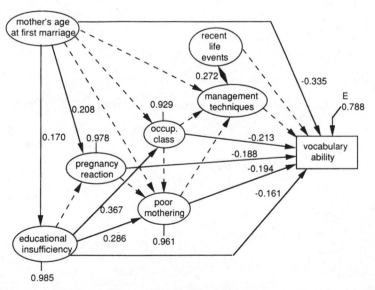

Figure 13.8   Path analysis: revised model:
vocabulary ability

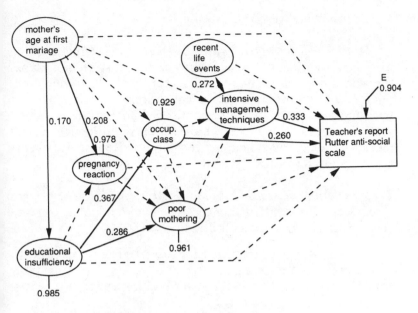

Figure 13.9   Path analysis: revised model:
antisocial behaviour (Rutter)

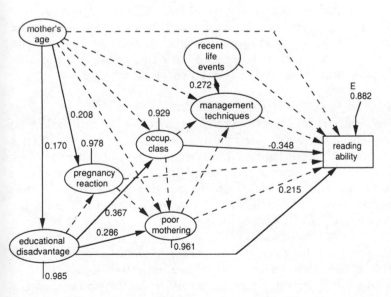

Figure 13.10   Path analysis: revised model:
reading ability

The following were the specific findings.

1   Mother's accounts of antisocial behaviour (Figure 13.6)
The only significant causal influence which stretched across the chronological sequence of factors was that which extended from mother's age to educational insufficiency, to poor mothering and finally to antisocial behaviour. However, mother's age also had a more direct causal influence, as did insensitive child management techniques. Recent life events also made an important contribution.

2   Non-verbal reasoning ability (Figure 13.7)   There were three sets of causal influences which extended across the chronological sequence as follows:

(i)   Mother's age at first marriage to pregnancy reaction to non-verbal reasoning ability.
(ii)   Mother's age to educational disadvantage to non-verbal reasoning.
(iii)   Mother's age to educational insufficiency to occupational class to non-verbal reasoning.

3   Vocabulary ability (Figure 13.8)   There were four sets of causal influences, three of which were identical to those described in relation to non-verbal reasoning ability. The fourth passes from mother's age to educational disadvantage to poor mothering and finally to vocabulary.

4   Teacher's reports of antisocial behaviour (Figure 13.9)
The causal influence extending across the chronological sequence followed the path from mother's age at first marriage to educational disadvantage, to occupational class and then to antisocial behaviour. Occupational class appeared to be the key mediating explanatory variable. The only other explanatory variable with a causal influence was insensitive child management techniques.

5   Educational attainment (reading ability) (Figure 13.10)
The same path as in (4) above emerged as significant. Educational disadvantage also made an important direct contribution and was another path directly extending across the historical sequence.

Path analysis across two generations
The same technique was used to study the influence that
social and environmental factors in grandparents and parents
(Generations I and II) had on the grandchildren's performance (Generation III). The study was confined to
families resident in Newcastle in 1980. Data relating to the
Red Spots as children were taken from the 1957 analysis for,
at this point, both generations seemed most alike in terms of
child-rearing.

The families selected fulfilled the following requirements:
they had lived in Newcastle throughout 1947–80; 95 of the
264 families interviewed fulfilled those conditions and 87
were included in the analysis. Most of the other eight were
excluded because the data were incomplete.

The explanatory variables
The explanatory variables selected were socioeconomic
status, degree of dependence on social welfare services, level
of marital disturbance and the extent to which the child
was cared for in his or her home. We also wished to investigate the influence of the neighbourhood environment upon
the performance of the children under consideration. To do
so it was necessary to have a measure of neighbourhood
environment for each of Newcastle City's 26 wards and this
is described in Chapter 7. A number of these ward characteristics were selected for investigation. A principal
component analysis clearly showed that all the social
characteristics of each ward could be reduced to a single
composite factor. Thus, each Generation II family was
allocated the appropriate composite score for the ward in
which they lived, and this acted as a neighbourhood explanatory variable representing social disadvantage for
Generation II families.

The proposed models
Two psychosocial models A and B were proposed (Figures
13.11 and 13.16). Each was investigated with respect to each
of the nine third-generation performance measures under
study. In Model A we examined psychosocial influences in
the following chronological sequence: Generation I — poor
care of child and home, dependence on social welfare services
and occupational class of the breadwinner; Generation II —

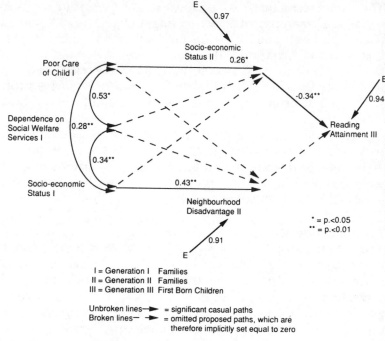

(See Gatzanis, 1985)

*Figure 13.11   Path analysis: psychosocial model A:
reading attainment*

occupational class of the breadwinner and an index of neighbourhood disadvantage.

Model B proposed that factors representing poor social
and marital functioning were likely to be important
mediators of poor care of the child and home. We examined
psychosocial influences in the following chronological
sequence: Generation I — Stage One — dependence on social
welfare services and marital disturbance — Stage Two — poor
care; Generation II — Stage One — dependence on social
welfare services and marital disturbance — Stage Two — poor
care.

Findings concerning psychosocial model A
Model A (Figures 13.11 to 13.15) shows that for five of the

Path Analysis: Psychosocial Model A
Child Performance

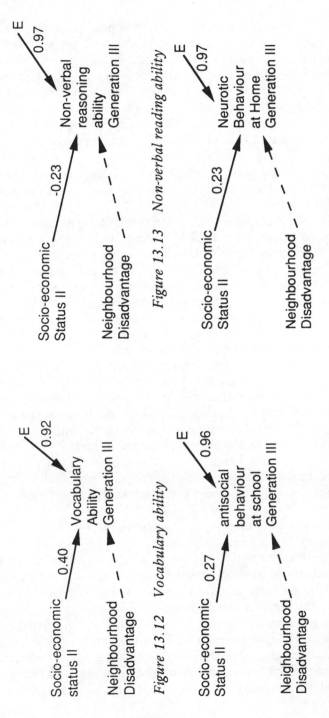

Socio-economic
status II — 0.40 → Vocabulary
Ability
Generation III ← E 0.92

Neighbourhood
Disadvantage

Figure 13.12   Vocabulary ability

Socio-economic
Status II — 0.27 → antisocial
behaviour
at school
Generation III ← E 0.96

Neighbourhood
Disadvantage

Figure 13.14   Antisocial behaviour at school

Socio-economic
Status II — -0.23 → Non-verbal
reasoning
ability
Generation III ← E 0.97

Neighbourhood
Disadvantage

Figure 13.13   Non-verbal reading ability

Socio-economic
Status II — 0.23 → Neurotic
Behaviour
at Home
Generation III ← E 0.97

Neighbourhood
Disadvantage

Figure 13.15   Neurotic behaviour at home

nine performance measures there appeared to be evidence in favour of intergeneration influences. In these models the occupational status of the child's family seemed to be the immediate prior causal influence on all five performance measures, namely reading ability, vocabulary and non-verbal reasoning ability, antisocial behaviour in school and neurotic behaviour in the home. Thus, for these path models, the occupational status of the child's own family constituted a key mediating variable. Further, the derived measure of neighbourhood disadvantage had no direct or indirect causal influence on any of the measures of child performance under consideration.

We must emphasize that the three first-generation explanatory variables were multicollinear with respect to causally influencing occupational status in the second generation. Therefore, any of the first-generation explanatory variables could have been chosen as the causal influence on occupational status in second-generation families. Although poor care of the child was chosen, we consider that very similar conclusions would have been reached if another first-generation variable had been selected.

Occupational status and neighbourhood influence were analysed simultaneously in every instance of model A, so that the relative influences of the home and the community in determining third-generation performance could be assessed. From the results we concluded that, while the former appeared to exert a powerful causal influence, the latter did not. We do not believe that this means that the neighbourhood has little influence, but rather that any such influence is likely to be overwhelmed by intrafamilial experiences.

Findings concerning psychosocial model B
(Figures 13.16 to 13.19)
In contrast to model A, each of the second-generation explanatory variables examined had a specific final pathway to a different area of child performance. The model suggests that, for the four measures of reading attainment, vocabulary ability, antisocial behaviour in school and home, there was evidence of intergeneration influences. Like model A, model B also demonstrated the influence, across two generations, of certain social variables on the reading attainment and vocabulary ability of the first-born children of a third

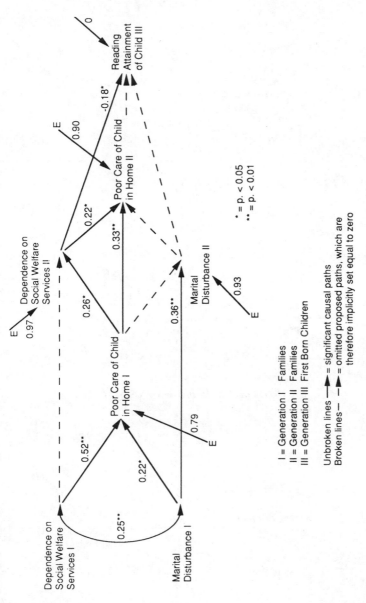

Figure 13.16 Path analysis: psychosocial model B: reading attainment

253

Path Analysis: Psychosocial Model B: Child Performance

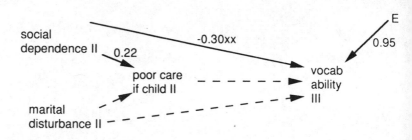

Figure 13.17   Vocabulary ability

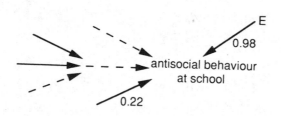

Figure 13.18   Antisocial behaviour at school

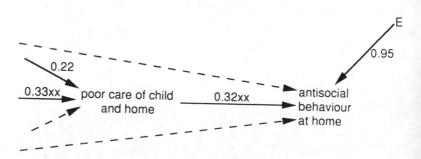

Figure 13.19   Antisocial behaviour at home

generation. Generation I variables of family dependence on social welfare services and marital disturbance had a causal influence on the quality of care experienced by the second-generation children. There also appeared to be a causal association between the experience of poor care as a child on the one hand, and dependence on social welfare services in adult life and poor care of one's own children on the other. The social deprivations of the two previous generations also appeared to be associated causally with lower reading scores and lower vocabulary quotients in third-generation children.

Antisocial behaviour (but not neurotic behaviour), in both the home and the school setting was adequately modelled by psychosocial model B. The prior causal influence on antisocial behaviour in the home was the poor care experienced by the child in that home; but for antisocial behaviour in the school, parental marital disturbance appeared to be a crucial prior causal influence. These results suggested that different aspects of a child's home environment were likely to have different influences on behaviour.

Also evident was intergeneration continuity extending from dependence on social welfare services and marital disturbance in Generation I to the intervening or mediating explanatory variable of poor child care. This in turn extended to dependence on social welfare services and poor care of the child in Generation II.

Some measures of child development and functioning, such as physical growth (height and weight) and neurotic behaviour reported by the child's schoolteacher had no identifiable significant pathways. Three possible conclusions might be drawn:

1 The explanatory measures were not sufficiently sensitive to discriminate between the difference in development.
2 The most appropriate variables were not considered in the models.
3 There were no such influences.

Comment
In this chapter we have examined the effects of explanatory variables using analysis of variance. Our conclusions are as follows:

*Concerning the effects of family deprivation
and occupational status in the family of origin*

Ability and achievements   Deprivation in the pre-school
years had a powerful and lasting effect on measured intelligence and achievement in both boys and girls. Occupational
status of the breadwinner had an important effect in boys
but less so in girls, but the effect of family occupational class
had mostly disappeared by mid-adolescence.

School attendance   Family deprivation in the pre-school
period had an important effect on adolescent school attendance both for boys and girls, but occupational status was
less important.

Behaviour and temperament   Deprivation strongly explained
concentration, persistence and criminal behaviour in males,
but occupational class had little effect.

*Concerning family deprivation at five and 10 years
and performance in adolescence and adulthood*
Deprivation in the pre-school years proved the more important factor. This finding was considered in terms of adult
performance and gave rise to the suggestion that, for boys,
deprivation in the pre-school or school years had no substantial implications for adult performance. However, there
were wider implications for the girls irrespective of whether
the deprivation occurred in their own families or that of their
spouses.

*Concerning the joint effect of deprivation
in the families of origin and formation*
Our conclusion was that deprivation in the families of origin
had less effect on psychological functioning of the adults of
the next generation than current deprivation, and that only
the latter had significant effect and then only in relation to
women. On the other hand, deprivation in the families of
origin had continuing effect on intellectual performance.

The next analysis related to performance in the third
generation where all the significant effects were in relation
to recent deprivation (such as in the family of formation).

Occupational class of parents explained antisocial behaviour and educational achievements; parental vocabulary ability explained educational achievements and non-verbal intelligence. However, when all children rather than only the first-born were studied, deprivation both in the families of origin and families of formation had significant effects in relation to antisocial behaviour in school.

We then moved to multiple regression analysis to predict the performance of the Red Spots in childhood. The most important explanatory variables were ordinal position and care of the child. In girls, poor mothering assumed great importance in prediction. In deprived families, the best overall predictor was again poor care of the child. Again, occupational status did not distinguish itself as a predictor, nor did unemployment.

We employed the same technique with those families having complete data in order to predict the performance of the children of the Red Spots. The most important predictors in order of importance were occupational status, age of mother at first marriage, birthweight and care of the child. When we varied the prediction set, the strongest predictors were occupational class, child management techniques, summed deprivation index, mother's age at marriage and recent life events.

Discussion: prediction analysis

Do our findings make sense?
We need to ensure that our major findings accord with what is considered sensible both on clinical grounds and from theoretical knowledge. To do so we look particularly at the findings relating to prediction of performance of the Red Spots as schoolchildren since this is based on relatively large numbers in a representative population.

It is well known that the *age of mother at marriage* is related to achievement on intellectual tests (Illsley, 1967; Neligan *et al.*, 1976). In the current study, this relationship is variably confirmed in terms of aspects of intelligence and behaviour. The predictive force of *gender* proved small but widespread in the case of intelligence, growth and antisocial behaviour of the Red Spots as children, which is consistent with previously published reports (Neligan *et al.*, 1976).

However, the influence of gender proved less widespread in relation to performance of children of the Red Spots, with the exception of antisocial behaviour.

In most previous research, *parental occupational status* has assumed a position of central importance in the prediction of all types of performance. The exception is where its influences have been weakened by the presence, in a prediction set, of other factors with which it is strongly associated (Neligan *et al.*, 1976). In the current analysis, home ownership is such a factor. In the Newcastle Child Development Study (Neligan *et al.*, 1976), the background factor of overriding importance was *mother's care of her child* at the age of three as assessed by the city's health visitors. It was therefore reinforcing in the present study to find that assessment of care of the child in the pre-school period proved a most powerful predictor of the performance of the Red Spots as schoolchildren. The well known widespread effects of ordinal position in the family (Illsley, 1967; Davie *et al.*, 1972; Neligan *et al.*, 1976) are confirmed in the current study, and the relatively small importance of birthweight as a predictor in comparison to social and family factors is also confirmed (Neligan *et al.*, 1976). Thus, we think that, in our study, the results of multiple regression analysis make sense both in terms of clinical expectation and previously published findings.

Patterns of prediction: the Red Spots as children

Previous work has emphasized the overriding importance of *poor care of the child and home*. This has also proved true in the current research, irrespective of the way in which the explanatory variables in the predictive sets were varied. Poor mothering in the early years of life also made an important contribution to subsequent performance. Another important conclusion was that *parental unemployment* in the pre-school years made little contribution to prediction of performance of the Red Spots as children.

A third finding was that, when the spread of families across occcupational strata was narrow (as occurred with deprived families), the contribution of occupational class to prediction became minimal. Fourth, our set of explanatory variables appeared to have a more important effect on the subsequent performance of boys than girls.

This may not be surprising, since it is already well known that, in early life, boys are the more vulnerable sex. Finally, the proportion of variance due to the sets of predictive factors was never very high, being more than 20 per cent only in the case of intellectual ability irrespective of how the samples were selected or how the set of explanatory variables varied.

Patterns of prediction: the children of the Red Spots

The sample used in this prediction analysis consisted of a new set of families derived from the combination of the stratified samples of first-generation families whose children were grown up with families of their own.

Poor care of the child and *poor mothering* continued to be important but *occupational status* eventually became of overriding importance. As we had confined the analysis in the third generation to first-born children, we could not study the effects of ordinal position and substituted the variable of family size in 1980, but this did not prove to be a sensitive predictor. On this occasion, mother's age at first marriage proved to be a major predictor. Birthweight again made only a moderate contribution to prediction. In this generation the set of predictors used accounted for a greater proportion of the variance of all types of performance than in the previous generation. It is not clear why this occurred; it may have been due to the nature of our reconstituted study group or the fact that our predictive and outcome variables were all measured at about the same time.

In summary, the patterns of prediction identified proved similar to those found in the previous generation, which strengthens our confidence in the validity of these patterns. It is not difficult to note and understand the causal connections between the predictors and the measures of performance, as already discussed. These analyses provide overwhelming evidence that poor child care and mothering in the early formative years have a powerful negative impact on the behaviour and intellectual development of children.

The prediction of adult family functioning from prior childhood factors

The most powerful childhood predictor of adult performance was poor intellectual ability measured at the age of 11 years.

While it is to be expected that intellectually dull children will do less well at school examinations, and are less likely to obtain vocational qualifications and well paid employment, it is to be noted that dull girls were likely to marry or cohabit earlier. Elsewhere we indicated that young mothers tend to be ineffectual parents. These findings underpin the clinical impression that dullness and immaturity are likely to constitute an unhelpful mix for mothering. A poor attitude to school in girls appeared to have both short- and long-term implications, as did a lack of success in subsequent education, early marriage or cohabitation, having a relatively large family, living in overcrowded circumstances and showing inadequate child management skills. It is also noted that male juvenile delinquency predicted the females' reaction to pregnancy; this suggests that a delinquent propensity may constitute a source of stress in the family, with the wife becoming apprehensive because she may have to care for the child without adequate support. Whatever factors determine poor attitudes to school or schoolwork and bad school attendance, these do not simply cease when the youth leaves school. The data suggest that an explanatory variable such as poor attitude to school may presage poor attitudes to work and thus the possibility of eventual dependency on state social and welfare benefits. In girls, poor social skills in pre-adolescence extends into poor skills in adult relationships; furthermore, the pre-adolescent girls who lack confidence also seem to lack skills (and possibly confidence) in relation to mothering.

Another important predictor in boys is accidents in childhood predicting social disadvantage in adulthood, which suggests that accidents may be a manifestation of social inadequacy in the family which has a tendency to repeat itself in the next generation. Further, poor concentration or impersistence in males (one of the characteristics of the so-called attention-deficit disorder syndrome of childhood) also predicts poor mothering by the spouse in the next generation. One possible explanation is that an attention-deficit disorder in childhood in one generation recurs in childhood in the next, and difficulties in coping with such children may be the basis of mothering problems. Finally, only one of the specified criteria of deprivation (educational disadvantage) was reasonably well predicted. Thus, the attempt to predict family deprivation from childhood explanatory variables gave moderate success.

The relative effects of two explanatory variables in predicting deprivation

First, few of the Red Spots with good ability or attainment at school, irrespective of exposure to deprivation in childhood, were multiply deprived in adulthood. Second, few of those who had been free from deprivaton in childhood, irrespective of dullness of intelligence or relatively poor attainments at school, were multiply deprived in adulthood. Finally, poor ability combined powerfully with multiple deprivation so that few of those with the double handicap escaped deprivation in their family of formation; more than half were in multiple deprivation in 1980. We concluded that 'non-deprivation' in childhood gave protection irrespective of ability and appeared to enhance resilience.

In addition, we found that responsiveness, initiative, self-confidence and concentration in the classroom all improved the resilience of those youths who had previously experienced deprivation, although none of the effects was statistically significant. However, good attitude to schoolwork and good attendance at school seemed to increase the resilience of those previously exposed to multiple deprivation and, furthermore, both of these attitudinal factors proved to be significant predictors of later deprivation.

Pathways from Generation I as adults to Generation II

Antisocial behaviour in childhood   The mother's young age at marriage, recent life events and insensitive management techniques appeared to have had a significant direct causal influence on antisocial behaviour. Another pathway was identified beginning with mother's age at marriage, passing to educational handicap and then to poor mothering and ending at antisocial behaviour.

Antisocial behaviour in school   Here the only direct influence was insensitive child management techniques but, in addition, one significant causal pathway was identified. It began at mother's age at marriage, passed to educational disadvantage, then to occupational class and finally to antisocial behaviour.

Reading   One significant causal pathway was identified identical to that described above and another began at mother's age at marriage, passed to educational disadvantage and finally to antisocial behaviour.

Non-verbal reasoning ability (Raven's Matrices)   Three significant causal pathways were identified, all starting at mother's age at marriage; the first passed to undesirable reaction to pregnancy then to non-verbal reasoning ability; the second, after educational disadvantage, went to occupational class and non-verbal ability; the third passed directly from educational disadvantage to non-verbal ability.

Vocabulary ability (Mill Hill)   The pattern is similar to that for non-verbal reasoning ability. A further pathway extends from educational disadvantage to poor mothering and then vocabulary ability.

Pathways from Generation I to Generation II to Generation III

These have already been fully discussed.

In model A, for reading attainments, the path extended from poor care (GI) to socioeconomic status (GII) to reading (GIII). Similar significant pathways occurred for vocabulary, perceptual ability, antisocial behaviour at school and neurotic behaviour at home.

In model B, for reading attainments, the path extended from social dependence (GI) to poor care (GI) to social dependence (GII) to reading (GIII). A similar path extended from marital disturbance (GI) and thereafter the links were the same.

The pathway was identical for vocabulary ability. For antisocial behaviour at school, the pathway extended from marital disturbance (GI) to marital disturbance (GII) to antisocial behaviour at school. For antisocial behaviour at home, the path extended from either dependence (GI) or marital disturbance (GI) to poor care (GI) to poor care (GII) to antisocial behaviour; a variation of this is from poor care (GI) to social dependence (GII) to poor care (GII) to antisocial behaviour.

The specific mediators of dysfunction have proved to be poor social and family circumstances (socioeconomic status, social dependence and marital disturbance) and poor care. While we must conclude that an adverse social ambience has an undesirable general effect, it is likely that the nature and quality of parental care is a crucial mediating process.

Limitations of path analysis
One of the major limitations of path analysis is that the causal path often accounts for only a small proportion of the variance. Stephenson and Graham (1983) reported that there were only slender and inconsistent links between indices of adverse family circumstances and subsequent child performance, and the variables which they studied explained only a small proportion of the variance of child dysfunction. Our findings matched this. Nevertheless, it may be partly a reflection of the insensitivity of the explanatory variables included as causal influences. For instance, in the path analyses from Generation II to III the network of clinically relevant variables selected for inclusion accounted for a relatively high proportion of the variance, ranging from 18–33 per cent in respect of behaviour and 19–38 per cent for cognitive measures (Table 13.11). However, when studying causal influences across three generations, we were constrained by our decision to focus on the same explanatory variables or influences operating at similar points in the generation cycle. The explained variance was then substantially less than in the previous set of analyses. For example, vocabulary ability is well explained in the first set of analyses but not in the second.

Table 13.11   *Path analysis: proportion of explained variance*

	Generations II to III %	Generations I to II to III	
		Model A %	Model B %
Antisocial behaviour (home reports)	33.1	–	9.8
Antisocial behaviour (school reports)	18.3	7.8	4.0
Reading	22.2	11.6	5.9
Vocabulary ability	37.9	15.4	9.8
Non-verbal ability	18.8	5.9	–

Further, in the model covering three generations, only the measures of occupational status and mothering were included whereas the model covering two generations included at least four other major influences:

1 educational disadvantage (probably a reflection of genetic inheritance as well as social);
2 undesirable child management techniques;
3 undesirable recent life events;
4 a measure of poor maternal competence which itself probably reflects a combination of lower intelligence, inadequate motivation and inadequate strength of personality.

In the circumstances, these findings are not surprising. They mean that the unknown variables responsible for the major part of differences in performance must be different in kind from those that have been measured. This was explained by Heath (1981) who wrote that many variables such as family size, overcrowding, health and employment records may add very little to prediction if they are strongly correlated with the variables already included. To discover more about the unknown sources of variation we must add variables not correlated with those already included.

Like Stephenson and Graham (1983) we concluded that, despite a presumed measurement error and the known relative inefficiency of path analysis for explaining social phenomena (Miller and Stokes, 1975), the results of path analysis are indeed of both theoretical and clinical interest. The techniques contain a potential to clarify the bases of complex networks of causal influences.

Notes

1　Regression does not merely consider the correlations between various predictive measures and subsequent performance but also takes into account the intercorrelations between predictive measures. Any predictive variable may be highly correlated with a measure of subsequent performance and yet have a low predictive weight in regression analysis because it is highly correlated with other predictive measures. The conclusions from these two different methods will not necessarily be identical or even similar. The correlative method considers each explanatory factor individually but tells nothing of the nature of its other associations.

whereas the more complex multiple regression method emphasizes the most predictive variables from a group.

2   For each explanatory variable we obtained a value for the coefficient of determination ($R2$) which represents the proportion of the total variance accounted for by that variable. The proportion of variance of each predictive measure is obtained by calculating the product of the appropriate correlation coefficient and the standardized partial regression coefficient (Guildford, 1956: p. 398).

PART VI
CONTACT WITH THE LAW

14   Deprivation and offending

Our study provided an opportunity to measure the incidence and prevalence of charges for indictable offences in the Red Spots up to 33 years of age and to compare families with or without evidence of deprivation. We studied three main hypotheses:

1   Underprivileged family environments are associated with criminal behaviour during the school years and thereafter.
2   Specific criteria of deprivation are associated with different patterns of criminality so that certain indices of social and family deprivation will be more closely related to offending than others.
3   The greater the degree of deprivation in a family the greater the risk of being charged with offences.

By 1957 35 families had moved away from Newcastle and we could not at that time keep in touch with them. Thus 812 families were included in the tenth year analysed.

In 1979–80 the sample of 296 children did include families who had left the city between 1952 and 1962. Since 96 per cent of those who were alive were traced, we infer that, theoretically, a similar proportion of the full sample of 847 was accessible. This was important because, if the full sample of Red Spots as adults is used as the base population without correction, the prevalence rates for offences are likely to be underestimated. Thus, when calculating offence rates a correction was achieved by using the 812 Red Spots living in Newcastle in 1957 as a notional denominator. This was equivalent to correcting for a 4 per cent attrition. Deprivation in the 812 families in 1957 when the Red Spots were 10 years of age are given in Table 14.1.

Findings
During the 1947–65 study, data on offending by children and adolescents to the age of 18.5 years were gathered from

*Table 14.1   Deprivation in Red Spot families when
the children were 5 and 10 years of age*

		1952 'n'	1952 %	1957 'n'	1957 %
A.	Degree of Deprivation				
	1. Not deprived	482	57	477	59
	2. Any deprivation (one or more criteria)	365	43	335	41
	3. One or two criteria	249	29	229	28
	4. Multiple deprivation (three or more criteria)	116	14	106	13
			((3) and (4) are included in (2))		
B.	Type of Deprivation				
	1. Marital instability	123	15	112	14
	2. Parental illness	103	12	88	11
	3. Poor domestic and physical care of the children and homes	107	13	98	12
	4. Social dependency	148	17	130	16
	5. Overcrowding	158	19	148	18
	6. Poor mothering ability	129	15	120	16
Total 'n'		847		812	

*Table 14.2   Newcastle upon Tyne 1947–65: delinquency:
children appearing in court by 18.5 years of
age from 760 boys and girls*

	No. of Appearances						
	1st				2nd	3rd	4th or more
	Boys (n=380)	%	Girls (n=380)	%	Boys %	Boys %	Boys %
By 15th Birthday	58	15.3	9	2.4	6.5	3.2	2.2
By 18.5 years	105	27.6	21	5.6	13.0	7.8	5.3

Note: Only three girls had more than one appearance before November 1965
(Miller *et al.*, 1974: 206).

local police records, and reported in the volume relating to the school years (Miller *et al.*, 1974). By that time, 28 per cent of boys had appeared in court, 5.3 per cent four or more times by their nineteenth year. In contrast, only 5.6 per cent of girls had been to court (Table 14.2).

In 1980 we obtained information from the official criminal records (CRO data) regarding convictions in adult life and earlier on 106 individuals. Cross-checking the CRO data and the '1,000 Family Records' showed some discrepancies, for the former contained information about convictions of Red Spots who had moved away or committed offences away from Newcastle between 1947 and 1962. On the other hand, the CRO records would have been reduced by 'weeding', which consists of the deletion of relatively minor offences and records of cautioning before an individual's seventeenth birthday. The '1,000 Family' material which was based on court appearances had not been subjected to that process and therefore probably provided a fuller account of offences up to the age of 18 years occurring within or near Newcastle. Combinations of data from these two sources provided a best estimate of lifetime offence rates. The form in which the data was held did not coincide precisely with official listings of delinquency or criminality, but we were able to code our data according to offences committed before and after the age of 15 years.

*Incidence of criminality based on
Home Office–CRO records: males and females*
These records showed that, by the age of 33 years, 13.1 per cent of the 847 Red Spots had committed offences (n=106). These data were analysed according to the degree and type of deprivation in the families and showed that rates of criminality increased markedly with the degree of deprivation. There was a more than fourfold increase from 6.3 per cent (n=30) in the non-deprived group to 29.2 per cent (n=31) in the multiply deprived group, the deprived group with one or two criteria coming in between, with 19.2 per cent (n=44).

The rates for individuals subjected to the six types of deprivation varied from 21 per cent of those exposed to marital disruption to 33 per cent of those from homes with poor domestic care and lack of cleanliness. The rates of offences in males were five times greater than in females. It must be remembered that these figures are unlikely to include all of the offences committed during the school years as some have been subject to 'weeding'. Finally, there was the question of the inclusion of minor motoring offences, but this seemed marginal. Over almost 20 years, motoring as a principal offence accounted for only seven of the 106 recorded cases and in all of these there was another associated indictable offence. Again, we suspect 'weeding'.

Incidence of offences derived from combining the two different sources of information ('1,000 Families' and CRO data)

To reach the best possible assessment of the incidence of offences from the combination of the two sources required certain considerations. First, no less than 14 (40 per cent) of the Red Spots in the 35 families who moved away from Newcastle between 1952 and 1957 had been convicted by the age of 33. We found this surprising and difficult to explain, since Osborn (1980) found that moving from London led to a decrease in delinquency.

Since the original study had recorded offences to the age of 18 years 6 months we were able to include in the total those offences which presumably because of 'weeding' did not appear in the Home Office records. We could also add those offences committed by the Red Spots away from the immediate vicinity of the city. Finally, we excluded non-indictable cycling/motoring offences which did not appear in the CRO records unless the person had also another indictable offence. By combining these data we were able to give a more complete estimate of offences in our 847 Red Spots (Table 14.3).

Eighty-three children offended before 15 years (the minimum school-leaving age) and three-quarters of them went on to commit further offences. In addition, 66 individuals later appeared in the criminal records for the first time. Thus, by 33 years, 149 individuals had offended, 10.2 per cent by their fifteenth birthday; 15.9 per cent between 15 and 33 years; and 18.3 per cent at some time up to 33 years.

At all ages, convictions were overwhelmingly due to offences committed by males and by 33 years of age more

Table 14.3   Offence rates in base cohort of 847
families corrected for losses

---

1. Overall incidence of offences (males and females)

By 15th birthday	83 of 812	— 10.2%
After 15th birthday	129 of 812	— 15.9%
Either	149 of 812	— 18.3%[a]

2. Offence rate (according to severity of deprivation and sex of offender)

(i) All males	125 from 404	— 30.9%[b]
All females	24 from 408	— 5.9%[c]
(ii) Males in non-deprived families	40 from 226	— 17.7%[d]
(iii) Males in deprived families (all grades)	85 from 178	— 47.8%[e]
(iv) Males in families with multiple deprivation (overlaps with (iii))	35 from 53	— 66.0%

3A. Offence rate (according to type of deprivation — males only)   3B. Rates of deprivation in offenders

		Males n=125		Females n=24	
Non-deprived families	17.7%	—		—	
Families in 1952 showing:					
Marital disruption	52.8%	28	22%**	10	42%***
Parental illness	51.1%	23	18%*	7	29%**
Poor physical/ domestic care	67.3%	33	26%***	7	29%*
Social dependency	59.4%	38	30%***	12	50%***
Overcrowding	55.8%	43	34%***	9	38%***
Poor quality mothering	60.9%	39	31%**	8	33%**

Notes: 1. Number of non-indictable motoring offences included: [a] = 5; [b] = 4; [c] = 1; [d] = 1; [e] = 3

2. Significance of difference from non-offenders: *$p \leqslant = 0.05$; **$p \leqslant = 0.01$; ***$p \leqslant = 0.001$.

3. A correction for a 4 per cent loss between 1952 and 1979–81 using 812 as a notional denominator representing the Red Spots in the families studied at the 10th year.

than one in four males had offended as against only one in 20 females. The proportions in males varied according to the degree of deprivation, ranging from one in six from non-deprived families, to more than six in 10 from multiply deprived families.

Having ascertained the proportion of offenders in the various deprived groups, we also asked what proportion of offenders had suffered deprivation in their early years. Table 14.3 shows that approximately one-fifth of the male delinquents experienced parental illness and marital disharmony in childhood and about one-third overcrowding, social dependency and poor mothering. In female offenders, the rates of such deprivation are much higher reaching 50 per cent for social dependency and 40 per cent for overcrowding and marital disruption.

Next we looked to see whether there were differences in rates of deprivation for those who committed their first offence before or after the age of 15 years (Table 14.4).

Table 14.4   Percentage of male offenders and non-offenders who experienced deprivation in early childhood

	Non-Offenders	First Offences Before 15 Years	First Offences After 15 Years	Chi-Squared	p
	n=279	n=67	n=58		
Marital instability	25 9.0%	20 29.9%	8 13.8%	21.4	< .001
Parental illness	22 7.9%	19 28.4%	4 6.9%	20.2	< .001
Poor physical/ domestic care	16 5.7%	18 26.9%	15 25.9%	30.3	< .001
Social dependency	26 9.3%	24 35.8%	14 24.1%	25.3	< .001
Overcrowding	26 12.2%	25 37.3%	18 31.0%	27.1	< .001
Poor mothering	25 9.0%	18 26.9%	21 36.2%	30.8	< .001

While a relatively small proportion of those who committed their first offence after age 15 had been exposed during childhood to marital instability or parental illness, those who offended before age 15 had frequent such experiences. Offenders at any age had been exposed as children to significantly higher rates of poor physical and domestic care, poor mothering and overcrowding. Social dependency appeared linked to offending before age 15.

From youth to adulthood
Nearly half (47 per cent : 52 of 110) of those males charged after 15 years had previous charges and only 5 per cent of those who did not offend after 15 years had done so earlier (15 out of 294). Boys charged before 15 years had a three in four chance of being charged again by 33 years (52 out of 67) whereas those not charged by 15 years had only a one in six chance by 33 years (58 from 337).

Female offenders
Only 24 females (5.9 per cent) were charged. Yet the rates rose from only 2 per cent of the non-deprived to 9 per cent of deprived and 15 per cent of those living in multiple deprivation. This rise was steeper than in the boys where the increase was three and four times, and not four and seven times as in the girls.

Mean number of convictions in relation to age (males: criminal record data only)
The mean numbers of offences committed by males at each age to 33 years are shown in Figure 14.1. The numbers have been calculated in relation to the degree of deprivation the individual experienced at five years of age. The picture is clear: the rates in pre-puberty (10 and 11 years) were low; there was then a steep rise through the teens with a peak at 16–17 years. The rate then fell away and at 33 years was almost as low as at the tenth-year level. The three curves soon diverged but from 26–27 to 32–33 years they again converged. At every band before 26 years those with multiple deprivation had the highest score, the deprived were intermediate and the non-deprived the lowest. Both deprived groups had a small secondary peak between 26 to 29 years. Thus, not only did a higher percentage of multiply deprived

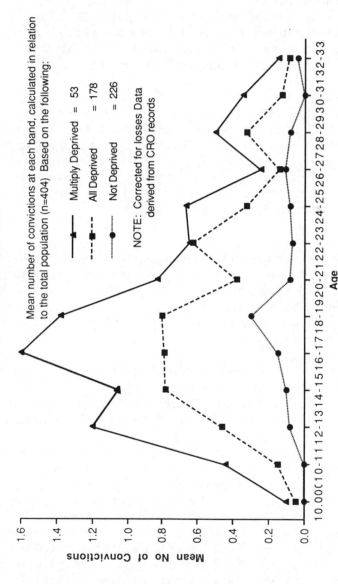

Figure 14.1 *Mean numbers of offences committed by males at each age to 33 years*

individuals commit offences, but the number of offences committed was also greater. After the age of 30 the mean number of offences committed was low.

Analysis of data from Home Office records (males and females)

Calculations were made on the basis of 477 non-deprived individuals, 335 deprived and 106 multiply deprived. Due to 'weeding', the rate should be regarded as minimal. For the principal offences of violence, sex, criminal damage and fraud/forgery the rates were all low, the highest being 3 per cent for violence in the multiply deprived group. Only burglary, robbery and theft (combined) show a gradient, from 20 offences (4 per cent) for the 477 non-deprived to 23 (22 per cent) for the 106 multiply deprived families. Offences other than principal offences were summed and slight gradients from the non-deprived to the deprived were seen as follows: criminal damage in the non-deprived (1 per cent), the deprived (4 per cent) and multiply deprived (8 per cent); taking and driving away (1, 5 and 10 per cent respectively); and motoring (1, 6 and 8 per cent respectively). However, none of the differences was significant except the item 'all other theft' where the rates are 3, 13 and 21 per cent respectively. We also found that the multiply deprived group had a higher percentage of both offences and repeated offences (Table 14.5).

These different offences were also studied in relation to the six criteria of deprivation experienced in the early years of life. When listed according to the highest and lowest rates of the different types of deprivation the following patterns emerged:

	Highest Percentage	*Lowest Percentage*
Violence	Poor care	Parental illness
Criminal damage	Poor care	Parental illness
Fraud/forgery	Social dependence	Parental illness
Theft	Poor care	Marital instability
Drink	Poor care	Overcrowding
Motoring	Poor care	Overcrowding

Despite what appeared to be small differences between the groups with the highest and lowest rates, the findings suggested that poor care of the child and home were the most powerful adverse influences in the family of origin and parental illness and overcrowding were the least adverse.

The pattern for males alone was more distinctive with most showing clear gradients from non-deprived to multiply deprived, suggesting that all types of offences, and particularly theft, increased in relation to the severity of deprivation in the family of origin. That pattern was confirmed by the characteristics of offences for males only (Table 14.5) which showed a steep increase in the mean number of convictions and mean time in custody according to the degree of deprivation. The multiply deprived began to commit offences earlier than the non-deprived.

Finally we attempted to use the profile approach developed by Gunn and Robertson (1976) to ascertain whether different types of deprivation were associated with distinctive profiles of offences. No such association was found. The only pattern broadly true for all types of deprivation consisted of high rates of theft and low rates of drug offences. The rest gave an indistinct picture.

Table 14.5   Convictions (CRO data) in relation to deprivation (1952)

Total Families	Non-Deprived n=226		All Deprived n=178		Multiply Deprived n=53	
(a) Number of males with criminal (CRO) records to age 33	27	(11.9%)	62	(34.8%)	27	(50.9%)
(b) Number of offences:						
1 to 5	20	(9%)	36	(20%)	14	(26%)
6 to 10	3	(1%)	9	(5%)	5	(9%)
11 or more	4	(2%)	17	(10%)	8	(15%)
(c) Mean number of offences	0.7		2.9		5.1	
(d) Mean time incarcerated (in months)	7.9		13.9		20.9	
(e) Mean age in years at first appearance	19.4		18.2		16.7	

Family factors

Some social factors and offending rates   There was a close relationship between offences and lower occupational status rising from 3 per cent of those from social classes I and II to 27 per cent of those from social classes IV and V. The association was even stronger for men alone; 5 per cent from classes I and II, 26 per cent from class III and 42 per cent from classes IV and V plus.

Another approach was to look at the data for non-offenders and offenders separately. Of the non-offenders, 12 per cent came from occupational classes I and II, 55 per cent from occupational class III, and 33 per cent from the lowest occupational strata. The percentages for offenders were 2, 42 and 56 per cent respectively. Offenders came from larger sibships with a mean sibship of 3.5 overall and 3.7 for males as compared to 2.6 overall and 2.5 for males who were not offenders. The fathers of families in the offending groups had an excess of unemployment.

Parental personality factors (Table 14.6)   Parental characteristics had been described and analysed in 1962 when the study team had known the families for 15 years and had

Table 14.6   *Predominant character traits of parents in relation to male Red Spots aged 15 years*

| Parental Characteristics | Fathers' Characteristics | | | | Mothers' Characteristics | | | |
| | Sons Non-Offenders | | Sons Offenders | | Sons Non-Offenders | | Sons Offenders | |
	n	%	n	%	n	%	n	%
Effective and kind	123	(48)	22	(20)	90	(35)	25	(23)
Ineffective but kind	46	(18)	31	(28)	27	(11)	38	(34)
Aggressive	46	(18)	32	(29)	47	(18)	18	(16)
Anxious	5	(2)	2	(2)	71	(28)	11	(10)
Others (includes non-applicable)	35	(14)	24	(22)	20	(8)	19	(17)
Total	255		111		255		111	

Note: Data not corrected for losses.

long acquaintance of the dominant character traits of the parents of the Red Spot children (Miller *et al.*, 1974). Our analysis showed that male offenders had an excess of parents characterized as 'ineffective', a moderate excess of aggressive fathers and a deficiency of parents who were 'effective and kind'.

Comment

The present data reconfirm the well known social origins of delinquency and criminality, in terms of poor occupational gradings of the breadwinner, excess of unemployment and large family size. But these were not the only origins, for parental personalities also seem to play an important part.

15 Non-deprived but delinquent: deprived but resilient

Introduction

Many youths from 'high-risk' backgrounds do not become delinquent while a small proportion of those from low-risk backgrounds do so (Rutter and Giller, 1983) and no theory of criminality can be complete without attempting to account for those who have slipped the hypothetical net. In so far as we are prepared to accept that criminality does have causal origins, we must accept that certain factors, which we term 'protective', serve to counter motivation to crime despite a high-risk background and, second, that certain other stress factors heighten criminal potential despite a non-deprived environment. Here we examine both 'protective' and stress factors (Kolvin *et al.*, 1988b).

Methodology

We divided our cohort into sub-groups (Figure 15.1). In the non-deprived group we tried to identify stress factors which discriminated between individuals who did and who did not become delinquent. Factors were then sought in the deprived group which helped to explain the resilience of those who did not offend. These are protective factors. An important question was whether protective factors operated across the spectrum of deprivation. We tried also to ascertain whether the two kinds of factors operated in a similar way in both boys and girls, but the low incidence of female delinquency confined us to a study of protective factors and prevented a study of sex differences in vulnerability to stress. Finally, we tried to discover if these factors remained potent over time (Werner, 1985) or changed in significance as the child developed. For these purposes, data have been drawn from the children's records at five, 10 and 15 years.

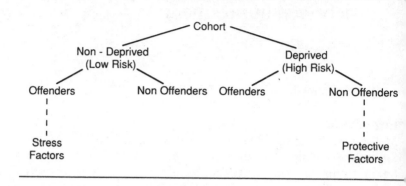

Note: Girls: Studied protective factors only.
Boys: Studied stress and protective factors.

Figure 15.1   Division of cohort into sub-groups

The first five years

Stress factors (Table 15.1)
By the time the boys were five years old, a small number of factors had already emerged in the non-deprived group which presaged later delinquency. The main ones were a relative decrease in personal territory, and 40 per cent of eventual delinquents in this group had experienced lesser personal 'space' (not of sufficient severity to be included as over-crowded according to our definition) as against 18 per cent of non-delinquents; mother relatively young at marriage (29 per cent as against 11 per cent); and the breadwinner being in semi-skilled/unskilled work or unemployed (33 per cent as against 18 per cent). They also showed relatively poor physical growth at three years of age.

Protective factors (Table 15.2)
Turning now to protective factors at age five, first the absence of specific deprivations against a background of general deprivation as reflected by less overcrowding and smaller family size, giving rise to greater living space, proved

Table 15.1 *Males: fifth-year and earlier — stress factors in the non-deprived; protective factors in the deprived*

	Non-Deprived (Score Zero)				Deprived (Score One or More)			
	Non-offenders %	Total 'n'	Offenders %	Total 'n'	Non-offenders %	Total 'n'	Offenders %	Total 'n'
Good mothering	NA		NA		68	111	46	85**
Semi-skilled occupation (father)	18	191	33	40*	50	111	61	85
Persons per room: 1.6 or more	18	191	40	40**	59	111	75	84*
Ordinal position: 3rd or later	15	191	23	40	26	111	51	85**
Poor maternal health at child's birth	8	190	8	40	18	111	32	4*
Family size when child 5: 3 or less	93	191	90	40	75	111	44	85**
Parent unemployed	NA		NA		23	111	40	85*
Height at 3 years > 36ins	56	156	31	29*	42	60	22	50*
Mother's youth at marriage (under 20)	11	189	29	38**	21	106	38	81**
Neonatal injuries	28	162	19	36	23	95	38	73*

*5% level of significance (two tailed)
**1% level of significance

to be important protectors. Second, 68 per cent of non-delinquents had had the benefit of good mothering against 46 per cent of delinquents in the deprived group; or of good maternal health (82 per cent against 68 per cent); good care of the children and home (93 per cent against 76 per cent); employment of the breadwinner (77 per cent against 60 per cent). But other factors were also identified. Being elder-born appears to mitigate the effects of underprivilege; 49 per cent of the deprived group who became delinquent were first- or second-born as opposed to 74 per cent of those who remained crime-free. There is also an undeniable statistical link with early physical development, the absence of a medical history (including relative absence of neonatal complications), fewer hospital outpatient attendances, and fewer accidents. All of these probably reflect a more favourable standard of child-rearing. The above simple statistics do not adequately reflect the relationship at the extremes of deprivation, offending and accidents. The rate of three or more accidents by five years is 8 per cent in non-offenders and 27 per cent in offenders; and the rate of hospital outpatient visits is 59 per cent and 77 per cent respectively. Thus, while there is no relationship in the non-deprived, among the multiply deprived there is a highly significant relationship between presence or absence of offending and frequency of accidents to year 5 (p < .01). Further, in the case of males, 18 per cent of non-offenders and 49 per cent of offenders had had one or more accidents by five years (p < .02).

Among the females, the protective factors (Table 15.2) identified by age five were smaller in number than for their male counterparts but nevertheless important. A secure socio-economic status of the breadwinner appeared to act as a bulwark against criminal activity as did a healthy mother and an accident-free early childhood. All of these factors may in turn reflect better care of the child. Another significant factor was dryness at night. Possibly this represented earlier biological maturation.

Table 15.2   Females: fifth-year protective factors in the deprived

	Non-Delinquent		Delinquent	
	%	Total 'n'	%	Total 'n'
Skilled employment	46	150	16	19
No social dependency	93	150	68	19*
No accidents before age 5	57	150	21	19**
Good maternal health	84	148	58	19
No bedwetting	73	132	42	19

*5% level of significance
**1% level of significance

The tenth–eleventh year

Stress factors (Tables 15.3 and 15.4)

By the age of 10, many more factors concerning the children's interaction with their social and school environments were measurable and the emergent stress factors seem to cover the whole range of a child's activities outside the family. They were of four main types: physical, temperamental, intellectual, and attitudinal. Although factors operative at age five did not cease to be significant, others became more prominent. School proved a major source of stress factors and the data all pointed to the conclusion that the scholastic underachiever, hostile to education, is more likely than the achiever to offend against the law. Further, the proportion of potential law-abiders exhibiting good concentration was more than three times the proportion of nascent delinquents doing so. A similar pattern occurred with those who were reliable in class. There was also a marked difference in abilities; intelligence and educational achievements in the core educational subjects differed considerably between the groups. Even by 10 years hostility to education and authority was apparent in 62 per cent of those who would become delinquent, against 35 per cent of non-delinquent. Whether a symptom or cause of antisocial behaviour, this was startling.

Protective factors

The converse of the above findings, that a good school career blunted the propensity to crime for children from deprived backgrounds was borne out by our findings. The proportion of the non-delinquent deprived group who performed well scholastically, concentrated in class, showed persistence and reliability or whose IQ was average or higher varied from between twice and five times that of the delinquent deprived. This is well demonstrated by the fact that only 16 per cent of the deprived delinquent group had an arithmetic quotient of 100 or above as against 56 per cent of non-delinquents. Good parental supervision also had an ameliorative effect; 28 per cent of delinquents, but only 10 per cent of non-delinquents, had been poorly supervised. Whereas 76 per cent of deprived children who later stayed out of trouble belonged to youth clubs, only 55 per cent of those who later

Table 15.3   Stress and protective factors in boys 10 and 11 years

	Stress Factors in Non-Deprived				Protective Factors in Deprived			
	Non-delinquent		Delinquent		Non-delinquent		Delinquent	
	%	Total 'n'	%	Total 'n'	%	Total 'n'	%	Total 'n'
Poor supervision	1	187	0	38	10	104	28	74*
Negative attitude to the police	35	158	62	34**	43	92	41	59
Membership of youth club	79	159	69	35	76	91	55	60**
Good reading	41	133	29	34	23	87	13	62
Good spelling	42	134	24	34	26	87	5	62**
Good reliability	69	134	41	34	61	87	29	62**
Good concentration	33	133	9	34	17	87	5	62
Poor persistence	24	133	38	34	31	87	61**	62**
Arithmetic quotient 100+	74	160	57	37	56	91	16**	67**

*5% level of significance
**1% level of significance

Table 15.4   Females: tenth year protective factors in the deprived

	Non-Delinquent		Delinquent	
	%	Total 'n'	%	Total 'n'
No loss of father	81	139	61	18*
Adequate supervision	93	139	72	18**
Good reliability	58	120	29	17*
Adequate sociability	92	120	71	17*

*5% level of significance
**1% level of significance

offended were members. This suggests that identification with positive peer group activities afforded some protection. Protective factors seemed even more effective in the multiply deprived group as seen in relation to achievements during the 11-plus examination, particularly the arithmetic quotient, and in reading and spelling as assessed by class teachers. A good reliability rating in the classroom was moderately protective. The majority of those who stayed out of trouble were members of youth clubs (72 per cent) as against the minority of those who did not (41 per cent). Absence of developmental delays, such as speech problems, was also moderately protective.

No less important were the protective factors in girls (Table 15.4). Twenty-eight per cent of the eventual delinquents experienced poor supervision as against 7 per cent of non-delinquents. The natural father was still present in only 61 per cent of the delinquent group against 81 per cent of non-delinquents. The future delinquent was also nearly twice as likely to be unreliable in the classroom and three times as likely to be unsociable as her non-delinquent contemporary.

The fifteenth year (Table 15.5)
As might have been expected, school factors operating *stressfully* at 10 years continued to do so five years later — particularly low intelligence, poor concentration, persistence and attitude to schoolwork. Not surprisingly therefore, only 36 per cent of the future delinquents expressed a desire to stay at school beyond the minimum school-leaving age against 61 per cent of the non-delinquents. What is more, the families' interest in maintaining contact with the school seemed to reflect their offspring's achievements there: 83 per cent of non-delinquent children had parents whose interest in their school career extended to maintaining contact, whereas only 48 per cent of the delinquent group had such parents. Only 32 per cent of the delinquent group as against 61 per cent of the non-delinquent group had fathers with an effective personality. The emergent stress factors at this age reflect a new-found discovery of a sense of independence, and the results of that discovery are now just as indicative of anti-social behaviour as intellectual and educational data; 43 per cent of those from non-deprived homes who became, or who were already, delinquent were missing at least one school day

Table 15.5   Males fifteenth year: stress and
protective factors

	Non-Deprived				Deprived (One or more criteria)			
	Non-delinquent		Delinquent		Non-delinquent		Delinquent	
	%	Total 'n'	%	Total 'n'	%	Total 'n'	%	Total 'n'
Mill Hill Vocabulary good	81	125	46	28**	52	73	34	44**
Reading poor	8	139	22	32*	24	82	45	65**
Concentration poor	30	140	56	32	48	80	75	61*
Persistence good	67	140	47	32*	54	80	25	61**
Hostile attitude to school	24	140	59	32**	38**	80	64	61**
Less than 90% school attendance	13	135	43	28**	39	80	61	59**
Willing to stay at school after 15	61	160	36	36**	34	93	25	72
Family interest in school	83	130	48	29**	55	74	27	60**
Youth joins family activities	70	161	45	39**	34	90	21	68
Father's effective personality	61	162	32	37**	26	94	14	74

*5% level of significance
**1% level of significance

Table 15.6   Females fifteenth year: protective factors
(deprived group only)

	Non-Delinquent		Delinquent	
	%	Total 'n'	%	Total 'n'
Height > 58ins at 13 years	70	130	42	19*
Concentration poor	46	123	78	18**
Persistence poor	56	123	72	18*
Hostile attitude to school	41	123	67	18*
Willing to stay at school	20	117	0	17**
Family interest in school	54	112	27	15**
Father always present	57	150	21	19**

*5% level of significance
**1% level of significance

in 10, as against only 13 per cent of those who did not become delinquent; 59 per cent of delinquents, as against 24 per cent of non-delinquents, had a hostile attitude to schoolwork. Furthermore, while only 45 per cent of the delinquent group participated in family activities, 70 per cent of the non-delinquent group did so.

A similar series of factors proved to be protective in the case of the deprived, and once again the factors reflecting positive motivation and attitude, particularly willingness to continue at school, good school attendance and attitude to schoolwork were prominent discriminators. One finding representative of the degree of protection afforded by positive temperamental factors was that while only one-quarter of the delinquent group concentrated well in class, over half of the non-delinquent group did so. Good intelligence and educational achievements and a positive family interest were powerful protectors. A few of these were also protective at the extremes of deprivation.

There was a smaller set of protective factors for girls (Table 15.6) and four of these were good concentration and persistence in class; non-hostile attitude to school; willingness to stay on at school; and a family that maintained contact with the school (which applied also to boys). The constant presence of the natural father was a powerful protector and, in the non-delinquent group, 57 per cent of fathers were always present against 21 per cent in the delinquent group. A new factor emerged of good growth at 13 years which seemed to complement the criteria of cessation of bedwetting by five years already mentioned.

16 Prediction of criminality

Introduction
Here we attempt to predict criminality using a number of criteria of deprivation, either alone, with other family factors or with factors personal to the child. We then apply the multivariate statistical techniques of multiple regression, discriminant function and log–linear analysis.

In the 1950s there were several attempts to develop formulae which would give reasonably accurate predictions of delinquency, and more recently a number of workers in the United Kingdom have again taken up this theme, notably West and Farrington (1977) and Farrington and Tarling (1985). The limitations of prediction studies have been summarized by Rutter and Giller (1983), with two telling conclusions: many of the youths theoretically at high risk do not become delinquent, while a substantial minority apparently not at high risk do so.

The subjects and their offending
It is important to note that our social, family and child data, collected prior to offending, were independent of the subsequent data gathered about criminal offences. The research assistant who coded the criminal records had no access to other information about the individuals.

Method: statistical techniques

Single-factor prediction
One way to study predictive efficiency is to view potential predictors as screen measures. 'False positives' are those individuals wrongly identified as potential offenders, and 'false negatives' are those for whom a 'no offending' prediction proved false. For our purposes, 'sensitivity' refers to the capacity of a measure to select offenders as a percentage of all offenders; 'specificity' refers to the capacity to

select non-offenders as a percentage of all non-offenders. The percentage agreement, or overall accuracy, gives the sum of valid positives and valid negatives in relation to the total number of subjects.

Loeber and Dishion (1983) have tried to identify antecedents of delinquency which show good predictive validity. They attempted to improve prediction and identify principal predictors by developing a formula in percentage form for relative improvement over chance (RIOC) of the many predictors studied. They then ranked the predictors according to that improvement.

They found the best predictors of criminal behaviour were family management techniques, the child's previous conduct problems, parental criminality and the child's poor academic performance. For some analyses we have followed their model.

Two-factor prediction
This involves combining two explanatory variables, one of which is always deprivation. The other consists of a variety of family factors or those features personal to the child such as growth, measured intelligence, achievements and classroom behaviour. These data shown in Tables 16.1 to 16.4 were analysed by log–linear analysis.

Multiple regression analysis
We used a multiple regression model to highlight the most important items in a set of explanatory variables. The attractiveness of this method was that all the explanatory variables were looked at simultaneously and their relative importance and interrelationship could be examined. We analysed data for males and females together and then re-analysed that for males alone; we then selected sets of explanatory variables and used ratings of delinquency or criminality as a measure of performance. In this way we sought a set of weightings which, applied to the explanatory variables, would maximize the correlation between their combined effect on the one hand and the measure of performance on the other (Maxwell, 1977). Discriminant function analysis was also undertaken with the same sets of data (using a dichotomous dependent variable).

Initially we used social and family factors as explanatory

variables and found that they predicted only 10 per cent of the variance. Subsequently, the sets of independent variables were expanded to include the personal differences of behaviour at school, attitudes to school and ability measures.

Simple models

Prediction using a single predictive factor

The factors selected related to the home environment, to events in the child's life and to data on behavioural and intellectual ability measures collected in school. Tables 16.1 and 16.2 give the results from this and several other studies and, for each, the relative improvement over chance (RIOC). On comparing the findings, we discovered that the false negative rate was usually low, except when the screen was the criteria of multiple deprivation or the measure of neighbourhood crime. On the other hand, the false positive rate was low when the screen consisted of three or more criteria of deprivation. That suggests that the multiple deprivation criteria tend to select only individuals who do commit offences. Sensitivity proved to be highest when using any one of our criteria and specificity was particularly high when the criterion was of 'multiple deprivation', as we have defined it.

The overall agreement in all the longitudinal studies was high except when using truancy as a screen measure (Robins and Hill, 1966) and when the Newcastle single criterion of deprivation was employed.

We also explored the use of other family factors as predictors (Table 16.2). The false negative rates were low for family size and family interest in the child as reflected by school contact. The presence of three or more children in the family proved to be a moderate predictor with poor sensitivity but with good random improvement over chance; the good specificity probably reflects poor social circumstances in large families. The parents' interest in the children, as shown by school contact, also gave rise to high specificity and reasonable overall accuracy and a high random improvement over chance. This factor probably reflected the quality of parenting in the family.

The factors relating to the final year in junior school suggest that certain kinds of school data were remarkably good predictors of late delinquency. Some, such as the intelligence and arithmetic quotients recorded at the 11-plus examination were totally objective and gave rise to high specificity, high percentage of correct predictions and good relative improvement over chance. The false negative rates were low for school achievements and the false positives were low for unreliable behaviour in the classroom. Some of the behaviour measures also proved to be good predictors. It seems that factors which reflected ability and scholastic achievements on the one hand and personality and temperament on the other were successful predictors, and others were reliability in the classroom, poor concentration and persistence at scholastic tasks. All showed good relative improvement over chance.

Data collected in the children's last statutory year at school were also used but are questionable predictors as the data were collected after some of the children had already committed offences. It was not surprising therefore that both poor school attendance and poor attitude to schoolwork showed a substantial improvement over chance in prediction. The latter also gave a low false negative rate and the former a moderately low false positive rate.

School predictors of adult criminality

An important question was whether judgements about children by school staff could predict adult criminality. When the children were 12 years of age they had been rated by teachers as to the likelihood of their becoming maladjusted or delinquent. Of 171 so rated 37 (21.6 per cent) later acquired a criminal record. Of the 558 otherwise rated, 50 (9 per cent) eventually offended. Thus, although the rates of adult criminality were more than twice as high in the group the teachers thought at risk, it would have been necessary to suspect five individuals for each offender.

Another way of looking at prediction is to study the later history of the 208 children who were considered to be maladjusted by doctors or to exhibit behavioural difficulties during childhood by teachers (Miller *et al.*, 1974). Some 24 per cent of that group acquired a criminal record against 7 per cent of children not rated as maladjusted, and over a quarter of the child population would have to be included to predict less than half the adult criminals. Looking backwards from those who were criminal, 43 per cent were predicted by

Table 16.1 Validity of predictors of delinquency

	'n'	False Negative	False Positive	Sensitivity	Specificity	Overall Agreement	RIOC[1]
Males: This Study							
Criteria of deprivation:							
One criterion	427	21.8	5.6	28.0	92.3	72.6	45.2
Two or more criteria	427	7.5	24.1	68.0	63.2	63.5	41.0
Neighbourhood crime (Newcastle Social Service 1979)[2]	388	33.0	10.8	64.4	83.5	56.2	29.1
Other Studies							
Truancy (Robins and Hill, 1966)	296	10.8	28.0	57.9	62.2	61.1	26.2
Aggressiveness (Mulligan *et al.*, 1963)	2063	5.8	9.2	31.0	90.0	85.0	21.5
Teacher ratings (Wadsworth, 1979)	1798	9.9	14.6	27.4	83.1	75.5	11.2
Attitude to schoolwork (Farrington, 1979)	409	12.0	14.7	38.8	81.8	73.3	21.1
Troublesome (peer and teacher) (Farrington and West, 1971)	373	6.2	19.0	43.9	78.6	74.8	26.4

Notes: 1. RIOC = relative improvement over chance.
　　　　2. Newcastle calculations assume zero attrition.

294

Table 16.2 Data from '1,000 Family Study'

	'n'	False Negative	False Positive	Sensitivity	Specificity	Overall Agreement	RIOC
Family Factors							
3+ children	427	10.3	22.9	45.3	79.1	66.6	39.2
Contact of family with school	303	10.2	19.0	57.0	84.1	70.7	46.3
Secondary School							
Score at 11-plus (dull = 90 or less)	356	16.6	13.2	49.6	80.3	70.2	33.5
Arithmetic quotient (100 or below)	358	9.8	15.1	59.3	80.0	74.6	43.1
Class ratings (bottom 20 per cent)	319	10.9	19.7	47.8	75.0	69.3	25.5
Poor reliability in class	317	24.0	10.1	45.7	81.9	66.0	29.9
Poor concentration/persistence	315	16.2	16.5	46.3	76.4	67.7	22.3
At 15 Years							
Poor attendance	299	16.4	12.0	49.5	82.2	71.6	36.3
Poor attitude to schoolwork	310	6.5	17.7	63.6	78.4	75.8	48.8

teachers and 56 per cent considered maladjusted. The insensitivity of these professional judgements is in line with reports from other research.

Neighbourhood factors and offending

So far we have described the relationship of intrafamilial influences and school assessments to offending. The literature has also underlined the effect of school and neighbourhood influences on behaviour (Power *et al.*, 1972; Gath *et al.*, 1977; Rutter *et al.*, 1979). We therefore looked for evidence in our study of any correlation between neighbourhood influences and offending.

Neighbourhood influences (Chapter 13) were then correlated with offending, and were highly significant for boys but not girls (Table 16.3). Yet, despite the high significance, the correlations were all low, the highest being with neighbourhood affluence, unemployment, adult drunkenness and crime. Similar results were obtained by chi square analysis.

Table 16.3   Correlation of neighbourhood factors and offending

	Male n=388		Female n=384	
	'r'	p	'r'	p
Neighbourhood affluence	0.19	< .001	0.12	< .01
Adult male unemployment	0.21	< .001	—	NS
Adult female unemployment	0.21	< .001	—	NS
Free school meals	0.18	< .001	—	NS
Adult crime	0.16	< .001	—	NS
Adult drunkenness	0.17	< .001	0.15	< .01
Families of concern to local authority	0.16	< .001	—	NS

Single-factor prediction in relation to sub-populations

So far we had studied single measures as predictors for the

males in our study. The next question was the ability of such measures to predict criminality within the various degrees of deprivation in our families. Table 16.4 shows that the 'percentage correct' prediction of delinquency differed for each of the three sub-populations, supporting the hypothesis that predictor measures are variably efficient for different populations. For instance, dull intelligence, as represented by an IQ of 90 or less gave rise to a 77 per cent correct prediction in the non-deprived group, but only 61 per cent for the group in which there was some deprivation; whereas the criterion of three or more children in the family was similar for each of the three populations. For other predictor measures the most efficient level for one population differed from that for another.

Table 16.4 Single-factor prediction: percentage correct in relation to different sub-populations

	Non-Deprived % Correct	1 or 2 Criteria % Correct	3 or more Criteria % Correct
3+ children in family	67	62	65
Accidents by 5 yrs (2+)	69	52	61
(1+)	54	45	67
IQ at 11+ (dull < 90)	77	61	65
Arithmetic quotient at 11+	80	65	69
Reliability	67	61	64
Poor response in class	79	64	51
Poor concentration/ persistence	74	69	53

Two-factor prediction: simple analysis —
stress and protection
This is an extension of the previous theme with the population classified by two explanatory variables allowing a view of their joint influence. To do this, adult males were grouped into the three categories of deprivation in their family of origin. A series of complementary variables were then considered in sequence as derived from Tables 15.1–15.4

(pp. 283, 284 and 286). The usefulness of this method can be seen in relation to family size — where offending became more common as the number of children in the family increases and the degree of deprivation becomes more severe. There was therefore a considerable contrast between men coming from small non-deprived families and from large families with multiple deprivation, for only 17 per cent (36 of 214) from the former compared with 70 per cent (23 of 33) from the latter category became offenders. Nevertheless, in families with four or more children, prediction was only marginally better in multiply deprived families (70 per cent) when compared to the deprived (63 per cent).

Another potential predictor of offending consists of accidents in the first five years of life. Again, if the two extreme groups are compared, a combination of predictors is more efficient than a single predictor. From non-deprived families with three or more accidents, only 21 per cent of men became offenders, whereas from multiply deprived families 82 per cent did so. Accidents appeared to have a different predictive significance in non-deprived families and in deprived families.

A similar picture occurred with height at the age of three. Only 9 per cent (9 of 96) of the tall boys coming from a non-deprived background became delinquent as against 69 per cent of the short boys coming from multiply deprived families. While non-deprivation is protective in respect of poor growth, the reverse is not true. A similar explanation can be advanced for the distinction between poor growth in children from non-deprived homes compared to deprived ones. In the latter, poor physical growth may, in addition to a familial predisposition to short stature, have a basis in poor nutrition or psychological stunting, or both. It is for this reason that poor growth may be efficient as a joint predictor. We need better explanations of such associations, and suggest that those influences which were additional to deprivation represented other components of social and economic stress within the family. Less than average growth probably reflected both adverse social factors and poor nutrition. Fortunately, log–linear analysis allowed us to ascertain the independent contribution of each of these factors.

We also examined a series of personality/temperamental, intellectual, and educational achievement factors gathered when the children were 11 years of age. The combination of reliability in class and degree of deprivation appeared moderately efficient. Similar patterns were found with initiative and concentration/persistence, each in combination with family deprivation.

Intelligence at 11 years was a strong predictor, but absence of deprivation was not strongly protective in the face of poor intelligence. Good arithmetical ability at the 11-plus examination was also strongly protective against deprivation and interacted strongly with deprivation so that no deprivation and multiple deprivation had rates of 15 per cent (21 of 139) and 69 per cent (24 of 35) respectively. In other words, from a group of boys with an IQ exceeding 100 and no family deprivation, less than one in six were likely to offend, compared to seven out of ten of those with an IQ below 100 and from a deprived home.

Similarly, attitude to schoolwork and school attendance at the age of 15 appeared moderate predictors of offending in the non-deprived group and strong predictors in the multiply deprived group. However, these ratings were made after some of the individuals had already committed offences. Self-confidence proved a poor predictor. Neighbourhood influences combined with family deprivation were moderate predictors of offending. Nevertheless the data suggest that neighbourhood factors increase vulnerability to delinquency, irrespective of home circumstance. Thus 76 (37 per cent) of 204 males coming from neighbourhoods with the highest level of crime became offenders and of the 181 who came from deprived families in the same neighbourhood, 81 (45 per cent) became offenders. These data suggest that, in adolescence, the locality of residence was almost as effective in predicting delinquency as was family deprivation. But there was also interaction between high level of neighbourhood crime and family deprivation and, where they coexisted, 50 per cent of the youths became offenders, whereas without either only 14 per cent did so. Nevertheless, this was little better than using deprivation alone as a screen measure for, although the deprived families included fewer than 50 per cent of the male adolescent population, about 45 per cent of them became offenders.

Two-factor prediction: log–linear analysis

So far we have studied the effects of two explanatory variables by examining their percentage distribution when presented in tabular form. However, it is useful also to obtain information about the relative importance of these explanatory variables. For this we used log–linear analysis, treating deprivation as an explanatory variable.

The findings are presented in Table 16.5. Irrespective of

Table 16.5   Two factor prediction of male offending in Generation II

		Log–Linear Analysis		
	Explanatory Variables	df	G2	Significance
(n=427)	Deprivation in Generation I	1	17.54	p < .01
	Family size at 5 years	1	20.32	p < .01
	(interaction)	1	4.01	p < .05
(n=356)	Deprivation in Generation I	1	6.83	p < .01
	IQ at 11+ examination	2	7.66	p < .01
(n=356)	Deprivation in Generation I	1	6.48	p < .05
	Arithmetic at 11+ examination	2	36.89	p < .01
(n=315)	Deprivation in Generation I	1	13.23	p < .01
	Concentration/persistence	1	12.11	p < .01
(n=324)	Deprivation in Generation I	1	11.65	p < .01
	Sociability	1	1.40	NS
(n=310)	Deprivation in Generation I	1	10.30	p < .01
	Attitude to schoolwork	2	36.03	p < .01
(n=310)	Deprivation in Generation I	1	17.87	p < .01
	Self-confidence	2	6.25	p < .05
(n=321)	Deprivation in Generation I	1	15.31	p < .01
	Reliable behaviour in class	1	10.12	p < .01
(n=298)	Deprivation in Generation I	1	7.66	p < .01
	School attendance at 15	2	30.48	p < .01
(n=388)	Deprivation in Generation I	1	12.88	p < .01
	Neighbourhood affluence	1	25.43	p < .01
(n=388)	Deprivation in Generation I	1	27.40	p < .01
	Neighbourhood male unemploy-			
	ment	1	6.14	p < .05
(n=388)	Deprivation in Generation I	1	29.27	p < .01
	Neighbourhood adult crime	1	5.48	p < .05

Note: Interaction significant in one analysis only.

which other explanatory variable was used, family deprivation always had a significant effect. Family size too had a highly significant effect, but variables representing accidents and growth did not: their effects were probably absorbed by family deprivation or its associations. Intelligence and scholastic achievements had significant effects ($p < .01$). Of the variables representing behaviour or temperament in the classroom at the age of 11, only reliable behaviour in the classroom and the composite variable of concentration/persistence proved to have significant effects, both at a very significant level. Self-confidence proved significant but at a lower level ($p < .05$). Both attitude to schoolwork and school attendance measured at 15 years had significant effects. A number of the indices of neighbourhood influence exerted significant effects — namely, both male ($p < .05$) unemployment, and neighbourhood affluence ($p < .01$). Surprisingly, neighbourhood adult crime exerted only a moderate independent effect ($p < .05$).

Models using multiple explanatory variables
These analyses allowed us to highlight the most important items in a defined set of explanatory variables. Two types of analysis were undertaken: multiple regression analysis to identify the best predictors; and discriminant function analysis which allows a maximum discrimination between offenders and non-offenders. In the former, a crucial finding was that the single variable of poor quality of care and mothering made a significant contribution to the prediction of offending up to the age of 33. No other family variable, including social status and neighbourhood influence, did so. On the other hand, the summed deprivation index was a good predictor and so too was family size.

Juvenile delinquency, some temperamental factors and intelligence have been implicated as good predictors of later criminality and they were included in a further multiple regression analysis. They made a strong contribution with the total prediction set accounting for almost 43 per cent of the variance.

Discriminant function analysis correctly identified as criminal or non-criminal between 71 and 77 per cent of the males (Table 16.6). However, when juvenile delinquency was included as a predictor, further analysis correctly identified

Table 16.6   Discriminant function analyses

	Correct as Criminal		Correct as Non-Criminal		Overall Accuracy		Improvement over Chance
	n	%	n	%	n	%	%
Set 1	86	72	196	77	282	75.2	20.5
Set 2	86	73	196	76	282	74.8	20.5
Set 3	96	63	230	75	326	71.5	16.0
Set 4	86	72	196	79	282	76.6	21.3

between 82 and 84 per cent of the males. Despite these impressive statistics the false positive rates remained extremely high so that a large proportion of the male population would need to be screened to identify merely two-thirds of the eventual delinquents. When environmental factors relating to neighbourhood or family were included as predictors in multiple regression analysis, they accounted for only a small proportion of the variance of offending. However, when measures from home and school and others such as individual differences of ability, achievement and temperament were added, a powerful prediction of criminality was obtained. This could be improved by including a measure of previous juvenile delinquency. The explanation would seem to be that predictors of the same broad type and source, such as occupational class and deprivation, may well be correlated and therefore tend to predict the same group of individuals who eventually become offenders. Ideally, predictors in multiple regression analysis should not be highly correlated in order that addition of each new predictor may add to the group of individuals at risk (Loeber and Dishion, 1983).

Parental occupational status, while a reasonable predictor on its own, did not prove to be a powerful influence within a set of explanatory variables. This was not unexpected, since previous workers have shown that occupational status is a poor predictor of recidivism in large and less selected populations (Wolfgang *et al.*, 1972). Both good parental care (McCord, 1979) and family size were important predictors. Intactness of the family did not make a substantial contribution.

Family factors appeared to vary in their influence in relation to offences occurring at different stages of development. The one powerful influence over the full period of risk, from adolescence to adulthood, was the summed index of poor care of the child and poor mothering and re-analysis of the data relating to offences before 15 years of age showed marital instability and parental ill-health were important.

Our school data indicated that a low level of measured intelligence and particularly underachievement in arithmetic were powerful predictors of offending. These predictor measures were gathered in the final year of junior school or the 11-plus examination prior to the onset of offending. Nevertheless, we do not know the youngest age at which poor educational performance becomes a stable predictor.

We did not have data on criminality of parents of the Red Spots but we did have a rating of adult neighbourhood delinquency, and found it did not make a significant contribution. Finally, we concluded that measures of parenting skills were the most important predictors of criminality.

Ideally, measures of prediction should be collected prior to any offending and in most of our analyses we used data collected up to the end of the junior school at 11 years, and the family predictors used were based on information gathered during the first five years of the child's life. We have argued that the neighbourhood influences were comparatively stable over the decades and therefore have depended on information collected in early adulthood but referred to a period 10 years earlier. Yet neighbourhood influences were of doubtful utility despite being impressive as a group predictor. We assume their influence was absorbed by other explanatory measures.

Discussion
This section contains three parts: on epidemiological considerations, on protective factors in high-risk backgrounds, and on prediction. The findings in each section have implications for the others.

Epidemiological considerations

Longitudinal research into criminality
This study, being longitudinal, has a number of disadvantages.

It was not possible to study the relative increase in female delinquency over the past 25 years which has altered the sex ratio within the total (Rutter and Giller, 1983). The longer the period covered in a cohort study the greater the chance that results will reflect temporal changes imposing their elements on analysis and interpretation. Rutter (1979) pointed to some of the difficulties. For example, alterations in law may entail certain behaviour moving into or out of the ambit of criminal law; criminal statistics can be affected by the level of police activity; police treatment of offenders does not remain constant; and the opportunity to commit crime is affected by social phenomena such as the increase in the number of self-service stores and motor vehicles. On the other hand, as the population of Red Spots was an age-cohort, both the criminal and non-criminal were simultaneously exposed to the changes in society, particularly the increase in frequency of criminal acts and the variations in police processing of delinquent acts which have occurred in the past 30 years.

Criminal records as a data source

In studying delinquency, it is axiomatic that a truer measure of delinquency will be obtained by relatively contemporaneous interviews than by a study of official records. Official records underrepresent the true extent of criminal behaviour. Self-report surveys show that less than 15 per cent of criminal acts result in police contact (West and Farrington, 1977). Even when the police contact is made, the processing of the individual concerned may well vary according to age, sex, race and previous record (Landau, 1981). Official record studies fail to recognize the offence or conviction as merely one facet of a delinquent lifestyle. For example, the Cambridge study showed official delinquents at 18 to be almost uniformly at the socially deviant end of a spectrum with an excess of alcohol problems, driving offences, sexual experience, unemployment, poor family relationships and anti-establishment attitudes (Farrington, 1979). It must also be remembered that, although the majority of young people may have committed delinquent acts, only a small minority enter the criminal records (Rutter and Giller, 1983).

Our work was confined to the use of criminal records to

establish the incidence and types of juvenile and adult indictable offences but we have confirmed that, in over 90 per cent of cases, we were dealing with the most delinquent and serious criminal acts committed by the cohort during the years from 1957–81.

While there is much criminal behaviour which cannot be identified by surveys of criminal records, on the positive side, our method was free from the distortions which can occur in studies relying on self-reports where there is a tendency to high rates of non-response in delinquent populations (Rutter and Giller, 1983).

Prevalence rates
A strength of the Newcastle research is that it comprised an entire birth cohort for the city with delinquency data collected until the individuals were 33 years of age. It therefore provided a good estimate of the prevalence of offending individuals from childhood to the age of 33 years — a period covering the main period of risk for new offences.

Three-quarters of the 83 individuals charged before 15 years of age went on to commit further offences afterwards. A further 66 offended for the first time after age 15, making 149 in all from a population of 847. Rates of offending are shown in Table 14.3 (p. 273). At all ages most offences were committed by males and by the age of 33, 31 per cent of men had been charged, but only 6 per cent of women.

These local rates, despite differences of definition and inclusion criteria, approximated closely to the national prevalence rates for both males (31 per cent), and females (6 per cent), born in 1953. The national statistics took into account only convictions included on the Home Office standard list which excludes less serious motoring offences, drunkenness, prostitution, and police cautions.

To date, the best measure of juvenile criminality within one cohort is the Cambridge team's study of 411 boys aged eight to nine years taken from six state primary schools in a working-class area of London in 1961–62. One in five of the group had been convicted as juveniles, and nearly one in three by 24 years of age (West, 1982). Farrington (1981) estimated lifetime prevalence by using official statistics based on a random sample showing estimated numbers of first convictions in each age group. He simply added the first-time conviction rate at each age and concluded that about one-third to one-half of males acquire a criminal record during their lifetimes.

The rate in our cohort at 33 years fell rather short of Farrington's (1979, 1981) estimates at 24 years. One possible reason was that Farrington's conclusions were influenced by the working-class composition of the Cambridge cohort, whereas the Newcastle population derived from a cohort of all births in the city over a defined period. Further, the Newcastle research displayed the often reported relationship between occupational class of the family of origin and contact with the law.

For men, the proportions ranged from one in six from non-deprived families to more than six in 10 from families in multiple deprivation, and some forms of deprivation appeared more harmful than others. Thus the risks were about five in 10 where there was marital breakdown, parental illness, overcrowding or social dependency; and about six in 10, with defective cleanliness and poor quality of mothering suggesting that the quality of parental care is of fundamental importance.

The cardinal finding of the Newcastle research was the dramatic increase in the rates of delinquency and criminality in relation to the severity of deprivation in the family of origin. Some 60 per cent of men from high-risk deprived families had a criminal record by 32 years. For girls, the rates were very much lower. In both sexes, the ratio of offences in the multiply deprived was much greater than the non-deprived — four times so in men and seven times in women (Kolvin *et al.*, 1988a).

Lifetime trends

Our data demonstrated another aspect of lifetime trends. The mean number of convictions peaked at 16–17 to 18–19 years and thereafter slowly declined (see, again, Figure 14.1, p. 276). Also, the mean numbers of convictions were closely tied to the severity of deprivation in childhood. The more severe the deprivation, the earlier were offences committed, peaking in late adolescence with a higher mean number of subsequent convictions. A secondary peak occurred at approximately 28–29 years, but we do not know any national or local circumstances which can explain this. West and Farrington (1973 and 1977) also reported 14 years as a peak age for first conviction and 17 years as the peak for both numbers of convictions and individuals convicted.

These findings support the concept of a group of boys at high risk for criminality who commit their first offences while still at school. Almost eight in 10 of the Newcastle males offending before 15 years of age committed further offences after leaving school, while only one in six of non-offenders at 15 years were offenders by 33 years of age. This agrees with other prospective surveys showing that a substantial proportion of youths convicted as juveniles were charged again in adult life. In the Cambridge study, Farrington and West found 61 per cent of juvenile delinquents were again convicted as young adults and only 13 per cent of convicted adults had no juvenile convictions. In the St Louis Study, 60 per cent of juvenile delinquents had been arrested for subsequent non-traffic offences by 43 years of age (Robins, 1966) and, from Massachusetts, McCord (1978) reported that 79 per cent of 139 men convicted of offences in the juvenile court from 1933–51 had again been convicted by 48 years of age.

In summary, not only are children from multiply deprived backgrounds at higher risk for later delinquency and criminality, but as a group are subject to many more convictions. It is not only that more of them are criminal, but they commit many more criminal acts. Nevertheless, in adult life there is a marked fall in the frequency of criminal behaviour and we can conclude that most juvenile delinquents do not become persistent offenders. In addition, few individuals commit their first offences in their twenties.

Types of offences (based on criminal data for males)
All types of offences, particularly theft, increased with the severity of deprivation, but we did not find any association between the type of offence and the nature of deprivation.

Previous research had demonstrated relatively high rates of adverse early life experience in the backgrounds of delinquents but, for men, the rates were low, running from 18–34 per cent for the different types of deprivation. In women, the rates were higher running from 29 to 50 per cent. Thus, while delinquency was a less frequent occurrence in females, where it did occur deprivation appeared to have had a potent influence.

While marital instability and parental illness were relatively commonly associated with offences before 15 years of age, in adult life this was uncommon. Poor care of the child and home and poor mothering appeared to have had similar associations with offences before and after 15. In addition, social dependency and overcrowding were important in relation to offences, but more so before than after 15 years.

Finally, while half the deprived and the majority of the multiply deprived men later committed offences a much smaller proportion (18–34 per cent) had experienced early life deprivation.

Family mechanisms

All of the criteria of deprivation had significant correlations with criminality. There was a strong relationship between delinquency and the mother's poor care of the home and child during the early years of life. Poor physical and domestic care of the child and home implies poor appreciation of the need for good parenting in the child's early years, and an inability to organize, plan or make wise provision for the future. In such circumstances, these mothers, or parents, fail to provide guidance, direction and supervision and are poor role models for their children. The two deprivations – poor quality of parenting and poor care of the home and children – appear to have had a much closer relationship with offending than did marital discord or family breakdown. Nevertheless, it is likely that they act both separately and together causing an atmosphere of family stress and disorganization and, to the child, a sense of lack of personal restraints (West and Farrington, 1973). It is tempting to suggest that these are the processes which lead to criminality. The work of McCord (1979) related child-rearing antecedents to criminal behaviour in middle age and demonstrated a significant link between home atmosphere in early life and adult criminality.

Significant predictors, considered to be direct measures of child-rearing, were parental conflict, supervision and mother's affection. Measures which reflected parental characteristics were parental aggressiveness, parental deviance and mother's self-confidence. All these proved to be significant predictors of either crimes against property or against persons, or both. Surprisingly, absence of the father failed to distinguish non-criminals from criminals, and elsewhere McCord (1982) commented that the focus should be turned from quantity of parenting to quality of parenting. However, the results of that important research were qualified by the nature of the families studied: all were reared in congested urban areas in the USA during the 1930s and 1940s. Nonetheless, it reinforced the view that family atmosphere during childhood has an important impact on subsequent behaviour. The Newcastle work, less subject to the limitations admitted by McCord, also suggests links between the quality of care and mothering and later criminality.

In our study the rate of male criminality in families dependent on the social services was at least three times higher than in non-deprived families. Nevertheless, it was lower than in families with poor quality of parenting and care of the home and children. Since, however, these criteria of deprivation were significantly correlated with each other it was not easy to estimate the independent or relative contribution of each. Again, an association with criminality proved stronger for deprivation than for occupational status of the parents, supporting the possibility that criminality has its origins in family deprivation and dysfunction (Rutter and Giller, 1983).

We demonstrated the usual ecological correlation between neighbourhood variables and offender rates, the latter ranging from one in six males in the more affluent areas to one in three in the poorest. Overcrowding in 1952 was also linked with a significantly higher rate of criminality in youths. We can advance all the usual explanations in terms of the social meaning of such circumstances to the inhabitants of a disadvantaged neighbourhood: lack of personal control over the social environment; lack of privacy; lack of a sense of safety (Rutter and Giller, 1983). However, it is important to remember that overcrowding does not often occur in isolation from other indices of deprivation and poor social and economic circumstances — such as poor care of the youth and the home, and social dependence — and these are likely to act in concert to produce their effects.

Another question was the significance of family size; 17 per cent of male offenders came from families with six or more children in contrast to 3 per cent of non-delinquents. These rates are lower than those in the Cambridge study suggesting a lower correlation of family size with delinquency when the data derive from a representative population. But it does not detract from the close relationship of criminality with large families and the latter with deprivation and circumstances in which children do not receive adequate care.

Parental factors: criminality and personality
While we did not have data on criminality in the parents of Red Spots we did have information about major trends of parental personality based on judgements reached over 15 years (Miller *et al.*, 1974). Table 14.6 (p. 279) shows the importance of the father's personality characteristics in relation to the son's criminality and suggests that children of ineffective parents are at high risk.

Conclusion
We have assessed the relationship between social and family variables and offences against the law. The study was not designed to look at those influences currently the object of interest of modern criminological research such as differences of intake of troublesome boys into secondary schools, perceptions of consequences of offending, situational factors and possible peer group influences (Roff *et al.*, 1972; Gath *et al.*, 1977; Rutter *et al.*, 1979). Even though those factors are likely to be more common in the presence of adverse social and family circumstances, the operative mechanisms remain unclear. Perhaps adverse social and family influences and parental attitudes make boys more vulnerable to current environmental factors; the effects of family influences may be mediated through individual characteristics in the boys, or there may be interactions between all these factors but in different combinations in individual delinquents.

Mechanisms and processes
In recent years there has been a steady accumulation of information showing how undesirable life experiences may influence development and behaviour. Bowlby's (1951) emphasis on the affectional components of mothering gave impetus to such research, but he overestimated both the universality and irreversibility of the psychological

consequences (Rutter, 1981a, 1985). From the viewpoint of our study, the most salient conclusion from recent investigations is that different undesirable experiences have different risk potentials in influencing cognitive and behavioural development (Rutter, 1985a) and that individuals vary in their degree of resilience to environmental experiences (Rutter 1985b).

Stress and protective factors
We have tried to establish stress factors associated with offences by the non-deprived and protective factors in deprived and multiply deprived non-offenders. Deprivation in our population was widespread, but deprivation in itself, while correlating highly with delinquency, was not a sufficient condition for its development. Other factors within the care-giving environment, and in the children themselves, appeared capable of modifying the influence of deprivation as defined.

The other influences have been categorized according to the three main periods in which the data were collected — roughly the pre-school years, the primary school and pre-adolescent years and, finally, the adolescent school years. This allows pinpointing of factors associated with vulnerability in the non-deprived and resilience in the face of major deprivation.

Summary of the findings
Important stress and protective factors are emphasized to provide an overview of the nature of vulnerability and resilience in childhood.

In the first five years the *resilient*, despite a background of some deprivation, were characterized by having good parental care, more positive social circumstances, and less adverse physical circumstances in the perinatal period and early childhood. The *vulnerable*, despite a background without deprivation as we defined it, were characterized by the experience of stressful social circumstances and their mothers' relative youth at marriage.

In the pre-adolescent period, the *resilient* were characterized by five different kinds of protective factors: a care-giving environment permitting good supervision of children; the absence of developmental delays; relatively good intellectual development and educational achievements; positive temperamental qualities; and positive responses from peers and social activities such as membership of a youth club. The features which characterize the *vulnerable* relate to the children themselves: their level of intelligence and achievement, temperament, behaviour and their attitudes, rather than to aspects of their care-giving environment.

In adolescence, some of the factors associated with *resilience* were similar to those found in pre-adolescence: good intellectual development, scholastic progress and positive school qualities. In this period we should question the validity of the concepts of stress and protection as delinquency had already occurred in the majority of cases. Nevertheless the pattern of factors identified in adolescence was similar to that in pre-adolescence and it is not unreasonable to suppose that many were merely continuations of earlier protective influences. In addition, there were two important parental and family factors: family contact with the school and, in girls, the continuous presence of the natural father.

The factors associated with *vulnerability* were again similar to those in pre-adolescence, but there were three additional family and parental factors: the family which showed little interest in maintaining contact with the school; the youth who did not participate in family activities; and the mother and father who lacked effective personalities.

The factors uncovered

We now consider the nature and the mechanisms of the factors referred to above. Are they responsible for, or merely associated with, resilience in the face of deprivation and vulnerability against a background of 'non-deprivation'? And how reliable are they as predictors?

Peer influences   It is often argued that delinquent activities may reflect the example set by friends of the potential delinquent. We examined the converse proposition that positive peer influences are associated with a decreased risk of delinquency in high-risk children. Taking the deprived group at 10 years of age we found that, while only 33 per cent of youth club members became delinquent, 54 per cent of non-members did so. Viewed retrospectively, only 55 per cent of delinquents as against 75 per cent of non-delinquents had been youth club members at 10 years of age. While it is difficult to disentangle cause and effect, this may be regarded as the resilience-conferring effect of youth club membership, on the basis that potentially delinquent youths choose delinquent friends whereas non-delinquent youths seek more approved forms of recreation provided in the youth club setting. Nevertheless, our findings do support the suggestion that beneficial social influences were associated with a measure of protection from delinquency even in high-risk children.

Family factors   Long before children reach the age of criminal responsibility, data obtained from the home environment can be used to forecast later delinquency as effectively as other predictors. For example, we found that 71 per cent of deprived children receiving poor maternal and domestic care before five years of age became delinquent, whereas good care was a powerful protector since only 39 per cent of recipients subsequently entered the criminal records. Those figures differed only slightly when care was measured at age 10. In other words, good parenting protects against the acquisition of a criminal record. Good affectionate mothering is complementary to good care and supervision and it was not surprising that a similar pattern emerges. Research data often imply that the mechanism by which good care is translated into relatively good behaviour is simply that the caring parent has jurisdiction over the child's choice of friends and recreation but, given the early age at which the correlation emerges, the argument must be that good parental care and supervision is itself capable of giving rise to beneficial personal qualities (such as internal controls) that influence behaviour at a later stage. 'Good parenting' is by no means the only way of measuring a family's beneficial involvement in a child's development, and other family correlates of later delinquency were uncovered whose influence continued well into the children's teenage years. For example, data were collected on whether the family was interested in maintaining contact with the child's school, and when that was so at 15 years old the probability of later delinquency was substantially reduced for high-risk children from 57 per cent to 28 per cent.

Positive behavioural qualities of the father appeared to go some way towards reducing the detrimental effects of a deprived background. For high-risk 15-year-old children, to have an 'effective' father decreased the probability of delinquency from around one-half to one-third, whereas among low-risk youths an 'ineffective' father raised the probability from 11 per cent to 28 per cent. The same increased vulnerability was found in youths who did not share or participate in family activities.

Social factors
Social stresses appear to have been operative in low-risk families even before the children were five. These include greater density of the home territory; the family breadwinner having low occupational status; and the mother being under 19 years of age when first married. The effect of these stresses taken individually is significant rather than startling, but their combined effects may be more substantial. On the other hand, smaller households, older mothers and employed breadwinners had a protective influence.

Childhood accidents
The word 'accident' carries many shades of meaning: at one extreme it describes in neutral terms an occurrence that was not intended or has no perpetrator. But the term also encompasses what the law would term 'negligence', such as an occurrence occasioned wholly or in part by the carelessness — momentary or inherent — of its caretaker or by a lack of foresight on the part of the child's supervisors, reflecting generally ineffective care and control. Where there is no deprivation, accidents in the pre-school years do not appear to be stress factors. However, since in the deprived group a relative absence of accidents proved to be associated with resilience, it is reasonable to speculate that, in the multiply deprived group, accidents represent a combination of carelessness and ineffective care or perhaps even physical abuse.

School factors
Research has shown an association between dull intelligence and delinquency (Rutter and Giller, 1983), and our own data compiled from the results of the 11-plus examination bear

this out. In the high-risk, multiply deprived group, 43 per cent of those who did not become delinquent had IQs above 100 as against 10 per cent of those who did. Similarly, only 16 per cent of deprived children who acquired criminal records scored more than the population mean of 100 while 56 per cent of those without convictions did so. Only 18 per cent of the high-risk group with arithmetical ability above the mean became delinquent, whereas 58 per cent of those whose ability was less than the mean did so. Results for ability in English were similar but not so impressive. It seems reasonable that positive attitudes to school, educational attainment and conduct in class should go hand in hand, but it is also noteworthy that positive temperamental and behavioural qualities in the classroom are strongly associated with a reduced risk of delinquency, even among deprived and therefore vulnerable children. Only 17 per cent of those vulnerable children who were described as having good ability to concentrate in class at 10 years of age went on to acquire a criminal record, but of those whose concentration was poor, over 45 per cent became offenders. On the other hand, low intellectual ability and scholastic achievements, and poor temperamental and classroom attitudes in youths from non-deprived backgrounds, appeared to render them more vulnerable. The great majority of these data were collected before the emergence of delinquency in most of the boys and support the notion that the sense of stability and esteem derived from meritorious school performance persists as a protective factor into later life (Rutter and Giller, 1983). Alternatively, factors encouraging positive academic performance might in themselves be protective. The mechanisms are still far from clear. For example, can a distressing home atmosphere be counterbalanced by a fulfilling school career? May the teacher react favourably to the high-risk, yet intellectually able, child and elicit from him a positive identification with the teacher's own values? Because of the complexity of interaction, anecdotal explanations are probably as near to the mark as any.

Male-female differences

Only a few factors protected girls against delinquency with any degree of significance and these differed considerably from those for boys. Furthermore, at 15 years, protective factors were associated with a smaller decrease in the risk of delinquency in males than in females. In other words, not only were females less predisposed to delinquent acts, but also they had stronger shields to guard against the risk. At age five, the major protective factors in the deprived female group were: a father in skilled employment; a family not dependent on social welfare; an accident-free life; and a mother in good health. A girl with any one of these factors was between three and four times less likely to acquire a criminal record than one without those attributes.

By the tenth year the importance of parental care was evident in the case of both males and females; one in ten of deprived boys who did not become delinquent was experiencing poor parental supervision in contrast to one in four of those who did become so. Among girls, the continual presence of a natural father was an important factor. Good reliability in the classroom was protective for both boys and girls and good ability to socialize was protective for females but not for males. The numbers of protective factors were fewer for females than males.

At age 15, a greater number of protective factors emerged in females — some also being common to males — but, when present, the protective element was as great or greater than in males. These overlapping factors mostly concerned scholastic ability and interest, level of concentration, attitude to schoolwork, willingness to continue at school, and families' interest in maintaining contact with the school. By that time, however, the majority of delinquents had actually declared themselves in the criminal records so that the presence of adverse attitudes may merely reflect an already acquired delinquent predisposition.

Nevertheless, the same cannot always be said of certain other factors, peculiar to girls, that are reflections not of attitude but development. For example, good physical growth at age 13 is associated with only 8 per cent delinquency rate, whereas poor growth portended a 63 per cent rate; bedwetting at age five or beyond entailed a threefold increase in risk for later delinquency. Finally, more than half of the females who did not offend had fathers who were continually present during the child's pre-school and school years, compared with only one in five of offenders. Certainly the continued presence of the natural father appeared to be an important protective factor in females. Presumably the quality of fathering is also important (McCord, 1982).

Summary
We have explored stress factors associated with vulnerability to delinquency in youths coming from non-deprived backgrounds and 'protective' factors associated with resilience in the face of family and social deprivation. A range of both 'stress' and 'protective' factors was identified, and the mechanisms by which they produced their influences proved to be complex. In girls, we could study protective factors only.

In boys, important stress factors included social factors, ineffective personalities of mother and father, accidents in childhood, relatively poor intelligence and educational achievements, negative temperamental characteristics, and negative attitudes to school and authority. In addition, absence of family cohesion and lack of interest in the youth's school progress proved significant. Protective factors were the reverse of the above with the additions of: a caring home environment despite a background of deprivation; participation in socially approved forms of recreation; and evidence of good physical growth.

In girls, the number of identified protective factors were fewer, important ones being good maternal health and social independence of the family despite a background of general deprivation; good parental supervision; the continuous presence of the natural father; family interest in the girl's school progress; good temperamental qualities; good physical growth.

Prediction of criminality

Introduction
Our work on prediction was limited in two ways. First, we had no information about criminality in the parents of the Red Spot children so, as a substitute, we used an index of adult neighbourhood criminality. The second was the use of police contact as our criterion variable. It is well known that a significant percentage of youth offences remain undetected, and we did not seek self-report data. But we

believe that our data, based on records of offending, included the most delinquent of the criminals in the local community.

Simple predictor factors
Prediction using simple factors revealed that these were efficient in different ways, some showing high specificity but low sensitivity, examples being three or more criteria of deprivation and three or more children in the family. None showed high sensitivity. School, rather than family, measures were the most efficient predictors of subsequent criminality.

We noted that the most efficient predictor for one population — for example, non-deprived families — may differ from that for others — such as multiply deprived families. For instance, two or more reported accidents by the age of five was a relatively efficient predictor only in the non-deprived; but one or more was the case in the multiply deprived. Similar contrast existed in the case of the measure of concentration/persistence and also the measure of sociability at school. These are excellent reasons for not using the same level of a particular measure (or even the same measures) when predicting delinquency in deprived inner city areas and non-deprived outer city neighbourhoods.

Two-factor prediction
Here we tried to obtain a view of the joint influence of two explanatory variables. This proved important for while, on the one hand, there was an evident trend for offending to become more common as the number of children in the family increased, on the other hand it seemed that small family size tended to protect boys from offending despite the presence of deprivation. In the same way accidents had a different significance in non-deprived and in deprived families. There were many other examples illustrating that there were complex relationships between the predictors studied and later offending. For certain pairings both predictors appeared important and efficient; however, some predictors seemed to function with differentiating efficiency only in the non-deprived group while others did so in the multiply deprived group. Nevertheless some combinations of predictors proved powerful in the sense that positive circumstances for both gave low rates of offending in the group concerned; and negative circumstances for both were

associated with high rates of offending. Those in which combinations of positive and also negative circumstances were powerfully predictive consist of the combination of the factor of deprivation and the following: number of children in the family; response in class; reliability; intelligence at age 11; and arithmetical ability at age 11.

Multivariate analysis: some comments

In the 1950s much was promised from sophisticated methods of predicting delinquency (Glueck and Glueck, 1950, 1959), but later there was disappointment. Much of their data was gathered retrospectively, and subsequent attempts to use their index have shown a poor predictive performance (Dootjes, 1972). However, recent work suggests that the multiple regression techniques give, if anything, worse prediction than the simpler Glueck methods (Farrington, 1985). However, the relative inefficiency of delinquency prediction may have less to do with statistical technique and more to do with the relevance of the explanatory variables selected. In this respect, our work was limited in two ways: first, by the absence of information about parental criminality (we tried to substitute for this by using an index of adult criminality in the neighbourhood rather than differences between families); second, by the use of police contact as our criterion variable, because of the low detection rate of youth offences.

Our data did, however, yield some important facts:

1 The only variable representing family atmosphere which made a significant contribution to prediction of criminality was poor child care and mothering. Marital disruption, parental illness, factors representing adverse social family circumstances, parental personality, mother's age at marriage, occupational status and neighbourhood influence all failed to make any contribution.
2 The deprivation index – the summed score of criteria – was a good predictor as too was family size, which probably directly reflects home circumstances.
3 While individual differences between children, such as measured intelligence and achievements and classroom temperament, made important contributions, classroom behaviour did not appear to do so.

Finally, we used four sets of predictors and found, irrespective of the size of the sample studied or the variation of the predictive measures contained in the set or their number, that those which proved to be significant did so across all the above circumstances. Using the same four sets of predictors in discriminant function analysis we found they correctly identified as criminal or non-criminal between 71–77 per cent of the males, between 63–73 per cent of the criminal and between 75–79 per cent of the non-criminal. This constituted a 16–21 per cent improvement over random predictions.

The literature suggests that juvenile delinquency is one of the best predictors of later criminality and it was therefore used as a predictor to two further sets of predictions. The first set included the summed deprivation score and reliability in the classroom at 11 years; the second set included all six deprivation criteria (the two child care criteria were combined) and concentration/persistence in the classroom instead of reliability. The other predictive variables were occupational class, family size, mother's age, IQ at the 11-plus examination, neighbourhood crime and parental personalities.

In the multiple regression analysis the first predictor set accounted for 33 per cent of the variance and the second 34 per cent. On both occasions, juvenile delinquency proved to be the most powerful predictor. Furthermore, using discriminant function analysis, 84 per cent and 83 per cent respectively of the youths were correctly classified as criminal or non-criminal. We also analysed juvenile delinquency committed before school-leaving, but this proved less well predicted. Perhaps one important difference was that, when the separate criteria of deprivation were included in the prediction set rather than the summed deprivation score, the predictors of criminality were different. While marital disruption, parental illness and parental ineffectiveness were significant predictors of offences committed during the school years, the 'poor mothering' index was a significant predictor of criminality after the age of 15 years.

McCord (1979) has addressed the question of whether or not home atmosphere during childhood has an effect upon personality development (Jessor and Jessor, 1977). Records collected during childhood, and coded prior to knowledge of adult behaviour, provided information about the family of origin and home circumstances of 200 men, and over 30 years information was collected from court records regarding their criminal behaviour. Multiple regression and discriminant function analysis indicated that six variables representing family atmosphere during childhood had important impact on subsequent behaviour. These were: parental supervision; mother's self-confidence; mother's affection; parental conflict; parental aggression; and father's deviance. Aggression, father's deviance and mother's self-confidence were considered to reflect parental characteristics, while the other three — parental conflict, supervision and mother's affection — were considered to be direct measures of child-rearing. Father's occupation and neighbourhood factors were also significantly related to criminality. In the prediction analysis, the effects of social status and parental characteristics were controlled to allow an evaluation of child-rearing practices. The prediction models accounted for between 36–39 per cent of the variance of which 24–26 per cent was contributed by the three direct measures of child-rearing. Subsequent discriminant function analysis, using the above six measures, correctly identified 74 per cent of the 200 men as criminal or non-criminal at any stage of their lives. The percentage correctly identified as criminal increased to 80 per cent when adult criminality alone was predicted. The importance of McCord's research is that, while home atmosphere was reliably related to criminal behaviour, parental absence failed to distinguish the criminal from the non-criminal. This contrasts with what had been reported in earlier work (Glueck and Glueck, 1950; Wadsworth, 1979). However, McCord's findings are limited in that all subjects were reared in congested inner city areas in the 1930s. The Newcastle measures did not account for such a great variance of criminal behaviour as did McCord's, and there could be several reasons for this. For example, hers was a more homogeneous inner city population, whereas ours was representative of the whole city. Furthermore, our study had no information about fathers' criminality.

PART VII
REVIEW AND
CONCLUSIONS

17 Perspectives, associations and statistics of deprivation

Historical perspectives

Brown and Madge (1982) identified a tradition of the documentation of poverty and deprivation in Britain. This was exemplified in the nineteenth century in the novels of Dickens and was followed by Rowntree's work on poverty in York in the first half of the twentieth century. However, in the years following the Second World War there was a change to the description of the needs of special problem groups. The 1970s and 1980s saw a resurgence of interest in poverty and other forms of deprivation. A major modern population study in which an attempt was made to address every facet of poverty was that of Townsend (1979) in *Poverty in the United Kingdom*. An account of multiple deprivation by Wedge and Prosser (1973), *Born to Fail?*, was based on data from the National Child Development Study. A different type of study by Coffield *et al.* (1981), concerning only four families, provided a minutely detailed account of the impact, experiences and processes of deprivation.

In the 1970s, following Sir Keith Joseph's watershed speech, the DHSS–SSRC supported other studies. Their research contracts into transmitted deprivation furthered work from: Tonge *et al.* (1975) on problem families in Sheffield; Brown and Cousins (1979) on unemployment; Ashley (1981) on income and poverty; Ineichen and Millerson (1977) on housing; Mortimore and Blackstone (1982) on education; Rutter and Quinton (1985) on experiences of care; and Graham and Stevenson (1983) on patterns of child development.

The Newcastle study described here was also supported by the DHSS–SRCC and other sources. Its foundation was the data of a study of childhood lasting from 1947–62. Operational criteria of deprivation were established and the children studied were visited as adults. Essentially similar strategies were used by Wedge and Prosser (1973) and Graham and Stevenson (1983).

Our earlier data were archival, which raised inevitable problems. First, there was the discrepancy between the data one would have liked to collect and the data actually available about the previous generation, these being determined by earlier objectives, perceptions and decisions of research method (Elder, 1973). Second, the recognized disadvantages of a particular period, such as deprivation in the 1930s, may have differing impacts on offspring in the family depending on age and psychological maturity. For instance, in the Great Depression, Elder (1973) reported that adolescents were exposed to greater personal distress than younger children. Earlier Mannheim (1952) had shown that generation units tend to vary in their response to environmental conditions according to age, sex and occupational class. Further, adversity does not necessarily have a uniform impact, even on members within the same family.

Associations
This study has emphasized associations between a variety of deprivation experiences and intellectual and scholastic under-achievement, disturbed behaviour, health and growth. The greater the number of criteria of deprivation that coexist in the same family, the more powerful the association. However, not all of these are necessarily new findings; the literature abounds with such evidence (Brown and Madge, 1982).

One such association is between socioeconomic status and scholastic achievement (Davie *et al.*, 1972; Neligan *et al.*, 1976); a second is between educational failure and broken homes or atypical family circumstances (Davie *et al.*, 1972; Essen, 1979) — although Lambert and Streather (1980) argue that the mechanism is largely economic, and Mortimore and Blackstone (1982) that poor school performance reflects teacher expectations towards children from broken homes; a third is between broken homes and delinquency and psychiatric disorders.

Most studies indicate that poor housing circumstances and overcrowding are associated with poorer ability and scholastic attainment (Douglas, 1964; Davie *et al.*, 1972;

Rutter *et al.*, 1970) and with childhood aggression and impulsiveness (Murray, 1974), but the mechanisms remain obscure.

Another association exists between family deprivation and poor parental health (Wedge and Prosser, 1973). Findings from the '1,000 Family Study' showed that parental ill-health does not affect children's health, although general deprivation, whether or not associated with parental ill-health, appears to be an important factor in enuresis and convulsions occurring in the absence of infective illness (Miller *et al.*, 1974). A strong association has also been demonstrated between chronic ill-health in parents and maladjustment in children (Rutter, 1966). Similarly Miller *et al.* (1974) and Richman *et al.* (1982) have reported an association between psychiatric disorder of mothers' and children's disturbance. Interestingly Douglas *et al.* (1968) showed that poor health in working-class parents, while associated with a decline in children's school attendance, was not linked with a corresponding deterioration in their attainments.

Overview of methods

Starting from the working definitions discussed in Part II, we presented information concerning the nature and extent of deprivation in two generations in a cohort of children born in Newcastle upon Tyne in 1947. This permitted a descriptive account of the social and family factors associated with contemporary deprivation as we defined it. Nevertheless, the study of the social and psychological characteristics of the families gave a comprehensive picture extending far wider than the criteria of deprivation.

We have given an account of the associations of deprivation in terms of growth, intellectual progress, scholastic achievements and behaviour.

We then examined continuities in deprivation, being concerned with continuity in two forms: within the families of origin and between those and families of formation. Archival data allowed us to examine continuities within the family of origin based on ratings of deprivation available in 1952 and 1957. Comparisons across generations were made on data available for 1952 and data collected in 1980. The chapters on change (Part IV) provide information about families which became deprived and those which escaped from deprivation in the next generation.

The richness of the data and the wide variety of findings, particularly of differences between groups, have allowed us to theorize about processes and mechanisms which underpin the effects of deprivation and its continuities. More evidence came from the study of change within and across generations. Finally, multivariate analyses revealed many patterns of association of family and environmental influences and individual functioning (networks) enabling us to generate ideas about underlying mechanisms.

Part VI on criminal behaviour provided many ideas: about the processes associated with becoming criminal; about the factors which protect deprived individuals from delinquency; and about factors which increase vulnerability to delinquency in those without deprivation. We also explored various predictors of criminal behaviour at different stages of the families' life cycles.

The statistics of deprivation

Over the last three decades there has been a steady increase in the absolute numbers of single parents and a dramatic decline in the stigma associated with single parentage. The Newcastle rate for single parents in 1951 was 7 per cent (Miller *et al.*, 1960). The 1971 Census reported that, in England and Wales, the total of married couples with children was 6.4 million and that there were 110,000 single male parents and 510,000 single female parents. Thus by 1971 about 10 per cent of all families with children were headed by a single parent of whom one in six was male. By 1978 a third of all marriages were remarriages for one or both partners (OPCS, 1980).

Previous reports from the '1,000 Family Study' indicated widespread adverse living circumstances in Newcastle in the post-war era. Re-analysis revealed two out of every five households experiencing one or more criteria of deprivation; multiple deprivation was present in one in seven households in our cohort.

There have been various attempts to estimate the rate of 'problem families' in the population. Tonge *et al.* (1975) in Sheffield offered a figure of 1.7 families per thousand as likely to show long-term social dependence. However, this was a narrow and rigorous concept and, when wider definitions are employed, rates have proved higher. While a family with multiple deprivation may not be a 'problem family', it is reasonable to assume that a high proportion of the multiply deprived are likely to be so. The rates of multiple deprivation range from 6.6 per cent (Wedge and Prosser, 1973), 6.9 per cent (Stephenson and Graham, 1983) to 8.8 per cent (Berthoud, 1980). In Newcastle the rate, both in families of origin in 1952 and families of formation in 1980, was 14 per cent, these being successive generations of the same families. This is rather high and is likely to reflect the social and economic ills of the Northern industrial regions of the country.

Issues in research into deprivation

Description or measurement
There are a number of ways of perceiving deprivation. Some authors have sought methods of quantifying social and family experiences (Wedge and Prosser, 1973; Townsend, 1979; Graham and Stevenson, 1983), but mere statistics cannot easily convey the emotional impact of deprivation upon a family and, until the work of Coffield *et al.* (1981), few modern workers had returned to the use of descriptive techniques to convey the quality of depriving experiences (Brown and Madge, 1982).

It is true that the essence of individual family distress may be lost when using quantitative techniques but unless one can find ways of measuring such experience the value of systematic description, analysis and generalization is reduced.

Defining, measuring and describing deprivation
Deprivation may be viewed as a range of undesirable circumstances experienced by a country, a city, a neighbourhood, a family, or offspring of the family. It may be viewed politically as lack of freedom, socially in terms of poor quality housing, economically in terms of material deprivation, psychologically in terms of poor parenting, or educationally in terms of inadequate opportunity for learning (Brown and Madge, 1982).

The choice of the criteria of deprivation to be used determines one's sampling frame (Silburn, 1978). Lawrence (1977) focused on a deprived city; Coffield *et al.* (1981) on a defined geographical area; Ineichen and Millerson (1977) on low-status council housing estates; and Brown and Cousins (1979) on areas of high levels of unemployment. All were areas where deprivation was concentrated. By contrast, our Newcastle research started with an urban cohort of newborn infants and focused on deprived families within it.

Our starting-point was the family. We viewed deprivation as any circumstance which was considered socially or psychologically undesirable in itself for normal family life. We speculated how one or more deprivations in a family might impair its capacity to organize its finances, day-to-day activities and care of children, and also hinder career planning and the children's education.

The first question posed was whether to define deprivation widely or narrowly. A broad definition — say, any one of six criteria — might have identified too many families as deprived and would have therefore suffered from lack of contrast between the deprived and the remaining families. Too narrow a definition — say, three or more criteria coexisting in the same family — would lose the potential for painting a full canvas of the extent of deprivation in the community. Our final compromise was to aim at a broad picture but retain the possibility of viewing in detail the circumstances of families with grave deprivation.

Another question was whether to use qualitative or quantitative measures. Some argue that we should define deprivation in terms of quantitative extremes — for instance, viewing the bottom 5 per cent of any population on a specified criterion as 'deprived'. However, with relatively affluent neighbourhoods quantitative extremes become meaningless. Such criteria may have more utility in relation to a total population.

Since we had neither resources, nor often the data, for a qualitative approach, we opted for the quantitative method. We drew on basic concepts from the literature and sought ways of defining these operationally. We then explored the archives of the '1,000 Family Study' to see whether the concepts could be confirmed from the data from the families of origin. We were able to identify 14 different items of deprivation and, for practical convenience, we sought ways of combining these individual items into meaningful composites. Six main types of deprivation were identified:

1 marital disruption;
2 parental illness;
3 poor domestic care of the child and the home;
4 dependence on social services;
5 overcrowding;
6 poor mothering.

Principal component analysis revealed a single important general component of deprivation in the data from the family of origin, and we concluded that the criteria could properly be summated.

When the Red Spots were adult we explored our data from the 1979–80 interviews expecting to identify a greater range, but identified only one additional deprivation — educational handicap. Our criteria and rationale for their selection then were as follows:

(a) Poverty Newcastle was an appropriate city on which to base a study of deprivation in that visible criteria of poverty were readily available. They included serious debt, unemployment and family dependence on National Assistance, which we defined as dependency on the social or welfare services. It was unlikely that the stress consequent on poverty would be solely economic; there were likely to be reverberations in the emotional climate in the home, together with a lowering of the parents' sense of self-esteem and the general morale of the family.

(b) Housing A nationwide improvement in housing circumstances since the Second World War was reflected in Newcastle by widespread slum clearance and by major re-building programmes so significant that the criterion of overcrowding became relatively unimportant in relation to our indices of deprivation. Osborn and his colleagues (1984) calculated from the 1951 Census data that the proportion of households in Great Britain living in overcrowded conditions in the 1950s was three times as great as in the 1970s. Butler and Sloman (1980) estimated that the proportion of private rented housing declined from 45 per cent in 1950 to less than 16 per cent in 1975. Similarly, home ownership increased from 29 per cent in 1950 to 53 per cent in 1975. Improvement in council house provision, together with extension of

owner-occupation, led to reduction of low-income families in private rented housing.

(c)   Family and marital factors   We had important evidence of marital disruption in two generations — that is, in the families of five-year-olds in 1952 and again in their own families when they themselves were 33. Meanwhile there occurred changes in divorce legislation — first, the Divorce Law Reform Act (1969) and, second, the Matrimonial Causes Act (1970) — both of which facilitated the formal conclusion of marriage. However, divorce or breakdown in interpersonal relationships is not the only reason for family disruption. We also considered the loss of a parent by death and, by 1952, 6 per cent of fathers and 5 per cent of mothers had died. Interestingly, the death of a parent does not seem to produce sequelae as damaging as loss through divorce and separation (Rutter, 1966). By definition, marital disruption did not occur in non-deprived families but rose steeply to one in three of deprived and almost one in two of multiply deprived. Almost invariably, when the family was disrupted, one child remained with the mother, and single parenthood in our sample was almost exclusively a female phenomenon.

We also found that the age of parents at first marriage or cohabitation proved a sensitive indicator of deprivation. The average age of mothers at marriage was two years less than that of fathers in the non-deprived, but three years less in the multiply deprived, when viewed in terms of deprivation in the family of origin. In terms of the family of formation, the difference rose from 1.4 years in the non-deprived to five years in the multiply deprived. Mothers in the multiply deprived group married at under the age of 20 on average and were less likely to have their own home but more likely to have experienced a range of social and financial problems, some of which may be attributed to their personal immaturity. There was a degree of circularity in this finding, but it was evident that deprived children were likely to come from families where the parents had married young, had poorer social origins and were less well educated. Furthermore, multiply deprived parents had larger families; the average number of children in non-deprived families in the first generation was 2.2 rising to 4.3 in multiply deprived families. However, family size reduced considerably over the three decades and, in the second generation, the average number of children in the non-deprived families was 1.9, and in the multiply deprived group 2.7 (although these were not strictly comparable because of the restricted age range of the Red Spots). In both generations, larger family size was likely to coexist with poorer social and housing circumstances.

Marital instability, parental disagreements, rows, accusations and counter-accusations and anticipated, or actual, loss of a parent were likely to cause the child stress, anxiety and a sense of insecurity. If the family did split up, secondary social and economic stresses were inevitable. There might also be distortions of affection including withdrawal or overindulgence.

(d) *Parental illness*   In the family of origin we made no distinction between physical and psychological ill-health of parents; in the family of formation data on psychological ill-health were probably stronger than on physical data. Illness readily brings repercussions. When one or both parents are ill the child may feel insecure and possibly anticipate loss. The parents may not be able to provide as much care or affection as previously. Both economic and emotional family resources may become overstretched.

(e) *Quality of mothering*   The work of Bowlby (1951) led to the appreciation of the importance of maternal deprivation as a major factor affecting the personality and psychological stability of children. We defined maternal deprivation as poor care (both child and domestic) and inadequate quality of mothering. Poor domestic skills may reflect poor attention to immediate necessities and poor foresight and planning of the home circumstances. Mothers who lack foresight in running their homes and lives are likely to constitute poor models for their children.

(f) *Educational handicap*   Osborn *et al.* (1984) have shown that the social origins of parents markedly influenced the likelihood of entry into grammar school and achievements in examinations. The Newcastle data similarly demonstrated how family deprivation adversely influenced such events. Poor educational and vocational achievements proved so widespread in the families of formation that we

were forced to focus on the extremes of such circumstances in either partner as constituting a 'deprivation', and this was the basis of our operational definition of educational handicap or insufficiency. But this was not a totally new idea as Halsey and colleagues (1980) had already highlighted the predictive importance of positive educational experiences and, in particular, their potential for bringing about changes in society.

(g) Combinations of factors   In his speech to the Pre-School Playgroups Association, Sir Keith Joseph (1972) postulated four factors as both interactive and cumulative in relation to the so-called cycle of deprivation: economic conditions, living conditions, personal factors and child-rearing practices. Townsend (1971, 1974) criticized Sir Keith's thesis chiefly on the grounds that the family factors identified were too narrow and did not attend to wider social issues. This criticism appears rather harsh as they broadly coincide with five of the six main criteria we identified in Newcastle first-generation families (families of origin), and with four of the six in families in 1980 (families of formation). Additional criteria identified in Newcastle were family disruption and educational handicap.

Deprivation and social inequality
The work of Osborn and his colleagues (1984) concerned social inequality in Britain and the way this affected five-year-old children. They considered poverty in the formative years restricted functioning of all kinds and impeded the child's opportunity for reaching his or her full potential. They argued for a wider concept of social class than that based solely on the breadwinner's occupation and developed a social index comprising eight variables hypothesized as being an index of a common socioeconomic dimension. When these were weighted and summed they demonstrated a strong association with occupational status.

It was often asked whether our research method could have been markedly simplified by using the lowest occupational stratum to represent deprivation. There were theoretical and practical reasons for not doing this and these broadly overlap with those outlined by Osborn and Morris (1979). First 'only economically active members of society can be classified reliably' and housewives, the unemployed and retired may be classified only according to past occupations or indirectly. Second, poor quality of care of the home and children, parental illness and marital disruption occur in every stratum of society; third, while it was likely that families with multiple forms of deprivation would be located in the lower occupational strata, this would not necessarily hold for lesser degrees of deprivation. Examination of our data revealed that, while our deprivation index was significantly correlated with social class (r = .49) and while the semi-skilled and unskilled were most at risk for social problems or deprivation, children in a semi-skilled family were not necessarily deprived in a material or psychological sense. Thus concentration on families coming from the lowest occupational stratum would have prevented the painting of a wider and comprehensive picture of deprivation and its effects in an urban community. Nevertheless, our index was in some ways comparable with that of Osborn *et al.* as it took into consideration a range of adverse life experiences.

Neighbourhood factors
There has long been awareness of the concentration of deprivation in British inner city areas. Political recognition came with the development of the concept of Educational Priority Areas (Plowden Report, 1967) and the White Paper Policy for the Inner Cities (1977). This was followed by an appreciation of need to revitalize deteriorating inner city areas with an Urban Aid Programme and, over the last 15 years, by a burst of research into social and personal problems existing in inner areas of large British cities. The Department of the Environment reported in 1977 that one in seven live in exceptional concentrations of poverty and deprivation in inner city locations. All were reviewed by Brown and Madge (1982).

Absolute and relative poverty
in relation to deprivation
While there has been a general rise in prosperity in Western European society, not everyone has benefited equally from it, and it has thus been argued that poverty and deprivation must be defined in terms relative to needs according to the

era or culture under focus, rather than in absolute terms (Townsend, 1979). In contrast, Brown and Madge (1982) made the crucial distinction between poverty and inequality, the former alone being identified as a target for social action. Our emphasis was on empirical criteria rather than social concepts in contemporary society. These were defined in relation to the circumstances in which families lived, since we decided that mere inequality was insufficient to represent deprivation.

'Pure' rather than overlapping deprivation
In our 847 families there was evidence of a single criterion of deprivation in only 165 families. If the six criteria occurred with equal frequency in these families then each criterion would appear on its own on 27 occasions. But the spread was very uneven and so the numbers for certain criteria were considered insufficient for analysis. Furthermore, when we examined all the families showing a particular criterion and noted the associations and effects, few specific patterns emerged. The most evident effects were usually in relation to greater severity rather than to different types of deprivation.

The Plowden Report (1967) described multiple deprivation as 'the seamless web of circumstances'. Our data allowed us to add some precision to this so-called 'web' by specifying the links and patterns of overlap between different social and family adversities. For instance, we have been able to demonstrate a 50 per cent overlap between poor physical care of the child and poor mothering, a 25 per cent overlap between overcrowding and social dependence, but only a 15 per cent overlap between family and marital disruption and overcrowding. In addition, each criterion of deprivation correlated at a highly significant level with the total deprivation score, suggesting a powerful clustering and interlocking of the criteria. Coffield and his colleagues (1981) also emphasized the complex interconnections of deprivations in problem families and saw these as impeding movement out of deprivation. Wedge and Prosser (1973) in the National Child Development Study found a high overlap between such criteria in disadvantaged households. Berthoud (1980) also reported that problems tended to cluster together. In general, while multiple deprivation is commonly reported in the literature, it is only recently that the degree of overlap between different forms of deprivation has been calculated with some precision. Thus, deprivations in families tend to go together — some more than others — and the overlaps vary from sample to sample and are highly dependent on the criteria selected and their definitions. For these reasons we did not find the concept of 'pure' deprivation useful. It is not a common event, and findings related to it are mostly academic and likely to have little bearing on the real world of social and family adversity.

The interlocking nature of multiple deprivation

We had to answer the question of how to evaluate the impact of two or more criteria coexisting in the same family. Brown and Madge (1982) suggested that multiple deprivation as an experience is more than a mere collection of deprivation items. When deprivations are summed, the combination has more than just an additive effect. Like Coffield and his colleagues (1981) they argue that this complex interlocking nature of multiple deprivation is central to the real meaning of deprivation.

One of the crucial findings of our research was the range and potency of the interlock. Multiple deprivation had powerful effects on so many of the measures of performance covering growth, cognition, scholastic achievements and behaviour. By focusing on a population cohort rather than a highly selected sub-group of problem families known to the social services, our data gave perspective to the strength and continuities of the interlock. Nevertheless, our overall impression is that such interlocks appear more powerful and destructive in individual 'problem' families than in a population sample of multiply deprived families. Brown and Madge (1982) raised the spectre of vicious circles occurring within multiple deprivation — for example ill-health leading to unemployment which in turn may lead to poverty and in turn to ill-health. The course of such vicious circles is best studied by using a descriptive ethnographic design consisting of a detailed study of a handful of families as was undertaken by Coffield *et al.* (1981).

18 Summary findings based on comparison of groups

Social and family deprivation is not necessarily an enduring phenomenon. Nevertheless we have demonstrated that deprivation identified at one point in the family life cycle is commonly preceded by evidence of other forms of adverse family circumstances and social malfunction.

The notion of deprivation, as we have defined it, is supported by evidence derived from a wide range of features of family disorganization beyond the definitions we employed. In comparing deprived and non-deprived families of origin, the salient features included higher rates of unemployment, poorer occupational status and fewer opportunities for the full-time employment of mothers. The index children tended to be born into larger families showing increased evidence of marital problems. The sleeping arrangements were generally poor and the availability and quality of parenting often suspect. Mothers were rarely absent from their families but often showed poor competence and undesirable aspects of character. By contrast, more fathers were absent and, when present, were seldom judged to be competent and caring. All in all these parents showed poor interest in their children. Such features were often present throughout the pre-school and school years.

Families of formation with deprivation tended to remain within or near to Tyneside. Relatives could easily keep in touch, although poor relationships often existed. The women in deprived families married earlier than in the non-deprived, usually with less than two years' acquaintance with their partners and, by the time of our survey, a higher proportion of these marriages had been dissolved. Men had higher rates of unemployment while more women undertook part-time employment. Many adults lacked any educational or vocational achievements. Membership of clubs or social organizations was infrequent. Women were at risk of both physical and mental health problems, particularly depression and suicidal thoughts. They also worried excessively about the health of husbands and children, about husbands' work, family finance and housing, their marriage, their own coping ability and their children's schooling. In addition to this catalogue of adversities, we recorded higher mortality rates for the grandparents.

Classification of families according to deprivation in family of origin or formation
Despite a degree of movement in and out of deprivation across the generations, about half of the Red Spots identified as living in multiply deprived families almost thirty years previously were in similar circumstances in the families of formation.

Rates of poor competence and social dysfunction in the second generation proved surprisingly similar for families whether classified according to deprivation in the family of origin or formation. The following picture emerged.

The children reared in deprived families tended, as adults, to contract earlier marriages. Current family deprivation was associated with higher levels of psychological and family problems; women had a higher incidence of physical and psychological ill-health while men were more prone to drink problems. Declared concern about everyday practical matters was, understandably, more closely related to the experience of current deprivation than to early life deprivation. Although worried about their finances and housing circumstances, the adults in the family of formation considered that society in general had treated them fairly.

The intellectual and scholastic associations of deprivation
At the 11-plus examination highly significant differences were found between children from non-deprived and deprived families in intelligence, arithmetic and English and, at 12 years, on the Raven's Matrices and Mill Hill Vocabulary Tests. Retesting at 15 years showed an apparent reduction of the differences on the Matrices but not the Mill Hill Vocabulary Test. It is reasonable to hypothesize that, during the secondary school years, the balance of home and school influences may have allowed deprived children to

make better use of their genetically determined potential. Our evidence suggested that deprived home circumstances can have a long-term depressing influence on children's intelligence and academic achievements. These are important findings as they relate to a substantial proportion of the city population; the moderately deprived represented 29 per cent and the multiply deprived a further 14 per cent of the total.

Similar initial findings were reported by Cox and Jones (1980) from their study of disadvantaged 11 year-olds; they showed that, over the primary school years, deprived children scored lower on measures of linguistic and scholastic achievements when intelligence was controlled. The rate of progress of children deprived during their junior school years was relatively slow and led to greater differences in attainments at age 11 than would have been predicted from their performance at seven. The question arises how much of the difference in intelligence between the Newcastle groups was due to deprivation and how much to intrinsic deficiencies of intellect. The data relating to the family of origin cannot provide the answer as the intellectual ability of the parents was not measured.

Our relatively culture-free measure of intelligence showed lesser differences between controls and deprived as opposed to multiply deprived; over time, the deprived almost caught up, but the multiply deprived failed to do so. Thus, we are left with two diverging trends: an increasing gap in performance as children proceed through their junior school years (Cox and Jones, 1980) and, on the other hand, a decreasing gap in performance as children proceed throughout their secondary school years. These apparently discrepant findings may have a simple explanation. Douglas (1968), for instance, asserted that the influence of family background on children's test performance is largely established by the age of eight, and family circumstances after this age would tend to have a less profound influence.

There is much evidence that extremes of environmental deprivation depress performance and achievement (Heber, 1968; Jensen, 1977) but that a certain degree of reversibility may occur when children are in normally stimulating environments. Shields (1980) and Clarke (1981) advanced the view that genetic factors are of prime importance in relation to normal conditions where the proportion of individual variations determined by genetic factors is about 80 per cent (Jensen, 1969, 1981). However, Cronbach (1969) argued that extremes of environmental circumstances may have the power to influence intelligence to the extent of about 1.5 standard deviations – about 25 IQ points. Our data showed differences in all types of functioning between children from non-deprived and multiply deprived backgrounds.

Our data on change had the potential of answering questions about environmental influences after the early formative years. We observed that, although the children of families who moved into deprivation over their junior school years did not perform significantly worse on formal measures of attainment in the 11-plus examination, they nevertheless showed an inferiority of performance and adjustment within the classroom. Their teachers reported they had weaker achievements in reading, showed poorer concentration, were less persistent and in general were less likely to make use of a children's library and, sadly, it was reported that a significant number of those children had never experienced visits to the country.

This suggested that early foundations were important and that subsequent breakdown of caring circumstances were not so damaging to general intellectual development. There were, however, signs of poorer achievements in reading, concentration and persistence in the classroom. Children who moved into deprivation eventually showed, during their school years, weaker job aspirations, an eagerness to leave school at the first opportunity and an increased risk of delinquency. We noted that all of these adverse features arose in children who, as a group, were of average intellectual potential.

It is not clear why there should be this distinction, or why deprivation in the primary school years had relatively little impact when it had such a dramatic impact in the pre-school years. We can only speculate about possible reasons. The foundation of intellectual performance may have already been laid down in the pre-school years and may become sufficiently robust so as to counter new adverse influences; or the effects on the intelligence of children who moved into deprivation in their junior school years may be transient, although this seems unlikely as the differences become significant at 15 years for the Mill Hill Vocabulary Test, Raven's Matrices, mathematics and manual dexterity. Another possibility is that there may be some self-correcting mechanisms operative at this time (Hinde, 1982). One other possible hypothesis is that there are age-dependent sensitivities to life stresses (Rutter, 1985b) so that cognition is more sensitive in the pre-school years and achievements and behaviour in the school years; but some would see this merely as a restatement of facts rather than a theory to explain them. Furthermore, we have provided evidence of differences in ability and achievement which appear after some five years from the time when the deprivation was measured. One possibility is that we are dealing with an effect which takes a fairly long time to emerge.

Children from both deprived and multiply deprived families in which deprivation was reduced over the junior school years performed better on ability tests at age 10 than those groups without reduction. Many of the differences were significant and were always greater in the deprived than the multiply deprived. The groups which improved had an average intelligence quotient four to five points higher than those who did not. Thus, deprived children who improved had a slight advantage over children from multiply deprived families who improved. This was greatest in scholastic achievement tests, but by 15 years the evidence of significant improvement had disappeared in the multiply deprived but persisted in the deprived. We concluded that emergence from family deprivation was associated with evidence of improved functioning in the children, provided that the deprivation was not severe. However, it should be noted that, while we have concentrated on degree of deprivation, the differences recorded must also be due to the nature of deprivation.

It is important to try to understand the mechanisms that determine these differences. One plausible explanation would attribute the differences between the groups of children to the changes in family circumstances over their second five years of life. This suggests that the adverse effects of milder deprivation can be appreciably attenuated by reduction in deprivation. However, the malign influences of serious earlier deprivation clearly exert a more enduring effect. Another possibility is that the differences between the groups of children are mostly determined by parental intelligence influencing both the reduction in family deprivation and the performance of their children. For instance, the lessening of deprivation may in part reflect the greater social competence of more able parents, which then re-emerges as identifiable differences in the next generation between the groups of children.

The continuing influence of environment
School-leaving attitudes partly reflect environmental influences. From non-deprived families, one child in five wanted to leave school as soon as possible but half of those in the multiply deprived did so. However, at 15 years, a smaller proportion of the deprived who wished to continue at school actually did so, probably influenced by the wider availability of work in the 1960s.

School-leaving examination
Non-deprived Red Spots had a significantly higher success rate than the deprived, but the husbands or partners of Red Spot girls showed little differences whatever the situation regarding deprivation in their families of origin. Nevertheless, there were some contrasts: the wives of men from deprived families had inadequate training for work, whereas husbands of women from deprived families did not. An appreciable number of women from multiply deprived homes married men brighter than themselves — that is, 'married up' — but multiply deprived men tended to marry their intellectual equals. This suggests that continuities in deprivation are more likely to occur in multiply deprived men than women.

Health effects
There is good evidence to show that we are becoming a healthier nation (McKeown *et al.*,1975; Brown and Madge, 1982) and both infant and child mortality are greatly reduced. On the other hand, wide geographical inequalities in physical health remain, with higher rates of ill-health likely to occur in high-density and poor inner city areas (Brown and Madge, 1982). Further evidence of a consistent correlation between social disadvantage and poor health comes from the survey conducted in the north-east of England by Townsend (1986), which is broadly in accord with the Newcastle '1,000 Family' data.

Physical

High mortality rates among brothers and sisters of Red Spots from multiply deprived families were revealed in the analysis of data in 1952, and our later analysis showed the same among their parents. The multiply deprived, when adult, had twice the rate of health problems of their spouses. The children of the deprived, especially the multiply deprived, suffered more ill-health and accidents. Unfortunately, we had no way of directly comparing rates of improvement in health for families of origin and formation since the definitions in our archival data inevitably differed from those used in the survey.

Psychological

Multiply deprived Red Spot males had an excess of drink problems, both in comparison with their spouses and with non-deprived males, and were also prone to antisocial behaviour. Their female counterparts, both Red Spots and spouses, were prone to depressed mood, suicidal thoughts and the use of tranquillizers.

A small group of multiply deprived in their secondary school years showed behaviour disturbances resembling 'attention-deficit disorder'. Disruptive behaviour in school, antisocial behaviour and scholastic failure were also common. Deficits of attention are known to be associated with antisocial behaviour in boys and educational problems, and debate continues on how these disorders are linked. Our data suggest that all three may have a common origin in deprivation, but does not clarify their interaction or direction of effect.

Growth

A significant failure of growth in height and weight of the multiply deprived Red Spot children was evident by the age of three and continued for all ages to 15. Since there was no significant difference in mean birthweight between multiply and non-deprived, we considered that the relative failure was related to postnatal factors and was more likely to be of environmental than genetic origin.

The childhood family background of adults of family of formation

We had data gathered prospectively about the childhood backgrounds of Red Spot men and women but only retrospectively about their spouses or partners. This retrospective information was more open to distortion but we checked on the validity of retrospective reports given by the Red Spot adults by reference to their original childhood data gathered at the appropriate time. Moderate validity was demonstrated in relation to individual criteria – marital disruption and poor care coming highest – and when they were summated to give a global measure the resulting correlation (0.64) reflected a reasonable level of validity.

We studied the extent to which individuals chose partners from similar family backgrounds, basing this on data gathered prospectively in the case of the Red Spots and retrospectively in the case of their partners. We found that the Red Spots did tend to choose partners from a similar background, especially at the extremes of our range – that is, Red Spots who, as children, had experienced either no deprivation or much deprivation. Yet one-third of the Red Spots, mostly females, who experienced multiple deprivation chose partners who reported no evidence of deprivation in their early childhood.

Networks

This section contains a gathering together of what has gone before. So far, associations have been studied both within, and across, generations and many significant influences have been highlighted. Initially, the focus was on direct influences of deprivation but, as it became evident that these were not the sole bases of subsequent dysfunction, it became necessary to attempt to make allowance for other influences. There were important sex differences in that some influences proved strong in males and others in females. There was also the question of whether we could identify processes or mechanisms by which effects were brought about. Although this could not be immediately answered by our data, we were able to examine:

1 the relative influence of two important explanatory variables, and;

2 the relative importance of a set of explanatory variables.

We now attempt to draw together these findings and provide a tapestry of the major explanatory variables and their cross-generation influences on performance as reflected in intellectual performance, achievement, behaviour and growth. In this we attempt to understand the nature of identified relationships in a social and psychological sense.

Indices of deprivation as predictors
All criteria chosen to represent deprivation in the families of origin and formation were potentially important on theoretical and clinical grounds. One difficulty in studying the effects of a particular index — for instance, marital disruption — was that we could not be sure that another variable with which it correlated highly was not the main source of any adverse effects (multicollinearity). Our solution was to study the indices both jointly and in association with other potential predictors in order to indicate which were the most important. We subsequently attempted to ascertain whether the same indices showed similar effects when studied in another population, and also examined the pathways to performance.

In the family of origin the most powerful predictor proved to be poor care of child and home during the child's pre-school years. This predicted both intelligence and behaviour in the secondary school years. Of the other five indices of deprivation only poor quality of mothering made a small contribution to performance.

In the family of formation the most important predictor proved to be occupational class of the family in 1979–80, followed by educational handicap and mother's age at first marriage or cohabitation. Poor care of child and home and poor quality of mothering made smaller contributions. Taking the two generations together it can be concluded that powerful predictors were poor care of child and home, occupational class and educational handicap. Other significant predictors were quality of mothering, large family size and home ownership.

We can only assume that the effects of marital disruption and parental illness, always considered important clinically, had been absorbed by the more influential measures of physical care and quality of mothering; that the effects of overcrowding as a predictor were absorbed by the variable representing family size; and that those of social dependency were absorbed by other more sensitive measures of social dysfunction, such as the family not owning their home and lower occupational class. Following Townsend (1979), unemployment was viewed both as a spectrum and as a dichotomy into employed and unemployed. However, unemployment as a separate explanatory index made little contribution, if any, to measures of performance studied, its effects presumably being absorbed by other more sensitive predictors with which it correlated. When explanatory variables reflecting care of children were examined, they were found to be of less importance in predicting the performance of daughters than of sons.

Path analyses suggested that mother's age at marriage had both direct and indirect effect on antisocial behaviour within the home and on verbal ability. The indirect effect passed from age at marriage to educational handicap which in turn influenced the following three performance variables: school-based antisocial behaviour, school achievements and non-verbal ability. Mother's age at marriage proved an important explanatory variable within a network of influences; but it probably reflects a host of other influences, namely lower intellectual ability, poorer judgement and poorer career motivation. But so too does educational handicap, which either directly or indirectly contributed to outcome in all causal paths leading to antisocial behaviour, poor ability and achievements. Occupational class was also an important explanatory variable in four of the five path analyses; and poor mothering in two of the five. (Earlier findings had led to expectation that poor mothering would make a greater contribution.) Unfavourable reaction to pregnancy was part of a significant pathway starting at mother's age of marriage and passing both to verbal and non-verbal ability. Perhaps these associations simply reflect a degree of dullness of intellect in young mothers, who may tend to view their pregnancies in a negative way.

The path analyses which dealt with networks across generations reinforced the importance of poor care of the child as a mediating influence in the development of antisocial behaviour both directly and indirectly. For instance, poor care in the family of origin influenced occupational status in the next generation and this in turn had an effect

on antisocial behaviour in the children of the family of formation. Verbal ability, vocabulary and reading achievements
appeared to be causally influenced in a similar way. Dependence on social services in one generation had a direct effect
upon educational achievements and vocabulary ability, and
an indirect effect upon antisocial behaviour in the next
generation. However, when other measures of social dysfunction were included, the influence of social dependence
was substantially reduced, suggesting that it was not a
sensitive explanatory variable. Marital disruption in the
family of origin proved a significant causal influence of
marital disruption in the family of formation and this in
turn had an effect on antisocial behaviour of the children
in the third generation.

Other explanatory variables in the network
A problem in prediction analysis is how to deal with an
abundance of potentially important explanatory variables,
many of which are significantly intercorrelated. One way
is to combine similar measures allowing a simpler and clearer
picture to emerge. When this was done, poor occupational
status and undesirable child management techniques proved
most significant, followed by the summed deprivation index
and mother's age at marriage and, finally, the index of undesirable recent life events.

Another question was which explanatory variables
predicted which measures of performance: occupational
status predicted verbal ability and antisocial behaviour; undesirable child management techniques predicted antisocial
behaviour; the summed deprivation index predicted verbal
ability and antisocial behaviour; mother's age at marriage
predicted verbal ability and school attendance; and recent
life events predicted school attendance and antisocial
behaviour.

We had anticipated that poor child management techniques
employed by parents in the family of formation would be
predicted by the major family variables identified in the
family of origin, but this was not so. However, such management techniques were well predicted by prior reports that a
parent had shown a poor attitude to school. Nevertheless,
poor management techniques and also the index of recent life
events proved powerful predictors of children's behaviour.

These findings are important. They suggest that parental management and recent life experiences have powerful influences on child behaviour and are relatively independent of other explanatory family variables, which of course have their own corporate effects. Child behaviour is not totally determined by family atmosphere and deprivation in early experiences.

From child to adult
So far attention has been confined to adult influences as predictors. An equally important question is whether we can predict adult functioning from prior childhood influences. It was not entirely surprising to discover that intelligence, measured at age 11, predicted not only educational handicap but a host of important family variables — occupational status, home ownership, age of marriage in females and size of family in males. Poor attitude to schoolwork in females predicted educational disadvantage, undesirable child management techniques, age at first marriage, number of children in the family and overcrowding. Poor school attendance predicted poor care of home and children in both males and females, social dependency in females and unemployment in males. Furthermore, poor sociability in childhood predicted marital instability, and self-confidence predicted later mothering abilities.

While the attempt to predict adult functioning from childhood variables proved only moderately successful, these variables are likely to be important mediators in the transmission of disturbance or deprivation across generations. Some of the mechanisms, such as poor attitude to school, may result from complex processes of conditioning while others, such as intelligence, are likely to have a significant genetic component.

The relative importance of major explanatory variables

Deprivation and occupational status In the family of origin, family deprivation in the pre-school years had a more powerful effect on intellectual performance of children at 11 years than did parental occupational class. By age 15 the effects of occupational status had virtually disappeared. While deprivation in the pre-school years had a powerful effect on school attendance at 15, occupational class had little effect. Similarly deprivation had a powerful effect on behaviour at secondary school.

Pre-school and primary school deprivation   While pre-school deprivation had a powerful effect on intellectual performance at 11 years, and on temperament and behaviour at secondary school, primary school deprivation had a greater effect on intellectual performance at age 15 and on school attendance in boys.

Deprivation in families of origin and formation in relation to performance in the family of formation   Deprivation in the family of origin had continuing effects on intelligence — first, in the school years and subsequently on the adults in the family of formation. In the same way, deprivation in the family of formation influenced intellectual functioning of children in the third generation.

Pre-school deprivation: parental occupation and intelligence   Again, the relative contribution of the explanatory variables varied according to the measure predicted. The best predictors of intelligence in childhood were deprivation and parental intelligence, which both proved powerful predictors of scholastic achievement. Deprivation proved a powerful predictor of antisocial behaviour at school; and parental occupational class a powerful predictor of antisocial behaviour within the home.

Cross-generation effects of deprivation in family of origin on antisocial behaviour in children in the family of formation   When only first-born children were studied, deprivation in the family of origin had no effect. Once the other children of school age were included, a cross-generation effect became evident.

Prediction
In his review, Clarke (1978) concluded that 'except in crude terms, long term prediction of individual human development is not very impressive; in group terms it is rather better'. Almost a decade later, the position remains mostly unchanged despite the benefit of hindsight, advances in research

design, the wide range of explanatory variables explored, and the availability of modern statistical techniques and powerful computer technology. His discussion merits reconsideration, and we offer observations from our present research.

Clarke demonstrated that earlier theories conceived of a model of human development whereby human characteristics were fixed and almost immutable from an early age. Subsequent research has eroded this view both in relation to intelligence and behaviour.

First, in relation to data from longitudinal studies, Clarke and Clarke (1972) noted consistent evidence of correlations decreasing over time, which led them to conclude that individual variability was as strong as consistency. Our data reveal that predictability and consistency over time is strongest in relation to antisocial behaviour. Nevertheless, while six out of 10 boys experiencing multiple deprivation in the pre-school years offend, it is difficult to predict which of them will offend. This was well demonstrated in prediction (multiple regression) analysis where only a small proportion of the variance of criminal behaviour was accounted for by family and environmental predictors. Only when individual differences in intelligence and temperament were included as predictors was a larger proportion of the variance of criminal behaviour accounted for. Continuation of antisocial behaviour during secondary school and post-school years was reflected by the fact that three-quarters of those offending after the age of 15 had also done so earlier. In contrast few offended for the first time after age 15.

Second, personal changes always followed marked environmental changes (Clarke and Clarke, 1972). Our data confirm that personal, intellectual and behavioural changes follow movement into or out of deprivation both within and across generations.

Third, the Clarkes (1972) indicated that development included substantial discontinuities as well as continuities. This is illustrated in the following chapter.

Fourth, the averaging of relationships over time can conceal important changes in a minority of individuals or sub-groups. For instance, the correlation between occupational class in Generations I and II proved moderate, but there were major changes in a relatively small number of families who, over a generation, moved from the lowest to the highest occupational stratum.

Fifth, multiple predictive measures are likely to be more powerful than a single measure (Clarke 1978) and even more so when distantly related or even unrelated to each other. This was demonstrated for criminality data where a reasonable proportion of the variance was explained only when totally unrelated explanatory variables were included in the prediction analysis. We conclude that using even the most sensitive of explanatory variables reflecting the same type of data is unlikely to be as successful as using additional variables from another source.

Sixth, evidence from longitudinal studies indicated that many competent adults had severely disturbing childhoods while many highly achieving children subsequently failed to achieve their predicted potential (MacFarlane, 1964). Yet there were small groups whose adult performance fulfilled the actual expectation. In his review of the New York longitudinal study Clarke (1986) concluded that the major picture was of inconsistency of characteristics in those who had childhood disorders and that correlations over short periods proved unimpressive. Study of these children into adulthood identified a number of significant links, but none proved substantial (Thomas and Chess, 1980; Chess and Thomas, 1984). Our account of change (Part V), particularly across generations, identified not only variability but also continuity at both extremes.

Seventh, behaviour has multiple determinants with a continuous interaction between person and situation; not only are we influenced by our situations but we influence them as well (Mischel, 1977). This is illustrated in our path analysis which showed how different pathways led to anti-social behaviour in the home as opposed to school.

Eighth, the previous rather narrow models which focused on the comparative effects of genetics and the environment have given way to examination of the wider interaction between person and environment.

Ninth, as far as mental ability is concerned:

(a)   the earlier the measurement and the longer the period predicted, the less the reliability. In our data, explanatory variables relating to the pre-school period were better predictors of data collected in the last year of primary school than the last year of secondary school;

(b) significant correlations which decrease over time cannot primarily be due to errors of measurement and must therefore mainly reflect genuine personal change (Clarke and Clarke, 1986).

Tenth, changes in psychological characteristics always move in the direction of environmental shifts; this suggests that, within limits, human development may be regarded as somewhat open-ended – at least potentially so (Clarke and Clarke, 1986).

In summary, from a number of themes relevant to our work, the evidence is strongly in favour of continuous process of change rather than predetermined development. Chance experiences in childhood can act as strong determinants of stability or change in the adult. There is also continuing individual variation in the face of environmental alteration – hence our awareness of the 'open-endedness of human development'. Despite this, it is now possible to forecast with broad accuracy the range of reactions that may occur within groups of individuals exposed to environmental change.

Finally, we have alluded to the danger of focusing on a single explanatory variable since its identified effects could be due to the other variables with which it is correlated. One way of dealing with this is to combine similar explanatory variables. Second, some explanatory variables have both direct and indirect influences on the way people perform while others have only direct effects. Third, criteria of deprivation have more powerful influences than others – for instance, poor child care and mothering and educational handicap have been identified as being of crucial importance. Fourth, prediction may be behaviour-specific – for example, neurotic behaviour in childhood is only poorly predicted, while antisocial behaviour and features representing attention-deficit disorder are well predicted. Prediction may also be specific. Fifth, opportunities should be sought to study the variation in the effects of deprivation during different periods of life. We found the effects of early life deprivation can disappear by late adolescence. Also the effects of deprivation in early and later childhood may differ;

deprivation in the school years appears to have greater effects on behaviour and intellectual ability in later adolescence than pre-school deprivation. Finally, adult performance may be influenced not only by family and environmental factors but also by those intrinsic to the child; in our study these included differences in intelligence and temperament, in behaviour and in attitudes to school.

19 Understanding deprivation

The life span perspective in understanding deprivation
Traditional theories have tended to view human development as becoming, in a sense, finalized in early life (Freud, 1949; Kohlberg, 1969; Piaget, 1972). In contrast, life span research has emphasized the pervasiveness of change throughout life (Baltes *et al.*, 1970; Baltes *et al.*, 1977; Lerner and Ryff, 1978). Of fundamental importance is the question whether behaviour can be viewed as quantitative increase or extension of what was present at an earlier stage (representing continuity); or whether behaviour in later stages of development is qualitatively different (representing discontinuity). Theories supporting the former hypothesis have been challenged by empirical research indicating that changes occur across the life span, and that these are multidirectional, showing both increase and decrease (Baltes *et al.*, 1970). Furthermore, changes have been linked to socio-cultural factors rather than being determined merely by chronological age (Baltes, 1979; Baltes *et al.*, 1977).

Our work emphasizes the importance of adopting a life span perspective in attempting to identify processes and mechanisms which explain behaviour. We have examined the contribution of early family deprivation in the pre-school period, and have been able to demonstrate differences in development in relation to early environmental change as well as recent life events. Like others, we have found that behaviour change phenomena are interdependent (Lerner and Ryff, 1978), are linked to a multiplicity of explanatory variables, and can be evaluated only by employing a wide range of theories in relation to the individual and his environment (Lerner and Ryff, 1978). While our empirical findings must be viewed and evaluated in the historical and local circumstances of Newcastle, this does not prevent generalization to other settings; rather they provide a refinement and difference in emphasis from earlier findings.

Continuities

We have noted that deprivation experiences in childhood gave rise to generally poor functioning in intelligence, school performance and behaviour and, in adult life, to neurotic problems in women and antisocial behaviour in men. Subsequently, we found evidence of poor parenting among these adults. Such associations proved especially powerful in the case of the multiply deprived. About half the multiply deprived in the family of formation had experienced multiple deprivation in their childhood. Nevertheless, such associations were not inevitable.

Continuities: parenting

We have identified some of the factors in childhood which played an important role in predisposing to deprivation in the next generation. We assume behavioural disturbance in childhood plays an important mediating role. Quinton and Rutter (1985), studying parenting in two generations, support this assumption for children admitted to residential care and show that, while adversities in childhood predispose to poor adult functioning, adaptive adult functioning is not formed by the end of childhood. Circumstances in adult life also determine functioning — for example, women happily married to a stable partner were likely to show good parenting. This suggests the chance of discontinuity for women in adversity who make good marriages, and our data suggest the same tendency. Advantageous marriage may mean gaining a partner who experienced better parenting, which introduces an important ameliorative element, as may other chance factors. On the other hand, there are many possible bases for continuity in deprivation as exemplified by women beginning their families very early or men having a criminal history. These processes are not inevitable precursors of deprivation in the next generation, but they may increase the risk.

We tried to quantify intergeneration continuities of deprivation and identify mechanisms and protective and stress factors involved. Many of these themes have been addressed in the section on multivariate analysis (Part V).

Continuities: occupational status

One approach is to study the similarity of earnings between

fathers and sons on the one hand and sons-in-law on the other. Atkinson *et al.* (1980) report a significant correlation (regression coefficient of 0.4 to 0.45) between fathers and sons and, surprisingly, a similar coefficient between fathers and sons-in-law. They suggest that this concordance is based on greater continuity among the affluent.

Townsend (1979) marshalls powerful arguments to support his view that the concept of social class is crucial to any explanation of the existence and scale of poverty. In a sense, social class reflects not only the individual's rewards but the privileges, responsibility and status conferred by society. It determines how he or she will be viewed by representatives of institutions both governmental and private, legal, medical or financial, and how a person is expected to act in society. He also suggests that social class has a tendency to institutionalize inequalities in society. However, there is a danger that, by concentrating on inequalities of social class, there will be a failure to emphasize the wider and more fundamental psychological and social qualities necessary for a satisfactory life.

While a social class index based on occupation, despite its relative crudity, has been found to be useful in a wide range of studies, the identified differences of behaviour, illness or mortality among the social strata are likely to be attributable to different standards of hygiene, behaviour and social and educational circumstances. Hence Osborne and Morris (1979) claim occupational class is singularly lacking in explanatory power in that it is not always clear what aspect of social class is the most significant predictor of a given measure of performance. Nevertheless, father's occupation has proved a powerful predictor in many studies of child health and development. Even after controlling for other socioeconomic factors postulated as contributing to the 'social' class effect (for example, housing, parental education), father's occupation still retains additional explanatory power.

Yet occupation itself cannot always be satisfactorily classified (Osborn and Morris, 1979). There are, for instance, problems of how to cope with occupational mobility and how to classify households with no economically active male head. Husbands and wives may be rated as belonging to different occupational classes, although their life styles are similar. The question also arises whether the occupational classes of single- and double-parent households are really comparable.

Osborn and Morris concluded there was need for indices of social stratification which relate directly to specific issues under investigation and embody a greater degree of explanatory power than does parental occupation alone. Thus, they compiled a wider social index which they hoped would have greater discriminative power. In practical terms, this index tended to contrast the most disadvantaged with the most privileged.

A number of important questions emerge from the literature on occupational status, the first of which is the extent to which the professional and managerial class is open to recruitment. The Oxford Mobility Study suggested that, in the recent past, there has been considerably more upward mobility into the professional–managerial class than previously supposed (Goldthorpe, 1980). Nevertheless, there remained differential recruitment, with movement into this class by offspring of the same class in the previous generation being three times as common as expected by chance, and that from the lowest stratum just half as common. Yet, while there was more entry into this occupational level by those with formal qualifications, this did not preclude entry from those without.

Second, there is the question of transmission of advantage and disadvantage. Research into unemployment, undertaken in a northern city by Brown and Cousins (1979), concluded that 'transmission of advantage was more likely than transmission of disadvantage, and it was the sons of fathers in the higher occupational groups who had a better chance of doing well themselves' (Brown and Madge, 1982).

Can our study provide any relevant answers to these questions? The key periods for studying occupation in our study were 1952 and 1980. In 1952 the index cohort were five years old and had started school; in 1980 they were 33 years old, and over 70 per cent had children of school age; it is, therefore, possible to compare occupations across the two generations. The social economy of the region changed considerably over these three decades. National censuses show a dramatic decrease in the availability of semi-skilled and unskilled manual jobs in developing new technologies, producing a moderate increase in non-manual jobs.

We combined strata derived from the Registrar General's 1951 classification to study social class mobility over the period for the total '1,000 Family' population and for the deprived groups. In the case of the former, the percentages in the semi-skilled and unskilled categories were twice as high in 1952 as in 1980, indicating substantial upward occupational mobility from the first generation to the second. However, the pattern of occupational mobility was an 'average' of the mobility of the subsamples. This can be most deceptive as such averages may mask subsample mobility in different directions. For instance, the non-deprived was a very large group (57 per cent of the original population) and showed good upward occupational mobility in the next generation but little downward mobility. The multiply deprived comprised a small group (some 14 per cent of the original population) and showed moderate upward occupational mobility but also substantial downward mobility. Nevertheless, we were impressed by the upward class mobility across generations of our different deprivation cohorts, suggesting that deprivation is not necessarily deeply ingrained.

The third question was whether our data provided any clues to explain the upward mobility across generations of families in the multiply deprived group. One possibility was that the multiply deprived Red Spot women who moved up in occupational class had married spouses of better intellectual potential than themselves. While the numbers were small there was evidence to support this in that multiply deprived females (n=26) had male spouses with a mean Mill Hill Vocabulary quotient of 99 compared to their own mean of 91 and a mean of 93 in their Red Spot male counterparts (n=32). Further, multiply deprived females married males who were on average about an inch taller than the Red Spot male counterparts. Hence part of the explanation of upward mobility is that some women 'marry up'.

Himsworth aptly comments:

Human societies exist in a state of flux. Always some individuals are rising in the social scale, some falling, and some remaining in the class in which they were born. Yet despite this continual interchange, class differences in health, as judged by such objective criteria as relative death rates, persist. (1984: p. 162)

Himsworth quotes Illsley's work in Aberdeen (1955) revealing that women who married into higher social classes were
more intelligent, spent longer at school, were more highly
skilled, had better-paid jobs, better physique, were more
healthy and had a better perinatal record than those who
married down the social scale. This suggests the importance
of genetic and personality factors in social mobility.
Himsworth proposes the importance of a factor of maternal
competence in that certain qualities of temperament and
background experience may enable a woman to benefit from
the advantages she possesses. He argues that the social origins
of adults are insufficient of themselves to prevent those
whose abilities differ from the average from being socially
mobile. This implies that, within each occupational stratum
there are variations in individual potential and performance.
He considers that there is a limit imposed by constitution
to the extent to which one can improve individual human
performance by environmental influences. On the other
hand, Heath (1981, p. 188) points out that 'social origins
and educational attainments may influence the kind of job
we get'. Yet the known influences that we are able to
measure are greatly outweighed by the unknown or un-
measured. Heath appears not to consider individual
differences of innate ability, which some regard as an
ideological block (Himsworth, 1984).

Discontinuities
We now have a comprehensive picture of the Red Spots over
their school years, of their scholastic achievements, their
interests and their activities, attitudes and aspirations, and
also any difficult or antisocial behaviour. At first glance, we
seem to have drawn a bleak picture of the multiply deprived
group, yet this may not be as bad as it appears. Whatever
feature we focused on, there was a sizeable proportion of the
multiply deprived who were rated as showing at least average
functioning. Over 60 per cent of these children received
satisfactory ratings for response in class, almost 70 per cent
for classroom reliability, 40 per cent for classroom initiative,
classroom concentration and persistence, and 90 per cent
for sociability. This implies that, in the school years, a
sizeable proportion of children coming from multiply
deprived homes were capable of showing adequate standards

of performance and behaviour in the classroom. Allowance also needs to be made for the so-called 'halo' effect, whereby a teacher's rating of children's personal qualities might be influenced by perception of their scholastic abilities and vice versa and also by knowledge of their home environment. In our data this possibility is hinted at by the similarity in the patterns of scholastic ability and behavioural functioning, as shown by about half the multiply deprived group. While we do not have direct evidence that these features occur in the same children, it is not unreasonable to speculate that they are likely to do so.

While comparative statistics may suggest significant differences between groups, they can mask the potential of individuals from deprived homes who may in fact constitute a substantial minority. The task of society is to seek a method of maximizing individual potential by a better use of social and educational resources, for there is clear evidence that intellectual achievement may be modified both by positive and negative mediators in the environment.

How does deprivation exert its effect?
The cardinal question is not whether deprivation is harmful but how it exerts its harmful effects. We simply postulated that deprivation gives rise to increased vulnerability which can be modified by a series of protective factors. This model hypothesizes that some who are exposed to deprivation are adversely affected, while others may be protected from its consequences by their intelligence, strength of character, pre-existing social skills, or by other positive personal and family qualities. Such qualities may not only protect against deprivation but create a 'steeling' effect by causing the individual to strive assiduously to overcome disadvantages experienced in his lifetime.

Mechansims

Family influences
A common belief holds that mothers rear their children according to the model of their own childhood. McGlaughlin and Empson (1983) examined this hypothesis and concluded that continuities in models of child-rearing were the exception rather than the rule, and that the idea of a cycle of

deprivation was hard to sustain. However, the work of Rutter and his colleagues (1983) suggested that mothers who experienced emotional deprivation in childhood will often, but not inevitably, prove less than adequate. They looked back to see how far childhood experience of mothers predicted placement and care of children and forward to the circumstances of parents who had been reared in institutions. They found that one-third of mothers who had been in institutions showed disturbed behaviour at school; 40 per cent had become pregnant by their nineteenth birthday compared to none of the controls; serious parenting factors were present in 20 per cent but in none of the controls; and half had ratings of poor parenting compared to one in 10 of the controls. This poor parenting constituted part of a broader pattern of poor psychosocial functioning.

The Sheffield research made an important contribution to the understanding of multiple problem families (Wright, 1955; Wright and Lunn, 1971). About a third of married adult children of problem families seemed themselves likely to form problem families. Daughters and their families seemed to do better at follow-up than sons and their families. However, subsequent Sheffield research (Tonge et al., 1983) suggested that deprivation has become less evident over time due perhaps to smaller families and to greater acceptance of divorce by society.

After reviewing the evidence, Brown and Madge (1982) concluded that specific forms of family deprivation are not reproduced from one generation to the next. However, our research suggests some degree of specific transmission especially in the area of marital disruption and, to a lesser extent, poor quality of care of children. Far more impressive is the fact that each type of deprivation in one generation was significantly associated with the sum score of deprivation in the next, prompting the conclusion that transmission of deprivation is more general than specific. However, certain forms of deprivation do appear more potent — particularly poor care of children and the home — but this probably represents a host of characteristics including inadequacy of foresight, organization, planning and supervisory skills. There was some movement out of the 'multiple deprivation' category over the generation, but the extent of continuity in the multiply deprived group was considerable — about 50 per cent.

Genetic versus environmental influences

There is a continuing debate about the relative importance of genetic and environmental factors and their interaction. Genetic factors could bring about their effects through temperament, personality and intelligence and may be modified by environmental influences. For instance, a child from a deprived background with relatively poor intelligence is likely to be in a less favourable position for planning a career or initiating a business venture, or even for competing successfully in the open employment market, especially in times of economic recession. The effects of genetic endowment are likely to be hampered or facilitated by the quality of parenting and of social stimulation (Waddington, 1966). Similarly, individual differences in temperament or personality could facilitate or reduce interpersonal relationships and encourage or impede job prospects. Yet matters are never so simple. While marked environmental deprivation may depress intellectual performance to a significant extent (Heber, 1968; Jensen, 1977), it is not easy to establish how much of that poor performance is due to genetic factors and how much to the deprived family environment. This is always the dilemma when trying to explain poor performance in children from multiply deprived homes. Brown and Madge (1982) in discussing one discrete physical variable such as height re-emphasize the distinction between genetic and environmental factors. Whereas the former gives rise to predictable individual differences in physical height in boys exposed to similar environmental circumstances, it is environmental factors which are mainly responsible for differences in average height between groups of boys living in different environments.

In our analysis, the question arose whether the poor ability of Red Spots from deprived homes was due to adverse environmental influence or to the poorer intelligence of their parents. Unfortunately it was not possible to check this, since IQ data on parents of the family of origin was not available. However, it was possible to check in relation to parental ability and deprivation in the family of formation. The measured vocabulary ability of both mother and father was averaged then expressed according to the dichotomy: quotient of 100 and above versus 99 and below. Analysis of variance was then undertaken. The findings revealed that both family deprivation and parental intellectual ability had significant independent effects. The most deprived children in Generation III (whose parents had an average quotient below 100) had a mean score below the non-deprived (in terms of environment and parental ability) of:

1   19 points in relation to non-verbal ability;
2   24 points in relation to vocabulary ability;
3   24 points in relation to reading ability.

Our data, therefore, indicate the importance both of genetic endowment and environment during the life cycle. They suggest that non-deprived environments allow genetically determined potential to develop, since children coming from parental backgrounds of similar intellectual potential show considerable discrepancies on mean scores according to the degree of family deprivation.

Our method of selection of groups allowed us to draw conclusions about genetic and environmental factors in relation to growth. As there were no differences in birthweight between our groups we could only conclude that the demonstrated differences in the pre-school and school years had a postnatal environmental basis. While differences in physical development within groups are likely to be due to genetic factors, the differences between groups are mainly determined by environmental factors. We have also to allow for the possibility of interaction between genetic factors and environmental deprivation.

There is suggestive evidence of the importance of genetic factors in personality and temperament (Rutter and Madge, 1976; Torgersen and Kringlen, 1978). It is generally held that what is transmitted is a genetic predisposition to behaviour (genotype), and, for the behaviour to become overt (phenotype), that predisposition needs to interact with environmental influences.

What contribution does our research make to this issue? Antisocial behaviour constitutes the only behavioural characteristic on which there were substantial differences between the non-deprived and deprived groups, both in the case of the Red Spots and their children — especially among boys. Among the Red Spots, measures of temperament obtained from their teachers proved to be helpful predictors of later criminality. Among the children of the Red Spots moderate differences were seen between the groups on the temperamental qualities of 'activity' and 'mood'. In the prediction of criminality we noted that only when measures representing intelligence and temperament were added to the set of family and social variables used was a substantial proportion of the variance accounted for. This suggested a small, but important, genetic component in the causation of criminality. We also found a modest relationship between clinical ratings of the personality of parents and criminality in their male Red Spot offspring, both as juveniles and adults. Yet the evidence in support of a genetic basis to criminality is modest (Bohman, 1978).

On the other hand, psychological theory and research provides evidence about the fundamental importance of environmental influences. These are of many kinds: child-rearing practices; influence of other adults in the environment (such as relatives, teachers, neighbours); socioeconomic factors, such as poor housing, poverty, unemployment and their repercussions. Coffield *et al.* (1981), after turning their microscope on problem families, offered the notion of a dense network of interconnecting socio-cultural factors. Our findings provide confirmation of the impact of this complex network on multiply deprived families.

Economic deprivation and its effects
Some authorities consider the quality of family life to be of greater importance than material welfare. Dependence on social services implies that a family will be on a limited budget with poor quality of consumer goods and clothing, which may give rise to crises of despair in parents (Brown and Madge, 1982). These problems have as much to do with the quality of material circumstances as with the quantity of material provision, although both may differ vastly from those of the rest of society (Coates and Silburn 1970; Coffield, 1981). Such depriving circumstances may lead to anxiety about money, a sense of entrapment with little hope of improvement and a family atmosphere of despair. This is particularly likely in multiple deprivation involving social dependence. It can be appreciated how, when she is incapable of making ends meet, it is difficult for the mother to give her undivided attention to planning the care of home

and children. Quarrels over debts may give rise to strained marital relationships. The children are likely to be living in a shabby home, often wearing outgrown clothes and consequently may develop a deep sense of humiliation.

Elder (1973) examined the ways in which catastrophic economic deprivation affects the family and advanced theories to explain the links. These concern the processes and mechanisms by which social changes influence behaviour. They suggest that economic deprivation gives rise to marital strains and, in due course, to an emotional estrangement of the family from the father. The mother may seek work but, in any case, the practical utility of her domestic role may affect the balance of power in the marriage. She may assume a central role in the family, and this is reflected in an emphasis on domestic socialization of daughters and lack of parental support for their further education. As a consequence the father's role and position may become reduced as the mother's is increased. In this paradigm, the father loses much of his attractiveness as a social and parental model, and his authority over his children is diminished. Thus we can advance the hypotheses that girls from economically deprived homes:

(a)   will identify more strongly with their mothers than their fathers;
(b)   will have less in the way of academic aspirations or achievement than those non-deprived;
(c)   will seek a solution in early cohabitation or marriage.

Equally, boys from deprived homes:

(a)   may accept a family leadership role and be motivated to become a competing provider;
(b)   will identify more strongly with the peer culture than with any positive family ideals;
(c)   are more likely to be attracted to antisocial behaviour through the diminution of parental authority and restraints.

In many ways, our work supports hypotheses (b) and (c) for both boys and girls. Deprived girls have little in the way of academic achievements and they cohabit or marry significantly early. Deprived boys are powerfully attracted to antisocial activities, particularly those from multiply deprived families. Our family data do not provide evidence in support of hypothesis (a), whether for boys or girls.

Different origins and mechanisms for different deficits

So far we have demonstrated that environmental deprivation may give rise to disturbance, but as Rutter (1981b) points out we need to go beyond the general conclusion that bad experiences may have bad effects. We need to search for the mechanisms by which deprived children are predisposed to develop specific types of deficit or disorder. There are some clues from specific events, such as hospital admission. A single hospital admission may give rise to short-term distress and disturbance in younger children, but lasting reactions are unusual (Rutter, 1981b). On the other hand, parental divorce usually follows a prolonged period of marital discord and the adverse psychological consequences appear to have a basis in this rather than in the actual separation (Rutter, 1981b). Nonetheless, there is evidence that the circumstances associated with divorce in themselves constitute additional stress which may precipitate or aggravate emotional difficulties (Hetherington *et al.*, 1978; Wallerstein and Kelly, 1980).

One of the key questions in deprivation research is whether the development of intellectual, scholastic, emotional and behaviour problems in deprived children are the result of the same influences and processes. One other group of workers has addressed this problem (Stevenson and Graham, 1983). They too assert that, among problem families, various types of deprivation tend to be found together and interact significantly but despite a degree of overlap tend to have different effects. They report three major findings: that social and material deprivations are linked to language and developmental delay; that the quality of family relationships also contributes to language delay; and that the quality of family relationships and the presence of external stress account for the development of behaviour and emotional disorders.

For our part, we have identified poor care of child and home as the most powerful predictor of lower intelligence and antisocial behaviour. Two other important predictors proved to be educational handicap and the relative youthfulness of the mother when first marrying or cohabiting. This is doubtless related to the fact that upwardly mobile women tend to postpone childbearing for a number of years. Occupational class also proved a powerful predictor and we believe that, in this circumstance, it reflects a combination of material advantage and stimulation. Two other significant predictors were family size and home ownership. We assume that the effects of marital breakdown and parental illness have mostly been absorbed by the other more sensitive measures of social and family dysfunction.

Life cycle changes and mechanisms
We have demonstrated that life cycle changes of deprivation status in the direction of improvement in one generation were associated with evidence of improved functioning in the next, provided that the deprivation was not severe. This proved true for physical development, intelligence and behaviour.

There was evidence that reduction in severe deprivation when the children were five was associated with better intellectual functioning when the children were 10. However, this improved functioning disappeared by the time they were 15 years old. Changes in deprivation status did not appear to affect physical development, but such changes did have some effects on behaviour and attitude to school.

It is important to try to understand the mechanisms that determine these differences. One plausible explanation would attribute the differences between the groups of children to the changes in family circumstances over their second five years of life. This would give rise to the suggestion that the adverse effects of milder deprivation can be attenuated by reduction in deprivation. However, the earlier adverse malign influences of serious deprivation seem 'robust' in the sense that they appear frequently to give rise to relatively enduring effects.

Another possibility is that the differences between the groups of children are mostly determined by an underlying parental cognitive factor, affecting both the reduction in family deprivation and the performance of their children. For instance, the lessening of deprivation may in part have reflected the greater social competence of intellectually more able parents, which then re-emerges in the next generation as identifiable differences between the groups.

This theory would carry with it the implication that, where deprivation is not severe, the range of parental intellectual ability is wide, thus allowing differences between the groups of children to emerge. However, where deprivation is severe, not only is the range of parental intellectual ability narrow, but the mean level is low, and this hampers the emergence of differences.

20   Final conclusions of the Newcastle study

Whatever deprivation a child may experience, our findings suggest that a fundamental family mechanism by which the child is affected is through inadequate physical and emotional care. Two of our criteria measured this directly. What of the other criteria that supposedly reflect social handicap — namely, social dependence and overcrowding? While poverty does not imply lack of affection and a caring attitude, the pattern of living enforced by poverty may not leave parents with adequate time and energy to devote to a particular child. And it is not only direct care which is important, but the skills of sensible organization, good housekeeping and planning of family activities which constitute a home, a family environment and a positive model for child development. We contend that, in large or 'overcrowded' families, the processes are not different in nature but merely more complex.

This leaves us with the two other deprivations of parental illness and marital disruption. We suggest that parental illness, especially in the mother, may give rise to poor care of the child but, where the family has other resources, the impact may be attenuated. Marital disruption, especially in the conflict-ridden phase of marital breakdown, will have similar effects on mothering and child care. In most cases these will be exaggerated by any attendant economic privation. It would be oversimplifying matters to suggest that these are the only routes by which deprivation brings about its effects, but we believe that parental care is a basic mechanism. Obviously, the effect will be modified by the specific circumstance of deprivation and by other strengths or weaknesses within a particular family.

A second fundamental mechanism involves educational handicap. The precise processes involved are not clear. In some families it may have a basis in intellectual dullness;

in others it may result from a tradition of disinterest in vocational or academic achievement, lack of opportunity, poor foresight and planning, or general lack of motivation and drive. Educational handicap seems to exert its effects in a multitude of ways and has many end results, and it is, as could be expected, an important predictor of low occupational rating and even unemployment. Nor is it surprising to discover that it is an important precursor of poor mothering ability. Many of the selfsame qualities required for the acquisition of educational and vocational achievements are also necessary in planning and organizing child care. Mere lack of achievement in a family may constitute a model for the child; the parents may be dull and may not have the enthusiasm or skills to stimulate their children, or there may be combinations of these factors. This is a recipe for less than adequate intellectual performance and scholastic achievement by children. Moreover, educational handicap has long-term effects. It is, for instance, an important predictor of low occupational status in the next generation and a significant link in the causal pathway to antisocial behaviour at home, at school and in the neighbourhood.

Our data also reveal that, while a single deprivation may have little effect, multiple deprivations, coexisting in the same family, can have impressive and widespread effects. But in such circumstances we are not necessarily able to tease out the important pathways to undesirable outcomes. While we have tried to establish broad patterns, it is likely that the underlying pathways to achievement or dysfunction in their offspring will vary from family to family.

It would be naive to conclude that childhood deprivations are the only important precursors of undesirable outcome. Other explanatory factors may contribute and may furthermore exercise different effects according to the circumstances of the family, one example being occupational status. It is possible to conceive of a large family whose breadwinner is in the lowest occupational status, with the members subject to financial and material privations in addition to overcrowding, and the parents lacking the personal resources to care for the family. At the other end of the continuum, in a financially secure family there may be not only absence of deprivation and the presence of good material resources and opportunities for care, but also parents motivated to stimulate their children and encourage cultural and scholastic achievements. Thus it is not surprising that occupational status proved such a good predictor of intelligence, achievements and behaviour.

Another important factor was mother's relative youth at first marriage or cohabitation. Our data suggest that dull girls from deprived homes are more likely to marry or cohabit early. How does this come about? Poor parenting skills may give rise to behavioural and socialization problems in their offspring, followed in turn by poor attitudes to school and schoolwork (both of which predict low age at marriage or cohabitation). These negative attitudes make for lack of motivation and unpreparedness for a career which, when combined with exposure to neighbourhood models of early cohabitation, increase the likelihood of early relationships.

There are two other important causes of child dysfunction. The first consists of undesirable recent life events. It is possible, though not inevitable, that any parental or family distress generated by such events may in turn, directly or indirectly, unsettle or distress the child. The second consists of socially and psychologically undesirable child management techniques by parents. We had planned our path analysis on the assumption that prior deprivation as represented by poverty or poor mothering experience in childhood would be associated with subsequent undesirable techniques in managing one's own children. However, this proved not to be the case and, on reflection, we concluded that these were two separate facets of negative child care. Poor care and poor mothering may often be due to lack of skills, imagination and social and economic resources and lead to acts of omission rather than of commission. In contrast, undesirable child management techniques are circumstances where negative or unpleasant measures are used to coerce the child, and are acts of commission. Undesirable management techniques proved significant predictors of antisocial behaviour in the home, neighbourhood and school. However, it is occasionally possible that this is an effect rather than a cause, with parents reacting punitively in their attempts to cope with their children's antisocial behaviour. Another possibility is that there are intrinsic qualities in a mother's personality which make a contribution to the negative way in which she manages her children. This hypothesis receives support from the fact that undesirable management techniques are powerfully predicted by the measure of poor attitude to schoolwork by the mother when a girl. Thus it seems there are intrinsic qualities in a mother's personality which contribute to the negative way in which she manages her children.

This brings us to qualities within the child which contribute to the processes underlying the major mechanisms. One cardinal factor is intelligence which is an important predictor of educational performance and occupational status in adulthood. In a similar way, attitude to schoolwork in a girl proved a powerful predictor of not only her adult achievements and her behaviour but also of other family factors. These included family size, undesirable techniques of child management and, at a lesser level, mother's age at first marriage and overcrowding in the home. This suggests that there are qualities in girls which, reflected in a negative attitude to schoolwork, are predictors of a series of adverse family circumstances in adult life. We can only speculate about their basis but suspect that they are qualities of personality which may be specific to girls.

Other qualities in schoolgirls were associated with a negative performance in adult life. Girls whose attendance at school was poor subsequently gave poor care to their children and were more likely to be dependent on social welfare services. Those who showed poor sociability at school had higher rates of marital disruption and those with poor self-confidence showed poor mothering ability. We also considered that there are intrinsic qualities in boys likely to evoke negative responses from their parents. This was supported by the finding that boys who were rated as showing poor concentration and persistence at school were children whose mothers were judged to show poor mothering abilities.

In recent decades there has been a steady accumulation of information showing how undesirable life experiences may influence development and behaviour. Bowlby's (1951) emphasis on the affectional components of mothering gave impetus to such research, but he overestimated both the universality and irreversibility of the psychological consequences (Rutter, 1981b, 1985b). From the viewpoint of our study the most salient conclusions are that individuals vary in their resilience to environmental experiences and that different undesirable experiences may have different risk potentials for cognitive, socioemotional and behavioural development.

In respect of individual differences of temperament, we conceived of poor concentration and persistence as tending to increase a youngster's vulnerability. No matter whether the genetic component underlying temperament is large or small, the question arises how such differences in vulnerability are converted into psychological disturbance (Plomin, 1983). There are several possibilities: teachers, and perhaps peers, are likely to respond more positively to the boy who can concentrate and show a good attention span, which in turn may lead to his increased confidence and self-esteem. In contrast, teachers and peers may respond less well to the boy of difficult temperament, which may reduce self-esteem and increase vulnerability even in the absence of environmental deprivation. Within the home, the temperamentally easy child is less likely to be the target of parents' irritability.

Similarly, in respect of intelligence and scholastic achievement, we envisage chain reactions whereby positive experiences with teachers and peers give rise to positive self-esteem. Abler children may be protected through better ability to understand the meaning of their experiences and to seek ways of solving social problems.

Our work emphasizes the importance of a network of social and emotional supports, especially in the pre-school years, as protection against environmental deprivation. Good mothering is likely to be reciprocated by positive attachment; good maternal health and absence of financial and employment problems mean better opportunities for management and supervision of the child; smaller family size enables better pre-school care, which is then likely to continue throughout schooling; relative maturity of age in the mother proves protective against delinquency in the child. Our findings suggest that a good relationship with a constantly present mother constituted the major source of protection in the pre-school years and school years for those deprived boys who did not become criminal. One important factor for girls was the continued presence of the father throughout the formative years. We assume that his presence implied a secure father–daughter relationship despite other forms of deprivation.

In conclusion, our data have given rise to speculation about a variety of important processes and mechanisms in one stage of the life span which underlie adverse experience and poor achievement in the next. Some of these are operative during childhood years and give rise to their effects in adult life; others operate in adult life and create their effects in the children of the next generation. We have seen that many children appear destined — due in part to the nature, attitudes and behaviour of parents and grand-parents — to experience a disproportionate burden of adversity, and we have attempted to unravel some of the complexities of cyclical deprivation. More encouragingly, we have identified some of the circumstances which enable individuals, despite initial disadvantage, to experience positive change and development in their lives. Desirable characteristics and protective factors are to be found in the nature of the child and parents and in aspects of family life: an equable temperament, scholastic ability, social competence, parents who plan and provide good physical and emotional care and close and appropriate supervision. Yet such positive and protective influences are not to be seen as discrete, isolated events. They appear to bring about their effects through chain reactions, often in social contexts, over the course of time.

Appendices

(Available from the Authors)

Appendix 1   Reliability and validity: deprivation data gathered in 1952

Table 1.1   Validity as expressed by factor loadings on principal component and correlation analysis

Table 1.2   Correlations of criteria rated in 1952 and 1957

Appendix 2   Inter-rater reliability: data gathered in 1979–1980

Appendix 3   Family of formation: principal component analysis

Table 3.1   Correlation matrix: family of formation

Figure 3.1   Principal component analysis (eigen values)

Figure 3.2   Principal component analysis

Appendix 4   Addendum to housing neighbourhoods in Great Britain

Table 4.1   Acorn classification of households 1980 categorized according to deprivation in family of origin (1952)

Appendix 5   Some precursors of current unemployment

Table 5.1   The precursors of unemployment in family of formation based on deprivation and unemployment in family of origin

Table 5.2   Predicting unemployment in family of formation based on unemployment in family of origin and intelligence of the Red Spots at 11-plus examination

Table 5.3   Two factor prediction of male unemployment in Generation II

Table 5.4   Predicting the effects of unemployment and deprivation in Generation II

Appendix 6	Two factors prediction of occupational class in the family of formation
Table 6.1	Two factor prediction of social class in Generation II
Table 7	Correlation of criteria of deprivation gathered prospectively (year 10) and retrospectively (year 30)
Table 8	Rates of unemployment according to degree of deprivation
Table 9a	Recommendation for job training
Table 9b	School attendance after 15th birthday
Table 10	Spouse self-report on school examinations
Table 11	Crighton/Mill Hill vocabulary scales: children of the Red Spots
Table 12	Reading performance of first-born children of family of formation
Table 13	Personal attributes of Red Spots in their final year at school
Table 14	Behaviour and illness in family of formation
Table 15	Housing of Red Spots in 1980 in relation to change in deprivation status 1952–1957
Table 16a	Criteria in 1980 shown by 35 families non-deprived in 1952
Table 16b	Families with three or more criteria of deprivation in 1952
Table 16c	Estimated degree of specific continuity from 1952–1980
Table 16d	Total declared income of families before deductions in 1980
Table 17	Correlation matrix of important explanatory variables
Table 18	Correlation of measures of behaviour in children in Generation III with explanatory variables
Table 19	Neighbourhood circumstances: ward rankings and offending by male Red Spots

References

Abel-Smith, B. and Townsend, P. (1965), *The Poor and the Poorest*, Occasional Papers on Social Administration no. 17, G. Bell & Sons Ltd.

Allen, S. and Smith, C.R. (1975), 'Minority group experience of the transition from education to work' in P. Brannen (ed.), *Entering the World of Work: some sociological perspectives*, London: HMSO, pp. 72–90.

Altus, W.D. (1966), 'Birth order and its sequelae', *Science*, 151, pp. 44–9.

Asher, H.B. (1983), *Causal Modeling*, Beverly Hills: Sage Publications, Inc.

Ashley, P. (1981), *Deprivation, Money and the Poor: problems and responses*, Final Report to the Joint Working party on Transmitted Deprivation, London: Heinemann.

Atkinson, A.B., Maynard, A.K. and Trinder, C.G. (1980), *From Parents to Children: living standards in two generations*, Final Report to the Joint Working Party on Transmitted Deprivation, London: Heinemann.

Baltes, P.B. (1979), *Life Span Development Behavior*, vol. 2, *Life Span Developmental Psychology: Some Converging Observations on History and Theory*, London: Academic Press, pp. 255–74.

Baltes, P.B., Baltes, M.M. and Reinert, G. (1970), 'The relationship between time of measurement and age in cognitive development of children: an application of cross-sectional sequences', *Human Development*, 13, pp. 258–68.

Baltes, P.B. Cornelius, S.W. and Nesselroade, J.R. (1977), 'Cohort effects in developmental psychology: theoretical and methodological perspectives' in W.A. Collins (ed.), *Minnesota Symposium on Child Psychology*, vol. II, Minneapolis: University of Minnesota.

Banks, M.H. and Jackson, P.R. (1982), 'Unemployment and risk of minor psychiatric disorder in young people:

cross-sectional and longitudinal evidence', *Psychological Medicine*, 12, pp. 789–98.

Berthoud, R. (1980), *Who Suffers Social Disadvantage?*, Report to the Joint Working Party on Transmitted Deprivation 1980 as cited in Brown and Madge, *Despite the Welfare State*.

Blaxter, M. (1981), *The Health of the Children: a review of research on the place of health in cycles of disadvantage*, London: Heinemann.

Bohman, M. (1978), 'An 18-year, prospective, longitudinal study of adopted boys' in E.J. Anthony, C. Koupernik and C. Chiland (eds), *The Child in his Family: vulnerable children*, New York: John Wiley.

Bosco, J.J. and Robins, S.S. (1980), 'Hyperkinesis: prevalence and treatment' in C.K. Whalen and B. Henker (eds), *Hyperactive Children: the social ecology of identification and treatment*, New York: Academic Press, pp. 173–90.

Bowlby, J. (1951), *Maternal Care and Mental Health*, Geneva: World Health Organization.

Brennan, M. and Stoten, B. (1976), 'Children, poverty and illness', *New Society*, 36, pp. 681–2.

Brewis, E.G. Davison, G. and Miller, F.J.W. (1940), 'Investigations into health and nutrition of certain of the children of Newcastle upon Tyne between the ages of five years (1938–9), City and County of Newcastle upon Tyne', Newcastle: Newcastle Health Department.

Bronfenbrenner, U. (1979), *The Ecology of Human Development*, Cambridge, Mass.: Harvard University Press.

Brown, G.W. and Harris, T. (1978), *Social Origins of Depression*, London: Tavistock.

Brown, M. and Madge, N. (1982), *Despite the Welfare State*, London: Heinemann Educational Books.

Brown, R.K. and Cousins, J.M. (1979), *Transmitted Deprivation and the Local Labour Market*, Final Report to the Joint Working Party on Transmitted Deprivation, London: Heinemann.

Butler, D. and Sloman, A. (1980), *British Political Facts, 1900–1979* (5th edn), London: Macmillan.

Chess, S. and Thomas, A.T. (1984), *Origins and Evolution of Behaviour Disorders from Infancy to Early Adulthood*, New York: Brunner/Mazel.

Clarridge, B.R., Sheehy, L.S. and Hauser, T.S. (1978), 'Tracing members of a panel: a 17 year follow-up' in K. Schnessler (ed.), *Sociological Methodology*, Jossey Bass.

Clarke, A.D.B. (1978), 'Predicting human development: problems, evidence, implications', *Bulletin British Psychology Society*, 31, pp. 249-58.

Clarke, A.D.B. and Clarke, A.M. (1972), 'Consistency and variability in the growth of human characteristics' in W.D. Wall and V.D. Varma (eds), *Advances in Educational Psychology*, vol. 1, pp. 33-52, London: University of London Press.

Clarke, A.M. (1981), *Adoption Studies: their contribution to our understanding of human development*, Thirteenth Hilda Lewis Memorial Lecture. Unpublished.

Clarke, A.M. and Clarke, A.D.B. (1986), 'Thirty years of child psychology: a selective review', *Journal of Child Psychology and Psychiatry*, 27, pp. 719-59.

Coates, K. and Silburn, R. (1970), *Poverty, the Forgotten Englishmen*, Harmondsworth: Penguin Books.

Coddington, R.D. (1972), 'The significance of life events as etiologic factors in the diseases of children; II. A study of a normal population', *Journal of Psychosomatic Research*, 16, pp. 205-13.

Coddington, R.D. (1979), 'Life events associated with adolescent pregnancies', *Journal Clinical Psychiatry*, 40, pp. 180-5.

Coffield, F., Robinson, P. and Sarsby, J. (1981), *A Cycle of Deprivation? A case study of four families*, London: Heinemann.

Cox and Jones (1983) 'Disadvantaged 11 year olds', a book supplement to the *Journal of Child Psychology and Psychiatry*, 3, Oxford: Pergamon.

Cronbach, L.J. (1969), 'Heredity, environment and educational policy', *Harvard Educational Review*, 39, pp. 338-47.

Davie, R., Butler, N.R. and Goldstein, H. (1972), *From Birth to Seven: a report of the National Child Development Study*, London: Longman.

Department of Employment (1978), *Family Expenditure Survey*, London: HMSO.

Dootjes, I. (1972), 'Predicting juvenile delinquency', *Australian and New Zealand Journal of Criminology*, 5, pp. 157-71.

Douglas, J.W.B. (1964), *The Home and the School*, London: MacGibbon and Kee.

Douglas, J.W.B., Ross, J.M. and Simpson, H.R. (1968), *All our Futures: a study of secondary school education*, London: Peter Davies.

Earls, F. (1980), 'The impact of family stress on the behavior adjustment of pre-school children', *Massachusetts Journal of Community Health*, pp. 7–11.

Elder, G.H. (1973), 'On linking social structure and personality' in G.H. Elder (ed.), *Linking Social Structure and Personality*, Beverly Hills: Sage Publications.

Elder, G.H. (1974), *Children of the Great Depression*, Chicago: University of Chicago Press.

Elder, G.H. Jr. (1979), 'Historical change in life patterns and personality' in P.B. Baltes and O.G. Brim Jr. (eds), *Life-Span Development and Behavior*, vol. 2, UK edition, London: Academic Press.

Elder, G.H. and Rockwell, R.C. (1978), 'Economic depression and post-war opportunity', in R.A. Simmons (ed.), *Research in Community and Mental Health*, Greenwich, Conn.: JAI Press.

Essen, J. (1979), 'Living in one-parent families: attainment at school', *Child Care, Health and Development*, 3 (5), pp. 189–200.

Essen, J. and Wedge, P. (1982), *Continuities in Social Disadvantage*, London: Heinemann Educational Books.

Fagin, L.H. (1981), *Unemployment and Health in Families*, London: DHSS.

Farrington, D.P. (1979), 'Longitudinal research on crime and delinquency', in N. Morris and M. Tonry (eds), *Criminal Justice: an annual review of research*, vol. 1, Chicago and London: University of Chicago Press, pp. 289–348.

Farrington, D.P. (1981), 'The prevalence of convictions', *British Journal of Criminology*, 21, pp. 173–5.

Farrington, D.P. (1985), 'Stepping stones to adult criminal careers' in D. Olweus, J. Brook and M.A. Yarrow (eds), *Development of Antisocial and Prosocial Behaviour*, New York: Academic Press.

Farrington, D.P. and Tarling, R. (eds) (1985), *Prediction in Criminology*, Albany: State University of New York Press, pp. 150–73.

Freud, S. (1949), *Outline of Psychoanalysis*, New York: Norton.

Fundudis, T., Kolvin, I. and Garside, R. (eds) (1979), *Speech-Retarded and Deaf Children: their psychological development*, London: Academic Press.

Garside, R.F., Birch, H., Scott, D. McI., Chambers, S., Kolvin, I., Tweddle, E.G. and Barber, L.M. (1975), 'Dimensions of temperament in infant school children', *Journal of Child Psychology and Psychiatry*, 16, pp. 219–31.

Gath, D., Cooper, B., Gattoni, F. and Rockett, D. (1977), *Child Guidance and Delinquency in a London Borough*, Institute of Psychiatry, Maudsley Monographs no. 24, London: Oxford University Press.

Gatzanis, S.R.M. (1985), 'The Newcastle Thousand Family Study. The influence of social and environmental factors', PhD thesis, University of Newcastle upon Tyne.

Gersten, J.C., Langner, T.S., Eisenberg, J.G. and Orzeck, L. (1974), 'Child behavior and life events' in B.S. Dohrenwend and B.P. Dohrenwend (eds), *Stressful Life Events, their Nature and Effects*, New York: John Wiley & Sons, pp. 159–70.

Glueck, S. and Glueck, E. (1950), *Unraveling Juvenile Delinquency*, Cambridge, Mass.: Harvard University Press.

Glueck, S. and Glueck, E. (1959), *Predicting Delinquency and Crime*, Cambridge, Mass.: Harvard University Press.

Goldthorpe, J.H. (1980), *Social Mobility and Class Structure in Modern Britain*, Oxford: Clarendon Press.

Goodchilds, J.D. and Smith, E.E. (1963), 'The effects of unemployment as mediated by social status', *Sociometry*, 26, pp. 287–93.

Goodyer, I., Kolvin, I. and Gatzanis, S. (1985), 'Recent undesirable life events and psychiatric disorders of childhood and adolescence', *British Journal of Psychiatry*, 47, pp. 517–23.

Goodyer, I., Gatzanis, S. and Kolvin, I. (1986), 'The impact of recent undesirable life events and psychiatric disorders in childhood and adolescence', *British Journal of Psychiatry*.

Graham, P. Rutter, M. and George, S. (1973), 'Temperamental characteristics as predictors of behaviour disorders in children', *American Journal of Orthopsychiatry*, **43**, pp. 328–39.

Graham, P.J. and Stevenson, J.E. (1983), 'The effects of family deprivation on pre-school children', in Nicola Madge (ed.), *Families at Risk*, SSRC/DHSS, London: Heinemann.

Guilford, J.P. (1956), *Fundamental Statistics in Psychology and Education*, London: McGraw-Hill.

Gunn, J. and Robertson, G. (1976), 'Drawing a criminal profile', *British Journal of Criminology*, 16.

Heath, A. (1981), *Social Mobility*, London: Fontana.

Heber, R. (1968), 'The role of environmental variables in the etiology of cultural–familial mental retardation' in B.W. Richards (ed.), *Proceedings of the First Congress of the International Association for the Scientific Study of Mental Deficiency*, Reigate: Michael Jackson.

Hepworth, S.J. (1980), 'Moderating factors of the psychological impact of unemployment', *Journal of Occupational Psychology*, 53, pp. 139–45.

Hetherington, E.M., Cox, M. and Cox, R. (1978), 'Family interaction and the social, emotional and cognitive development of children following divorce', Paper presented at the Symposium on the Family, *Setting Priorities*, Washington DC, 17–20 May.

Himsworth, H. (1984), 'Epidemiology, genetics and sociology', *Journal of Biosocial Science*, **16**, pp. 159–76.

Hinde, R.A. (1982), *Ethology*, London: Fontana.

HMSO (1977), 'A Policy for the Inner Cities', White Paper Policy, London: HMSO, Cmnd 6845.

Holmes, T.H. and Rahe, R.H. (1967), 'The social readjustment rating scale', *Journal of Psychosomatic Research*, 11, pp. 213–18.

Housing Act (1936).

Illsley, R. (1955), 'Social class selection and class differences in relation to still births and infant deaths', *British Medical Journal*, 2, pp. 1520–4.

Illsley, R. (1967), 'Family growth and its effect on the relationship between obstetric factors and child functioning' in R. Platt and A.S. Parkes (eds), *Social and Genetic Influences on Life and Death*, Edinburgh: Oliver and Boyd.

Ineichen, B. and Millerson, G. (1977), *Housing Factors in Transmitted Deprivation: a feasibility study*, Final Report to the Joint Working Party on Transmitted Deprivation, London: SSRC.

Iversen, G.R. and Norpoth, H.N. (1976), *Analysis of Variance*, London: Eagle.

Jahoda, M. (1979), 'The impact of unemployment in the 1930s and the 1970s', *Bulletin of the British Psychological Society*, 32, pp. 309-14.

Jensen, A.R. (1969), 'How much can we boost IQ and scholastic achievement?', *Harvard Educational Review*, 39, pp. 1-123.

Jensen, A.R. (1977), 'Cumulative deficit in IQ of blacks in the rural South', *Developmental Psychology*, 13, pp. 184-91.

Jensen, A.R. (1981), 'Raising the IQ: the Ramey and Haskings study', *Intelligence*, 5, pp. 29-40.

Jessor, R. and Jessor, S.L. (1977), *Problem Behaviour and Psychosocial Development: a longitudinal study of youth*, New York: Academic Press.

Joseph, K. Sir (1972), 'The cycle of deprivation', Speech at Conference of Pre-School Playgroups Association, 29 June.

Kagan, J. (1980a), *The Second Year: the emergence of self-awareness*, Cambridge, Mass.: Harvard University Press.

Kagan, J. (1980b), 'Perspectives on continuity' in O.G. Brimo and J. Kagan (eds), *Constancy and Change in Human Development*, Cambridge, Mass.: Harvard University Press, pp. 26-74.

Kenny, D.A. (1979), *Correlation and Causality*, New York: John Wiley and Sons.

Kohlberg, L.A. (1969), 'Stage and sequence: the cognitive-developmental approach to socialization', in D.A. Goslin (ed.), *Handbook of Socialization Theory and Research*, Chicago: Rand McNally.

Kolvin, I., Wolff, S., Barber, L.M., Tweddle, E.G., Garside, R.F., Scott, D. McI. and Chambers, S. (1975), 'Dimensions of behaviour in infant school children', *British Journal of Psychiatry*, 126, pp. 114-26.

Kolvin, I., Miller, F.J.W., Garside, R.F. and Gatzanis, S.R.M. (1983a), 'One thousand families over three generations:

method and some preliminary findings', in N. Madge (ed.), *Families at Risk*, London: Heinemann.

Kolvin, I., Miller, F.J.W., Garside, R.F., Wolstenhome, F. and Gatzanis, S.R.M. (1983b), 'A longitudinal study of deprivation: life cycle changes in one generation — implications for the next generation', in M.H. Schmidt and H. Remschmidt (eds), *Epidemiological Approaches in Child Psychiatry, II*, Stuttgart and New York: Thieme Verlag.

Kolvin, I., Miller, F.J.W., Garside, R.F., Gatzanis, R.M. and Scott, D. McI. (1988a), 'Parent, child, grandchild, the transmission of deprivation', in E.J. Anthony and C. Childand (eds), *The Child in His Family*, New York: Wiley, pp. 535–59.

Kolvin, I., Miller, F.J.W., Fleeting, M. and Kolvin, P.A.K. (1988b), 'Social and parenting factors and offending findings from the Newcastle 1,000 Family Study 1947–1980', *British Journal of Psychiatry*, 152, pp. 80–90.

Kolvin, I., Miller, F.J.W., Fleeting, M. and Kolvin, P.A. (1988c), 'Risk protective factors for offending with particular reference to deprivation', in M. Rutter (ed.), *The Power of Longitudinal Data: studies of risk and protective factors for psychological disorder*, Cambridge: Cambridge University Press.

Lambert, L. and Streather, J. (1980), *Children in Changing Families*, London: Macmillan.

Landau, S.F. (1981), 'Juveniles and the police', *British Journal of Criminology*, 21, pp. 27–46.

Lawrence, D. (1977), *Transmitted Deprivation in Jarrow and Nottingham: a feasibility study*, Report to Joint Working Party on Transmitted Deprivation, London: SSRC.

Lerner, R.M. and Ryff, C.D. (1978), 'Implementation of the life-span view of human development: the sample case of attachment', in P.B. Baltes (ed.), *Life-Span Development and Behavior*, vol. 1, pp. 1–44.

Little, C.B. (1976), 'Technical–professional unemployment: middle-class adaptability to personal crisis', *Sociological Quarterly*, 17, pp. 262–74.

Loeber, L. and Dishion, T. (1983), 'Early predictors of male delinquency: a review', *Psychological Bulletin*, 94, pp. 68–99.

McCord, J. (1978), 'A thirty year follow-up of treatment effects', *American Psychologist*, 33, pp. 284–9.

McCord, J. (1979), 'Some child-rearing antecedents of criminal behaviour in adult men', *Journal of Personality and Social Psychology*, 9, pp. 1477–86.

McCord, J. (1982), 'The relation between paternal absence and crime', in J. Gunn and D.P. Farrington (eds), *Abnormal Offenders, Delinquency and the Criminal Justice System*, Chichester: Wiley.

Macdonald, K.I. (1977), 'Path analysis', in C.A. O'Muircheartaigh and C. Payne (eds), *The Analysis of Survey Data*, 2, Chichester: Wiley.

Macfarlane, J.W. (1964), 'Perspectives on personality consistency and change from the guidance study', *Vita Humana*, 7, pp. 115–26.

McGlaughlin, A. and Empson, J. (1983), 'Sisters and their children: implications for a cycle of deprivation', in N. Madge (ed.), *Families at Risk*, London: Heinemann.

McKeown, T., Record, R.G. and Turner, R.D. (1975), 'Interpretation of the decline in mortality in England and Wales during the 20th century', *Population Studies*, 29, pp. 391–422.

Madge, N. (1983a), *Families at Risk: studies in deprivation and disadvantage*, London: Heinemann.

Madge, N. (1983b), 'Annotation: unemployment and its effects on children', *Journal of Child Psychology*, 24 (2), pp. 311–19.

Mannheim, K. (1952), *The Sociological Problems of Generations. Essays on the Sociology of Knowledge*, New York: Oxford University Press.

Manpower Services Commission (1977), *The Coventry Report*, London: HMSO.

Matrimonial Causes Act (1970).

Maxwell, A.E. (1977), *Multivariate Analysis in Behavioural Research*, London: Chapman and Hall.

Miller, F.J.W., Court, S.D.M., Walton, W.S. and Knox, E.G. (1960), *Growing up in Newcastle upon Tyne*, London: Oxford University Press.

Miller, F.J.W., Billewicz, W.Z. and Thomson, A.M. (1971), 'Growth from birth to adult life of 442 Newcastle upon Tyne schoolchildren', *British Journal of Preventative and Social Medicine*, 26, pp. 224–30.

Miller, F.J.W., Court, S.D.M., Knox, E.G. and Brandon, S. (1974), *The School Years in Newcastle upon Tyne*, London: Oxford University Press.

Miller, F.J.W., Kolvin, I. and Fells, H. (1985), 'Becoming deprived: a cross-generation study based on the Newcastle upon Tyne 1,000 Family Survey', in A.R. Nicol (ed.), *Longitudinal Studies in Child Psychology and Psychiatry*, Chichester: John Wiley and Sons.

Miller, M. and Stokes, C.S. (1975), 'Path analysis in sociological research', *Rural Sociology*, 40, pp. 193–210.

Mischel, W. (1977), 'On the future of personality measurement', *American Journal of Psychology*, 32, pp. 246–54.

Monaghan, J.H., Robinson, J.O. and Dodge, J.A. (1979), 'The children's life events inventory', *Journal of Psychosomatic Research*, 23, pp. 63–8.

Morris, Sir Parker (1961), *Homes for Today and Tomorrow*, Ministry of Housing and Local Government, London: HMSO.

Mortimore, J. and Blackstone, T. (1982), *Disadvantage and Education: Final Report to the Joint Working Party on Transmitted Deprivation, 1980*, London: Heinemann.

Moylan, S. and Davies, B. (1980), 'The disadvantages of the unemployed', *Department of Employment Gazette*, 88, pp. 830–2.

Mulligan, G., Douglas, J.W.B., Hammond, W.H. and Tizard, J. (1963), 'Delinquency and symptoms of maladjustment', *Proceedings of the Royal Society of Medicine*, 56, pp. 1083–6.

Murray, R. (1974), 'Overcrowding and aggression in primary school children', in C.M. Morrison (ed.), *Educational Priority*, vol. 5, London: HMSO.

Neligan, G.A. Kolvin, I., Scott, D. McI., and Garside, R.F. (1976), *Born Too Soon or Born Too Small*, London: Spastics International Medical Publications.

Office of Population Censuses and Surveys (1973), *General Household Survey: Introductory Report*, London: HMSO.

Office of Population Censuses and Surveys (1980), *Marriage and Divorce Statistics*, London: HMSO.

Osborn, A.F. and Morris, T.C. (1979), 'The rationale for a composite index of social class and its evaluation', *British Journal of Sociology*, 30 (1), pp. 39–60.

Osborn, A.F., Butler, N.R. and Morris, A.C. (1984), *The Social Life of Britain's Five-year-olds: a report of the Child Health and Education Study*, London: Routledge and Kegan Paul.

Osborn, S.G. (1980), 'Moving home, leaving London and delinquent trends', *British Journal of Criminology*, 20, pp. 54–61.

Paykel, E. (1974), 'Recent life events and clinical depression', in E.K. Gunderson and R.H. Rahe (eds), *Life Stress and Psychiatric Illness*, Springfield, Ill.: Charles C. Thomas, pp. 134–63.

Piaget, J. (1972), 'Intellectual evolution from adolescence to adulthood', *Human Development*, 15, pp. 1–2.

Plomin, R. (1983), 'Developmental behavioral genetics', *Child Development*, 54, pp. 253–9.

Plowden Report, Central Advisory Council for Education (England) (1967), *Children and their Primary Schools*, London: HMSO.

Policy Services Department of the City of Newcastle upon Tyne (1974, 1980), *City Profiles : Occasional Publications*, Newcastle.

Power, M.J., Benn, R.T. and Morris, J.N. (1972), 'Neighbourhood, school and juveniles before the courts', *British Journal of Criminology*, 12, pp. 111–32.

Raven, J.C., Court, J.H. and Raven, J. (1976), *Manual for Raven's Progressive Matrices and Vocabulary Scales*, (revised 1978), London: H.K. Lewis and Co. Ltd.

Registrar-General's Office (1951), *Classification of Occupations*, London: HMSO.

Richman, N., Stevenson, J. and Graham, P.J. (1982), *Preschool to School: a behavioural study*, London: Academic Press.

Richman, N. (1974), 'The effects of housing on preschool children and their mothers', *Developmental Medicine and Child Neurology*, 16 (53), pp. 53–8.

Robins, L.N. (1966), *Deviant Children Grown Up*, Baltimore: Williams and Wilkins.

Robins, L. and Hill, S.Y. (1966), 'Assessing the contributions of family structure, class and peer groups to juvenile delinquency', *Journal of Criminal Law, Criminology and Police Science*, 57, pp. 325–34.

Roff, M., Sells, S.B. and Golden, M.M. (1972), *Social Adjustment and Personality Development in Children*, Minneapolis: University of Minnesota Press.

Rutter, M. (1966), *Children of Sick Parents: an environmental and psychiatric study*, Maudsley Monograph 16, Oxford: Oxford University Press.

Rutter, M. (1967), 'A children's behaviour questionnaire for completion by teachers: preliminary findings', *Journal of Child Psychology and Psychiatry*, 8, pp. 1–11.

Rutter, M. (1979), *Changing Youth in a Changing Society*, London: Nuffield Provincial Hospitals Trust (1980); Cambridge, Mass.: Harvard University Press.

Rutter, M. (1981a), 'Stress, coping and development: some issues and some questions', *Journal of Child Psychology and Psychiatry*, 22 (4), pp. 323–56.

Rutter, M. (1981b), *Maternal Deprivation Reassessed* (2nd edn), Harmondsworth: Penguin Books.

Rutter, M. (1983), 'Statistical and personal interactions: facets and perspectives', in D. Magnusson and V.L. Allen (eds), *Human Development: an interactional perspective*, New York: Academic Press.

Rutter, M. (1985a), 'Family and school influences: meanings, mechanisms and implications', in A.R. Nicol (ed.), *Longitudinal Studies in Child Psychology and Psychiatry*, Chichester: John Wiley and Sons.

Rutter, M. (1985b), 'Resilience in the face of adversity: protective factors and resistance to psychiatric disorder', *British Journal of Psychiatry*, 147, pp. 598–611.

Rutter, M. and Giller, H. (1983), *Juvenile Delinquency: Trends and Perspectives*, Harmondsworth: Penguin Books.

Rutter, M. and Madge, N. (1976), *Cycles of Deprivation: a review of research*, London: Heinemann Educational Books Ltd.

Rutter, M., Maughan, B., Mortimore, P., Ouston, J. with Smith, A. (1979), *Fifteen Thousand Hours: secondary schools and their effects on children*, London: Open Books; Cambridge, Mass.: Harvard University Press.

Rutter, M. and Quinton, D. (1985a), 'Parenting behaviour of mothers raised "in care"', in A.R. Nicol (ed.),

Longitudinal Studies in Child Psychology and Psychiatry, Chichester: John Wiley and Sons Ltd.

Rutter, M. and Quinton, D. (1985b), 'Family pathology and child psychiatric disorder: a four-year prospective study', in A.R. Nicol (ed.), *Longitudinal Studies in Child Psychology and Psychiatry*, Chichester: John Wiley and Sons Ltd.

Rutter, M., Quinton, D. and Liddle, C. (1983), 'Parenting in two generations: looking backwards and looking forwards', in N. Madge (ed.), *Families at Risk*, London: Heinemann Educational Books Ltd.

Rutter, M., Tizard, J. and Whitmore, K. (eds) (1970), *Education, Health and Behaviour*, New York: Longman.

Shaffer, D. (1985), 'Brain damage', in M. Rutter and L. Hersov (eds), *Child and Adolescent Psychiatry: modern approaches*, London: Blackwell Scientific Publications, pp. 129–51.

Shields, J. (1980), 'Genetics and mental development', in M. Rutter (ed.), *Scientific Foundations of Developmental Psychiatry*, London: Heinemann Medical Books.

Silburn, R. (1978), *A Report Summarising and Comparing the Sub-contracts of the 'Socio-economic' Group*, Report to the Joint Working Party on Transmitted Deprivation, London: SSRC.

Sinfield, A. (1981), *What Unemployment Means*, Oxford: Martin Robertson.

Spence, J.C. and Miller, F.J.W. (1941), *Infant Mortality in Newcastle upon Tyne*, City and County of Newcastle upon Tyne.

Spence, J.C., Walton, W.S., Miller, F.J.W. and Court, S.D.M. (1954), *A Thousand Families in Newcastle upon Tyne*, London: Oxford University Press.

Steinhausen, H.C. (1983), 'Life events in relation to psychopathology among severely and chronically ill children and adolescents', *Journal of Child Psychiatric Human Development*, 13, pp. 249–58.

Steinhausen, H.C. and Radtke, B. (1986), 'Life events and child psychiatric disorders', *Journal of the American Academy of Child Psychiatry*, 25 (1), pp. 125–9.

Stevenson, J.E. and Graham, P.J. (1983), 'The effects of family deprivation on pre-school children', in N. Madge (ed.), *Families at Risk*, London: Heinemann Educational Books.

Tennant, C. and Andrews, G. (1978), 'The pathogenic quality of life event stress in neurotic impairment', *Archives of General Psychiatry,* 35, pp. 859–63.

Thomas, A. and Chess, S. (1980), *The Dynamics of Psychological Development,* New York: Brunner/Mazel.

Tizard, B. and Hodges, J. (1978), 'The effect of early institutional rearing on the development of eight year old children', *Journal of Child Psychology and Psychiatry,* 19, pp. 99–118.

Tizard, B. and Rees, J. (1974), 'A comparison of the effects of adoption, restoration to the natural mother and continued institutionalisation on the cognitive development of four year old children', *Child Development,* 45, pp. 92–9.

Tonge, W.L., James, D.S. and Hilam, S.M. (1975), 'Families without hope: a controlled study of 33 problem families', *British Journal of Psychiatry,* 11.

Tonge, W.L., Lunn, J.E., Greathead, S., McLaren, S. and Bosanko, C. (1983), 'Generations of "problem families" in Sheffield', in N. Madge (ed.), *Families at Risk,* London: Heinemann Educational Books Ltd.

Torgersen, A.M. and Kringlen, E. (1978), 'Genetic aspects of temperamental differences in infants', *Journal of the American Academy of Child Psychiatry,* 17, pp. 433–44.

Townsend, P. (ed.) (1971), *The Concept of Poverty,* London: Heinemann.

Townsend, P. (1974), *The Cycle of Deprivation,* British Association of Social Workers' Conference, Manchester University.

Townsend, P. (1979), *Poverty in the United Kingdom,* Harmondsworth: Penguin Books.

Townsend, P., Hillmore, P. and Beattie, A. (1986), *Inequalities in Health in the Northern Region,* Northern Regional Health Authority and University of Bristol.

Vincent, K.R. and Rosenstock, H.A. (1979), 'Relationship between stressful life events and hospitalized adolescent psychiatric patients', *Journal of Clinical Psychiatry,* 40, pp. 262–4.

Waddington, C.H. (1966), *Principles of Development and Differentiation,* New York: Macmillan.

Wadsworth, M. (1979), *Roots of Delinquency: infancy, adolescence and crime,* Oxford: Martin Robertson.

Wallerstein, J.S. and Kelly, J.B. (1980), *Surviving the Break-up: how children and parents cope with divorce*, New York: Basic Books; London: Grant McIntyre.

Warr, P., Jackson, P. and Banks, M. (1982), 'Duration of un-employment and psychological well-being in young men and women', *Current Psychological Research*, 2, pp. 207–14.

Watts, A.F. (1948), *The Holborn Reading Scale*, London: George G. Harrap & Co. Ltd.

Wedge, P. and Prosser, H. (1973), *Born to Fail?*, London: Arrow Books.

Werner, E.E. (1985), 'Stress and protective factors in children's lives', in A.R. Nicol (ed.), *Longitudinal Studies in Child Psychology and Psychiatry: practical lessons from research experience*, Chichester: Wiley.

West, D.J. (1982), *Delinquency: its roots, careers, and prospects*, London: Heinemann.

West, D.J. and Farrington, D.P. (1973), *Who Becomes Delinquent?*, London: Heinemann Educational Books Ltd.

West, D.J. and Farrington, D.P. (1977), *The Delinquent Way of Life*, London: Heinemann Educational Books Ltd.

Wolfgang, M.E., Figlio, R.M. and Sellin, T. (1972), *Delinquency in a Birth Cohort*, Chicago: University of Chicago Press.

Wright, C.H. (1955), 'Problem families: a review and some observations', *The Medical Officer*, 94, pp. 381–4.

Wright, C.H. and Lunn, J.E. (1971), 'Sheffield problem families, a follow-up study of their sons and daughters', *Community Medicine*, 126, pp. 301–7, 315–21.

Zlatch, D., Kenny, T.J., Sila, U. and Huang, S.W. (1982), 'Parent–child life events relation to treatment in asthma', *Journal of Development Behaviour Pediatrics*, 3, pp. 69–72.

Index

Abel-Smith, B., 74
ability
    achievements and, 212–14,
        256
    attainments, 232, 247, 248
    testing (of parents), 123–4
absenteeism (school), 110–11,
    118
accidents, 54, 105, 136, 314
achievement, ability and, 212–
    14, 256
Acorn system, 101, 158–9
adolescence, 60, 216–17, 256
adult
    criminality (predictors), 293,
        296
    family function, 234–6, 259–
        61, 349
    performance, 217–18, 256
age, height/weight by, 105, 106,
    134, 156
alcohol problems, 53, 54
Allen, S., 85
Altus, 129
analysis of variance, 211–12
Andrews, G., 61
antisocial behaviour
    at home, 83, 135–6, 245,
        248, 251, 254, 261, 262,
        263
    at school, 83, 135–6, 220,
        247–8, 251, 254, 261,
        262, 263, 350
arithmetic, 214, 238
Asher, H.B., 241
Ashley, P., 325
asthma, 60
Atkinson, A.B., 24, 357

attainments, 232, 247, 248
    deprivation and, 107–19
    see also ability
attention-deficit disorder, 260,
    344
attitudes to school, 116–17,
    157, 238–40

Baltes, P.B., 355
Banks, M.H., 85, 88
behaviour
    as adults (Red Spots), 124–7
    antisocial, see antisocial be-
        haviour
    attention deficits, 260, 344
    of children of Red Spots,
        134–6
    predictions (factors intrinsic
        to child), 232–4
    problems (pre-school), 60
    at school (Red Spots), 114–
        19, 157
    in secondary school, 214–
        16
    see also temperament, con-
        centration/persistence
behavioural data, 152–3
behavioural performance, 139–
    40
Berkeley study, 161–3
Berthoud, R., 21, 336
birth, children at, 187
bivariate correlations, 241
Blackstone, T., 325, 326
Blaxter, M., 141
Bohman, M., 365
Bosco, J.J., 139
Bowlby, J., 310, 333, 373

boys
    delinquency, 282–3, 286,
        288, 289
    economic deprivation, 366–7
    performance prediction, 224–
        5
    school attendance, 214, 215
Brennan, M., 88
Brewis, E.G., 8
Bronfenbrenner, U., 161, 162
Brown, G.W., 60, 61, 85, 141
Brown, M., 4, 21, 72, 88, 161,
        325–6, 329, 335–7, 343,
        358, 362–3, 365
Brown, R.K., 325, 330, 358
Butler, D., 331

Cambridge study, 304–7 *passim*,
        310
care (physical and domestic),
        17–20, 22, 28–9, 31, 44,
        78, 372–3
Careers Advisory Service, 114
'catch-up' longitudinal design,
        120–23
causal path analysis, 241–3
change across generations
        (1952–80)
    analysis of groups/change,
        169–70
    change across generations,
        204–6
    characteristics of families,
        175
    continuity, 175
    criteria and change in criteria,
        170–75
    extremes (comparison), 175–
        90
    extremes (movement
        between), 190–204
    life cycle changes, 206–7
    measurement, 166–9
change within generations
        (1952–62)
    becoming deprived, 149–54

    comparison of families, 155
    in deprivation, 145–9
    deprivation status changes,
        158–65
    moving from deprivation,
        155–8
Charles, G., 74
Charles, J.A., 8
Chess, S., 232, 352
child
    care patterns (1962), 177–
        9
    management, 189, 372–3
    -rearing, 230, 361–2
childhood
    experiences, 42–8
    factors, 234–6, 259–61
children
    care of, 17–20, 22, 28–9, 31,
        44, 78, 372–3
    health and development,
        187–90
    in school years (comparison),
        179–83
    of unemployed, 88
children, Red Spots as (1947–
        62)
    physical factors, 105–6
    at school, 107–19
children of Red Spots (1979–
        80)
    accidents, 136
    behaviour, 134–6
    physical growth, 134
    at school, 129–33
    summary and comment, 136–
        42
City Profiles (Newcastle), 100–
        102
Claridge, 25
Clarke, A.D.B., 351, 353
Clarke, A.M., 340, 350–52, 353
Coates, K., 365
Coddington, R.D., 60, 61
Coffield, F., 61, 325, 329, 337,
        365

cognitive
  development of first-born,
    129-33
  functioning, scholastic pro-
    gress and, 83, 88-9
  performance (summary),
    137-9
  see also ability
concentration/persistence, 236,
  238-40, 260, 344, 374
continuities of deprivation, 5-7,
  175
  study background, 3-13
  study planning and method,
    14-34
  summary findings, 351, 356-
    60
Court, J.H., 27
Cousins, J.M., 325, 330, 358
Cox, 340
Crichton vocabulary test, 27,
  130, 132
criminal records (data source),
  304-5
Criminal Records Office, 271-5,
  278
criminality, 158
  see also delinquency;
    offending
criminality (prediction)
  analysis, 319-21
  epidemiological con-
    siderations, 303-11
  introduction, 290
  method, 290-92
  prediction of, 317-19
  simple models, 292-9
  stress and protective factors,
    311-17
  subjects and offending, 290
  two-factor predictions,
    300-303
Cronbach, L.J., 341
cross-generation effects,
  350

cycle of deprivation, 3-5, 334
  change across generations,
    204-6
  see also life cycle changes

Davidson, G., 8
Davie, R., 258, 326
Davis, B., 87
deficiency (deprivation
  category), 12
deficit, types of, 367-8
delinquency, 117-18, 183, 270
  fifteenth year, 287-9
  first five years, 282-4
  introduction and metho-
    dology, 281-2
  tenth-eleventh year, 285-7
dependence (deprivation
  category), 12
  see also social dependence
dependent variables, 243-4
Depression, 160-62, 326
depression (in women), 217
deprivation
  associations, 326, 327
  continuities, *see* continuities
    of deprivation
  criminality prediction, 290-
    321
  cycle, *see* cycle of depri-
    vation
  delinquency and, 281-9
  discontinuities, 351, 360-61
  economic, 365, 367
  family (effects), 212-20
  family income and, 73, 74
  final conclusions (of
    Newcastle study), 370-75
  housing and, 90-95, 97-9
  occupational status and, 64-
    71
  offending and, 269-80
  personal development and,
    105-28
  pre-school, 350

deprivation (cont.)
  research issues, 329–37
  review, 325–37
  routes to/from, *see* statistical
    indicators
  summary findings, 338–54
  transmission of, 16–17, 358
  understanding, 355–69
deprivation (changes in)
  changes in individual criteria,
    148
  improvement in individual
    families, 148–9
  prevalence and change, 145–8
  see also changes across
    generations (1952–80);
    changes within generations
    (1952–62)
deprivation (criteria of)
  and change in criteria, 170–
    75
  composite index, 47–8
  definitions, 17–21, 23, 28–30
  in families of formation, 29–
    34, 57–9
  in families of origin, 29, 39–
    40
  'pure', 336–7
deprivation (understanding)
  continuities, 356–60
  discontinuities, 360–61
  effect, 361
  life span perspective, 355
  mechanisms, 361–9
deprived, 14, 16
  becoming (1952–7), 149–54
  delinquency and, 281–9
development (of children),
    187–90
difficult–easy child index, 232
discontinuities of deprivation,
    351, 360–61
discriminant function analysis,
    291, 301–2, 320, 321
Dishion, T., 291, 302

Divorce Law Reform Act
    (1969), 332
Dootjes, I., 319
Douglas, J.W.B., 89, 108, 326,
    327, 340
downward mobility, 71, 149–
    50, 159, 359
dysphoric mood, 125, 128, 217

Earls, F., 60
economic deprivation, 365–7
education
  of Red Spot children, 107–19
  social behaviour and, 189–90
  see also examinations; school;
    training
Education Act (1944), 12
educational attainment, 232,
    247, 248
  deprivation and, 107–19
educational data, 152–3
educational handicap, 333–4,
    370–71
educational insufficiency, 29–
    30, 32–4
Educational Priority Areas, 335
Elder, G.H., 88, 160–62, 326,
    366
electoral wards (Newcastle), 90,
    91
eleven-plus examination, 107–8,
    180–82, 236–8
emotional state (of parents),
    186–7
employment, 76, 185
  preference for, 113–14
  see also unemployment
Empson, J., 361
English ability, 214
entrance events, 61
  see also life events
environment, influence of, 343,
    363–5
epidemiological considerations,
    303–11

Essen, J., 88
examinations
  eleven-plus, 107–8, 180–82,
    236–8
  external, 112–13, 120, 121
  school-leavers, 343
exit events, 61
  see also life events
explanatory variables, 221–2,
    233–6, 249, 261
  effects of pairs, 211–12, 236–
    40
  multiple (models using),
    301–3
  in network, 345–50
external examinations, 112–13,
    120, 121

Fagin, L.H., 88
false negatives, 290, 292–3, 294–
  5
false positives, 290, 293, 294–5,
    302
families
  changing, see change across
    generations (1952–80);
    change within generations
    (1952–62)
  characteristics, 175
  classification, 339
  'problem', 328–9, 337
  with multiple deprivation,
    see multiple deprivation
  with one criterion, 172
  with two criteria, 173
families of formation, 16–17,
    339, 345, 350
  adults, 183–4, 217–18
  criteria of deprivation, 29–
    34, 57–9
  income and family size, 74–5
  occupational status, 256–7
  other factors, 218–20
  parents (ability tests), 123–4
  predicting deprivation, 236–
    40

recent life events, 60–63
  social and family data, 50–54
  social and family factors,
    54–60
  unemployment and, 79–80,
    82–4
families of origin, 16–17, 91,
    339, 350
  criteria of deprivation, 29,
    39–40
  deprivation in, 63, 72–4
  discussion, 48–9
  occupational status, 212–17,
    256–7
  parental illness/loss, 38–9
  social data, 37, 38
  social and family factors,
    40–42
  spouses, 42–8
family
  background, 345
  care patterns, 177–9
  data, 37, 50–54, 150–52
  deprivation (effects), 212–20
  disruption, 17–20, 22, 28–30,
    44, 370
  experiences, 42–8
  income, 72–89, 186
  influences, 361–2
  interviews, 25–7
  mechanisms, criminality and,
    308–10
  relationships, unemploy-
    ment and, 82, 87–8
  shortcomings, 11–12
  size, 31, 74–5, 240
  see also fathers; mothers
Family Expenditure Survey,
    75
family factors, 240, 313–14
  marital and, 332–3
  1962, 40–42
  1979–80, 54–60
  offending rates, 279–80
Family Practitioner Com-
  mittees, 23

Farrington, D.P., 290, 304, 305–6, 307, 308, 319
fathers, 41, 150, 152, 178, 179, 374–5
fear, 217
first-born children, 83, 129–36, 190
flow-chart (1,000 family cohort), 14–15
Freud, S., 355
Fundudis, T., 232

Garside, R.F., 135, 226
Gath, D., 296, 310
Gatzanis, S.R.M., 243
gender
    effects on prediction, 257–8
    sex differences in behaviour, 127–8
General Health Questionnaire, 85
General Household Survey, 21, 99
generation I, 6
generation II, 6, 23
    male unemployment, 78–82
    see also Red Spots
generation III, 6, 83, 107
    deprivation and other factors, 218–20
    see also children of Red Spots
generations
    change across (1952–80), 166–207
    change within (1952–62), 145–65
    occupational mobility over, 67–70
genetic factors, 363–5
genotype, 364
Gersten, J.C., 60
Giller, H., 281, 290, 304–5, 309, 314–15
girls
    delinquency, 282, 284, 286–9
    economic deprivation, 366–7

performance prediction, 225
    school attendance, 214, 215, 373
Glueck, E. and S., 319, 321
Goldthorpe, J.H., 358
Goodchilds, J.D., 84
Goodyer, I., 60–61
Graham, P.J., 21, 233, 240, 264, 325–6, 329, 367
'group validity', 48
growth, *see* physical growth
Gunn, J., 278

Halsey, A.H., 334
Harris, T., 60, 61, 85, 141
health
    data (1947), 37
    and development of children, 187
    effects, 343–4
    and other worries (second-generation women), 53–4
    of parents, 186–7
    of Red Spots as adults, 124–7
    summary of findings, 140–41
    unemployment and, 81–2
Heath, A., 264, 360
Heber, R., 340, 363
height by age, 105, 106, 134, 156
Hepworth, S.J., 85, 88
Hetherington, E.M., 367
Hill, S.Y., 292
Himsworth, H., 359–60
Hinde, R.A., 160, 342
historical perspectives, 325–6
Hodges, J., 139
Holborn Reading Scale, 27, 130, 132–3
Holmes, T.H., 60
Home Office, 277–80, 305
home provision, 188–9
hospital attendance/admission, 188
household amenities, 95–7

housing
circumstances, 158-65
'facilities index', 99
overcrowding, 18-20, 22,
28-32, 44, 92-6, 99-101,
370
ownership, 95, 96, 100, 331-
2
personal unit standard, 92
93
post-war programme, 145
tenure, 79-80
types, 94-5
housing (and neighbourhood),
90-91
and deprivation, 97-9
discussion, 99-102
type and quality, 92-
7
Housing Act (1936), 31, 78

Illsley, R., 257-8, 360
income, 72-4, 186
independent variables, 243-4
individual criteria, changes in,
148
individual families, improvement
in, 148-9
Ineichen, B., 325, 330
intellectual development, 156
ability, 216-17
assessment, 109-10
data, 152-3
scholastic associations of
deprivation and, 339-43
intelligence, 213-14, 236-8, 374
deprivation and, 107-19
intentions (Red Spot children),
116-17
interests (Red Spot children),
116-17
interviews, family, 25-7
Iverson, G.R., 212, 221

Jackson, P.R., 85, 88
Jahoda, M., 88

Jensen, A.R., 340, 341, 363
Jessor, R. and S.L., 320
Jones, 340
Joseph, Sir Keith, 3, 325, 334
juvenile courts, 183

Kagan, J., 206
Kelly, J.B., 367
Kenny, D.A., 241-2, 243
Kohlberg, L.A., 355
Kolvin, I., 135, 156, 207, 226,
281, 306
Kringlen, E., 364

Lambert, L., 326
Landau, S.F., 304
language and verbal ability, 232-
3
law, contact with
deprivation and offending,
269-80
deprived/non-deprived and
delinquency, 281-9
prediction of criminality,
290-321
Lawrence, D., 329
Lerner, R.M., 355
life cycle changes, 58, 164,
206-7, 368-9
life events, recent, 60-63, 372,
373
life span perspective, 355
lifestyles, 184
lifetime trends (criminality),
306-7
Likelihood Ratio Chi Square,
238
Little, C.B., 85
Local Government Act (1974),
91
Loeber, L., 291, 302
log-linear analysis, 238, 240,
291, 294-7, 298, 300-303
longitudinal data, 14-16
longitudinal research (criminality), 303-4

Lunn, J.E., 362

McCord, J., 302, 307–9, 317, 320, 321
Macdonald, K.I., 242
MacFarlane, J.W., 352
McGlaughlin, A., 361
McKeown, T., 343
Madge, N., 4, 5, 21, 72, 87–8, 161, 241, 325–6, 329, 335–7, 343, 358, 362–5
Mannheim, K., 326
marital disruption, 17–20, 22, 28–30, 44, 370
marital factors, 332–3
marital problems, 126, 127
maternal failure, 18–20, 22, 28–9, 31, 41–2, 44, 333
Matrimonial Causes Act (1970), 332
Maxwell, A.E., 291
mechanisms (of deprivation), 361–6
    different (for different deficits), 367–8
    life cycle changes and, 368–9
men
    behaviour and health, 125, 127
    criminality, 271–2, 274–80, 300, 307–8, 315–17
    fathers, 41, 150, 152, 178, 179, 374–5
    predictive force of gender, 257–8
    unemployment, 72–89
    see also boys
mental ability scores, 156, 216–17
method and planning (of study)
    catch-up longitudinal design, 120–23
    criteria of deprivation, 30–34
    deprivation in 1952, 17–21
    deprivation in 1979–80, 28–30

family interview/school visits, 25–8
    longitudinal data, 14–16
    psycho-social models, 242, 244–8
    tracing and follow-up, 21–5
    transmission of deprivation, 16–17
methods (overview), 327–8
Mill Hill Vocabulary Test, 26–7, 109, 123–4, 130, 132, 182, 190, 200–201, 214, 217–18, 232, 262, 339, 341, 359
Miller, F.J.W., 4, 8, 9, 13, 17–18, 41, 69, 76, 105, 108–9, 116, 150, 155, 207, 271, 280, 293, 310, 327, 328
Miller, M., 264
Millerson, G., 325, 330
miscarriages, 41
Mischel, W., 352
Monaghan, J.H., 60
Morris, T.C., 334, 357–8
Morris Committee, 99
Mortimore, J., 325, 326
mothers
    accounts of antisocial behaviour, 83, 135–6, 245, 248, 251, 254, 261–3
    age at marriage, 347, 368, 372
    attitudes to pregnancy, 187
    maternal failure, 18–20, 22, 28–9, 31, 41–2, 44, 333
    quality of, 333, 374
Moylan, S., 87
multi-collinearity, 221, 243, 252, 346
multiple deprivation, 14, 16, 21, 173–4, 362, 371
    extremes (comparison), 175–9

multiple deprivation (cont.)
extremes (movement between), 190–204
interlocking nature, 337
multiple explanatory variables, 301–3
multiple regression analysis, 211, 221, 223, 227–8, 232, 242–3, 257, 291–2, 301, 302, 320, 321
multivariate analyses
of criminality, 319–21
prediction by, 220–25
Murray, R., 327

National Assistance, 18, 46, 331
National Child Development Study, 21, 325, 336
National Health Service Act (1946), 12
National Study of Child Health and Education, 68
National Survey of Health and Development, 88
neighbourhood, 97–9, 249, 296, 335
Neligan, G.A., 257–8, 326
networks, 345–50, 374–5
neurotic behaviour, 135, 136, 251
Newcastle Child Development Study, 258
Newcastle upon Tyne
final conclusions, 370–75
historical development, 7–8
housing and neighbourhood, 90–102
study background, 3–13
summary findings, 338–54, 370–75
non-deprived, 14, 16
comparison of extremes, 175–90
delinquency, 281–9
movement between extremes, 190–204

non-verbal reasoning, 246, 248, 251, 262, 263
Norpoth, H.N., 212, 221

Oakland study, 161–2
occupational class/mobility, 371–2
as continuity, 356–60
deprivation and, 212–17, 256–7, 349–50
downward mobility, 71, 149–50, 159, 359
extremes of deprivation, 176–7
findings, 65–71
method, 64
movement into deprivation, 154
study families, 64–5
upward mobility, 68, 70, 71, 159, 358–60
offences (types), 307–8
offending
findings, 269–77
Home Office data, 277–80
Office of Population Censuses and Surveys, 23, 328
organization of study, 9–10
Osborn, A.F., 68, 331, 333, 334, 357–8
Osborn, S.G., 272
outcome variables, 234, 235
overcrowding, *see* housing
'overlapping' deprivation, 336–7
overseas families, 26–7
Oxford Mobility Study, 358

parental care, *see* care (physical and domestic)
parental factors (personality), 279–80, 310
parental illness, 18–20, 22, 28–9, 31, 38–9, 42, 44, 333, 370
parental stress, 23

parents, 51-2, 88, 130, 356,
    361-2
    ability testing, 123-4
    attitudes to eleven-plus, 180-
    82
    education of, 181, 182
    health of, 186-7
    occupation and intelligence,
    350
    recollections, 51-2, 78
    separation from, 188
    see also fathers; mothers
path analysis, 240-42, 347
    across two generations, 249-
    55
    covering two generations,
    243-8
    limitations, 263-4
pathways from Generation I as
    adults to Generation II,
    261-2
pathways from Generation II
    to Generation III,
    262-3
Paykel, E., 60, 61
peer influence (criminality),
    312-13
performance
    in adolescence, 216-17, 256
    adult, 217-18, 256
    last year at school, 118-19
    predictions, 222-31
    variables, 221-2, 233, 234
personal attributes, 118-19, 182
personal development
    children of Red Spots, 129-
    42
    Red Spots as children, 105-
    19
    spouses and Red Spots, 120-
    28
'personal unit' standard, 92, 93
personality, criminality and, 310
personality factors
    parental, 279-80, 310
    school-based, 238-40

phenotype, 364
physical factors, 105-6
physical growth, 156, 180, 217,
    240, 344
    children of Red Spots, 134
    Red Spots and spouse, 128
    summary of findings, 141-2
physical health, *see* health
physical punishment, 189
Piaget, J., 355
Plomin, R., 374
Plowden Report (1967), 335,
    336
police record, 158
population — baseline, 14-16
poverty, 68, 72, 74, 75, 331
    absolute/relative, 335-6
Power, M.J., 296
precursors of unemployment,
    84
prediction
    adult family functioning,
    234-6, 259-61
    analysis (discussion), 257-
    64
    behaviour, 232-4
    deprivation, 236-40
    multivariate analysis, 220-25
    patterns, 258-9
    performance, 222-31
    summary findings, 350-54
    two factor, 291, 297-303,
    318-19
    see also criminality (predic-
    tion)
predictors, 227-30, 294, 346-8
pregnancy, 60, 187
pre-school deprivation, 350
pre-school experience, 129,
    189-90
prevalence rates (criminality),
    305-6
primary school, 350
'problem families', 328-9, 337
Prosser, H., 21, 65, 325-7, 329,
    336

protective factors, 281–9 *passim*
  criminality, 297–9, 311–17
  psychiatric minor morbidity, 85
  psychiatric morbidity, 85
  psychiatric symptoms, 125
  psychological disorders, 23, 60,
    61, 81–2, 344
  psychological well-being, 84–5
  psychosocial models, 242, 244–8
    model A, 249–52
    model B, 249, 252–5
  psychosomatic behaviour, 135,
    136
  punishment (by parents), 189
  'pure' deprivation, 336–7

Quinton, D., 325, 366

Radtke, B., 60
Rahe, R.H., 60
random controls, 14, 16
Raven, J.C., 27
Raven Progressive Matrices, 27,
    109–10, 130–32, 154,
    182, 190, 201, 214, 217,
    262, 339, 341
reading ability, 27
  children of Red Spots, 130,
    132–3
  family of formation, 123–4,
    219–20
  path analysis, 247–8, 250,
    253, 262–3
  Red Spots, 26, 109, 123–4
recent life events, 60–63, 372,
    373
recollections (of parents), 51–2,
    78
records (of study), 10–11, 12–13
Red Spots, 11
  as adults, 124–7, 183–4
  behaviour at school, 114–19,
    157
  as children, 37–49, 105–19
  children of, 129–42
  spouses and, 120–28

Rees, J., 139
Registrar General, 51, 64, 67,
    359
relative improvement over
    chance, 291, 292, 294–5
research issues, 329–37
residual coefficients, 243
resilience, 311–12, 313, 317
retrospective accounts (family
    · experiences), 42–8
Richman, N., 232, 327
Robertson, G., 278
Robins, L.N., 25, 292, 307
Robins, S.S., 139
Rockwell, R.C., 160, 161,
    162
Roff, M., 310
Rosenstock, H.A., 60
Rowntree Study, 24, 325
Rutter Behaviour Scale, 28,
    83, 134, 188, 220, 226
Rutter, M., 61, 134, 160, 206–
    7, 241, 281, 290, 296,
    304–5, 309–11, 314–15,
    325, 327, 332, 342, 356,
    362, 364, 367, 373
Ryff, C.D., 355

scholastic performance, 88–9,
    339–43, 374
school, 12–13
  absenteeism, 110–11, 118
  antisocial behaviour, 83,
    135–6, 220, 247–8, 251,
    254, 261–3, 350
  attendance (data), 110–11,
    182–3, 214, 215, 240,
    256
  attendance after fifteen
    years, 114, 157–8
  attitudes to, 116–17, 157,
    238–40
  -based personality factors,
    238–40
  children of Red Spots,
    129–33

school (cont.)
  experience, unemployment
    and, 80–81
  factors, criminality and,
    314–15
  leavers, 84–5, 113–14
  -leaving attitudes, 111–12,
    180, 343
  -leaving examinations, 343
  predictors of criminality,
    293, 296
  Red Spots at, 107–19, 182
  secondary, 108–10, 182,
    214–16
  selection after eleven-plus,
    108–9
  visits, 27–8
school years (background), 12–
  13
schooling, previous, 186
secondary school, 108–10, 182,
  214–16
self-esteem, 84–5, 88, 162, 374
self-report data, 120–23, 304,
  305
sensitivity, 290, 292, 294–5, 318
sex differences in behaviour,
  127–8
Shaffer, D., 116
Shields, J., 340
siblings, 51–3, 110
Silburn, R., 329, 365
simple models (criminality),
  292–9
simple predictor factors, 318
Sinfield, A., 87
single-factor prediction (criminality), 290–91, 292,
  294–5, 296–7
Sloman, A., 331
Smith, A.J., 8
Smith, C.R., 85
Smith, E.E., 84
social behaviour, 189–90
social circumstances of unemployment, 87

social class, *see* occupational
  class/mobility
social data, 37, 38, 150, 151
social dependence, 18, 19, 20,
  22, 28, 29, 31, 44, 370
social factors (offending), 279,
  314
social and family data, 50–54,
  150–52
social and family factors, 40–42,
  54–60
social inequality, 334–5
social mobility, 64–71
social perceptions (Generation
  II), 78–9
socio-economic stress, 23
sons and sons-in-law, 69
specifity, 290, 292, 293, 294–5,
  318
speech defects, 105
Spence, J.C., 4, 8
spouses of families of origin,
  42–8
spouses of Red Spots
  behaviour and health, 124–7
  parents in families of for-
    mation, 123
  physical growth, 128
  sex differences in behaviour,
    127–8
statistical indicators
  comment, 255–7
  effects of family deprivation,
    212–20
  effects of explanatory
    factors, 211–12, 236–40
statistical techniques
  analysis of variance, 211–12
  bivariate correlations, 241
  causal path analysis, 241–3
  correlation coefficients, 243
  discriminant function
    analysis, 291, 301–2, 320,
    321
  Likelihood Ratio Chi Square,
    238

statistical techniques (cont.)
log-linear analysis, 238, 240, 291, 294–7, 298, 300–303
multiple regression analysis, 211, 221, 223, 227–8, 232, 242–3, 257, 291–2, 301, 302, 320, 321
path analysis, 240–55, 347
prediction, 290–92
relative improvement over chance, 291, 292, 294–5
residual coefficients, 243
single factor prediction, 290–91, 292, 294–5, 296–7
two factor prediction, 300–303
statistics of deprivation, 328–9
'steeling' effect, 361
Steinhausen, H.C., 60
Stevenson, J.E., 21, 240, 264, 325–6, 329, 367
Stokes, C.S., 264
Stoten, B., 88
Streather, J., 326
stress factors, 281–3, 285–8
criminality prediction, 297–9, 311–17
subsistence levels, 73, 74–5
suicide, 82, 128
summary findings, 338–54

Tarling, R., 290
teachers
ratings of behaviour, 214–16
reports of antisocial behaviour, 83, 135–6, 220, 247–8, 251, 254, 261–3, 350
temperament, 256
concentration/persistence, 236, 238–40, 260, 344, 374
difficult–easy child index, 232
parental reports, 135, 136

teacher ratings, 214–16
Tennant, C., 61
tenth-year population, 14
testing
children of Red Spot, 130–33
see also reading ability; vocabulary ability
32–33 year families, 16–17
Thomas, A., 232, 352
'1,000 Family Study', 8–13, 327, 330
offences data, 271–5, 295
Tizard, J., 134, 139
Tonge, W.L., 141, 325, 328, 362
Torgersen, A.M., 364
Townsend, P., 68, 74, 91, 101, 325, 334, 336, 343, 347, 357
tracing
and follow-up, 21–5
long distance children, 26
overseas families, 26, 27
training, 23, 30, 32–4, 53, 186
after school (spouses), 120, 122–3
school leavers preferences, 113–14
transmission of disadvantage, 16–17, 358
two-factor prediction, 291, 297–303, 318–19

unemployment, 41, 185, 217, 225
duration, 76–83, 84–7
incidence, 77–8
male, 55, 56
unemployment, male (and family income)
data, 76–84
discussion, 84–9
findings, 72–5
introduction and method, 72

upward mobility, 68, 70, 71,
 159, 358–60
Urban Aid programme, 335

variables
 dependent, 243–4
 explanatory, 221–2, 233–6,
  249, 261
 independent, 243–4
 outcome, 234–5
Vincent, K.R., 60
vocabulary ability, 26–7, 109,
 123–4, 130, 132, 182,
 185, 190, 200–201, 214,
 217–18, 232, 246, 248,
 251, 254, 262–3, 339,
 341, 359
vulnerability, 311–12, 314, 317

Waddington, C.H., 363
Wadsworth, M., 321
walking, children at age of, 187
Wallerstein, J.S., 367
Warr, P., 84, 85, 86
Watts, A.F., 27

Wedge, P., 21, 65, 88, 325, 326,
 327, 329, 336
weight (by age), 105, 106, 134,
 156
Werner, E.E., 281
West, D.J., 290, 304, 305, 306–
 7, 308
Whitmore, K., 134
Wolfgang, M.E., 302
women
 behaviour and health, 124–7
 criminality, 271–2, 275,
  277–80, 315–17
 predictive force of gender,
  257–8
 social and family data, 52–4
 see also girls; mothers
worry, 217
Wright, C.H., 362

young unemployed, 84–5
Youth Employment Service,
 113

Zlatich, D., 60